Sissieretta Jones

Sissieretta Jones

"THE GREATEST SINGER OF HER RACE"
1868–1933

Maureen D. Lee

THE UNIVERSITY OF SOUTH CAROLINA PRESS

© 2012 University of South Carolina

Published by the University of South Carolina Press
Columbia, South Carolina 29208

www.sc.edu/uscpress

Manufactured in the United States of America

21 20 19 18 17 16 15 14 13 12
10 9 8 7 6 5 4 3 2 1

Library of Congress Cataloging-in-Publication Data
Lee, Maureen D.
Sissieretta Jones : "the greatest singer of her race,"
1868–1933 / Maureen D. Lee.
pages cm
Includes bibliographical references and index.
ISBN 978-1-61117-072-6 (cloth : alk. paper)
1. Black Patti, 1869–1933. 2. African American singers—
Biography. 3. Black Patti Troubadours. I. Title.
ML420.B6325L44 2012
782.0092—dc23
[B]
2011050452

This book was printed on a recycled paper with
30 percent postconsumer waste content.

For my husband, John Lee,
and my mother, Helen Petterson,
who have supported me with their love and encouragement

CONTENTS

ILLUSTRATIONS

PREFACE

Some biographers claim their subjects choose them. Such was my experience with Sissieretta Jones. I first heard about her while visiting family in my native state of Rhode Island. My brother, George Donnelly, was working with others in Providence to create a unique Rhode Island history exhibit called "Rhode Island Treasures." The idea behind the exhibit was to feature artifacts and historical documents seldom seen by most Rhode Islanders. Two of those items were dresses worn by Matilda Sissieretta Jones, the African American soprano who is the subject of this book. Sissieretta, born in Virginia in 1868, grew up in Providence and retired there after a lengthy singing career.

From the moment I read a brief description of her life and saw her photograph, I was fascinated and wanted to know more about her. Soon after I retired from Clemson University, I began researching more about her life. My husband, John, and I visited the Moorland-Spingarn Research Center, Manuscript Division, at Howard University in Washington, D.C., where Sissieretta's scrapbook and three of the nearly twenty medals she received for singing are kept in the Dr. Carl R. Gross Collection. It was a thrill to touch the scrapbook Sissieretta must have held in her hands many times, to see her photographs, and to hold three of the medals she wore.

After reviewing the newspaper clippings in the scrapbook, most of which are not dated and many of which do not bear the name of the newspaper, John and I began a four-year task of methodically reviewing old New York entertainment weeklies and two prominent African American newspapers (the *New York Age* and the *Indianapolis Freeman*) that provided news of the stage. We examined these newspapers, which were available on microfilm, for the years 1885 to 1915 (the year she retired from the stage). With the information we gathered, we put together a schedule of her whereabouts, month by month, for the years she performed on the stage. (See appendix B for a sample of her touring schedule, this one for the 1901–2 theater season.) Using these schedules, as well as newspaper articles and reviews about her concerts and shows, I was able to piece together details about her career and chronicle her professional life. Unfortunately Sissieretta did not leave diaries or letters that might have provided more insight into her private life.

I must ask readers to forgive the demeaning language and derogatory terms quoted in the text from newspaper articles written during Sissieretta's career. These words reflect some of what she and other African Americans were subjected to in their daily lives in the late 1800s and early 1900s. I have tried to ensure that these derogatory terms and prejudicial comments have been placed in historical context, as well as to show how African Americans led the movement in the early 1900s to remove these harmful words from use.

The pages that follow describe Sissieretta's early years, how she became a singer, and her rise to fame on the concert stage. The second half of the book traces her career as the head of her own road company, the Black Patti Troubadours, later called the Black Patti Musical Comedy Company. The final chapter tells what little is known about Sissieretta's retirement years in Rhode Island before her death in 1933. I have enjoyed adding to the knowledge about this remarkable singer. I hope my work will help to foster the recognition Sissieretta Jones so richly deserves.

ACKNOWLEDGMENTS

In the nine years I have worked on this biography of Sissieretta Jones, I have had the good fortune to receive assistance from many people. The first person I want to thank is my husband, John, for his constant support and encouragement. Without it I would not have finished this biography. I also wish to thank him for the countless hours he helped me search reels of microfilm of old newspapers for information about Sissieretta, compiled her performance schedules, and read numerous drafts of my work.

I want to thank the staff of the Interlibrary Loan Department and the Government Information, Microforms and Newspapers Department at the Thomas Cooper Library, University of South Carolina in Columbia. For four years the Interlibrary Loan Department, particularly Jo Cottingham (now retired), responded quickly and patiently to my many requests for years of old newspapers as well as hard-to-find publications. With borrowed microfilm reels in hand, my husband and I viewed the film on the machines in the Government Information, Microforms and Newspapers Department. Thanks to director Bill Sudduth and his excellent staff for all the assistance they gave us.

Many other libraries and librarians helped me. They include Eric Nitschke, reference librarian, Woodruff Library, Emory University, Atlanta; the Library of Congress; the Richland County Public Library, Columbia, South Carolina; Robert Hetilewigs, Norfolk (Virginia) Public Libraries, History Department; Tricia Roush, former reference librarian, and Kirsten Tanaka, head librarian, Performing Arts Library, Museum of Performance and Design, San Francisco; Joellen ElBashir, chief curator, and Ida Jones, assistant curator, Moorland-Spingarn Research Center, Manuscript Division, Howard University, Washington, D.C.; Portsmouth (Virginia) Public Library; Jennifer Lee, Rare Book and Manuscript Library, Columbia University; Nicolette Bromberg, Special Collections Division, University of Washington Library; J. D. Kay and the staff of the Rhode Island Historical Society Library; and the Providence (Rhode Island) Public Library. I am indebted to the librarians and photo reproduction staff at these institutions for helping me find the materials I needed to complete my research and for providing the photos included in this book.

I also want to thank several people who shared their experience and knowledge with me. Thanks to Joaquina Bela Teixeira, former executive director of the Rhode Island Black Heritage Society, for providing information about African American history in Rhode Island and giving me a copy of a 1911 letter Sissieretta wrote to her attorney. I also received great marketing tips and helpful information from Ray Rickman, a scholar of African American history in Rhode Island. Thanks to Glenn Laxton, former reporter for Channel 12 News in Providence, for helping me search for Sissieretta's grave in the Grace Church Cemetery in Providence. Thanks also to Mrs. Linnear H. Horne, music director (retired), Congdon Street Baptist Church in Providence, who shared the history of the church with me as well as stories about her grandfather William Younger, who would have been the choir director when Sissieretta retired to Providence in 1915. Sissieretta sometimes sang with the choir during her retirement years. My husband enjoyed singing at the church during our visit there while Mrs. Linnear accompanied him on the pipe organ.

John T. Meyers, archivist (retired) at Providence City Hall, was incredibly helpful in my search for information about Sissieretta's estate. I thank him for locating the estate documents in archived probate court records and for also guiding my search of Sissieretta's property records. A special thanks goes to Rob Hudson, associate archivist at Carnegie Hall, who not only supplied program information from Sissieretta's performances at the famous New York City landmark, but also sent me several helpful newspaper reviews. Rob's guided tour of Carnegie Hall provided me with great background about the early days of the concert hall. Thanks also to Mae Breckenridge-Haywood, executive director, African American Historical Society of Portsmouth, Virginia, for the additional information about Sissieretta and her native city, Portsmouth, and for introducing me to the historical library staff at the Portsmouth Public Library, who also assisted me.

I also wish to thank two people who helped me find some old court records related to Sissieretta's life. Bruce Abrams, Division of Old Records, County Clerk and Clerk of the Supreme Court, New York County Court House, tracked down a copy of the July 1893 lawsuit between Sissieretta's manager, James B. Pond, and Sissieretta and her husband, David. Thanks too to Andrew Smith, then administrative assistant at the Rhode Island Supreme Court's Judicial Record Center, who located copies of Sissieretta's and her mother's divorce decrees.

A very special thanks goes to two gentlemen who helped me with the writing process. Richard Layman, president of Bruccoli Clark Layman, a company that produces reference books in literature and social history, generously read a very early draft of two chapters of my manuscript and gave me a detailed, lengthy, and helpful critique. His comments guided my subsequent rewrites. The other gentleman, Don Judson, served as my writing coach for almost two years. He carefully reviewed my work after I completed each chapter and gave me instructive editing suggestions. His knowledge, expertise, and encouragement were invaluable to me. Thanks.

I have enjoyed working with everyone at the University of South Carolina Press. A special thanks goes to acquisitions editor Alexander Moore, who believed in my manuscript from the first and whose enthusiasm for the project sustained me during the acquisition process, and to Jonathan Haupt, assistant director for sales, for his marketing expertise.

Finally I want to thank my friends and family for their love, understanding, encouragement, and support these last nine years. Thanks to my three wonderful stepchildren (Lisa, Nancy, and John) and their spouses (Pauley, Kevin, and Lisa), my seven beautiful grandchildren (Sally, Nathan, Chase, Sara Kate, Annslee, Sidney, and Aaron), my mother (Helen), sisters (Patti and Nancy), and my brother (George), who first introduced me to Sissieretta. I love you all!

Prologue

Slowly Sissieretta Joyner walked toward the taxi parked in front of her nine-room home on Wheaton Street high above the capital city of Providence, Rhode Island, in the area now known as College Hill near Brown University. She had a dollar in her purse, borrowed from her friend and benefactor, William P. Freeman, to pay for the cab ride to Rhode Island Hospital on this somewhat cool fourteenth day of June 1933.[1] Freeman, a realtor and past president of the local chapter of the National Association for the Advancement of Colored People, had helped keep her afloat financially for the last several years. He may have even been there that day to wish her well. As she sat down in the back of the taxi, she took what would be her final look at her home of thirty-five years. Sissieretta died on Saturday, 24 June, from cancer of the stomach with metastasis to the liver.[2] She was sixty-five and a half years old.

Most likely no one at the hospital knew about Sissieretta's famous and glorious past, when she was billed as the "greatest singer of her race" and called Madame Sissieretta Jones or "Black Patti," a nickname created by the press to suggest a comparison to the world-famous European prima donna Adelina Patti (1843–1919). The doctors and nurses had probably never seen Sissieretta in her younger days, dressed in elegant evening gowns, wearing sparkling rings and necklaces of gold and precious stones. Instead they saw an old, heavy-set African American woman who was very sick and ailing, with no family members to comfort her during her final days. Funeral services were held at her church, Congdon Street Baptist, where she had worshiped and sometimes sung with the choir since leaving the stage eighteen years before. Freeman saw to it that she received a decent burial at Grace Church Cemetery, where her mother was buried, and was not left to rest in a pauper's grave, although her grave, to this day, has no headstone.

Sissieretta Joyner Jones and her parents moved from Portsmouth, Virginia, to Providence when she was very young. She got her start singing in Providence's black churches. She studied classical singing in Providence, Boston, and New York, sang opera and concert selections, and went on to become a household name in the field of popular entertainment. Sissieretta sang before four U.S. presidents; toured throughout Europe, Canada, the West Indies, and South America; sang at Madison Square Garden and Carnegie Hall in New York City; and entertained thousands in music halls and opera houses around the United States as the star of her own troupe, the Black Patti Troubadours. At one time she was the highest-paid African American female performer. Many black actors, musicians, dancers, composers, and comedians got their start in her troupe, with several of them becoming famous later in their careers. Sissieretta was a pioneer among African American entertainers. She was one of a handful of early black female concert singers who showed white America that black Americans could do much more than sing minstrel songs. At the same time, she was a source of pride to the people of her race. As biographer William Lichtenwanger said of Sissieretta in *Notable American Women,* "Despite a white public inclined to overlook her artistry and treat her as a freak, despite a Negro public too poor and uneducated to support her effectively, despite biased critics and mediocre management, Madame Jones forced the musical and theatrical worlds in the United States to accept the Negro in a new image."[3]

Sissieretta left a legacy of achievement during her twenty-eight-year career, taking advantage of many opportunities available to her, but she failed to reach her full potential because racial discrimination presented obstacles and limitations she could not overcome. Today's music lover will never know how Sissieretta's voice sounded, for she made no recordings, even though the technology was available during the latter part of her career.[4] Newspaper accounts from critics of her day describe a beautiful and powerful soprano voice that charmed audiences, both black and white.

Sissieretta's accomplishments might have been lost to time had it not been for a distant relative, Willia Estelle Daughtry, who wrote her doctoral dissertation, "Sissieretta Jones: A Study of the Negro's Contribution to Nineteenth Century American Concert and Theatrical Life," about the accomplished soprano and later penned a biography of her life. Daughtry's 1968 dissertation became the basis for much of the information about Sissieretta found in reference books about famous musicians and historical figures. Sissieretta left no diary or cache of letters, making it impossible to know her private thoughts and feelings. The only thing she kept until her death that captured some of her achievements on the stage was a scrapbook of press clippings, mostly from her concert years.[5]

In 1911 black theater critic Lester Walton wrote, "Mme. Sissieretta Jones is really a remarkable woman—an artist whom biographers cannot overlook in days to come when giving historic references to performers past and present and their accomplishments."[6] Yet Sissieretta has been in large part overlooked.

This biography attempts to correct that by providing more details of her professional life and a sense of how she fit into the entertainment world of her day. The work also explores the obstacles and limitations she faced because of her race as well as the opportunities she seized upon to become a famous and successful prima donna.

1

Rhode Island

Sissieretta was born Matilda Sissieretta Joyner on 5 January 1868,[1] three years after the close of the Civil War and seven months before the adoption of the Fourteenth Amendment, which gave black Americans the rights and privileges of citizenship and provided them equal protection of law. Her birthplace was a house with two apartments on Bart Street in Portsmouth, Virginia, between Chestnut and Effingham Streets.[2] Her father, Jeremiah "Jerry" Malachi Joyner, had been born into slavery in 1833 in North Carolina. At the time of Sissieretta's birth, he was a carpenter as well as pastor and choir leader of the African Methodist Church in Portsmouth.[3] He could read and write. Sissieretta's mother, Henrietta, was an illiterate washerwoman, also from North Carolina. She was born about 1845, making her twelve years younger than her husband.[4] They married in October 1862.[5] Henrietta was an exceptional soprano and talented musician who sang in the choir at the nearby Ebenezer Baptist Church, the first black Baptist church in Portsmouth. Sissieretta, whose family called her by her first name, Matilda, or her nickname, "Sissy," was the oldest of three children born to Jeremiah and Henrietta. From an early age, Sissieretta enjoyed singing, often climbing on chairs or tables in the house to sing before her mother chased her out.[6] Sissieretta's sister, Isabella, born in August 1869, died a year later of "teething," according to Portsmouth death records. Her brother, Jerry Jr., was born in March 1871, but he died 10 October 1876 at the age of four and a half from an "abcess [sic] in [the] bowels."[7] After Jerry's death, likely in late 1876, the family moved to Rhode Island in search of a better life.[8] Even though Virginia had been readmitted to the Union in January 1870, the state still suffered the aftermath of the war and Reconstruction. Most black residents of the South were poor, were subjected to inadequate schooling, lived in substandard housing, and had limited economic opportunities and health care.[9] Jeremiah had been offered a ministerial position at an African American church in Providence and probably seized on this opportunity to improve living conditions for his family.

In 1876, the year the Joyners moved to Providence, the United States celebrated its one hundredth anniversary as a free country with a Centennial Exposition in Philadelphia. Ten million people visited the thirty thousand exhibits during the six-month run of the exposition, where Alexander Graham Bell personally demonstrated his telephone. The exposition, with themes of unity, strength, and prosperity, featured machinery, agriculture, horticulture, arts and crafts, and cultural displays all centered around middle-class life—white middle-class life. African Americans had no exhibit of their own, and there were no African American women featured in the exposition's Women's Building. The only time blacks were included was when they appeared in stereotypical roles singing plantation songs and playing banjos in concessions named "The South" and the "Southern Restaurant."[10]

Although the Civil War had freed African Americans from slavery, it had not guaranteed that whites would accept them readily into American society. By 1876 the Reconstruction period in the South was coming to an end. Federal troops were withdrawn the following year, leaving southern white leaders free to impose their control once again. Segregation returned, lynchings increased, and intimidation and terrorism by white supremacist organizations such as the Ku Klux Klan became more prevalent. In the North black citizens maintained their legal rights, but most whites made sure African Americans "knew their place" and kept to themselves.

When the Joyner family arrived in Providence, they found a thriving, vibrant capital city whose population and wealth had doubled in the decade of 1860–70. The profitable sugar and slave trade of the 1760s and early 1770s had been replaced by industrial wealth, with big gains coming from textile and manufacturing industries. For fifty years following the Civil War, Rhode Island was an attractive place to live. "For the state, it was the beginning of a fabulous era of wealth and middle-class comfort."[11] Providence, a city of residential neighborhoods and businesses, had an urban transit system with horsecars on rails linking various parts of the city. Racial segregation of the public schools had been abolished in 1866 throughout Rhode Island, making it possible for seven-year-old Sissieretta to attend Meeting Street Primary School and later Thayer Street Grammar School.[12]

The number of African Americans living in Providence was small compared with the white population. Many black citizens living in the city could trace their roots back to the South. Jeremiah and Henrietta probably felt comfortable settling into life in Providence's black community on the East Side near the Benefit Street area. Jeremiah's ability to read and write gave him an advantage as he tried to adjust in this northern city. The family's first documented address was 20 Congdon Street, across the street from the Congdon

Street Baptist Church, one of the city's black churches.[13] By 1870 Providence's African American population had at least five different churches of their own to attend, all of which originated from the African Union Meeting House. In addition to those five, the black community began six other churches.[14] Jeremiah had moved his family to Rhode Island to preach in one of these churches, but it is not known which one.

Surely the African American church community embraced the Joyners and helped them establish themselves in Providence. Churches were an integral part of African American life. In addition to worship services, these institutions provided a social network that helped people find jobs, introduced strangers, spread news of the community, and provided charity to those in need. The church also was a gathering place where people came together for church suppers, lectures, and musical performances.

Unfortunately for Sissieretta, the Joyner family did not stay together long once they settled in Providence. Sometime in 1878 Jeremiah and Henrietta stopped living together. By 1880, when the federal census was conducted, Henrietta listed herself as the head of household with no mention of Jeremiah. Henrietta, then age thirty-five, and twelve-year-old Sissieretta were living at 7 Jackson Court, still on the East Side of downtown Providence. Henrietta supported herself and Sissieretta by taking in washing and ironing in her home. Census takers reported Henrietta's status as a widow, a term occasionally used for women who were divorced or separated as well as for widows.[15] Years later, in 1889, Jeremiah divorced Henrietta, claiming she was "guilty of the crime of adultery and other gross misbehavior and misconduct in violation of and repugnant to the marriage covenant." Her reply to these accusations was not included in the existing court records.[16]

Henrietta no doubt struggled to provide food and shelter for herself and her young daughter. Jeremiah stayed in Providence at least until 1893. He lived most of those years at 8 Gould's Lane and worked as a carpet cleaner.[17] It is unknown whether he tried to see Sissieretta or helped pay for his daughter's care. Despite the hardships at home, Sissieretta kept singing. "When I was a little girl, just a wee slip of a tad, I used to go about singing. I guess I must have been a bit of a nuisance then for my mouth was open all the time," she recalled.[18] Little "Sissy" or "Tilly," as her classmates called her, delighted the other students on "singing teacher day" with her beautiful voice. A schoolmate said her distinctive voice carried over the rest of the class.[19]

Not only did Sissieretta sing at school, but she also sang at church, especially at programs and festivals held at the Pond Street Baptist Church. One can imagine the small black child dressed in a stiff, uncomfortable white dress that rustled as she walked on the stage, taking her place before a church hall filled with expectant faces all trained on her. "Oh, I was scared so I could hardly catch my breath," Sissieretta said, recalling one of her first stage appearances. "When the applause came I almost fell off the stage. But timidity was soon replaced by confidence, and I kept on singing in charitable enterprises."[20] By 1883, when Sissieretta was fifteen, she began formal musical training at the Providence Academy of Music, "under the tutelage of Baroness Lacombe, an eminent Italian preceptor, and Mr. Monros, also eminent in the world of music."[21] It is a wonder how she or her mother would have paid for this music instruction.

At age fifteen Sissieretta had things on her mind other than music. That year she met David Richard Jones, a handsome mulatto from Baltimore who was working as a hotel bellman at the fashionable, eight-story Narragansett Hotel on the southwest corner of Dorrance and Weybosset Streets in Providence. The two were married 4 September 1883 by Baptist clergyman John C. Stockbridge. Although marriage records said Sissieretta was eighteen and David was twenty-four, she was actually fifteen and he was about twenty-one.[22] The young couple lived with Henrietta. The following spring, on 8 April 1884, seven months after their wedding, David and Sissieretta's daughter, Mabel, was born.[23] Her middle name, Adelina, may have been chosen in honor of the famous soprano Adelina Patti, who was very popular when the child was born.

By the time Mabel arrived, David was supporting his family working as a waiter at the Narragansett Hotel while Sissieretta and her mother cared for the infant. David, who often went by his middle name, Richard, was ambitious, working his way up from bellman to waiter at the hotel and being elected vice president of the Narragansett Hallmen, a group of African American men working at the city's luxurious, 225-room hotel.[24] During the 1880s many blacks living in Providence had a rich community and social life, as well as being comfortable financially. "In no other city in the Union will you find a colored community better off than in Providence, when it comes to money," said the *New York Age's* Providence correspondent in 1888.[25] The *New York Freeman* often carried columns about various African American organizations and clubs in Providence that took steamboat cruises together on Narragansett Bay, hosted balls and grand receptions, or sponsored recitals and cultural programs at halls and churches. David Jones's organization, the Narragansett Hallmen, had the distinction of giving one of the finest balls ever held by Providence's African American community. The only other organization to give a grander reception was the Apollo Club, but the black press criticized this group for inviting some white guests who were staying at the Narragansett.[26] As good as conditions were for many African Americans in Providence, the "color line" existed there. For example many skilled mechanics who were black could not get jobs in Providence because of their skin color. Another example: white clerks would not rent skates to "colored peo-ple" at the Providence Roller Skating Rink.[27]

Sissieretta continued studying vocal techniques and began singing at more church concerts and performing with other musical groups such as the Excel-sior Brass Band. Her name began to show up in the Rhode Island column of the black *New York Freeman* newspaper more often after appearing in various concerts. The "coming soprano" was usually referred to as Mrs. Richard Jones or Mrs. M. S. Jones.

On 21 May 1885 Sissieretta joined a well-known black singer in Provi-dence, Flora Batson, at a concert and reception hosted by the Fourth Battal-ion Drum Corps. Sissieretta shared the concert stage with Batson before a "packed" audience at Providence's Armory Hall.[28] This was a very important contact for the young singer to make because Batson was well established in the black community as a concert singer and later helped open doors for Sissieretta. Batson (1864–1906) was born in Washington, D.C., but moved to Providence at an early age to live with her widowed mother, Mary A. Batson. Flora Batson did not have formal training, but she had a powerful voice with a soprano-baritone range. She gained experience singing in church choirs in Providence. By the time Sissieretta met her, Batson had performed for three years, 1883 through 1885, at the People's Church in Boston and had sung in many other concerts, including a European tour and a temperance revival in New York City.[29] Batson got a big career break in 1885, when she was hired to perform in a Bergen Star Concert on 15 October 1885 at the Providence Music Hall. Bergen Star Concerts were led by John G. Bergen, a white concert man-ager who promoted black singers and arranged concerts to entertain black au-diences. He had planned for the nationally famous African American soprano Mme. Nellie Brown Mitchell to sing at the October concert, but for some unexplained reason, Mme. Mitchell canceled her appearance. Bergen hired Batson to replace her.[30] From that point forward, Batson became the lead singer in the Bergen Star Concerts. Two years later, on 13 December 1887, Bat-son and Bergen married. With Bergen as her husband and manager, Batson's career advanced quickly, and soon "she was booked all over the country and the world."[31]

Nellie Brown Mitchell (1845–1942), one of the first classically trained Afri-can American female singers, attended Boston's New England Conservatory, where she earned a music certificate and later received a music degree at the New England School of Vocal Arts in Boston. She sang professionally with the Bergen Star Concerts until early fall of 1885, when she went out on her own and did an extended tour of the South, one of the first black concert singers to perform in that part of the country.[32] Batson and Mitchell were two of a small group of black female concert singers during this period who performed on stage before black and white audiences and who defied the stereotypes portrayed in minstrel shows of shiftless, joke-cracking, banjo-plucking, plantation-singing African Americans. White audiences were curious about, even fascinated by, these early black prima donnas. The first of the prima donnas was Elizabeth Taylor-Greenfield, born a slave in Natchez, Mississippi, sometime in the mid-1820s. She taught herself to sing and performed mostly in the Northeast. White people who heard her were amazed by her dazzling, although untrained, soprano voice, but at the same time they were amused by a black woman singing serious music rather than minstrel or plantation songs. She had to withstand many degrading comments because white audiences were uncomfortable with this new role for a black woman. Some claim she could have matched any of the white divas of her day had she been given proper training. She traveled to Great Britain in 1853, where she received some musical tutoring and also gave a command performance for Queen Victoria at Buckingham Palace on 10 May 1853. After returning to the United States in 1854, she continued to sing some concerts and opened a music studio for private teaching.[33] She died in 1876, the year seven-year-old Sissieretta and her family moved to Providence and the year another black concert artist, Marie Selika (1849–1937), made her professional debut. Selika had a two-octave range from C to C. Like Taylor-Greenfield she was born in Natchez. Her real name was Marie Smith, but she took the pseudonym Marie Selika from the main female character, Selika, in the opera *L'Africaine*. Selika reportedly was the first black female concert singer to perform at the White House, appearing before President Rutherford B. Hayes in 1878. She too toured Europe, and in 1893, with her career declining, she returned from Europe and the West Indies to settle in Ohio, where she opened a music studio and continued to sing concerts. In 1916 she retired from the stage and began teaching music in New York City's Harlem. She died in 1937.[34]

Like Batson, Selika, Mitchell, and Taylor-Greenfield, Sissieretta had her sights set on singing classical music. Concerts and opera were two of several entertainment forms that people of the late 1800s enjoyed. But there were other, less sophisticated kinds of amusements, such as minstrel, vaudeville, or burlesque shows, that likely appealed more to the majority of people toward the end of the nineteenth century. Vaudeville was just beginning to become popular in the 1890s and would remain so up though the 1930s. Minstrelsy, an American form of major significance to the growth of American entertainment, began in 1843 in New York.[35] Before the Civil War, most minstrel shows featured white men wearing burnt cork on their faces to imitate blacks. After the Civil War, many black performers began to play in minstrel shows, with some organizing their own companies. Many people, particularly Northerners, wanted to see "authentic" former slaves rather than white men in blackface.[36]

African American musicians and entertainers joined the minstrelsy ranks, even though the shows reinforced negative stereotypes of black people, because it was the only way at that time for black singers, musicians, and dancers to gain stage experience while earning a living. By the 1890s black minstrelsy "evolved" into ragtime operetta[37] and black musical comedy shows.

Sissieretta continued to sing at church concerts, local festivals, and special events such as the one held 29 October 1885 at Providence's Amateur Dramatic Hall. The show featured New York's black dramatic actor John A. Arneaux playing Shakespeare's *King Richard III.* The audience braved stormy weather that night to see the performance and to hear Sissieretta's solo, which came before the play started. The evening's program earned favorable press reviews, including some in the white press. The *Providence Evening Telegram* said, "It is certainly a favorable sign of the times, as well as the making of a new era of intelligence and education among the colored people when they are found enacting Shakespearean plays. Last evening witnessed a new departure in the amusements of our colored citizens, instead of joining in a cake walk they were participants in an entertainment that possessed many elements of merit."[38]

Two months after the Shakespearean event, Sissieretta got a big break. On 3 December 1885 she appeared at the Providence Music Hall in a Grand Selika Concert starring black prima donna Marie Selika. Sissieretta, along with the Brown University Glee Club, mandolin player Carrie Melvin, and elocutionist Benjamin Lightfoot, was part of the "local talent" featured in the concert.[39] She surely was thrilled to appear on the same program as the world-renowned Selika, a signal that Sissieretta's musical career was beginning to blossom. As 1886 began, the eighteen-year-old vocalist was getting more opportunities to perform with other groups and singers and not only at church concerts. In January she got an invitation to sing later that year at Steinway Hall in New York City. But tragedy struck that cold winter when her two-year-old daughter, Mabel, died of "pharyngitis and croup" on 23 February.[40] Sissieretta was grief stricken and reported to be "quite ill."[41] Eventually she recovered and turned back to music, concentrating on developing her voice. By mid-May she was performing again at a Providence concert sponsored by the Fourth Battalion Drum Corps.[42] After a summer in Providence, she went to Boston to continue her musical studies at the Boston Conservatory of Music, according to an article in the 21 August 1886 edition of the *New York Freeman.*[43] In later years some newspapers said she had studied at the New England Conservatory, while others continued to say it was the Boston Conservatory of Music. There are no records of her attendance at the New England Conservatory, and the records at the Boston Conservatory for that period no longer exist.[44] While Sissieretta studied in Boston, David Jones continued working at the Narragansett Hotel, now selling newspapers there. He and Sissieretta had been living with Henrietta at 7 Jackson Court on Providence's East Side, but by 1887 Henrietta moved to nearby 5 Jackson Court.[45]

At the end of 1886 and the beginning of 1887, Sissieretta began appearing more often with Flora Batson both in Bergen Star Concerts and in independent concerts with her. She also did concerts with other entertainers and musicians, including a performance with the internationally renowned "Blind Tom" in late December 1887 at Providence's Music Hall.[46] "Blind Tom," whose real name was Thomas Wiggins Green Bethune, was born into slavery near Columbus, Georgia, in 1849. Blind from birth, Bethune showed an aptitude for music as early as his fourth birthday.[47] He was a piano prodigy, known for being able to "reproduce instantaneously, after just one hearing, any passage played for him on the piano."[48] Beginning at age five, he composed more than one hundred piano and vocal compositions in his lifetime. "Blind Tom" played all over the United States and Europe and was famous by the time he came to perform in Providence.[49] Certainly, with her musical studies behind her and a concert tour, likely arranged by her husband, planned for early 1888 to Baltimore, Boston, and other New England cities, Sissieretta was well on her way to achieving her goal—a career in music. Rather than having to accept the life available to most black women back then—working as a domestic servant or laundress—Sissieretta was able to use her God-given musical talent to do something that gave her joy and great satisfaction while earning money to help support her family. She probably never would have achieved her goals without the love and assistance of her mother, Henrietta, who recognized Sissieretta's gift and apparently encouraged her to fulfill her dream of performing. Sissieretta developed a strong bond with her mother, one that would last throughout her lifetime. David helped her career as well, arranging concerts for her and accompanying her on concert tours. He too recognized her talents and likely realized her earning potential. His motives for pushing Sissieretta's career were not as noble as Henrietta's, as the starry-eyed young vocalist would later learn.

Sissieretta joined Batson once again on 5 April 1888, in a Bergen Star Concert held at New York City's Steinway Hall, her first appearance in New York City. The benefit concert for the Odd Fellow's Building Fund gave Batson top billing but called Sissieretta "the rising soprano of Providence." Although the concert was described as a "notable artistic success" in one newspaper review, it was a financial failure because bad weather kept people from the various lodges from attending. Gross receipts for the night were $328.50, while expenses were $368.40. Sissieretta, along with many of the other performers, received praise for her work. "Mme. M. S. Jones, the soprano from Providence, has a voice of wonderful roundness and peculiarly sweet intonation and distinctness."[50] The following month Sissieretta appeared in another Bergen Star Concert in Philadelphia on 3 May 1888. She and Batson performed before nearly eight thousand people, most of whom were probably black, at the city's Academy of Music. Batson, who had planned to sing three songs, was recalled many times and had to sing eleven encores to satisfy the audience. Sissieretta, making her Philadelphia debut, made a favorable impression. "Her voice is sweet, sympathetic and clear and her enunciation a positive charm," one review said.[51] One can only imagine what it must have felt like for the young Sissieretta to be onstage before eight thousand people, singing in a city where she had never before performed. Like Batson, Sissieretta also was asked to sing encores.

Sissieretta's career began to move quickly after the Philadelphia concert. Sometime that spring, either at her Steinway Hall performance in New York City or her concert at Providence's San Souci Gardens, William Risen, musical director of the Little Tycoon Opera Company and an agent for the New York management firm of Abbey, Schoeffel, and Grau, heard Sissieretta sing. He telegraphed Henry Abbey, who was in Europe at the time, and said he had found a "phenomenal singer, who had no equal in the race."[52] Abbey's management group was in charge of the Metropolitan Opera Company at the time and had represented Adelina Patti on her South American tours.[53] Patti (1843–1919), a white Spanish-born opera singer, was the most famous soprano of the last half of the nineteenth century.[54] Abbey sent a reply telling Risen to hire Sissieretta for a tour of the West Indies.[55]

Sissieretta reportedly signed a two-year contract with Abbey, Schoeffel, and Grau.[56] She left Rhode Island at the end of July 1888 and appeared Wednesday afternoon, 1 August, for a rehearsal at Wallack's Theatre on Broadway and Thirtieth Streets in New York City, a theater where no other "colored" singer had ever appeared. The first-class theater was between engagements, having recently closed an opera performed by the McCaull Opera Company. The rehearsal was for the Tennessee Jubilee Singers, a company of African American singers, a pianist, and their white manager, who were leaving the following day on a two-year tour of the West Indies, the Windward Islands, and South America. James R. Smith was the company's manager, in partnership with Charles H. Matthews, who worked for Abbey, Schoeffel, and Grau.[57] One researcher speculates that Smith and Matthews likely organized the tour themselves for their own profit rather than under the auspices of Abbey, Schoeffel, and Grau.[58] Sissieretta and Will Pierce, a Providence tenor, were billed as stars of the touring group. The rest of the company included Annie Smith and Mattie Brown, sopranos; Kate Johnson, alto; George Richards, second tenor; Joseph G. Stevens and John Wolford, bassos; Louis L. Brown, baritone; and A. K. LaRue, accompanist and musical director. David Jones accompanied his wife on the tour.

One press report, written three years after Sissieretta's 1 August 1888 performance, said that she sang that day at Wallack's Theatre before all the newspaper critics of New York City and that the newspapers published glowing statements about her, including one by the *New York Clipper*, a white entertainment paper, that called her the "Black Patti," comparing her with Adelina Patti.[59] No such press statements could be found in the July or August issues of the *New York Clipper*, although Sissieretta, later in her career, also attributed the nickname to that particular newspaper. New York's black newspaper, the *New York Age*, called her "Black Patti" when it reported on 4 August 1888 that "Mrs. Jones is called the Black Patti by such men as Abbey, Schoeffel and Grau, who should be competent to judge such matters."[60] The use of these stage names or sobriquets, as they are often called, was widespread in the late 1800s. In fact "it was common from the 1880s on to associate black singers with their famous white counterparts or to label them with superlative epithets." For example Flora Batson was called the "Queen of Song," Maire Selika was called the "Brown Patti" and the "Creole Patti," and Elizabeth Greenfield was known as the "Black Swan."[61] Regardless of who first penned the name "Black Patti," it stuck with Sissieretta for the remainder of her years on stage and was quite useful to her managers in terms of publicity and name recognition. Sissieretta said she did not like the name. She once told a reporter for the *Detroit Evening News* that "it rather annoys me to be called the 'Black Patti.' I am afraid people will think I consider myself the equal of Patti herself. I assure you I do not think so, but I have a voice and I am striving to win the favor of the public by honest merit and hard work. Perhaps some day I may be as great in my way, but that is a long way ahead."[62]

With a two-year contract to sing professionally on a tour that would take her far from the United States and her home in Providence, the twenty-year-old Sissieretta said her goodbyes and prepared for her trip. She had never left the country before and had never had the starring role in a singing company such as the Tennessee Jubilee Singers. No doubt she had heard of the famous Fisk Jubilee Singers, a group of black student singers from Fisk University in Nashville, who, under the direction of their white music instructor, began touring in 1871, performing concerts to help raise money for the Fisk building program. They sang black folk music throughout the United States and Europe.[63] The success of the Fisk Jubilee Singers sparked the creation of many other copycat groups, including, apparently, Sissieretta's new company, the Tennessee Jubilee Singers. It remained to be seen how successful she and her fellow musicians would be. One thing was for sure: Sissieretta was about to embark on a journey few black women of her day could imagine.

2

West Indies and South American Tours

As Sissieretta boarded the steamer *Athos* in New York with her husband to begin their journey on 2 August 1888 to Kingston, Jamaica, she likely wondered what to expect of her upcoming tour as the star of the Tennessee Jubilee Singers. She had never ventured too far from the East Coast of the United States and was probably traveling by ship for the first time. Neither had the twenty-year-old vocalist ever been on an extended tour, especially as the prima donna of the company. What she was about to encounter would have been a bit overwhelming for most young people, but Sissieretta proved to enjoy the limelight and benefit from her many experiences.

She got a taste of what was to come when the company landed in Jamaica on 10 August 1888 and prepared for their first concert, which took place the following evening at the Theatre Royal. The concert hall was packed and included many prominent citizens. Before the troupe's arrival in Jamaica, publicity about the concerts appeared in newspaper pieces designed to motivate people to come and see the choral singers. The audience was thrilled with the concert, although it apparently lasted too long, with eighteen numbers on the program and numerous encores. Sissieretta sang "The Night Birds Cooing" during the first part of the program and opened the second half with the descriptive song "The Ship on Fire," by Henry Russell. Reviewers noted her great voice, precise enunciation, and powerful delivery of "The Ship on Fire." Two days later Sissieretta and company performed again and received "enthusiastic" reviews. This time she sang "Magnetic Waltz Song" and "Marguerite's Farewell," as well as repeating "The Ship on Fire." One of her encore selections was "Home, Sweet Home." In describing that particular number, one reviewer said, "Mdme. Jones created a genuine feeling of pleasure and pensive sadness in the large and sympathetic audience . . . by the sweet and expressive rendering of the well-remembered tones."[1] Not only did Sissieretta and company receive high praise in the local Jamaican press, but her successes were also noticed back in America as well. The *New York Times* reported on 27 August 1888 that "Mathilda Jones, whom Mr. Matthews advertises as his 'black Patti,' astonished the natives with her singing, and she is being lionized wherever she appears."[2]

The Tennessee Jubilee Singers stayed on the island of Jamaica until 22 October 1888. They sang concerts and benefit concerts in Kingston and toured the 4,450-square-mile British island several times, performing at small inland towns during their ten-week stay. In a newspaper interview in the *Indianapolis Freeman* (13 July 1889), Will Pierce, the group's tenor, described some of the travel difficulties the company faced while getting from one island town to another:

> It would have amused you to have seen us riding from Kingston to New Castle on small mules. Well you would have burst your sides had you have noticed "Lew" Brown and myself hitching our mules together and then trying to drag Miss Jones' and Miss Brown's behind us.
>
> But the funny thing was at St. Ann's Bay, our manager had a guarantee for a packed house to play at the court house. He sent Mr. Jones in advance with the advertising, the distance was fifteen miles, and Mr. Jones had often boasted of his superb horsemanship. He started on a two-year-old filly, which had not been broken to saddle. He had been gone about two hours when we discovered him coming back leading the horse, covered with mud from head to foot. The horse had evidently been trying to ride Mr. Jones.[3]

The Tennessee Jubilee Singers prepared to leave Kingston on 22 October 1888 and sail to Panama on the steamer *Medway*. Shortly before they left, several members of the cast were presented with gifts. Sissieretta and Katie Johnson were each given a gold medal, and Will Pierce was given a silver medal. John Wolford received a silver watch, and Hattie Brown received a necklace and pendant. After singing several songs for those gathered at the wharf to see them off, the company sailed for Panama, a Colombian province, where they arrived two days later.[4]

Pierce said the company's first stop was in the city of Aspinwall, located on the Atlantic side of the Isthmus of Panama. Aspinwall, whose name was officially changed to Colón in 1890, was founded as a result of the California Gold Rush. Americans came to the swampy, unsanitary, squalid city in 1850 to build a railroad (completed in 1855) from the Atlantic coast of Panama across the land to the Pacific coast, thus creating a way for people to travel by ship from the eastern United States, ride the train across Panama, and take another ship to California rather than having to travel across the United States to reach the West Coast.[5] In 1878 a French company won the rights to build a canal across the Isthmus of Panama, connecting the Atlantic and the Pacific, but it went bankrupt in 1889, a year after the Tennessee Jubilee Singers visited the country.[6] When Sissieretta and her fellow performers appeared in the city, it was still under French influence. Ultimately the United States completed the Panama Canal in 1913 and opened it for business in 1914.

Pierce said the Tennessee Jubilee Singers played to their "most cultured" audiences of the tour in Panama and that Mme. Jones was "first styled the Black Patti" in this country. While there the company played in the Sarah Bernhardt Theater, which Pierce described as the most handsome theater he had ever seen.[7] The Jubilee Singers only stayed in Panama for two weeks, although Smith had said the singers would be there for six weeks. The city, despite some improvements by the French, was still poor, dirty, and disease ridden. Poor living conditions, low ticket sales, and language differences may have contributed to Smith's decision to leave Panama and return to Kingston. Arriving back in Jamaica on 5 November, the group performed two more concerts and left two days later aboard the *Medway*, headed to Barbados, a 166-square-mile island owned by Great Britain.[8]

The troupe performed six concerts while in Barbados and earned great reviews, especially Sissieretta. One newspaper, the *Barbados Globe*, said she kept her audience "spell-bound" and was received with "rapture."[9] Reviews such as this were a new experience for Sissieretta. Following her concerts back in Rhode Island, she had barely received mention for her work. At most she was called a "rising soprano." Here in the relatively poor country of Barbados, she was a star and the center of attention, a rather heady experience for the young vocalist. In recognition of her work, during the intermission of the company's 26 November concert, two citizens of Barbados presented Sissieretta with a gold medal from the governor and citizens of Bridgetown.[10]

The company left Barbados at the end of November and arrived in Trinidad, an island off the coast of Venezuela, where they gave five concerts, the first of which was Saturday, 1 December 1888. Once again Sissieretta earned glowing reviews in the local newspaper and received another gold medal, this time from the citizens of Port-of-Spain.[11] Pierce said that while in the British territory of Trinidad, the company was given a grand reception in the Princess Building. About 1,200 people attended, and 500 couples took part in a grand march.[12] If Pierce's description of this party was accurate, it would have been a new and impressive experience for Sissieretta, who had grown up in modest circumstances in Providence's black community.

The Tennessee Jubilee Singers' next stop was British Guiana (now Guyana), where they arrived sometime between 10 December and 13 December 1888.[13] Rough seas on the trip caused most of the young performers to get seasick and forced them to cancel their first show. "After leaving port generally the only food that was consumed by most of the party was soup, but our party seemed to take great delight in feeding the fishes. Mr. Jones seemed to have a particular fancy for it," said Pierce. He mentioned that the company "first met the green-eyed monster" of prejudice in Georgetown, British Guiana's main town.[14] The opening night concert was only moderately attended. The second night the audience was small as well, which prompted manager Smith to shorten the concert to just an hour and to refund the audience's tickets rather than canceling the performance entirely. When the program was over, Smith addressed the audience, saying that "he did not wish the members of his company to be insulted by being the victims of colour prejudice."[15] The company prepared to leave for Surinam. While getting ready for the upcoming trip, Smith learned that a petition was circulating in Georgetown disputing the accusation of prejudice and requesting one more concert. He decided to offer another performance on 19 December, and after it was successful, he later scheduled three benefit concerts. At an evening concert held Saturday night, 22 December 1888, Sissieretta received a gold medal from her admirers, her third gold medal of the trip.[16]

Smith, in an interview with the *New York Age* (30 March 1889) following the completion of the tour, talked about the prejudice the troupe encountered in Georgetown and Barbados. He said his company was refused accommodations at two main hotels in Georgetown "in a country that is maintained by colored people, where positions of trust and dignity are held by the colored race and their descendants." He also described his experiences in Barbados. On opening night he discovered race prejudice was hurting ticket sales. Smith said he told the audience he had gone to great expense to bring a talented company to perform for them and would not be insulted by such a "slim" audience. He allowed the concert to proceed for those who had "dared to brave prejudice" but canceled further concerts. Eventually, after various groups pleaded with him to permit more concerts, he agreed, but said he would not allow "a white man or woman nor one of your prejudiced half-casts [sic] to enter the hall." The next concert was packed, he said. In contrast to the initial trouble in Georgetown and Barbados, the troupe was treated "royally" in Jamaica, Colón, Trinidad, San Fernando, Surinam, Antigua, and St. Kitts, Smith said.[17]

It is unknown what the racial mix of the concert audiences was on this tour; however one researcher who has studied this trip in depth, John Graziano, believes the audiences in most of these countries had both white and black patrons.[18] Pierce, in remarks made after the tour, confirmed the presence of black audience members. He said the blacks they encountered on their tour were of mixed races. He called the two main groups either Creole Spaniards or "Colliers," adding that the Creole Spaniards favored choral singing while the Colliers preferred solos and secular music. "The low class are called niggers there, the same as the high class here," Pierce said. "They are particularly fond of the humorist, and a man does not have to be much of a comedian to set them wild. High tragedy would go there for they like something excitable.[19]

On 28 December, the troupe sailed for Surinam, the Dutch-owned country next to British Guiana on the northeast coast of South America, and landed there 7 January 1889, just two days after Sissieretta's twenty-first birthday. They stayed for a week, performing for people who could not understand English. Their tour was winding down. The company may have visited Brazil for a short time and then headed back to Antigua for two concerts. By 31 January the Tennessee Jubilee Singers boarded the ship *Barracouta* and sailed for New York, stopping in St. Kitts to give two concerts there to "overflowing houses."[20] Arriving back in New York City in mid-February, Sissieretta and a few other performers took up residence at Sumner House,[21] the largest "colored hotel" in the city, located on West Thirty-Seventh Street between Broadway and Sixth Avenue. While Sissieretta and David were getting settled once again in the United States, exciting news was being made in France, where the country was preparing for the Paris Exposition of 1889. The 986-foot Eiffel Tower, designed and constructed by Alexandre Gustave Eiffel, was completed 28 March 1889 and ready to be unveiled at the exposition in May. It was one of the first tall buildings in the world to use passenger elevators.

As Sissieretta once again walked the busy streets of New York City and Providence, she must have had fond memories of her six-month tour, where she achieved unmatched success for a "colored soprano" in the countries she visited. Her trunk was filled with favorable newspaper reviews of her performances as well as eight medals, seven of which were solid gold; three gold necklaces; two silver bracelets; and eight sovereigns from Colón.[22] "Nightly the stage was perfectly covered with floral tributes presented by the ladies," tenor Pierce said. Sissieretta came back to New York from her international tour a more seasoned, mature, polished, and confident singer than when she had left. She had begun to grow into her role as a prima donna, learning how to acquit herself both on and off the stage. The tour was an apparent financial success, according to Pierce. He said manager Smith made about four thousand U.S. dollars for the six-month tour once traveling expenses were deducted. The singer said the troupe traveled first class everywhere they went.[23]

Smith, in his interview with the *New York Age* a month after the tour ended, had nothing but praise for his troupe. He said he was familiar with the West Indies because he had taken six trips there previously to remodel several theaters and to learn about the people who lived there. When he decided to take a troupe of black performers there, he said he felt it would either be "a most pronounced success or a most dismal failure, there would be no happy medium. It proved the former. My next anxiety was to surround myself with a coterie of artists that could not only command artistic recognition, but social consideration as well. Suffice it to say that I found them. They stand today the only medallion decked organization of its kind."[24] Smith said he planned to take the troupe to Europe in about six weeks. Before then the company would perform about five concerts in and about New York, as well as appear in Philadelphia, Baltimore, and Boston. The first concert was held 3 April 1889 at Mount Olivet Baptist Church in New York City, with proceeds from the concert going to the church. Tickets were fifty cents for adults and twenty-five cents for children. Most of the church was filled on the night the Tennessee Concert Company made its metropolitan debut. The program included a variety of music—"ballads, love ditties, and plantation melodies." The audience appeared to like the jubilee songs better than the classical selections. Sissieretta sang well, managing her voice and her trills. She was persuaded to give an encore. Pierce and baritone Louis Brown also were well received. The audience responded enthusiastically, and the concert was a financial and artistic success. The only person missing was Smith, who was said to be "much indisposed" and who had sold his rights and interest in the concert group to another white man, George M. Dusenberry.[25]

The story behind Smith's nonappearance at the concert and his selling the rights to the company was brought to light by *New York Age* reporter Florence Williams. Smith told Williams the company had disbanded because of a misunderstanding between members and manager. He claimed the singers had become "swell-headed" and were unwilling to give him any credit for his part in bringing them to the world's attention. He said the company had rebelled against him and broken their contract. However, two members of the company, Kate Johnson and Louis Brown, told Williams a very different story. They said they did not break their contract; the manager had. Both claimed the company had been duped by the "wily ways" of the manager. By contract Smith was supposed to pay all traveling expenses, including board, from concert receipts. Up until the breakup, the boardinghouse proprietors had not been paid as promised. Johnson asked Smith to pay her board, and Smith reportedly told her "to go and hustle." Brown also asked for his money and had it out with Smith "in the style of 'nip and tuck.'" The astonished Smith decided to sell his rights to the concert at Mount Olivet Baptist Church to Colonel Dusenberry. When the company heard about this before the concert, they grew suspicious and said they would not perform until their claims were settled. Eventually the artists were paid. "When Mr. Smith found out upon the turning over of the receipts by Dusenberry that he had been outwitted he denounced the company as ingrates and surrendered them their right to act for themselves."[26]

No longer under any obligation to Smith, Sissieretta returned home to Providence for a short time on 4 April 1889 to sing at an Irish Home Rule meeting held that evening at the city's Music Hall. The *Providence Journal* said the purpose of the meeting was to "express condemnation of the base plot concocted by the London Times and the Tory Government against Charles Stewart Parnell and other Irish National leaders."[27] Sissieretta was not listed in the newspaper as one of those appearing at the event, but in an 1893 newspaper clipping pasted in her scrapbook, she said she performed at the Providence meeting.[28] For her appearance she received a medal from her "Providence Friends" with the date "April 4, 1889" engraved at the top of the medal just below her name. The medal must have had particular significance to her, because she kept it until the day she died, one of only three medals she saved throughout her lifetime.[29] Shortly after this presentation, Sissieretta, along with Louis Brown and Will Pierce, appeared with the Excelsior Quartette, "one of the most successful black professional vocal harmony groups of the era," and along with other popular stars, played at Dockstader's Theater on Broadway. The group was billed as "The Georgia Minstrels." They opened 8 April 1889 and performed for a week. The show consisted of jubilee selections and minstrel antics.[30] This was probably Sissieretta's first appearance in a minstrel show, and it is unknown what selections she sang. In early May she advertised her availability to perform during the summer months and said she could be reached through Florence Williams at the *New York Age* or at her Rhode Island residence, 7 Jackson Court, in Providence.[31]

Later that month Sissieretta and baritone Louis Brown began a short southern tour under the management of twenty-four-year-old Benjamin F. Lightfoot, an African American actor and elocutionist from Providence. The tour included concerts in five Virginia cities, Maryland, Washington, D.C., and Delaware, concluding in Stonington, Connecticut, on 6 June.[32] At some point in mid-June, Pierce replaced Brown. In addition to the concerts Lightfoot scheduled, Sissieretta's husband, David, arranged and managed two concerts, 26 and 27 June, to benefit the Asbury Methodist Episcopal Church in his hometown of Baltimore. The organizational name for the concert group was the Cawtee Star Concert Company, and it consisted of Sissieretta, Pierce, and Lightfoot along with the Phoenetic Quartette of Baltimore. The audiences were small both evenings, but the concerts were well received.[33]

One of the city's wealthiest black men, Elijah Johnson, and his wife gave a reception to honor Sissieretta when she was in Baltimore. With the success of her singing career, she and David were traveling in new circles. Neither of them had probably ever imagined she would become so celebrated. Sissieretta gave her farewell concert in Baltimore at the North Street Baptist Church to a large and enthusiastic audience. Church members wanted her to stay for a reception after the concert, but she declined, saying she had to return to New York City to tend to business related to another possible trip to the West Indies.[34]

David Jones must have been pleased with himself for presenting his wife to Baltimore's African American community by arranging and managing several concerts for her in his hometown. He even received a mention for his efforts in the 6 July 1889 issue of the *New York Age*: "D. R. Jones is showing himself a sufficient manager by his qualities of stick and go-a-head."[35] Instead of working primarily behind the scenes, as in the past, he was taking a much more active role in advancing his wife's career and would continue to do so in the upcoming months.

During the last half of 1889, the press reported that Sissieretta was planning to leave on another West Indies tour, this time with Florence Williams (the former reporter for the *New York Age*), who had created her own troupe, the New York Star Concert Company. The company set sail Sunday, 20 October, on the steamer *Athos* for Kingston, Jamaica, but Sissieretta and David were not aboard. Sissieretta, from her home in Providence, sent word to Williams that she and David were not going. Apparently there was some kind of a contract dispute between Sissieretta and Williams. Williams, who had already advertised extensively in the West Indies that Sissieretta would perform with the company, was left without her starring soprano. She hired Mme. Allen of New York at the last minute to take Sissieretta's place. Williams also left without an accompanist when, just before sailing, the pianist she had hired opted not to go.[36] During the last half of 1889 and into 1890, David Jones continued to book concerts for Sissieretta. In August she sang in places such as Newport, Rhode Island, and New York's Richfield Springs and Saratoga. Sissieretta also reportedly hired Italian and French singer Adeil Byround de Combries to tutor her during this time.[37]

Meanwhile things did not go well for Williams in the West Indies. The touring company she had brought there failed to please audiences. Williams returned to New York City in mid-December 1889 to search for some new entertainers for the company.[38] While she was in New York, a letter from Kingston merchant A. E. Lunan, dated 6 January 1890, appeared in the *New York Age* (1 February 1890) explaining why Williams's troupe had been such a failure. Lunan was one of Williams's agents in Jamaica, and he had advanced money for the troupe to travel there. In his letter he said he had told Williams before she left New York that if she brought a first-class company to Kingston, she would be "almost certain of success." Unfortunately, Lunan said, she only brought three worthwhile singers—Madame Allen, Miss India Bell, and Mr. Brown. Many of the men in the troupe, particularly Mr. W. Watts, spent their time off in rum shops and barrooms, "which lowered the company to such an extent that Miss Williams became entirely helpless." Watts gave Williams all kinds of trouble before finally quitting, which left the troupe short of performers. It was at that point that Williams decided to leave her troupe in Kingston and return to New York to find some additional singers. Lunan called her a "brave little woman" and said Williams's friends in Jamaica "are anxiously waiting to see her reap the reward she deserves."[39] Little is known about Williams except that she had worked as a reporter for the *New York Age* and was most likely an ambitious black woman who thought herself capable of managing a troupe of performers at a time in history when it was unusual for a black woman to do so. She obviously convinced Lunan she could manage a troupe, because he advanced the money for the company to travel to Jamaica and agreed to act as its agent.

Williams, upon returning to New York City in mid-December, began negotiating with Sissieretta and her husband about joining the New York Star Concert Company and returning with her to Jamaica. In mid-March 1890 Williams sailed for Jamaica, accompanied by Sissieretta and her husband as well as a pianist, Mr. Jackson, from Providence. She also added Louis L. Brown, the baritone who had been so well received in the West Indies when he toured with Sissieretta and the Tennessee Jubilee Singers, and Mr. Boswick, a basso. Katie Johnson, a soloist and jubilee singer, was also hired, but she missed the boat and had to sail two days later. These singers joined the three remaining members of the troupe in Jamaica—Mme. Allen, Miss India Bell, and Mr. Brown.[40]

Somewhere out on the ocean between New York City and Jamaica, the name of the concert group changed from the New York Star Concert Company to the Star Tennessee Jubilee Singers, because that is the name that appeared in newspaper reports. Perhaps David Jones persuaded Williams to use a name that capitalized on the previously successful Tennessee Jubilee Singers rather than using the New York Star Concert Company name, which had earned a poor reputation during its short tour in Jamaica. The similar name, the Star Tennessee Jubilee Singers, would make it easier to secure bookings, because people in the West Indies would associate it with Sissieretta's first tour there. It appears that Williams and David Jones entered into a partnership to manage the troupe together, as both are referred to as managers in later newspaper reports about the troupe's performances.

The Star Tennessee Jubilee Singers arrived 20 March in Kingston, and the townspeople came to the wharf to greet the new members of the company. Williams, who wrote about the group's arrival for the *New York Age,* said

Sissieretta's name was on everyone's lips. Residents sent her flowers every day, so much so that her room resembled a bower, "where sweet fragrance of appreciation mingles with the sweetest of roses." Sissieretta probably loved being the center of attention once again. Louis Brown and Katie Johnson were also well received, and the former members of the New York Star Concert Company, Allen, Bell, and Brown, were glad to see the new singers and welcomed them with open arms. Williams said, "The company has every prospect of being successful in their tour."[41]

Williams sent a condensed article from the *Jamaica Post* about the company's third performance late in March to the *New York Age,* which published it on 3 May 1890. Every account of the troupe's performances that Williams sent to the *Age,* whether written by her or condensed from local press reports, must be measured against her vested interest in making the concerts appear wonderful and successful. The article said the troupe's performances had been "unqualified successes and this has been owing as much to the high class nature of the entertainments as to the wonderful powers they exhibit." The Saturday night performance opened with a piano solo by Jackson, followed by the company singing the Lord's Prayer together. Katie Johnson sang "Till the Snowflakes Come Again," which pleased the audience so much they demanded an encore. Following that the company sang the jubilee song, "Judgment Will Find You So."

Finally it was Sissieretta's turn. A burst of applause erupted when she was announced. Dressed in a blue velvet gown, she sang "When the Blue Birds Build Again." Throughout this song, the newspaper said, Sissieretta showed her phenomenal range of voice with its purity and sweetness. "Her mastery over every note, her expression, her trills and shakes tell at once why she has been termed, and rightly termed, the Patti of her race." Sissieretta nearly brought the house down with the way she sang her encore, "No Sir." Following Sissieretta, Louis Brown sang "Only to See Her Face." The audience, impressed with his magnificent baritone voice, wanted an encore. The rest of the program featured several solos and duets before the long evening came to an end with the entire company singing "God Save the Queen." At the end of the concert, Brown, speaking on behalf of the company, thanked the audience for their patronage and announced there would be no performance the following week because it was Holy Week.[42]

Williams, who was serving as a special correspondent for the *New York Age,* said the troupe continued to sing in Kingston and had performed two concerts outside the city in Old Harbor and Port Royal. The troupe planned to visit outlying parishes and towns later in May. She reported good attendance for the company's shows and said audiences were most pleased with Sissieretta and Brown.[43] Unfortunately Brown died at some point in May, and no reason for his death was provided in press reports. By early June David Jones returned to New York City for about a week to gather some additional talent for the company and brought news to America of Brown's death. He signed up tenor Will H. Pierce, singer Hattie Brown, and Alice M. Franklin, an elocutionist and dramatic specialist. They returned with him to Jamaica.[44]

The company continued to perform in Jamaica for most of the summer, but by 24 August 1890, the group left for the French-speaking country of Haiti, with plans to go later to Cuba. The company's management was reportedly "reorganized," but no details were given to explain what that meant and how it affected the troupe.[45] David Jones continued to make statements to the press about the company's concert plans, and Williams continued to write descriptive accounts of the troupe's concerts, which indicate that both were still involved with the company's management, although David may have taken on a more leading role.

Williams's account of the Star Tennessee Jubilee Singers' performance at the palace of Haiti's president, Florvil Hyppolite, in Port-au-Prince before a group of the country's elite chronicles a magical evening, one Sissieretta likely remembered all her life. As the company approached the outside of the palace, they saw Chinese lanterns, flags, and streamers of the national colors, with beautiful ferns and native plants hanging on the broad, white portico of the well-guarded palace. "Broad avenues of white pebbles glistened like snow flakes, and the tread of the guards could be heard as they tramped back and forward crying their challenge 'qui vive?' (Who comes there?)," Williams said. The palace was huge, with eight massive pillars and iron shutters and bars. Within an iron and stone fence, guardhouses stood every ten or fifteen feet apart. On the evening of the concert, the troupe arrived at the palace about 7:45 P.M. in carriages sent by President Hyppolite. When the ladies arrived, they were escorted up the broad staircase to their dressing room. After leaving their wraps, they were brought downstairs, and the entire company went to meet the president. Following introductions, they walked down a long hallway to the music hall at the back of the palace, where they found wine, fruit, and perfumery for their enjoyment, Williams said. The stage was set off with ferns, palms, and roses, and a beautiful rug covered the floor.[46]

The concert opened with a grand overture from the palace band followed by a chorus from the company. The audience applauded and called for an encore. Sissieretta was the hit of the evening. "No queen could have been received with greater homage and demonstration. The great hall rang from dome to pit with cheers of 'L'etoile, L'ange' [star, angel]," Williams said. At the close of the concert, Haiti's secretary, on behalf of the president, presented Sissieretta with a large bouquet of roses. Then she and the rest of the company were once again escorted to the reception hall, "where a sumptuous repast, such as only the French are capable of getting up, was served. Toasts, addresses, and flattering compliments were plentiful."[47]

President Hyppolite, who spoke in French, praised the company. A translation of his speech was published in the *New York Age* (27 December 1890): "Ladies and gentlemen of the Tennessee Singers: I am proud of having had the pleasure of listening to such accomplished singers as yourselves. The sweetness, richness, and harmony far surpass anything that I have yet heard on this island, and I feel a pride in complimenting you all upon the great advancement and intelligence you have acquired. I feel proud to see the enlightenment my people are making throughout the world. I say my people, because we have all sprung from the African race. I hope that you will ever meet with success as you travel, and we shall ever bid you welcome whenever you wish to return to Port-au-Prince."

Sissieretta's husband responded on behalf of the company. After speeches members of the company shook hands with the president and his family before returning to their hotel. Williams, in writing about the evening, expressed surprise that the company, which sang no French songs, was so well received in a French-speaking country where few people spoke English. "I asked a French gentleman why it was so, and he told me that the French are music loving people, and as long as there was sweetness and harmony, they would be just as successful in Paris," Williams said.[48]

The Star Tennessee Jubilee Singers achieved great success in Haiti, despite the language barrier and having to compete with two circuses that were in Port-au-Prince at the same time.[49] On New Year's Day 1891, just days before the company's departure for St. Thomas, Sissieretta received a medal that said "Black Patti, Republique 1891 D'Haiti" on the front and "Presented to Mme. M. S. Jones by Inhabitants of Cape Haytien, January 1891" on the back.[50] This is another of the three medals that Sissieretta kept until her death, which may indicate what wonderful memories she had of this country and her reception there.

Arriving in St. Thomas on 5 January 1891, Sissieretta's twenty-third birthday, the company found a beautiful island with a large harbor. Williams described the city's houses as colorful, large, and airy, built two or three stories high in the style of the Dutch or English. They were surrounded by velvetlike lawns, shade trees, and attractive flower gardens. Several old castles belonging to early Danish settlers were also visible. Gaslights lit the city, which had wide streets paved with concrete. Five daily and three weekly newspapers served the city, and telegraph and telephone services were available. The company stayed at the Commercial Hotel, one of the best hotels in the city. It faced the sea and had a beautiful promenade and pavilion with a music stand, where bands played every other day. Sissieretta and her fellow entertainers found something special there: ice, "a godsend in these melting places," Williams said. It was shipped from New York and came at a high price, as much as fifty cents a pound.[51] In St. Thomas the Jubilee Singers gave eleven concerts during their three-week stay.

From the end of January until early July, the Star Tennessee Jubilee Singers crisscrossed the West Indies and toured in a few cities in South America, coming back to some places multiple times. They sang concerts in Barbados, Grenada, British Guiana, Antigua, St. Kitts, Montserrat, and Nevis.[52] In April, while in Georgetown, British Guiana, a city Sissieretta's former manager James Smith had accused of being prejudiced against black people, the citizens there presented her with a gold tiara as a token of their appreciation. The tiara was adorned with three stars accented by a diamond at the center of each star.[53] In addition to its obvious monetary value, it symbolized the growing recognition and adoration she was receiving from her fans—a perfect gift for an up-and-coming prima donna.

In early July the troupe boarded the steamship *Muriel* and left St. Kitts, arriving in Brooklyn on 6 July 1891. When the ship arrived, two of Sissieretta's trunks, along with those of several others, had not been declared. Officials decided to send the bags over to New York City "for appraisement," which apparently meant they would be cleared there through customs and assessed for tax purposes. David Jones "rushed about the various Barge Office departments in perspiration to hurry up matters." Meanwhile the entire company had to wait. Sissieretta paced up and down "with dramatic nervousness," while two wagons stood ready to pick up the baggage. Finally, two hours later, everything was straightened out, and the party left with their baggage.[54] Sissieretta and David were home once again.

Sissieretta's second tour of the West Indies and parts of South America, which lasted sixteen months, and her first, six-month tour were similar in that they both included countries that had large, predominately poor, black populations with smaller populations of white Europeans who made up most of the business and governing class. But they were different in several ways. First many of the musical selections on the second tour were different from those of the first tour. Sissieretta's new repertoire included "Il Bacio" by Arditi and Gounod's "Ave Maria." Tenor Will Pierce added several new pieces as well, including one of the earliest "coon songs," "A New Coon in Town," by Paul Allen. This piece was probably the most remarkable addition to the company's repertoire, because it was far removed from the spiritual selections for which most jubilee troupes were known. It shows how David Jones and

A young Sissieretta Jones poses for her portrait in New York City. She is wearing several of the medals she received from countries in the West Indies and South America after her tours there in 1888 and 1890. Photograph courtesy of the Dramatic Museum Portrait Collection, Rare Book and Manuscript Library, Columbia University.

Florence Williams were willing to try something totally new to draw in audiences. Music scholar John Graziano writes that the troupe presented "a musical program that ignored minstrel show stereotypes and demonstrated a versatility of musical styles and genres."[55]

The second difference in this tour was its management. Instead of a white man with major financial backing and management experience running the day-to-day operations of the company,[56] two African Americans with limited funds and supervisory experience directed the troupe—a woman, who was a former newspaper reporter, and the husband of the company's star. With his new management role, David was emerging as an important factor in the development of Sissieretta's early career. He had apparently observed and learned a great deal while traveling with Sissieretta on her first tour. Williams, with her writing and reporting expertise, seems to have been adept in handling publicity and press relations. The descriptive concert reports she sent to the black press in the United States gave American readers a fascinating look at the troupe's travels and its warm reception in these foreign countries. These reports, many of them featuring Sissieretta's performances, enhanced the young soprano's reputation back in the States while she was traveling in the West Indies.

The final difference between these two tours was the fact that Jones and Williams did not try to portray this troupe as an extension of the Fisk Jubilee Singers as manager James Smith did on Sissieretta's first tour. Smith told audiences that the Fisk Jubilee Singers had split into three factions and that his troupe was one of those factions.[57] Unlike Smith, Jones and Williams did not claim or imply that the Star Tennessee Jubilee Singers were trying to raise money for Fisk University or any black college. By not pretending to be part of the Fisk Singers, the performers and managers on the second tour were free to arrange their own musical program rather than limiting themselves to spirituals.

All in all the second tour was a tremendous success. "They had managed to sustain this second tour from their own resources for over a year and had returned with unimaginable riches as well as new fame," Graziano writes.[58] These riches included personal gifts to Sissieretta from officials and citizens of countries she visited—gold medals, five hundred dollars in gold from the Haitian president, a diamond-studded tiara, four pearls, one emerald, one ruby, and one large diamond.[59] Sissieretta had cinched her status as an international star with this second tour, and now, back in the United States, she had to try and capitalize on her new standing and earn a place on the American entertainment scene. The black press appeared ready to sing her praises shortly after she returned home. The *Indianapolis Freeman* wrote, "The story of her triumph, measured by years is a short one, but within the same time, we know of no Afro-American songstress who has so filled the measure of brilliant achievement upon the lyric stage as this young song bird of the western world."[60] Sissieretta would not disappoint her admirers, as they would soon see.

3

"I Woke Up Famous"
1892

With the success of two West Indian and South American tours behind her, Sissieretta returned to New York in July 1891, more experienced and eager to advance her concert career in the United States. She rejoined Flora Batson Bergen to sing with her in a few Bergen Star Concerts managed by Batson's husband, John. He booked the two singers to appear together at several church concerts during October in Brooklyn, New York City, and Philadelphia. In Brooklyn the concert at the Bridge Street Church on 8 October 1891 was well attended, with people paying fifty cents for a ticket. By the time the choir sang the opening chorus at 8:25 P.M., all the seats were filled, including chairs placed in the aisles, and some people in the audience had to stand for the entire performance. Batson and Sissieretta, who was making her first appearance in Brooklyn, were the stars of the evening. Both were praised in a newspaper review of the concert. One critic wrote that Madame Jones had a sweet voice of splendid range and excellent control and an "exceedingly pleasing" stage presence, and he predicted that, "if all the conditions were equal, there is no question but that she would in time become as great a favorite in the United States as she is in the West Indies."[1]

By early December 1891, Sissieretta was no longer singing with the Bergen Star Concert Company and was reported to be touring the South, perhaps at concerts arranged by her husband.[2] Shortly after plans for a southern tour were announced in the press, the *Indianapolis Freeman* reported that "Black Patti" was touring the West, although it is unknown whether she actually toured the South or the West at the end of December. As the new year began, Sissieretta celebrated her twenty-fourth birthday and apparently decided to start using her musical-sounding middle name rather than her first name, Matilda, in advertising and other publicity materials. By early 1892 Sissieretta's name began to appear in newspaper articles and advertisements as Mme. M.

Sissieretta Jones rather than Matilda S. Jones, which she had used in her ear-lier concerts and on her tours of the West Indies and South America.

Since her return from the West Indies, Sissieretta had been performing before largely black audiences, mostly at African American churches, the typi-cal venue for black musicians and singers who performed serious or classical music. On 18 February 1892 she sang at a testimonial concert in Brooklyn to honor the prominent African American pianist Mrs. Albert (Georgiana) Wil-son, who had on occasion accompanied Batson and who later became Sissie-retta's accompanist. A number of leading black citizens attended the concert at Jefferson Hall, Court Square, in Brooklyn. The stars of the evening were Mrs. Wilson, violinist Walter Craig, and Sissieretta. Others appearing were tenor Henry Jackson, soprano Maggie Scott, and basso William Jackson. The black press said the testimonial was one of the best entertainments of the year and described it as a "notable artistic and social success."[3] A few days after the testimonial concert, Sissieretta went to Washington, D.C., to perform Mon-day evening, 22 February, at the Metropolitan African Methodist Episcopal Church, located at Fifteenth and M Streets. The audience that evening was the largest the church had ever experienced.[4] Every available seat was taken and many people had to be turned away.

With a successful Washington debut before a black audience behind her, Sissieretta was poised to make history in the capital city, this time appearing before a select white audience—the president of the United States and his guests. Although not the first black singer to appear at the White House, she was one of the first African American female vocalists to perform there. Sissieretta went to the White House to give a luncheon concert in the Blue Room. How she came to be invited is unknown. Sissieretta, escorted by David Jones and her accompanist, Charles Dunger, arrived at the Executive Mansion at 10 A.M. on Wednesday, 24 February. Wearing a gown with a bodice covered in medals from her West Indian and South American tours, Sissieretta stood before President Benjamin Harrison, his family, and his guests and sang Stephen Foster's "Swanee River," a folk song she would sing hundreds of times in her career and one that would become her signature song. She also sang Bishop's "Home, Sweet Home," a waltz by Pattison, and the cavatina from Meyerbeer's *Robert le Diable*. Caroline Harrison, a profes-sional musician before becoming first lady, was so pleased with the concert that she presented Sissieretta with a bouquet of White House orchids.[5] Sissie-retta returned to the White House several times during her career, reportedly singing before four consecutive presidents: Benjamin Harrison, Grover Cleve-land, William McKinley, and Theodore Roosevelt. To date no details about these other performances have been found.[6]

A photograph of Sissieretta taken during a session at a New York photography studio. Photograph courtesy of the Dr. Carl R. Gross Collection, Moorland-Spingarn Research Center, Howard University.

A week after her first White House performance, the *Washington Post* published an article that described Sissieretta as having "pure negro blood," which was proved by her "charcoal complexion and unmistakably African cast of countenance." "Nevertheless," the newspaper continued, "she is of a very pleasing appearance and, according to the testimony of the ablest musical critics, undoubtedly gifted with a marvelous voice, rivaling in strength and sweetness the tones of the world's most famous prima donnas."[7] The black newspaper the *Washington Bee* had high praise for Sissieretta. "Madame M. Sissieretta Jones is the name of the lady who has won a reputation of which she should feel proud, one who is an honor of the colored race."[8]

By the end of April, Sissieretta was in New York City, booked to sing at a three-day "Grand Negro Jubilee" before a mixed-race audience at Madison Square Garden—an event that ultimately helped to make her famous in the United States. Sissieretta's husband, David, was largely responsible for getting her top billing at the Grand Negro Jubilee and cakewalk. By the spring of 1892, Sissieretta had only been back in America from her West Indian tour for a short time, yet somehow David was able to get Sissieretta hired as the prima donna for this show. Manager John Bergen had been trying to secure the key singing position for his wife, Flora Batson, but David found a way to defeat Bergen's efforts. This outcome upset Bergen, who responded by billing his wife as the "Real Patti," a name that stayed with Batson to some degree until her death in 1906.[9] The event surely strained the formerly cordial relationship between the Bergens and the Joneses. Manager S. Goodfriend had secured Madison Square Garden for 26–28 April (Tuesday through Thursday) to hold the Grand Negro Jubilee that the *New York Dramatic Mirror* said would in-clude "singing, cake-walking, and other diversions illustrative of the customs of our dusky citizens." Goodfriend had originally arranged to hold the final night of the Jubilee on Saturday, 30 April, but gave up that date to help organ-izers for the Actor's Fund Fair, who needed the Garden free that night so workers could get ready for the organization's three-day fund-raising event scheduled to begin early the following week.[10] Goodfriend's action was re-warded, as many prominent theatrical and entertainment people bought boxes and seats for the opening night of the Grand Negro Jubilee. Articles in the *New York Times* leading up to the opening night said the event would feature Jules Levy, a white bandleader born in London, his military band playing in-strumentals, and Sissieretta singing along with the "Alabama Quartet" and a chorus of four hundred "colored people" to add to the harmony. The news-paper said that the upcoming program would include a double banjo quintet and that the night would end at eleven o'clock with a championship cake-walk.[11] The cakewalk was "a duple-time dance with simple syncopations," whose beginnings could be traced back to pre–Civil War plantations, where enslaved couples competed for a cake or other prizes by performing a "high-stepping" promenade.[12] Some scholars say slaves developed this kind of danc-ing "into a parody of the mannerisms and fashions of the white southern elite."[13] After the Civil War, black minstrels often performed cakewalks as the grand finale of minstrel shows. Cakewalk competitors in stage shows dressed in fancy, colorful outfits, often with silk hats for the men and highly decora-tive hats for the women. They attempted to show off their own distinctive, creative moves while parading before judges and the audience. By the 1890s the dance became popular first among African Americans, and later white people became fascinated with it. The cakewalk at the Grand Negro Jubilee would have seventy-five couples in the competition, including some of the best-known black cakewalkers: Blackburn, Snow and Schudder, Luke Pully, and Dandy Jim. Cash prizes, a gold badge, and the "cake" would be awarded the winning contestants.[14]

By 9 P.M. on the opening night of the jubilee, 26 April, 5,000 people, nearly 3,700 of whom were white, were seated in the auditorium of Madison Square Garden. The boxes and arena seats were filled "by people whom one would not often see at a cakewalk."[15] Many of the ladies wore "dazzling" dresses and jewelry, and most men were in evening dress. Earlier in the day, the *New York Times* had published an article naming many of the prominent theatrical and business professionals who planned to come to the event. The newspaper said the most "important feature" of the evening would be the "first" public appearance in New York City of the "famous" prima donna Mme. Sissieretta Jones, known as the "Black Patti."[16] Apparently the newspaper was unaware that Sissieretta had first performed in New York City at Steinway Hall back in 1888 with Batson at a Bergen Star Concert. One can assume that the white patrons in the audience were curious to see what a black jubilee was like and to hear a black prima donna who had been likened to Adelina Patti, one of the few performers of her day who could draw a crowd large enough to fill Madison Square Garden.[17]

The Madison Square Garden building where the jubilee took place, completed in 1890, was the second of four such buildings to bear that name in the past one hundred years. Designed by architect Stanford White, the yellow brick and white terra-cotta building with a tower that reached 320 feet from the street was considered the "central palace of pleasure" in New York City, hosting various entertainments such as balls, concerts, ballets, boxing exhibitions, and horse shows. The auditorium, with its pale red walls and eighty-foot ceiling, seated eight thousand people, with room on the floor for several thousand more. On the northwest corner of the Garden complex there was a 1,200-seat theater, and on the southeast side, a 1,500-seat concert hall. The grand entrance, constructed of lavender marble and featuring a Roman colonnade, was along Madison Avenue.[18]

As the concert began that evening with several selections by the band, twenty-four-year-old Sissieretta, while waiting to make her entrance, would have time to think about her upcoming debut before one of the largest mixed-race audiences she had ever sung for. Was she anxious? Probably. Was she confident she could win them over? Perhaps. After the band played, the Jubilee Chorus sang some songs, followed by a "Southern shuffle executed by three colored damsels." Next came an "amusing" fake fight, which one newspaper called a "Battle Royal" or "Hit a Head When You See It" by four black men wearing soft gloves. Finally it was Sissieretta's turn. Wearing long white gloves, a pearl gray gown, and a chestful of medals, Sissieretta smiled broadly as she walked confidently up the steps to the platform in the center of the huge amphitheater. If she was nervous, she did not let her audience see any evidence of it. The *New York Herald* described her as being "very black, but with pleasing features" and said she was "perfectly self possessed." Standing at the center of the stage, she began singing the cavatina from Meyerbeer's opera *Robert le Diable*. The audience appeared enchanted and applauded loudly when she finished, calling for an encore. Sissieretta responded with "Swanee River." Again the audience asked for more, and she sang "Maggie, the Cows Are in the Clover." When she had finished, the audience gave her a standing ovation. After a brief intermission at 10 P.M., some dancers took the stage to perform "buck dancing" and a "buzzard lope dance." The dancers were followed by more selections from Levy's band and more singing by the Jubilee Chorus. Next came a "skirt dance," and then it was Sissieretta's turn to come back and sing. This time she sang "La Farfalla" by Gelli and "Sempre Libera" from Verdi's *La Traviata*. The final event of the evening was the cakewalk. The *New York Herald* reporter attending the event said the contestants were still walking after midnight and that no one had taken the cake by the time he had to file his report.[19]

After the concert the *Herald* writer spoke with Charles F. Chatterton, who had been in the audience to watch the Jubilee. Chatterton was responsible for looking after Adelina Patti for her manager, Mr. Abbey. The *Herald* reporter asked him what he thought about the Black Patti, to which he replied, "This colored woman is certainly a very good natural singer, and while I should hardly feel like comparing her voice with Mme. Patti's, I find her negro dialect much better, as shown in her rendering of the 'Suwanee River.'"[20] The *Herald* reporter also interviewed Sissieretta in her dressing room after the performance. She told him she had not been nervous on the stage and had found the acoustic properties of the Garden superb. She said the last time she had sung in New York had been when Frederick Douglass lectured at Cooper Union. Sissieretta said she was living at the Hotel Venus, on West Seventeenth Street. The reporter described the young vocalist as well spoken but said she tended to be somewhat reserved and hesitant. Years later, while thinking back on her 1892 performance at Madison Square Garden, Sissieretta said, "I woke up famous after singing at the Garden and didn't know it."[21] In the days before radio, television, and the Internet, entertainers had to rely on newspapers, handbills, advance agents, and word of mouth to help them realize fame and recognition, and that took time. Other than the immediate positive reviews of her performance at the jubilee, it would be months before Sissieretta learned the extent of her success.

Newspaper critics were not overly impressed with the jubilee. One said the show might have been better on a stage rather than in the large arena, where the banjo playing and choral singing echoed, spoiling the sound for the audience. The newspaper said the "sparring" and "skirt dancing" showed "neither science nor art."[22] The critics, however, gave Sissieretta's performance special attention. A reviewer for the entertainment newspaper the *New York Dramatic Mirror* appeared surprised with the quality of her voice.

> The negro jubilee . . . would be worthy of little note were it not that it brought to the attention of New Yorkers a singer, who leaving her color altogether out of the question, has one of the most pleasing soprano voices ever heard in this city. We confess that the advance notices of Sisieretta [*sic*] Jones, the singer in question, did not predispose in her favor. The announcement that she was "the Black Patti" and the wearer of more medals than any other singer in the world savored of palaver and vulgarity. She appeared on stage, however, in a modest and becoming gown of pearl gray; she stood quietly and seemingly at ease; and she sang the cavatina from Robert le Diable with a purity of tone, an accuracy of phrasing, and a richness and a power that the audience, which hitherto had been bored, applauded and cheered. . . .
>
> No manager need be afraid to have Sisieretta [*sic*] Jones in his company. She is an artist, and the statement made by her manager that she is the greatest singer of her race should be altered to the statement that she is one of the best of any race.[23]

Another New York City newspaper called Sissieretta's performance the "piece de resistance of the bill." The writer said, "If godless people went to the Garden last night to 'guy' [ridicule] the 'Black Patti' they were humiliated in the extreme, for there was everything in her voice and method to commend and nothing to deplore."[24] Still another New York review, published in the African American newspaper the *Detroit Plaindealer,* called Sissieretta "A Patti with a soul." The reviewer said, "The soul of a nightingale seems to have lodged in that throat. She sings with remarkable passion and depth of feeling." The writer's closing comments would prove prophetic regarding Sissieretta's stage career:

> It is rather pitiful to think of the way in which her career may be hampered because of her race—not because of prejudice exactly, but she certainly cannot appear in opera, in which she would undoubtedly succeed, unless one were written especially for her, and then almost insuperable

Early 1890s; Sissieretta loved jewelry and enjoyed wearing beautiful gowns.
Photograph courtesy of the Dramatic Museum Portrait Collection,
Rare Book and Manuscript Library, Columbia University.

difficulties would attend its production. She will be limited to concert, and even there, after the novelty has died out, her color will be an unpleasant circumstance to those over-fastidious people who demand an angel in face as well as in voice for their delectation at a public performance.

But if, after the canaille has sated its curiosity it forsakes the "Black Patti" to run after some pink and white singer of opera bouffe, or the next sensation, Miss Jones may be sure she will be able to secure an audience of true music lovers as long as she keeps that glorious and thrilling voice, the wonderful gift of God to this young woman—this raven that is yet a nightingale.[25]

Sissieretta's performance at Madison Square Garden was the turning point in her concert career. Prominent people recognized her talent, and many opportunities in terms of professional management and singing engagements became available to her. Some have said there was talk about hiring Sissieretta to play "dark roles" in *Aida* and *L'Africaine* at the Metropolitan Opera House, but she was never given that opportunity.[26] With her appearance at Madison Square Garden, she had extended her reach by successfully entertaining a large, mixed-race audience in a major cosmopolitan venue. Black music critic Sylvester Russell, writing years later about Sissieretta's 1892 concert at the Garden, said, "It was on this occasion that Sissieretta Jones, billed as Black Patti, made her American reputation that carried her fame the world over."[27] Authors Langston Hughes and Milton Meltzer, in their 1967 book about the history of black entertainment, wrote that Sissieretta was one of the greatest black concert singers and listed her 1892 performance at Madison Square Garden as one of thirty-six milestones in the history of the "Negro's participation in American entertainment": "Of the all-time greats among Negroes in the various fields of entertainment, there can be little argument concerning the place of such names as Ira Aldridge, Buddy Bolden, Black Patti, Ernest Hogan, Bert Williams, Florence Mills or Bojangles, whose talent and popularity history confirms, or whose sparks of personality still light the memories of living spectators old enough to have once seen or heard any of them."[28]

Two nights after the jubilee closed, Sissieretta sang a concert on Saturday evening, 30 April, at the Academy of Music in New York City, sharing the stage once again with Jules Levy and his military band and with the Alabama Quartet. Goodfriend, fresh from his jubilee starring Sissieretta, scheduled the young singer for a limited tour of large cities such as Philadelphia and Boston. She appeared in Philadelphia on 9 May at the Bethel A.M.E. Church and was back in New York by 18 May, when she sang at Brooklyn's Academy of Music. During this time an article about Sissieretta was published 14 May 1892, in the *Message,* a newspaper that said it was endeavoring to "become an educator among the Afro-Americans and whites so as to lead them into closer relations with each other." The article described how she looked: "Madame Jones is a woman of exceedingly pleasing presence. Tall, well rounded shape, she moves with a natural, but seductive grace that suggests thoughts of a Cleopatra. Her skin has a soft lack-lustre tint as of blue plush in shadow. Her eyes are expressive and intuitively play sympathetically a colloquial part. Her teeth would be the envy of her fair sisters and the despair of dentistry. Her rather thin lips are fond of exposing their even rows, snowy white, whether in song or conversation. Her hair is straight. She is agreeable in manner, but rather reticent in conversation. Her bearing is not marked by any uncertainty of speech, though she lingers over her sentences to select and shape them."[29]

Sissieretta's next big career break came two months after her Madison Square Garden appearance. A prominent white manager and promoter, Maj. James B. Pond, approached Sissieretta about handling her. He managed Levy and his military band, with whom Sissieretta had shared the stage at the Grand Negro Jubilee. Pond was a major player in the field of entertainment. He owned and operated the American Lecture and Musical Agency, which represented many famous musicians and authors, including Charles Dickens, John Greenleaf Whittier, Mark Twain, and later Paul Laurence Dunbar. Sissieretta and her husband signed a one-year contract with Pond on 8 June 1892, with an option for him to renew it for two additional years. The contract, which gave Pond exclusive rights to manage Sissieretta, had two different payment schedules—one for concerts before 14 November 1892 and one for concerts after that date. Sissieretta was required to give Pond 15 percent of all monies received for singing concerts scheduled before 14 November 1892, except when he agreed to secure a concert for her and pay her a set amount for that performance. Pond had the right to pay for as many single concerts between 8 June and 14 November 1892 as he thought "judicious." The terms of the contract make it appear that Sissieretta had some concerts already scheduled before 14 November and that Pond was willing to let her meet those obligations before he took total control of her schedule.[30]

The arrangement changed after 14 November 1892. Beginning on that date and until 1 June 1893, the agreement called for Sissieretta to sing no more than seven concerts a week or less than five and to keep all singing engagements of any kind "whatsoever" that Pond arranged. Beginning 14 November 1892 Pond would pay Sissieretta a flat fee of $150 a week (equal to about $3,650 in purchasing power in 2009)[31] plus traveling expenses (sleeping car on the train, carriage expenses, and first-class hotel accommodations) for Sissieretta, her husband, and her maid. She was to be paid every Saturday. Pond gave Sissieretta the option of hiring her own accompanist instead of a maid, which she did. He agreed to pay the accompanist $35 a week (the equivalent of about $850 in purchasing power in 2009)[32] and required the accompanist to play all of Sissieretta's concerts. The contract further spelled out what the financial arrangements would be if Pond decided to take Sissieretta to England to sing during the 1892 or 1893 season. She would receive one-half of the net profits of a European tour after all traveling, living, advertising, and other necessary expenses were paid for Sissieretta, her husband, and Pond. Pond said that he would pay for all expenses in the event the concert receipts did not cover them. The contract was witnessed by William Glass and musician Jules Levy.

This contract would make David and Sissieretta quite wealthy. If Sissieretta worked the typical forty-four-week entertainment season, she would make $6,600 for the year. The average annual wage for workers in 1892, excluding farm laborers, was $495. The average annual wage for one of the highest-paid worker categories in 1892, federal employees, was $1,096.[33] She would be making more than six times that much. It appeared that David's years of promoting Sissieretta either behind the scenes or by managing her concerts and Sissieretta's hard work to improve and master her voice were about to pay off now that Pond was going to manage her career. Pond would handle the logistics and business side of her career—booking concerts, handling publicity, making travel arrangements—so she could concentrate solely on performing and perfecting her singing. With the signing of this contract, the soft-spoken twenty-four-year-old was poised to become a true prima donna with someone to handle her every need as she traveled from one singing engagement to another. She would wear fine clothes, stay in first-class hotels, and have her own accompanist. She would make a great deal of money, and there was a possibility she might travel to Europe to sing. All this for the little girl with the big voice who got her start singing in church in Virginia and then Rhode Island. She would be able to send money to her mother in Providence, who continued to make her living by taking in washing and ironing. When David and Sissieretta signed their names to the contract on 8 June 1892, they must have been thrilled and brimming with great expectations for the future. But, as they would later learn, everything comes with a price.

A week after signing the contract with Pond, Sissieretta sang at a benefit concert on 15 June to raise money for the poor. The city's black fraternal organization, the Society for the Sons of New York, sponsored the event. Most likely the concert had been arranged before Pond came on the scene. The all-black performance, featuring Sissieretta and Jeannette Doyle as sopranos, was held at Carnegie Hall, which had been open for about a year. The sold-out event did not take place in the main hall but rather in the 1,200-seat lower-level auditorium, which was then called "Recital Hall" (known today as Zankel Hall). It was the second time African Americans had performed onstage in any part of Carnegie Hall.[34] The recital hall, "jammed almost to suffocation" and stifling with the mid-June heat, prompted audience members to wave souvenir fans in an effort to cool themselves. Performers that night included Harry T. Burleigh, baritone; W. S. Durham and J. W. Cochran, both tenors; Burr Edwards, bass; Walter F. Craig and Martinius G. Knowlton, both violinists; and Georgiana Wilson, pianist. Sissieretta sang Gounod's "Ave Maria," Verdi's "Sempre Libera" from *La Traviata*, and later, by request, "Swanee River." Just before she came onto the stage for the first time, the audience began to give her round after round of applause. A review of the concert in the *New York Echo* said that her notes were "clear as a mocking bird's and her enunciation was perfect."[35] The audience loved her.

With her Carnegie Hall experience behind her, Sissieretta focused on Pond's plans for her career. In June he announced that she, along with Levy and his military band, would be touring all the large U.S. cities the following season.[36] Before sending Sissieretta on tour with Levy, Pond first had her travel with a small troupe of white European musicians. This was the first time she had ever starred with a group of white music professionals. The clever manager probably realized that most white American entertainers would not tour with or appear on the same stage in a troupe starring an African American singer. By featuring Sissieretta in a company of foreign musicians and vocalists, Pond avoided this problem and, at the same time, may have attracted white concertgoers eager to hear European performers. As one music scholar wrote, "This novel arrangement was certainly a brave move on his part, since there was no precedent for a mixed-race 'high art' troupe in the United States just twenty-six years after emancipation.[37]

Pond booked Sissieretta in a number of festivals and other venues where she would be seen by large, predominantly white audiences and her appearances reported on by the white press. One of her first engagements was in the New York resort town of Saratoga Springs. On Monday, 6 August 1892, more than five thousand people assembled in the lake pavilion at the town's Congress Spring Park to hear her sing. Saratoga Springs, nestled in the foothills of the Southern Adirondack mountain region of upstate New York, was the perfect place for Sissieretta to encounter a white, "upper-crust" audience who were receptive to listening to her sing operatic and concert music. These were people who had come to the resort town to relax and spend time in the healing spring waters or perhaps gamble at one of the oldest racetracks in the United States. They were people on summer holiday, open to being entertained while sitting in the beautiful Congress Springs Park gardens and probably curious about a black woman singing serious music. The concert began with three selections by the orchestra. Then Sissieretta made her entrance and sang an aria from *Robert le Diable*. Following a "rousing" response from the audience, she gave an encore, "Maggie, the Cows Are in the Clover." She sang a third encore before leaving the stage. Later in the evening she sang Gelli's "Farfalla" with great expression. Again she was called on to give two more encores, "The Song of the Bobolink" and "Swanee River." The highlight of the evening came at the close of the program, when she sang Gounod's "Ave Maria." She left the stage even though the audience applauded and asked for more. A review in the *Saratoga Union* the next day described Sissieretta's voice as "beautiful, clear, steady and resonant. There is neither brass in her notes nor thickness in her phrasing. Her enunciation is also perfect. The exquisite crispness with which she executes complicated scales in rapid time delighted all. Withal she sings intelligently, without affectation, and with much feeling."[38]

Sissieretta next sang at the Auditorium in Asbury Park, New Jersey, where she did two performances on 11 and 12 August with the European group formed by Pond. The group consisted of Sissieretta, violinist Princess Lily Dolgorouky, the "Lutteman Swedish Male Sextette," and pianist Herr Rudolph Von Scarfa. Princess Dolgorouky, born in Spain, was related through marriage to the reigning family of Russia, where she had studied and conducted the orchestra that played for the empress of Russia.[39] The program included four selections by the Lutteman Sextette, two piano solos by Von Scarfa, two vocal solos by Sissieretta, and two violin solos by Princess Dolgorouky. Both Sissieretta and the princess were singled out for praise in newspaper reviews following the concerts. Although concertgoers may not have been familiar with Black Patti and Princess Dolgorouky, they had heard of the women's agent, Major Pond, and had confidence in the talent he typically presented. One newspaper credited Pond for the full houses at these concerts.[40] Clearly Sissieretta was benefiting from her manager's outstanding reputation.

On Sunday, 14 August, Sissieretta sang a sacred concert at Congress Spring Park. The following day she appeared at the park again, this time singing to the largest crowd ever gathered there. People began to stream into the park an hour before the concert was to begin, quickly filling every available chair, bench, or seat. About 60 percent of the people who came to hear Sissieretta had to stand for the entire program. The little lake with the pavilion in the center where she performed was surrounded on all sides by the crowd of five thousand to six thousand people. Sissieretta, greeted by applause, acknowledged the crowd with a graceful bow and made her way to the platform to sing her first selection. "As her first notes broke upon the vast crowd, there was the most intent quiet, which remained to the end, and then the applause broke out heartily and continued until the singer responded."[41] Sissieretta sang two encores familiar to the audience, "Maggie, the Cows Are in the Clover" and "Every Rose Must Have Its Thorn." As with her previous performance at Congress Spring Park, she opened the second half of the concert with "La Farfalla" and then sang two familiar encores, "Swanee River" and "The Song of the Bobolink." She again closed the concert with Gounod's "Ave Maria." Although the audience applauded for a long time after she finished her final selection, she did not sing an encore. Instead she bowed to show her thanks and left the stage. The *Daily Saratogian* called her a "phenomenal woman."[42]

Two days later Sissieretta appeared at the Buffalo Exposition (16–18 August). Once again Major Pond had chosen the perfect venue for her to gain wider exposure and to extend her fame. On her first night in Buffalo, she drew huge crowds and received extensive press coverage. When she finished her opening night performance, she put on her cloak to leave the stage, but the audience would not have it. They wanted more. The exposition's manager jumped onto the platform where Sissieretta was standing and spoke with her briefly, after which she laid down her cloak and stepped forward to sing once again. As requested, she sang what had become her signature song, "Swanee River." The audience stopped talking and listened intently. "The room, with the exception of the noise of the engines, was as still as death. The voice of the sweet singer rang out loud and clear in the familiar strains of that old melody and when the last notes died away not a person stirred. It was a full thirty seconds before anyone made a move and then the house nearly came down with the thunderous applause," one newspaper reported.[43]

Sissieretta returned to Congress Spring Park in Saratoga Springs for two additional performances on 27 and 28 August. The Saturday evening concert was done in conjunction with an orchestra. The audience of about 2,500 was "distinguished and cosmopolitan" and represented every section of the country. All the seats were taken despite the cool weather. Extra chairs were even placed in the pavilion where the orchestra was set up, which gave the band barely enough room to perform. A review in the *Daily Saratogian* (29 August 1892) said, "Mrs. Jones has every reason to feel proud of her reception in Saratoga, and her success has rivalled, if it has not exceeded, that of the most famous prima donnas who have favored Saratoga with their presence."[44] The next evening, Sunday, she did a sacred concert, which began with Millard's "Ave Maria" sung in English. The local newspaper said the sacred concert in the park was "equally brilliant and successful," as had been her Saturday night performance. In all Sissieretta reportedly sang before more than sixty thousand people at the Congress Spring Park concerts during that three-week period in August 1892. She also had great successes at the Buffalo Exposition and with her concerts at Asbury Park. "Clearly, the Major's initial gamble paid off, both artistically and financially: as these reviews demonstrate, the public had a genuine fascination to see and hear the Black Patti. And once they heard her, they were enchanted by the exceptional qualities of her voice," wrote one music scholar.[45]

While Sissieretta was entertaining audiences in the North, traveling first class, and making a name for herself, African Americans elsewhere, particularly in the South, were being subjected to segregation, diminished civil rights, and violence. Of the 6.5 million African Americans residing in the United States between 1880 and 1900, nine out of every ten lived in the South, and 80 percent of them lived in rural areas. During this period more blacks began to move to southern cities such as Nashville, Montgomery, and Raleigh. A small percentage of African Americans lived in northern states, mostly in urban areas. By the 1890s Jim Crow laws had been instituted throughout the South.

These laws segregated African Americans in public places such as schools, theaters, restaurants, trains, and streetcars. Southern states also passed laws restricting the right of black citizens to vote by instituting literacy and property requirements and charging poll taxes.[46]

Laws passed after the Civil War and during Reconstruction that had given African Americans equal rights were rewritten and "reinterpreted" when federal troops were pulled out of the South, thus changing the standard of justice for black and white citizens. "The most terrible outcome of this erosion of rights was the denial of due process of law: People who committed crimes against African Americans failed to be arrested or prosecuted, and African Americans who were accused of wrongdoing were not assured of a fair trial."[47] African Americans were often subjected to violence—lynching in rural areas and mob violence in cities. More than one hundred people were lynched annually between 1882 and 1901, most of them black people living in the South. According to official reports, about two thousand African Americans were lynched in those decades, although there were likely many more incidences that went unreported. Black journalist and activist Ida B. Wells railed against lynching, writing articles about it and speaking to women's groups, churches, and meetings of African Americans. In October 1892 she published a pamphlet called *Southern Horrors: Lynch Law in All Its Phases*.[48] Sissieretta had to have been aware of the racism and injustices against her people. Unfortunately she left no diaries or journals to tell how deeply this violence and these injustices troubled her.

Until her big break at Madison Square Garden, Sissieretta had performed mostly for black patrons, primarily at churches and community halls. Now, under the direction of Major Pond, she was performing to mostly white audiences. While making her first appearance in Toronto in mid-September 1892, Sissieretta granted an interview to a reporter for the *Empire* and talked a little about her new white patrons. She told the reporter that she had been singing ever since she was a little girl, "but always among my own people. It is only recently that I have sung to white audiences, and only in last March that I came out in New York." The reporter asked whether she liked singing before white audiences as much as for black audiences. " I do not feel as much at home with them yet," she replied. "I am a little shy lest they should not like me. But so far they have proved most kind." During the interview the reporter asked her if she would like to sing opera. She said, "I have had an offer to sing in the new opera 'Scipio Africanus,' by the composer of 'Cavalloria [*sic*] Rusticana.' But I do not know whether I should like it. I prefer the concert platform for the present."[49] No evidence of this offer has been found other than Sissieretta's comments to the reporter in Canada, but if indeed she was approached about singing opera, she may have decided to stick with the lucrative concert arrangements she had with Major Pond rather than risking something new and untried.

The *Empire* reporter conducted the interview with Sissieretta at the Metropole Hotel, where she greeted him "in the simple unaffected manner that is one of her chief platform charms." He said that she had a gentle voice, spoke with a "clear, pure accent of a gentlewoman," used words sparingly, and was "modest and retiring." In his report the writer described how she had appeared on the stage: "She has a perfect figure, a pretty, natural carriage, and a pleasant, girlish face lit with dark, soft eyes. Her dress is the perfection of richness and good taste; a combination of form and color that gives the dusky skin effective setting. Her hair, of heavy, dusky black, without ever a kink or curl, is coiled in a Grecian knot at the nape of the neck showing a prettily shaped head. The front of her bodice is aglitter with medals, her dark fingers ablaze with rings. As she stands before her audience, we understand for the first time something of the fascinations of the dark-hued women of the Orient."[50]

By the end of September, Sissieretta had started performing with Levy and his military band. Pond negotiated a twenty-five-day appearance for Levy and his band at the Pittsburgh Exposition. Levy's group started at the exposition on opening day, Wednesday, 7 September. Pond later arranged for Sissieretta to appear at the exposition as well. The annual exposition was similar to today's large state fairs, with food booths, displays, and exhibits (such as one in the machinery hall that featured natural gas appliances for the home), as well as musical entertainment and a large carousel. Musical shows were given in a large concert hall that included a gallery and balcony with seating for about two thousand. Sparkling mirrors stood behind the band, reflecting its movements to the audience. A placard in front of the band showed the audience the next selection on the program.[51]

Levy, the balding cornetist with a handlebar moustache, led a band of forty men, all first-rate musicians. The exposition audiences loved the band selections and Levy's solos. They played many encores to satisfy the large crowds who came to hear the band concerts every afternoon and for the two evening performances at seven and nine each day. While Levy's band entertained the crowds during the first two weeks of the fair, exposition manager J. H. Johnson began negotiations with Major Pond for Sissieretta's services. On 24 September Pond sent Johnson a telegraph that said, "All right. 'Black Patti' will be on hand to-morrow. Ovation in Washington last night. Basket of flowers from Mrs. President Harrison, who though ill, but heard the sweet singer before. Hundreds turned away."[52]

In advance of Sissieretta's arrival at the Pittsburgh Exposition, newspapers in that city ran large ads on 25 and 26 September announcing her upcoming appearance. In addition thousands of small handbills were printed and posted in conspicuous public places within a few hours following the announcement that she was coming to sing at the exposition.[53] These were the promotional tools available to Pond and Johnson before the days of television and radio. Sissieretta made her debut at the exposition on Monday, 26 September, at 4 P.M. She found it challenging to deal with more than 3,500 noisy school-children who had come to the exposition that day. Although teachers and policemen could not keep the children quiet, Sissieretta persevered and finished her hour-long concert. The evening concert from 9 P.M. until 10 P.M. was much easier without the distraction of the "unruly" children. The audience was "wildly enthusiastic" as she sang old-time favorites and other songs with which they could identify.[54] Her selection of familiar songs, no doubt, was a crowd-pleaser. "If Mme. Jones could have been prevailed upon to sing so long the audience would have encored her until the hour of closing," one newspaper said. Sissieretta delighted the audience not only with her pure, strong soprano voice but also with her easy manner and "personal magnetism that at once draws the audience to her."[55]

A local newspaper said the "young colored woman" sings like Patti without the slightest visible effort. The article said Sissieretta's high notes showed she could handle difficult compositions, and her low tones were particularly "deep, intense, and masculine." The reporter had high praise for Sissieretta but used words to describe her that would be unacceptable today: "This sable diva is highly cultivated, of profound insight into the spirit of her art. Yet she sings intelligently, wholly without affectation and with sound musical feeling. Her voice coming from a skin as white as her teeth would be counted the wonder of all lands—it is a strong and beautiful voice, that sounds with the steadiness of a trumpet. Though is does not ring with passion, it shakes the heart, not your ears, with the pathetic warmth that marks all negro singing."[56]

A week later, after one of her evening concerts, another reporter described Sissieretta's appearance onstage. She wore a "chocolate-hued dress" upon which were pinned seventeen large medals all inscribed to Mme. Matilda Jones, her name when "she hadn't sense enough to cling to her musical middle name, Sissieretta." The reporter described several of the medals and gifts given to Sissieretta on her West Indian and South American tours. They included a medal from President Hyppolite of Haiti, a bracelet of old coins (one of which was 135 years old) from the governor of St. Thomas, a box full of diamond rings, an Egyptian necklace, and a pear-set locket pendant. Sissieretta told the reporter about a diamond tiara set in gold that the mayor of Demerara had given her. She wanted to show the tiara to the reporter but gave up hunting for it, explaining that her husband had been cleaning the jewelry and had probably slipped it into his pocket to show someone. Sissieretta said, "Men are so powerful tricky."[57] This comment may have hinted at

*Early in her concert career, Sissieretta frequently wore many of the medals
she had received from foreign dignitaries during tours of the West Indies and
South America. Photograph courtesy of the Dramatic Museum Portrait
Collection, Rare Book and Manuscript Library, Columbia University.*

some trouble brewing in Sissieretta's and David's nine-year marriage. Although
there are no documents to prove it, some familiar with David described him
as a "gambler" and "infamous spendthrift."[58] One writer recounted a story,
supposedly typical of David's behavior, that said he once told a young ticket
taker who had collected twenty dollars in ticket proceeds at the door of one
of Sissieretta's concerts to keep the money "for pocket change."[59] Sissieretta
would eventually file to divorce David in 1898 for drunkenness and non-
support, so it is entirely possible that they began to have marital trouble in
1892 once she started to earn more money while working under Major Pond.

David's involvement in booking concerts and making arrangements for Sissieretta had been curtailed under Pond's management, apparently leaving him without much to do other than to accompany his wife as she sang at venues such as the Pittsburgh Exposition. If he was a spendthrift, he certainly had more money available to him now that Sissieretta was earning so much more.

Sissieretta was a big hit with the crowds attending the exposition. From 1,200 to 20,000 people, including many African Americans, attended the exposition each day. Pittsburgh residents, as well as people who came to the event on train excursions from nearby states, flocked to her afternoon and evening concerts, where she entertained them with operatic selections and familiar favorites of the day such as "The Last Rose of Summer," "Maggie, the Cows Are in the Clover," "Home, Sweet Home," and a waltz. Many asked her to sing "Swanee River," written by Pittsburgh's own Stephen Foster. She became an audience favorite because she was modest and without affectation.[60] On the evening of 28 September, the hall where she was to sing was packed "almost to the point of suffocation," yet the audience wanted to hear Sissieretta so much that no one made a sound as she began her first selection. After another song she responded to an encore by singing "Swanee River." The building "shook with applause" when she finished. She thanked the audience by singing four more encores.[61]

On Saturday, 1 October 1892, Levy and Sissieretta gave their farewell concerts. Thousands of people "of all classes of society and of all sizes, ages, and nationalities" packed the hall to hear Levy and Black Patti. Reports said the concert crowd was the largest in the exposition's history. Sissieretta took the stage at 9:20 P.M. and received an ovation "seldom witnessed in Pittsburg [sic]." When the crowd quieted down, she began her soulful rendition of "Swanee River." "The faintest whisper, the dropping of a pin could be heard as the song went on. And when she finished, the cheers of the multitude rang out again, drowning every recall given."[62] Sissieretta, hand in hand with Levy, came forward once more and sang "The Last Rose of Summer." When she finished the crowd applauded loudly for about five minutes. Then she sang her final number, "Comin' thro' the Rye," and once again there was a "deafening applause" when she finished. She bowed as manager Johnson stepped onto the stage and presented her with a basket of roses. As the crowd began to leave the concert, people found the building so overcrowded they could barely move. Several women fainted but were not injured. About three hundred to four hundred people were lifted over the fence because they could not make their way out of the turnstile doors of the main gate.[63] With the close of Sissieretta's successful run at the exposition, one reviewer said, "Black Patti sang her way into the hearts of the people on the first afternoon, and she is probably the most talked about woman in this town."[64] Another said few singers ever heard in

Pittsburgh caused the sensation that Sissieretta had at the exposition. "It was a pleasure to hear her. Patti, the first, who has charmed millions, never sang better than did this cultured daughter of slave parents. . . . A very successful season is ahead for both manager and star."[65]

After Pittsburgh, Sissieretta began touring the East Coast with the Russian violinist Princess Dolgorouky. They appeared in Boston, where they performed for the opening concert of the thirteenth season of the Boston Star Course concert series, and then traveled to Toronto. While Sissieretta was singing in Boston and Toronto, Pittsburgh Exposition manager Johnson was negotiating with Major Pond to bring her back for the closing week of the exposition. On Saturday, 15 October, Johnson announced he had successfully rehired Sissieretta "at considerable expense." He had to buy out her concert appearances scheduled elsewhere. Johnson called her a "great and glowing star" and said he was confident she would draw large crowds for the fair's last week. The *Pittsburgh Chronicle* (17 October 1892) said Black Patti had proved to be one of the greatest attractions ever seen at the exposition building. The newspaper attributed her success, in part, to her willingness to sing songs familiar to the audience.[66]

Sissieretta opened her second engagement at the exposition on Monday, 17 October, before five thousand people. She was accompanied by Ellis Brooks's band, a New York group that had succeeded Levy's band at the exposition. Although they did not have time to rehearse, Sissieretta and the band worked well together, as if they had been a team for many years.[67] One report compared Sissieretta's voice with that of Clementine DeVere, an accomplished soprano and attractive prima donna who had been at the exposition the previous week. The reviewer said although DeVere had a sweeter voice than Sissieretta's and every song "showed marks of cultivation," her voice was not powerful enough to be heard all around the hall. "Patti, on the other hand, selects songs which bring her in sympathy with her audience, and then lets her voice out so that every word is audible in every part of the building."[68] During the week she sang familiar selections that she had sung during her first exposition appearance. Sissieretta obviously knew what pleased her audience. On Friday, 21 October, which was Columbus Day, she added two songs to her repertoire—"The Star-Spangled Banner" and "In Old Madrid," a song to honor Spain, under whose flag Christopher Columbus sailed to the New World. She sang her final exposition concert the next day.

During the last two months of 1892, Sissieretta toured with Levy, and at times Princess Dolgorouky accompanied them. Sissieretta and Levy played several towns in New York, Massachusetts, Ohio, and Pennsylvania. On Monday, 14 November, Sissieretta and Levy and his band entertained at the Music Hall in Cleveland. Levy escorted Sissieretta to the stage for her opening

Sissieretta posing by a chair at a photography studio in Pittsburgh,
taken, perhaps, when she was appearing at the Pittsburgh Exposition.
Photograph courtesy of the Dr. Carl R. Gross Collection,
Moorland-Spingarn Research Center, Howard University.

number, "Robert, Toi Que J'aime." She sang several of her standard ballads
and closed her concert with "Swanee River," which she sang "with taste and
feeling that won her all the applause the large audience of five thousand was
capable of giving."[69] Levy too garnered audience recognition for his "execution and command" of the cornet. A newspaper review complimented him on
his courteous treatment of Madame Jones, "escorting her on and off the stage.
In this and other things he evidences his gentlemanly teaching and that broad

mindedness that should characterize all great artists." The review ended with praise for Pond. "The Black Patti–Levy combination is really an exceptionally strong one and Maj. Pond, the amusement caterer, again demonstrates his ability in his line of business to the entire satisfaction of Cleveland's amusement seekers."[70] This comment shows how Sissieretta's contract with someone of Pond's influence and reputation was so important to advancing her career.

The combination of Sissieretta and Levy made for good business, and apparently the professional relationship suited the two performers as well. An interesting front-page column called "The Rounder's Chat," published in the African American newspaper the *Cleveland Gazette* shortly after Sissieretta's visit to Cleveland, provided some insight into the relationship between her and the English-born Levy.[71] "The Rounder," actually *Gazette* editor Harry C. Smith, wrote that he and two friends, Messrs. Eubanks and Myers, had dropped by the grandest hotel in Cleveland, the elegant eight-story Hollenden, the morning after Sissieretta's concert to visit with the singer and her husband, David, in one of the hotel's parlors. David, whom Smith described as having a slight build, light brown skin, and the loss of sight in one eye, and Sissieretta, a pretty, "exceptionally tasty dresser," agreeable conversationalist, and "very, very dark complexioned lady," were talking with the three men about the concert the previous night. About five minutes into the conversation, Levy walked by the parlor door, and David invited him to come in and meet the men. As Levy entered he went over to Sissieretta, knelt before her on one knee, and kissed her hand "with all the dignity that could possibly characterize the most gentlemanly foreigner." Smith wrote, "Such courtesy is so seldom extended in this country that I declare I almost fell off the chair. I have seen a good many things that astonished me, but never have I seen the like of Mr. Levy's action."[72] In the next issue of the *Gazette,* Smith reported that several readers doubted his story about Levy kneeling before Sissieretta and kissing her hand. "It was a fact, nevertheless—just as I wrote it—to which the other two local gentlemen present will testify," he wrote. Smith noted that in the few minutes Levy visited with them and Mme. Jones, Levy described how they had dealt with racial discrimination they encountered at hotels and restaurants while on the road. Levy told the men how he, Mme. Jones, Mrs. Levy, and Mr. Jones avoided trouble while going to meals. He said the two women entered as a couple and the two men did the same. "Thus far things have moved along smoothly and nicely," Levy told Smith.[73]

As 1892 came to a close, Sissieretta was able to look back at how quickly her fame had grown since her spring appearance at Madison Square Garden and her subsequent contractual arrangement with Pond. Word of her amazing voice had spread by word of mouth and by favorable newspaper reviews in both the black and white press. Thousands of people had attended her concerts, most of them curious to see the black prima donna with the powerful soprano voice. Often newspaper reviews of Sissieretta's concerts in 1892 described how attractive, dignified, and well-dressed she was and how her voice was highly trained, as if the critics were surprised. People apparently had not expected such an accomplished singer with the stage presence she had. Frequently reviews in white newspapers commented on Sissieretta's physical appearance—the color of her skin, the size of her lips, the whiteness of her teeth, the texture of her hair—and on her graceful, confident manner onstage. Some music patrons during this period probably came to her concerts expecting to see Sissieretta sing stereotypical songs associated with minstrel shows rather than classical pieces and familiar ballads. An article in the *Boston Journal* following a 10 October 1892 concert in that city typified the reaction Sissieretta received in the white press as her fame grew. "Mrs. Sissieretta Jones, the 'Black Patti,' as she is called, was welcomed with a good deal of curiosity, for much had been said about her voice as being something remarkable. She proved more than an entertaining singer; not only was her singing pleasing, but it was excellent from a critical standpoint," the newspaper review said.[74] Sissieretta, for her part, continued to develop her voice, studying with Louisa (Kapp-Young) Cappiani in New York, in between concert appearances in 1892 and for several years beyond that. Cappiani, born in Austria in 1835, was a well-known voice teacher who lived in New York City. Sissieretta's studies helped to add to her classical repertoire and gave her a balanced and varied selection of ballads, arias, and virtuoso songs to perform.[75] As important as her voice studies were, they were certainly no more important than the experience she had gained during 1892. She developed great stage presence and appeared quite comfortable entertaining large audiences. People seemed to find her charming, modest, friendly, and approachable. She appeared to reach her audience on an emotional level with songs that were familiar to them, such as her signature "Swanee River," and yet she also pleased the crowd with her classical and operatic selections. By the close of 1892, Sissieretta's growing fame had African American newspapers asking who was the greatest black prima donna—Sissieretta, Marie Selika, or Flora Batson Bergen. It was not uncommon to see newspaper critics compare the singers. Many argued for Selika, calling her a "finished artist" and identifying Sissieretta as a great singer but not the "greatest colored singer."[76] By and large, though, Sissieretta had taken center stage among African American concert divas by the end of 1892. Her success at Madison Square Garden, her contract with Pond, and her fall tour with Levy "mark the point at which she stepped beyond her competitors to become the era's undisputed black 'Queen of Song.'"[77]

4

Trouble on the Horizon
1893

As Sissieretta's fame grew, critics began to take more notice of her and hold her to higher standards than when she first began performing. Nowhere was this more evident than following her Chicago debut in January 1893. Her first appearance in the country's second largest city was at the Central Music Hall under the auspices of the (white) Star Lecture Course, "a recognition seldom accorded one of the Afro-American race."[1] As might be expected in a city the size of Chicago, there were many critics to review her performances. Sissieretta saved copies of these newspaper reviews in her scrapbook. She performed at the Central Music Hall 5 January through 7 January and again on 10 and 11 January. Although she appeared with several other performers, she had top billing. Her manager for these concerts was F. Wight Neumann, who apparently contracted with Major Pond for her services. Sissieretta's concerts were well publicized prior to opening night, which helped fill Central Music Hall to near capacity on 5 January, the evening of her twenty-fifth birthday. The audience included many African Americans as well as white music enthusiasts curious to hear a black singer whose nickname, "Black Patti," likened her to the great Patti. Despite Sissieretta's growing reputation as a singer, curiosity was still a major reason people came to her concerts for the first time, particularly white music patrons. The novelty factor may have helped her gain entrance to some predominantly white venues, such as this Chicago concert series, but then it was up to her to prove herself to her audiences. The *Chicago Journal* said theater goers who came to see Sissieretta out of curiosity "went away satisfied that the colored singer was a phenomenon."[2] An unnamed Chicago newspaper clipping in her scrapbook said she was "the first vocalist of her race to whom a place in the ranks of artistic singers may be accorded, and as such she claims and has received greater attention than she would perhaps were she of other nationality or color."

CENTRAL MUSIC HALL

SISSIERETTA JONES.

THURSDAY EVENING, JAN. 5, AT 8:15

FRIDAY EVENING, JAN. 6, AT 8:15

SATURDAY EVENING, JAN. 7, AT 8:15

AND ONE MATINEE ONLY

SATURDAY AFTERNOON, JAN. 7, AT 2:30

THE ARION LADY QUARTETTE.

THE BLACK PATTI

*The Greatest
Singer of Her Race*

HER FIRST AND ONLY APPEARANCE
.... IN CHICAGO

ASSISTED BY

SENOR ENCARNACION GARCIA

SOLOIST ON THE SALTERIO

Invented and Constructed by Himself
Upon the Ancient King David Psaltery

THE ONLY INSTRUMENT OF ITS KIND IN THE WORLD

WILLIAM SHERMAN BAXTER

THE POPULAR BANJO VIRTUOSO

AND

THE ARION LADY QUARTETTE

UNDER THE DIRECTION OF THE

STAR LECTURE COURSE

F. WIGHT NEUMANN, MANGR.

ARIEL NICHOLS.   ADELE V. HOLMAN.   AMELIA HEDEN.   MARIE HEDEN.

*Sissieretta's first appearance in Chicago, January 1893, was at the Central Music Hall
under the auspices of the Star Lecture Course. Courtesy of the Museum
of Performance and Design, San Francisco.*

Sissieretta's selections for the Chicago concert series included the "Waltz Song" by Pattison, a selection by Centemeri, "Farfalla" by Gelli, the cavatina "Robert, Toi Que J'aime" by Meyerbeer, "Sempre Libera" from *La Traviata*, a song from Meyerbeer's *Les Huguenots*, an aria from Meyerbeer's *L'Africaine*, as well as popular ballads such as "Comin' thro' the Rye," "The Song of the Bobolink," "Swanee River," "Maggie, the Cows Are in the Clover," and "Every Rose Must Have Its Thorn." The other musicians on the program were the "Arion Lady Quartette," banjo player William Sherman Baxter, and a Mexican musician, Signor Garcia, who played the saltori, an instrument similar to a zither. Sissieretta and the other musicians gave two performances each day— one at 2:15 P.M. and the other at 8:15 P.M. The Arion Lady Quartette sang the opening number, followed by two selections by Baxter. Then Sissieretta performed one selection and likely sang an encore or two. Following her, Garcia, the Arion Lady Quartette, and Baxter each performed a musical piece before Sissieretta once again took the stage to sing a selection and an encore.[3]

For her opening night concert, Sissieretta wore a long gown with a train. The *Chicago Inter-Ocean* newspaper described the "sable singer" as a "fine representative of her race" with a good figure, a "bright, intelligent face," and a graceful carriage. "She seemed indeed like a veritable Aida, in a Parisian costume," the newspaper said. In describing Sissieretta's voice, the *Inter-Ocean's* critic said it was difficult to compare her voice with other singers. "It is an organ of large range, clear and bright in its uppermost tones, rich in the breadth and timbre of its lower ones, almost contralto, all being pervaded with the peculiarly African sympathetic quality, pathetic in its warmth."[4]

Apparently Sissieretta got off to a rocky start on opening night when she sang her first number, Meyerbeer's cavatina "Robert, Toi Que J'aime," for her predominately white, musically discerning audience. The *Chicago Inter-Ocean's* critic said the audience was "curiously cold in its greeting" to the black singer and that this reception initially appeared to rattle Sissieretta as she attempted to sing the "difficult and ambitious" piece. The critic said, "The execution in descending scales and semi-tones was not as smooth nor as finished as might possibly have been expected as there were slight variations in tone and resort to mezzo voce effects. In this selection there was an absence of the limpid quality, absolute purity of tone, and brilliancy of execution— too much, possibly, to expect at the first hearing, but demanded by reason of precedent. The fact is that she gave evidence of possessing a remarkable natural voice and real musical intelligence, without that finer phrasing that betokens the great artist."[5] The critic for the *Chicago Times* also noted "deficiencies" in Sissieretta's vocalization and method, but said she sang "Robert, Toi Que J'aime" with so much feeling and expression that one could overlook those deficiencies. This critic did not find Sissieretta's waltz selection very effective but said when she gave an encore selection of "Swanee River," she "carried her audience by storm," singing the "plaintive melody" with much depth of feeling. The *Chicago Times* critic said Sissieretta's rendition of this song was better than any of the great artists who had performed it before in Chicago.[6]

The *Chicago Tribune*'s critic found Sissieretta's tones in the lower and middle registers to be of "surpassing beauty," while those in the upper registers often had a clear, "bell-like" quality to them, especially when she sang softly or with medium power. When she sang in full voice, the critic said, her tones had an "indescribable quality" to them "that can scarcely be called harshness, but which suggests a great natural voice which cultivation has not freed entirely from its original wildness." The *Tribune* critic also made note of the "plaintiveness" in Sissieretta's voice, saying that it was the most "individualizing element in the voice" and that no amount of schooling or training could remove it, not that one would want to do so. "It is the heritage the singer has received from her race, and it alone tells not only of the sorrows of a single life but the cruelly sad story of a whole people."[7]

Not all reviews were so positive or sympathetic. One Chicago critic took Sissieretta to task for using the name "Black Patti," which the critic said was "an unnecessary reflection on her race . . . and detracts from the favorable impressions which much of her work makes." The critic called her an uneducated singer with a naturally pure and strong voice that, under proper instruction, "would no doubt improve to an extent that would win her renown." The critic added that many other black sopranos, less well known than Sissieretta, "sing with a greater degree of finish, although they may not possess the natural gifts of Mrs. Jones."[8] Another Chicago critic praised her natural ability but criticized her lack of training: "Nature has been lavish in the bestowal of this rare voice, but not so generous in providing the higher quality of intellect that should guide such a vocal organ to its greatest sphere of usefulness. The voice has been fairly well cultivated, but not to the extent that it deserves nor in the measure that it demands. Much of her singing is still without the stamp of art, being crude and at times almost amateurish. Mrs. Jones owes it to herself and her art to continue her studies in the higher branches of vocalization; she has the foundation, now let her add the finishing touches."[9]

These critical assessments of Sissieretta's voice and her training, given by those used to judging high-level musical talent and ability, indicate that she needed more training and experience to reach the level many white sopranos had achieved. However, several of the critics found her emotional delivery of the music superior to those who were more skilled in the finer points of singing. Without a doubt she had a beautiful, natural voice that would only improve over time as she acquired more tutoring and experience. Sissieretta survived her Chicago experience, and despite some harsh criticism, her Chicago debut was generally hailed as a success. As one reviewer said, "The colored race has every reason to be proud of such a fine exponent of song; and Mrs. Jones has reason to feel pleased over her enthusiastic reception."[10]

In early February Sissieretta traveled to Brantford, Ontario, where on 2 February and 3 February she sang with several local performers at the Brantford Opera House. Extensive preconcert publicity resulted in a large and "fashionable" audience at her opening concert on Thursday evening. Many, of course, were curious to see the black singer who likened herself to Adelina Patti. Those who saw her were impressed with her remarkable voice, clear enunciation, and her grace and stage presence. "Miss Jones is well worth hearing," one reviewer said. "Her color doubtless does much to enhance her reputation, but apart from that she has a splendid and well-trained voice."[11] Sissieretta sang many of her concert standards—"Song of Page" from *Les Huguenots*, "Comin' thro' the Rye," "Every Rose Must Have Its Thorn," and "Maggie, the Cows Are in the Clover." Two encores, "The Song of the Bobolink" and "Swanee River," were two of the biggest crowd pleasers. She received positive reviews for her performances both evenings, with critics calling her a "delight" with a "marvelous" voice that possesses "exquisite richness, great compass and singular sweetness." One critic noted her well-cultivated voice had "little traces of roughness and unevenness."[12] The concerts were successful both professionally and financially. Sissieretta reportedly received about $250 for the two concerts.[13]

A week after her Canadian concerts, Sissieretta went to Detroit to sing concerts there on 10–11 February at the request of Maggie Porter-Cole, a black voice teacher and soloist. Porter-Cole joined in the performances along with her Porter-Cole Chorus and local soloist George Owen. Porter-Cole had been born into slavery in Lebanon, Tennessee. At the age of thirteen, she was one of three hundred students who attended Fisk University the first year it opened. After two years at the school, she became a teacher at the Bellevue school, a few miles from Nashville. The Ku Klux Klan burned her schoolhouse while she was away for Christmas vacation. She moved to another district and taught school until 1871, when she joined the famous Fisk Jubilee Singers. While a member of this organization, she visited Europe three times, singing concerts throughout England, Scotland, and Germany. By 1886 she had moved to Lansing, Michigan, where she conducted voice classes and participated in concerts in other cities.[14]

Unfortunately Sissieretta had to compete with strong attractions at the Detroit Opera House those evenings, which affected the size of the crowds who came to hear her. Black attendance was "poor, very poor," numbering about three hundred African American patrons the first night and two hundred the second, rather than the one thousand that had been expected each night. Had it not been for the white patrons, who largely outnumbered the African Americans, the concert would have been a "big financial failure."[15] Although the audience was small, Sissieretta was well received. The *Detroit Plaindealer,* a black newspaper, praised her, saying that "no singer has appeared in Detroit in years, colored or white, who sings the most difficult airs with more ease, or whose voice is sweeter and grows each time it is heard. Her voice is sweet and bird-like, and when she warbles it is like listening to the sweet bubbling music of the running brook." The *Plaindealer* said the concert proved whites will attend high-class concerts and that white people in Detroit "now know that Afro-Americans can sing other kinds of music than the jubilee with credit."[16]

Shortly after Sissieretta's Detroit appearance, she left her midwestern tour to return to New York, where she got involved in African American musician and composer Will Marion Cook's seven-month effort to stage a black opera, *Scenes from Uncle Tom's Cabin,* at the upcoming Chicago World's Fair, better known as the World's Columbian Exposition. Cook, born in Washington, D.C., on 27 January 1869, was a highly trained concert violinist who had studied at the Oberlin Conservatory in Ohio, then in Berlin under Josef Joachim, and later at the National Conservatory of Music in New York.[17] An article in the *Indianapolis Freeman* (11 February 1893) said "colored people" had tried unsuccessfully for the past two years to be represented at the Columbian Exposition. Although African Americans had been excluded from the National Board of Commissioners that planned and managed the fair and had been denied any "place of honor,"[18] Cook was determined to showcase a black opera at the 1893 exposition. He enlisted help from Frederick Douglass, who took Cook to the White House and introduced him to President Benjamin Harrison. Douglass urged the president to help Cook in his efforts to produce the opera, based on *Uncle Tom's Cabin,* at the Columbian Exposition. Cook said Sissieretta would be the soprano in his production. Harry Williams of the London Conservatory would sing the tenor part, and Mme. Waring, who was then singing at La Scala in Milan, was to be the contralto. The president gave Cook a letter of support that secured him the right to give concerts at the World's Fair grounds. To pay for the costumes, training, scenery, and other expenses, the promoters planned to give benefit concerts in key American cities, the first of which was to be in New York at Carnegie Music Hall on Monday, 13 February 1893.[19] Those advertised to perform at Carnegie Hall with Sissieretta included the original Fisk Jubilee Singers; baritone Harry Burleigh of the National Conservatory of America; Lloyd Gibbs of Baltimore, a tenor who was one of the "best-known colored composers" in the United

States; the Phonetic Quartet of Baltimore; Paul C. Boler, a talented young pianist; contralto Louise "Lulu" Hamer; Cook playing the violin; and an orchestra of fifty banjoists. The program was to be a selection of representative "Negro music."[20]

The Columbian Exposition, honoring the four hundredth anniversary of Columbus's arrival in the New World, had been dedicated in October 1892 and was scheduled to open to the public on 1 May 1893. The site for the exposition was on seven hundred acres of reclaimed marshland along the shores of Lake Michigan. Four hundred buildings were built and covered in a "white plaster-like material" that looked like marble. These buildings housed the various exhibits that included "halls for machinery, new inventions, agricultural products, painting, sculpture and exhibits by foreign nations." The mass of buildings, built in the Beaux Arts style that resembled ornate classical temples, came to be known as the "White City." At night thousands of electric bulbs lit the White City, making it look all the more spectacular. To the west of the White City there was a "mile-long recreational area" called the Midway Plaisance, from which the term *midway* came to be used in American fairs and carnivals. Visitors could buy food and drink at the Midway Plaisance, or they could see sights such as Thomas Edison's kinetoscope, which showed moving pictures, or ride George Washington Ferris's new invention, a huge, two-thousand-passenger, 265-foot-tall mechanical wheel, built especially for the Columbian Exposition. Nearly thirty million people came to the exposition during the six months it was open.[21]

Prominent society people were reportedly interested in Cook's ambitious plan to bring a black opera to the exposition. At the suggestion of Douglass, Cook arranged the benefit concert at Carnegie Music Hall to raise funds for the opera as well as to test whether there was enough interest in the project among New Yorkers. Douglass planned to come from Washington to give a short address. The concert, which was to begin with "wild plantation melodies" and end with Gounod's "Ave Maria," was designed to demonstrate "the progress in music made by the colored race."[22] On the night of the concert, a winter storm kept many people at home, so the concert hall was not totally filled; however, many prominent members of society and patrons of the arts attended the event. Their names were listed in newspaper reviews. This was the first time African Americans had performed in the main hall at Carnegie Music Hall. An article in the *New York Review* noted this breakthrough and said, "we feel sure the management can no longer discriminate on account of color." The concert was a success, although the audience was disappointed that Cook played little and Harry Burleigh did not perform at all, but the audience enjoyed the Fisk Jubilee Singers and singer Louise Hamer. Douglass was not at the concert as planned. Some "misunderstanding" had kept him from being there to deliver opening remarks.[23] Yet it was Sissieretta, with her sweet, clear voice and careful enunciation, who held the audience "spellbound from beginning to end." She sang Centemeri's "Grand Aria," a selection from Meyerbeer's *L'Africaine,* and "Ave Maria." A newspaper review gave special mention to David Jones, who served as stage manager for the show; Cook, who directed the program; and attorney Charles Morris, who served as general manager. Sissieretta later performed at a few other concerts organized by Morris to raise funds for *Scenes from Uncle Tom's Cabin.*[24]

One of those sitting in a box at Carnegie Hall that evening was a prominent New Yorker, Judge Charles Andrews, and his wife. The couple invited Sissieretta to sing for a party of thirty ladies at their Fifth Avenue home the next day, 14 February—Valentine's Day. The women who came to the party included society women such as Mrs. Vanderbilt and Mrs. Astor. Sissieretta was scheduled to sing at Mrs. Astor's home the following week. The chief justice of India, also a guest at the party, reportedly gave her a valentine that contained a check for one thousand dollars. In addition she received a solid silver basket filled with special flowers. "The ladies pronounced the singing superior to [Adelina] Patti's and then sat down to lunch with Mme. Jones."[25]

With the benefit concert for the opera behind her, Sissieretta closed out February in Washington, D.C., performing there twice before returning to New York City, where her husband booked two concerts for her—one in Harlem on 2 March and the other in Brooklyn, 6 March, at the Bridge Street Church. These two concerts would lead to serious problems between Sissieretta and her manager, Major Pond. Under the agreement the Joneses had with Pond, Sissieretta and David were supposed to let Pond book all her performances or contract with other managers for her services, as was the case in mid-March, when he arranged for Sissieretta to work for a limited time under contract with E. S. Jones (a white man) of Velder and Jones of New York. Under the terms of the contract, Velder and Jones were supposed to advertise the concerts, pay all the expenses, and pay Sissieretta $150 a night to perform. Velder and Jones planned for Sissieretta to appear at concerts in three Ohio cities—Cincinnati, Columbus, and Dayton—as well as in Indianapolis.[26]

Sissieretta's first concert under Velder and Jones was at the Music Hall in Cincinnati, where it was reviewed by John Smith Van Cleve, a Boston-educated musician, teacher, author, and former music critic for the *Cincinnati Commercial.* Writing about Sissieretta's performance, Van Cleve said that she was an "artist of high and genuine abilities" and that he was impressed with the sweetness of her voice, with its "melancholy warmth which characterizes the voices of her race." He said her performance of the aria from *L'Africaine* "was a delight long to be remembered." During one of her encore numbers, Van Cleve said Sissieretta sang the A above the staff and held it for about fifteen seconds "in a way to display that supreme domination over the breath, which seems to be a lost art among our asthmatic and hyper-dramatic, so-called singers, whose efforts to soar do not resemble those of the eagle, but do bear a painful likeness to the struggles of a barnyard fowl." Although he was impressed with her performance, the critic took issue with her nickname, "Black Patti," saying it both helped and hurt the singer. "It certainly does pique curiosity and draw people into the concert room, but it sets up a standard of comparison, which neither she nor any other vocalist of our generation can successfully meet." In reference to her race and his obvious surprise with her voice and her accomplishments, Van Cleve said, in words that would be offensive, demeaning, and completely unacceptable today, "Every true Christian and every sincere philanthropist must rejoice to find a member of the African race arising this high in the noble art of music."[27]

The Cincinnati concert met expenses, and the troupe moved on to Columbus for the scheduled 20–21 March concerts at the Board of Trade auditorium. Ticket sales for the 20 March performance only totaled about one hundred dollars, not enough to cover expenses. About nine o'clock that night, E. S. Jones went to Grub's music store, where the tickets had been sold, and took all the money collected for the concert. Next he went to the Board of Trade auditorium and paid for whatever expenses the money would cover. Jones then left the auditorium during the concert, saying he would return in a few minutes. That was the last anyone heard of him for a few days. He left his baggage and unpaid bill at his hotel and skipped town.[28] One newspaper report said, "Mme. Jones has been meeting with poor business recently and it was said that the money taken by [E. S.] Jones was due him."[29] That report is questionable in that Sissieretta's concerts had been well attended prior to Jones taking over as her manager. Perhaps he had not been advertising the concerts sufficiently. The concert scheduled for 21 March was canceled by the theater's management, and purchased tickets were refunded. Sissieretta, clearly upset and embarrassed by the incident, wrote a letter to the newspaper's editor to set the record straight. The letter was published the next day, 21 March. She explained that E. S. Jones was not her manager, as most people likely thought, and that her manager, Maj. James B. Pond, had contracted with Jones and Velder for Sissieretta to perform in Columbus. Sissieretta wrote, "I am very sorry that anyone has been misled in the matter, and that on account of Messrs. Jones and Velder not meeting their obligations, those friends who had purchased tickets for the concert advertised for tonight have been disappointed."[30]

Velder and Jones had booked Sissieretta's next concert in Dayton for the following evening, 22 March. Even after the fiasco in Columbus the previous night, Sissieretta and her accompanist, Georgiana Wilson, went to Dayton, not knowing what to expect. News about the concert's financial difficulties in Columbus had already spread there, where it was reported initially that the 22 March concert would not take place. However, D. A. Sinclair, secretary of the YMCA, decided to open the organization's Association Hall rather than disappoint people who had already bought tickets, and Sissieretta agreed to sing for free. She was joined that evening by several local black performers, including African American poet and Dayton native Paul Laurence Dunbar.[31] Despite "the misfortune suffered through the trickery of the agent," the large audience gave Sissieretta a "hearty welcome." Singing both "high-class" music as well as simple, popular ballads, she "captivated" those who came to hear her with "her entrancing and harmonious notes resounding throughout the hall with great melody and distinctness."[32]

Sissieretta's association with Velder and Jones's concert series ended in Dayton. She traveled to Louisville for two concerts, 27–28 March, at the Masonic Temple Hall, arranged by Major Pond. This likely was the farthest south she had ever performed. By 1893 Jim Crow laws segregating the races were well established in the South, as Sissieretta was about to experience firsthand. The audience for the opening night concert was seated separately, with black concertgoers filling the gallery and white ones sitting in the "parquet and dress circle seats" on the first floor. The gallery was packed, while the orchestra section was only about half-full. This segregated seating disappointed and displeased Sissieretta so much that she spoke about it during a newspaper interview in her dressing room following the first night's concert. She said she found it "strange" to put all the "colored people" in the gallery and leave all those vacant seats downstairs. "I never have met with anything like it before," she said. The *Louisville Commercial* reporter asked her to explain what she meant, to which she replied, "Why, putting the colored people off in the gallery and leaving all those vacant seats down stairs. Why, the house would have been crowded if 'they' had allowed them to have seats down stairs. I felt very much disappointed; I have never before had such an experience and I could not help feeling it. Don't you think there ought to have been a division of the house downstairs?"[33]

Sissieretta continued her conversation with the reporter about the racial segregation she had just encountered. Speaking softly yet showing disapproval through her demeanor, she said, "I think people of my race ought not to be shut out in this way. The gallery, you could see, was crowded and no more could go up there and still all the back part of the house was not taken. I didn't know about it, or course. That's a business affair." Sissieretta went on to tell the reporter how difficult it had been for her and Georgiana Wilson to find suitable lodging in Cincinnati. "We had to search and search before we, Mrs. Wilson and I, could find a nice place." In reply to the reporter's question about where they were staying in Louisville, Sissieretta said they were housed at the Gault House, although the reporter said that the way she said it suggested the accommodations left a lot to be desired.[34] Sissieretta and her accompanist were the first African Americans to stay at the Gault House.[35] Wilson assured Sissieretta that things would be better when they got to Evansville. "Evansville is in Indiana," she said, implying they might not encounter Jim Crow laws there.

Despite her ill feelings about the segregated seating, Sissieretta most likely was pleased with her performance and her mostly positive, although condescending, newspaper reviews. As in other cities, many white concert patrons were curious to see and hear a black woman who advertised herself as the "Black Patti." Apparently from the reviews after her concerts, those who came were both surprised and pleased with what they saw and heard. One critic said that she had grounds for a libel suit against the parties responsible for her lithographic advertisements. "Coarse-looking and bemedaled, they prepared a very great surprise to those present last evening. What people saw was a negress of light color, attired in a very becoming gown, en train, which revealed a superb figure, surmounted by a head and face bespeaking plainly intelligence and refinement. She carried herself with dignity, save when once she courtesied [sic], and with much grace."[36]

Sissieretta's first number was an aria from *Robert le Diable,* which she sang with "apparent ease and clearness." For an encore she sang "Comin' thro' the Rye." Her second selection was a waltz, "La Farfalla," followed by two encores—"Maggie, the Cows Are in the Clover" and her signature song," Swanee River." Her last number was an audience request—"Home, Sweet Home." Several critics praised her singing, calling it agreeable, effective, and delightful but not in the same league as that of Adelina Patti. One newspaper reported that Sissieretta had a three-octave voice range, from low C to high E.[37] Interestingly one reviewer, after hearing her opening night concert, said the "beauties of her voice" stemmed from her training more than "from endowment." Previously critics in many other cities and towns had attributed her success to her natural voice, calling it a gift and a wonder, while criticizing her degree of training. This reviewer said that Sissieretta, who had lately been studying under the direction of Mme. Cappiani in New York, had acquired a "beauty of execution, a power, although a too penetrating one, which verges dangerously on the shrill, and an accuracy which entitles her to a high position and which pleases."[38] The same critic also differed with many previous reviewers about the warmth, pathos, and expression in Sissieretta's voice. In the past several critics said the feeling conveyed in Sissieretta's voice when she sang songs such as "Swanee River" and "Home, Sweet Home," almost brought tears to many in the audience. This critic had a different reaction: "She sings with grace of execution, but lacks in delicacy of expression. She seemed last night to fail to grasp the spirit of the waltz and sang 'Suwanee River' with beautiful technique, but failed entirely to strike that note which forces feeling. The same may be said of 'Home, Sweet Home,' which was sung with every mark of the trained singer, but failed to touch that chord which makes the song so dear. She is a mistress of singing, but not of song."[39]

Sissieretta's last appearance of the 1892–93 concert season booked by Major Pond was in St. Louis on 1 April 1893 at Entertainment Hall. A notice in the local newspaper said she would return to New York following the concert to rest for her World's Fair engagement.[40] Her St. Louis concert was a success, and she enjoyed her time there as guest of the "Leading Commandery of St. Louis" for an Easter reception and also was entertained at the Lindell Hotel during her stay.[41] Although the St. Louis concert had been billed as her last concert before returning to New York, the *Indianapolis Freeman* (9 April 1893) reported that Sissieretta was scheduled to appear 17–18 April at the Lyceum Theatre in Baltimore, her husband's native city. These concerts, as well as one at the Amphion Theatre in Brooklyn on 16 April, were arranged and managed by David and were therefore outside the contractual arrangement David and Sissieretta had with Major Pond. They were about to find out how Pond would deal with their contract violations.

When David and Sissieretta returned to New York, the city was abuzz with news of the upcoming May opening of the 1,595-foot-long Brooklyn Bridge, built across the East River to link Brooklyn and Manhattan. In the music world, New Yorkers were awaiting the finishing touches on the Metropolitan Opera House, which was being rebuilt after fire destroyed it in August 1892. Things had changed on the national political scene as well with the inauguration in March of Grover Cleveland, former president from 1885 through 1889, as the twenty-fourth president of the United States.

No sooner had the Joneses adjusted to life back in New York than Pond's attorneys filed a motion with the Superior Court of New York 25 April 1893 to stop Sissieretta from singing concerts under anyone's management but Pond's or his designees. Pond asked for damages and court costs. The court issued a summons to David and Sissieretta, which was served on 4 May 1893, just before she went on stage to sing a concert at Madison Hall in New York City. A hearing was set for 10 May but was subsequently moved to 17 May.[42]

Pond, in a sworn affidavit on 2 May, said that Sissieretta's 16–18 April concerts violated the terms of the contract she and David had signed with him on 8 June 1892, because he had not authorized the couple to book these events. Her singing at these concerts, he said, hurt his business because they prevented him from booking concerts in the same place and made it impossible for him to arrange future dates there. He also claimed Sissieretta was "pretending that she is too tired to sing" at concerts Pond arranged, and then "without his knowledge or consent, she goes and makes contracts through the agency of her said husband to sing for her own benefit." Pond, who swore he had fulfilled his end of the 8 June 1892 contract, said that he had spent lots of time and money arranging and advertising concerts for the black soprano. He added that he would lose the benefit of many engagements and the large sums of money he had already spent in advertising Sissieretta and "introducing her to the public" if the public learned she was making contracts for herself without him. Pond's attorneys gathered sworn affidavits from several people—F. A. Sadles, Sabina C. Glass, Frank L. Shopp, and Oscar Murray—to prove Sissieretta had given concerts on these April dates without permission from Pond. One of the statements included press clippings from Baltimore newspapers about the 17 April concert.[43]

On 6 May, between the time Pond provided his sworn testimony and David and Sissieretta answered Pond's claims, the American stock market crashed. The country stood on the brink of an economic disaster—a financial depression that lasted from 1893 until 1897. In the ensuing weeks and months after the crash, companies collapsed and declared bankruptcy.[44] "By the end of the year, 16,000 businesses and 500 banks had failed. Seventy-four railroads (including the Philadelphia & Reading, the North Pacific, the Erie, and the Santa Fe) went into receivership. Banks called in loans, the number of soup kitchens grew in the cities, and the unemployment rate reached 20% of the workforce."[45] The teetering economy would affect many Americans in the coming months, including Sissieretta, David, and Pond, who depended on the public to spend money to buy tickets for entertainment.

By 15 May David and Sissieretta answered Pond's claims by providing sworn statements of their own as well as those of several supporting witnesses, including Sissieretta's accompanist, Georgiana Wilson. Clearly Sissieretta had achieved great fame under Pond's management, but as the court documents showed, problems had developed between the Joneses and Pond by November 1892, five months into their three-year contractual relationship and just days after Pond was supposed to start paying Sissieretta a fixed salary of $150 a week to sing concerts. David Jones claimed that on 8 November 1892, the day Sissieretta was singing a concert in Troy, New York, Pond told David and Sissieretta that after her upcoming concert in Boston on 27 November 1892, he would have to "give up the band, and it would be necessary to make a different arrangement."[46] The "band" apparently referred to Jules Levy and his military band, whom Pond was going to take off the road. As for the "different arrangement," Pond could have meant he would not be able to pay Sissieretta a weekly salary of $150. He also may have been referring to the practice of contracting Sissieretta's services to other concert managers, as described in a brief item in the *Cleveland Gazette* (24 December 1892) that said Pond "now sells the 'Black Patti's' services to concert managers who desire her to sing."[47] David Jones said that in his presence Pond told bandleader Levy that he could have David and Sissieretta because Pond wanted "to get rid of them." There was no supporting documentation from Levy in the court file. In his statement David said that Levy was in New Orleans, and therefore he was unable to obtain an affidavit from Levy confirming the conversation with Pond. Jones said that he told Pond that November day that he and Sissieretta had no means of support other than money earned from her singing concerts. Jones said Pond agreed to make concert arrangements for Sissieretta on a percentage basis when he could and gave David permission to book additional concerts and make arrangements for Sissieretta on his own.[48]

Then David told about a meeting he and Sissieretta had in December 1892 with W. S. Angleman, Pond's agent and representative, at an office at 158 West Fifty-Third Street in New York City. According to David's affidavit, Angleman told them Pond was unable to pay Sissieretta a salary of $150 a week as called for under the contract. The contract signed in June 1892 had stipulated that up until 14 November 1892, Sissieretta would give Pond 15 percent of all money received for singing concerts except when Pond agreed to pay her a fixed sum to sing at a concert he booked. After 14 November 1892 Pond was supposed to pay Sissieretta a flat $150 a week plus traveling expenses for her and David, as well as $35 a week plus traveling expenses for her accompanist. In return Sissieretta was to sing no more than seven or less than five concerts a week. According to David, Angleman told him and Sissieretta in December 1892 that Pond would have to give up managing Sissieretta. "It was then and there agreed that such management should be terminated," David said. Still Sissieretta continued to sing many concerts booked by Pond under special arrangement with David. David also booked concerts on his own, without Pond's involvement. For example he arranged for Sissieretta's performance at the 13 February 1893 concert at Carnegie Music Hall in New York City to benefit the production of *Scenes from Uncle Tom's Cabin* at the Chicago World's Fair. He also booked the March 1893 concert in Harlem and the 6 March concert in Brooklyn. David said that these concerts were publically advertised and that Pond had to have known about them. He said that Pond did not object to any of them until the April concerts named in the lawsuit. Up until that point, David said, all parties—himself, Sissieretta, and Pond—had not considered the 8 June 1892 contract in force and effect.[49]

In her affidavit Sissieretta said she believed Pond's lawsuit was initiated "for the express purpose of harassing and annoying her and was not instituted in good faith." She gave no reasons why Pond would be harassing her. She denied his claim that she had refused to sing any concerts he had arranged, adding that she had "often sung when physically unfit so to do and against the advice and orders of her physician." Further, she said, she had sung "under compulsion and under threats" from Pond or his agent that unless she did so, she would not be paid for any of the services she had already rendered or might render in the future upon such trips. Sissieretta claimed Pond had failed to advertise her concerts and "contribute as fully" as agreed to in the 1892 contract. As for his arranging contracts for her service with other concert managers, Sissieretta said that she did not think she and David got their "proper portion" of the proceeds under these arrangements. She said she was "informed and believes" that Pond received as much as nine hundred dollars a week and upward for concerts she had sung under his direction but that Pond had kept more than the 15 percent to which he was entitled. Like David, Sissieretta said that Pond had "in no way" abided by the terms of the 8 June 1892 contract since December 1892 and, since that time, that all parties had treated the contract as "null and void." Because Pond had failed to live up to the contract for concerts already given, Sissieretta asked the court for damages of five thousand dollars.[50]

David and Sissieretta provided affidavits from two people to support their claim that Pond had given up total control of Sissieretta's schedule and had agreed to let David do some of her bookings. James H. Durham said he had arranged with David for Sissieretta to sing a concert on 6 March 1893 at the Bridge Street Methodist Church in Brooklyn. After making the arrangement with David, Durham said that he called on Pond to ask him whether David had the authority to book the concert. Durham said that Pond told him, "Yes that is all right. Jones and I have arranged all that; he is to give some concerts and I arrange others."[51] A second affidavit was provided by Charles S. Morris, who said he called on Pond in January 1893 to see if he could obtain Sissieretta's services to give concerts throughout the west. Morris, a dramatic reader and lawyer who was married to the daughter of Frederick Douglass,[52] said that Pond told him he was anxious to get rid of Sissieretta and David and would arrange to release any claim he might have on them. Morris said that Pond gave him permission to contract with Sissieretta. Morris said he called on Pond again on 5 April 1893 because he wanted to hire Sissieretta to sing concerts in Virginia for a week. Morris said that W. S. Angleman, Pond's general agent and person in charge of his office, told him that Pond could not make those arrangements "as he no longer had anything to do with her."[53]

David and Sissieretta submitted sworn statements from two additional witnesses to back up their story. D. W. Robertson, a musical and entertainment manager and agent, provided an affidavit about a conversation he had on

10 May 1893 with S. M. Spedon, the editor and owner of *Talent,* a publication about concerts and entertainment. Robertson, who visited Spedon in his office, saw a memorandum written by Pond to Spedon asking the editor to remove "Black Patti" from an advertisement Pond was running in that issue of *Talent.* Robertson said that in the memorandum Pond said he no longer wanted to manage people "who cause him so much trouble." The final affidavit the Joneses supplied came from Sissieretta's accompanist, Georgiana Wilson. She said she had entered into an agreement on 1 August 1892 to be Sissieretta's accompanist and had played for her from that point up until the lawsuit was initiated, except for a period from 7 November until 1 December 1892, when Sissieretta was traveling with Levy's band. Wilson claimed she had not been paid the weekly $35 salary agreed to under the contract with Pond and that Pond still owed her this money.[54]

The sworn statements from Pond, David, and Sissieretta show that their relationship had soured to the point that they were unable to work out their contract differences in private rather than involving the legal system. Apparently all parties had violated the original contract in some way during the past year. David and Sissieretta needed Pond to pay Sissieretta $150 a week and to book concerts for her because Sissieretta's singing career was the only means of support the Joneses had. If Pond had failed to keep his end of the contract, David probably felt compelled to make his own concert arrangements for Sissieretta so that he could keep her working and bringing in money. Pond apparently found it difficult to work with David and Sissieretta. If he wanted to be free of them, it is unclear why he would have clamped down on their contract compliance and brought legal action to stop them from making their own arrangements, unless, perhaps, his lack of contract enforcement was making him look weak and ineffective to other agents and clients.

On 17 May 1893 Judge John Sedgwick, chief judge of the New York Superior Court, heard the case of *James B. Pond v. Sissieretta and David Jones* and weighed the evidence. Former New York judge A. J. Dittenhoefer and attorney William C. Beecher represented Pond, and attorney Job E. Hedges represented David and Sissieretta. Sedgwick denied Pond's motion to prevent Sissieretta from singing in concerts other than those arranged by him but did so without prejudice and with permission to renew the request, which Pond later did on 2 June.[55] With her initial court victory paving the way for her to sing without Pond's consent, Sissieretta performed a sacred concert 21 May at the Providence Opera House in her home state of Rhode Island.[56] She returned to New York to sing a concert at the Brooklyn Tabernacle church in conjunction with a flower show being held there and then gave a concert 6 June at the Lee Avenue Congregational Church in Brooklyn.

Pond's renewed case against Sissieretta and David was assigned to New York Superior Court Judge David McAdam in early June. The judge issued a temporary injunction on 10 June 1893 requiring Sissieretta to let Pond and no one else arrange and manage her concert appearances until a hearing on the motion was held 17 June at 10 A.M. The judge allowed her to sing concerts arranged prior to his issuing the temporary injunction but required that any money earned from these concerts was to be deposited with attorney Job Hedges to await further orders or judgment from the court.[57]

On 17 June 1893 Judge McAdam heard the case. Ten days later he found in Pond's favor, granting him an injunction that prohibited Sissieretta from singing any engagements except under Pond's management.[58] David could no longer make contracts for Sissieretta to sing. Hedges was not present when the ruling was made and had to be sent a copy of the judge's order. The court documents that remain on file with the New York court system do not include a transcript of McAdam's courtroom remarks,[59] but the *New York Dramatic Mirror* (8 July 1893), an entertainment newspaper, found the case interesting enough to print the judge's remarks. Apparently, according to the judge's comments published in the newspaper, Pond and the Joneses disagreed not only on whether both parties were conforming with the 8 June 1892 contract, but also on an extension clause within the contract that allowed Pond to extend the initial year's contract for two additional years under the same terms. Had the judge not recognized the validity of the contract for three years, the Joneses could have argued that their one year under the contract had been completed on 8 June 1893. McAdam's opinion offers additional insight into the lawsuit and the relationship between Pond and the Joneses:

> The "Black Patti" has great musical talent, and her performances are special, unique, and extraordinary within the meaning of the rule allowing injunctions in cases of this character. She was professionally unknown to the world, and had no hold on public favor until after she met the plaintiff [Pond]. She had the genius but no opportunity of exhibiting it before critical and appreciative audiences in order to earn a professional reputation. She was without means, and applied for aid to the plaintiff as a manager of musical and literary celebrities and lecturers, as well as in conducting the business of a first-class musical and lecture agency. It was a happy thought. He appreciated her wonderful talent, and made a contract with her which, at the time, was extremely fair and liberal. By it she put herself under his "exclusive" management. The contract was made June 8, 1892, and was to continue for one year with the privilege given to the plaintiff of continuing it for two additional years, on the

same terms. The plaintiff elected to continue the engagement and the contract is to be read as if the term "three years" had been inserted in it originally. The agreement contains mutual covenants, the details of which are therein stated with particularity.

The defendant opposes the application upon two grounds: First: That the contract is inequitable: Next, that the plaintiff violated its conditions on his part. In reference to the first, the situation of the parties at the time the contract was entered into must control. The defendant was then unrecognized as a professional or as having merit. She needed an introduction to the public by some successful manager, one whose high character would command confidence and carry weight. She required to be advertised in a manner to attract attention and to be introduced at places worthy of her talent and aspirations. No one was better qualified for the duty than the plaintiff, and he did his work well. Indeed, so satisfactorily that her reputation is now well established and her fame precedes her wherever she goes. She is a pronounced success, so much so that she feels and acts as if she can get along hereafter without further assistance from her benefactor, and she has therefore thrown down the ladder on which she ascended to the position she now enjoys. Every sense of gratitude requires her to be loyal to the manager who furnished her the opportunity for greatness, and every principle of equity requires that she be compelled to perform her engagement according to its spirit and intent. Talent is of little value without opportunity, and history records on its bright pages the names of many who would have died in obscurity but for opportunity. Opportunity is a golden word, and is itself more precious than rubies. In view of the facts there is now [no?] ground for declaring the contract inequitable. Equity, as applied to this instrument, means nothing more nor less than giving to each party his due, according to justice, equality of rights—fairness in determination of conflicting claims.

The second objection is without merit. The onus of proving a breach by the plaintiff is on the defendant, who asserts it in his defense. It is fully denied and disproved. Indeed, it is difficult to believe that the plaintiff intended to furnish the defendant with a legal excuse for not performing a contract, he was pecuniarily interested in having carried out in all its integrities [*sic*].

The plaintiff is therefore entitled to an injunction enjoining the defendant from singing, except under the management of the plaintiff, and in conformity with the contract before referred to.[60]

Judge McAdam's ruling reprimanded Sissieretta, claiming she was ungrateful and disloyal to the manager who had made her a star. Faced with the same evidence that Judge Sedgwick used to rule in Sissieretta and David's favor, McAdam interpreted the facts in the case differently. With the restraining order in place, David, for the next two years, would not be able to get involved in Sissieretta's career, and she would be subject to whatever arrangements Pond made for her. Although Sissieretta was no longer free to sing when and where she wanted, presumably, based on the judge's ruling, Pond would have to pay Sissieretta $150 a week as stipulated in the original contract. With the economy turning sour, a steady paycheck would be welcome. An interesting item related to the lawsuit appeared in the *Cleveland Gazette* (15 July 1893), which indicated that the Joneses and Pond, despite the judge's ruling, may have reached an out-of-court compromise favorable to both parties. "Eighty percent of the proceeds of future concerts until the contract expires [June 1895] will go to the 'Black Patti,'" the newspaper reported.[61] If this were true, the arrangement would have left Pond in charge of Sissieretta's bookings, without having to pay her a weekly salary of $150 plus expenses.

With the lawsuit behind her, Sissieretta began her second season under Pond's direction. Pond took out an advertisement in the *Indianapolis Freeman* (9 September 1893) listing her scheduled concerts and announcing her availability for bookings for the 1893–94 season. Sissieretta began the new season on 2 August 1893 in Asbury Park, New Jersey, then went to Saratoga Springs, where she was already well known with the summer visitors, on 12–13 August and 15 August.[62] Her 2 August opening at the auditorium in Asbury Park was a huge success. After a selection by the Fifth Regiment Orchestra and a harp solo by Edwin Smith, Sissieretta took the stage to sing. When she made her entrance, most of the audience stood up to welcome her. She sang "Ocean Thou Mighty Monster," which earned her an "uproarious" applause from the audience. Then she sang "The Last Rose of Summer" as an encore. Later in the program she sang "Fleur des Alpes," and after a thunderous applause she sang an encore, "Maggie, the Cows Are in the Clover." The audience continued to applaud, persuading her to come back on the stage one last time to sing "Swanee River." The auditorium was filled to capacity, making it necessary to turn away nearly a thousand people who came and could not get seats. To satisfy these people, concert manager Fred J. Long arranged for Sissieretta to appear again on the evening of 25 August, the same date she had agreed to sing in Chicago at the premiere of *Scenes from Uncle Tom's Cabin* on "Colored Folks Day" or "Negro Jubilee Day" at the World's Columbian Exposition.[63]

The story behind Colored Folks Day at the Columbian Exposition shows how poorly African Americans were treated in 1893 and how their leaders responded. It is also interesting in light of Sissieretta's initial commitment to Cook's black opera to be presented that day and her subsequent decision not to appear. From the beginning most of the African American press was opposed to Colored Folks Day at the exposition because fair officials had denied African Americans any role or place of honor within the fair management, programming, or planning efforts, and many blacks felt that fair officials, by giving African Americans this special day at the fair, were simply "throwing them a crumb to entice them to turn out in large numbers and spend lots of money."[64] Ida B. Wells, an African American journalist and civil rights activist, joined with Ferdinand Barnett, the editor of the black newspaper *Conservator,* where Wells worked, and with Frederick Douglass to publish a booklet titled *The Reason Why the Colored American Is Not Represented in the World's Columbian Exposition.* About ten thousand copies were distributed during the exposition.[65]

Somehow Cook's idea for a black opera based on *Uncle Tom's Cabin* got co-opted by exposition officials, who were eager to make it the "one alluring aspect of their otherwise unappealing plans for 'Colored Folks Day.'"[66] Cook's opera was to be one of the entertainment highlights of the day, although apparently that was not his original intention. At one point, in early March 1893, the *Detroit Plaindealer* reported that the story of *Uncle Tom's Cabin* in Cook's black opera was going to be modified in a way that was causing "great excitement and indignation" in some "Southern Democratic journals." According to the newspaper, Uncle Tom would not die by the lash, as in the original story, but instead would be burned to death like Henry Smith, a deranged black man who had been accused of murdering a four-year-old white child.[67] At least ten thousand spectators looked on and cheered as Smith was slowly tortured and burned alive in Paris, Texas, on 1 February 1892.[68] The newspaper said that the scene would be as realistic as possible in order to give the audience "a general idea of this late piece of barbarity." Some southern journals were calling on the managers of the World's Fair to stop this scene from being enacted. The *Plaindealer* said the southern journals "uphold the barbarity, but they think its representation will place a stigma upon the South. In that, they are right. They deserve the stigma. They encourage such fiendish acts. Let them abide by the consequences."[69] Two scholars think this report about the burning scene may have been "disinformation" intentionally "planted by opponents of the Colored Folks Day program."[70]

More controversy about Colored Folks Day emerged in July, when newspaper accounts in the black press said that fair officials had arranged to have hundreds of watermelons placed around the exposition on that day. Wells, in a letter published in the *Cleveland Gazette,* said the horticulture department at the exposition had "pledged itself to put plenty of watermelons around on the ground with permission to the brothers in black to 'appropriate them.'"[71] These watermelon rumors prompted John H. Cook, secretary of the Chicago World's Fair, to write a letter published in the *Indianapolis Freeman* (12 August 1893) denying the rumor that two thousand watermelons were to be placed about and that the grand jubilee was to be presented to show only "the ridiculous side of the most illiterate race." Secretary Cook also denied this day had been set apart "on account of the prejudice against the colored people. This is a mistake." He said every distinct nationality and race represented by a great number of people in the United States, such as the Irish, Polish, and Italians, had been given a special day to celebrate with appropriate ceremonies. Cook said the program to be presented on 25 August was to be one of the "highest merit" and was to include scenes from the opera of *Uncle Tom's Cabin* by Will M. Cook and sung by Black Patti, Harry Burleigh, Sidney Woodward, and a trained chorus of one hundred voices. "Mr. Cook's opera has been highly commented upon by eminent musical critics of the New York press, Sissieretta Jones declaring it to be the most beautiful music she has ever heard. The Thomas Exposition Orchestra of 114 pieces will accompany Mme. Jones and will play a suite of Negro dances, composed by Mr. Strothotte, a teacher in the National Conservatory of America. The orchestra will be directed by Will M. Cook." The fair secretary went on to describe more of the scheduled entertainment, which would include the Fisk Jubilee Singers.[72]

In the end there were no watermelons on the ground on 25 August for Colored Folks Day. Not only were the watermelons missing, but so too were many of the prominent black speakers, singers, and actors who had been advertised to be there, including Sissieretta. There also was no performance of *Scenes from Uncle Tom's Cabin,* although Woodward and Burleigh sang an excerpt from the opera toward the end of the day's musical program.[73] The *Cleveland Gazette* said the African Americans who had made some of the arrangements for Colored Folks Day—Joseph Banneker Adger of Philadelphia and Will Marion Cook and Charles S. Morris of Washington, D.C.— "ought to [be] ashamed of their connection with the alleged affair."[74]

Douglass was the most prominent African American to appear on Colored Folks Day. He delivered a powerful "extemporaneous" speech before the start of a classical musical program, a program that included mezzo-contralto Madame Deseria Plato rather than Sissieretta, baritone Harry T. Burleigh, violinist Joseph Douglass, and poet Paul Laurence Dunbar. Frederick Douglass's remarks included a strong statement about the fair's and the country's prejudice against African Americans. "That we are outside of the World's Fair is only consistent with the fact that we are excluded from every respectable calling, from workshops, manufactures [*sic*] and from the means of learning trades. It is consistent with the fact that we are outside of the church and largely outside of the state," Douglass said. Ida Wells, who had been against Douglass's participation in Colored Folks Day, was so taken with his speech after reading it in the newspaper the next day that she went to the fair to beg his pardon for criticizing him.[75]

Although Sissieretta had been advertised to appear at the exposition on Colored Folks Day on 25 August, the *Indianapolis Freeman* had reported as early as 12 August she would not be there. One of the newspaper's correspondents had seen a telegram from Major Pond in which he said that "under no circumstances" would she appear on that day.[76] After she failed to sing at the event, Charles S. Morris made a public apology for Sissieretta's absence. According to Morris "opponents of colored American day at The Fair had written and misled her and her husband in regard to the good character of the celebration. This was done after her manager, Major Pond, had signed an agreement for her to make three appearances here for the sum of $800, of which $300 was paid by telegraph."[77] Pond had another explanation. He said Sissieretta "did not appear because the guarantee money reached him by wire . . . too late to get the word to her at Asbury Park in time to catch the last train to Chicago."[78] Still another story about Sissieretta's nonappearance was published in a long letter to the editor in the *Conservator* (9 September 1893), the black newspaper Wells worked for and that was edited by Ferdinand Barnett, another opponent of Colored Folks Day. The writer of the column, an anonymous person who went by the name of "Rambler," provided an "insider" account of the affair sprinkled with irony throughout. Sissieretta pasted a copy of this column in her scrapbook. "Rambler" called Will M. Cook and Charles S. Morris a "precious pair of straw colored pets, . . . who blarneyed a confiding people by one of the boldest confidence games ever seen in Chicago." He said their work was "so slick that you hardly know whether it was rascality or genius." "Rambler" said Morris came from New York and hooked up with Cook. They forced out a Philadelphia man named Adger, who had been working for six months to line up music for "watermelon day" and had already engaged Selika and others to sing at the event. Cook and Morris were soon managers of "watermelon day" with the understanding that the more people they packed into the hall, the more dollars would jingle in their pockets. "Rambler" continued:

> That was a picnic and they proceeded to make the most of it. They had no stock on hand but two dandy imaginations and two eighteen caret [*sic*] tongues warranted to stand any test which the emergency might require. They first fastened on two good singers, [Harry] Burleigh and [Sidney] Woodward, who were here [Chicago] visiting and hence didn't cost very much. Then they resurrected Cook's scheme of his great Afro-American opera, "Uncle Tom's Cabin" which he says he has written and which

we are expected to believe will knock out all the operas that the white people ever knew or heard of. They billed this opera and as a climax advertised that Mme. Sissieretta Jones would appear in the title role. . . . Sissieretta Jones was the drawing card and the managers knew it. They did not stop to perfect the engagements so as to have her here. What they were after was the crowd and the dollars the crowd would bring. If Sissieretta Jones got here all right, if not, neither of the slick managers would die of heart ache.[79]

About fifteen hundred people came to the fair on Colored Folks Day to hear Douglass and the Black Patti. After Douglass's speech the crowd waited in vain for the African American opera to begin and to hear Sissieretta. "Rambler" said that folks began to get restless. "They saw her name outside on bills, saying she would be there, but they didn't know that Black Patti was warbling in New York at the time. But Morris and Cook knew it, and Morris went out on the platform with a search light smile on his face and a sugar coated whopper in his mouth, and told the people that Sissieretta would not be there because some parties in Chicago had conspired to keep her away."[80] This aroused some anger in the crowd. "Rambler" said Black Patti was not there because Morris and Cook had not sent money in time for her to be there. They had sent one hundred dollars to Pond and promised to send the additional two hundred. They supposedly "held up" Douglass and "squeezed him for a pair of hundreds to fetch Sister Jones," "Rambler" said. They sent the two hundred dollars, but it was too late.

> Back came the answer that Sissieretta Jones could not be present. But that didn't stop the confidence game from going on. All day of the concert Black Patti was billed to appear, while the managers had a telegram plainly saying that she would not. Some people call this kind of work cute and slick, but I call it highway robbery. You may call it what you like. . . . Morris and Cook drew down over $500 and they can afford to smile at their brilliant success.
>
> There are only two other people who can get any smile out of the affair, they are the Black Patti and her manager, Pond. When Morris and Cook found that Patti would not come, they thought, of course, they would get their $300. The "mon" didn't come, so they sent for it. You can imagine the smiling match which occurred in New York between Sister Jones and her manager as they looked at the $300 and considered the suggestion of sending it back.
>
> "Do you see anything green in my eye?" asked Manager Pond of Mrs. Jones. The lady smiled sweetly and assured him that there wasn't a sign of green there. "Are there any flies on Black Patti," suggested the

only Mrs. Jones, and the manager said it was past fly time. Then they divided the $300 between them and telegraphed Mr. Morris that they would have to keep the $300 for damages.[81]

It is likely Cook never intended to dupe the public about his black opera, but instead found he could not deliver on his promises. Unfortunately for him, his ambitious desires got caught up in all the controversy surrounding Colored Folks Day. "By most accounts, it was a result of Will Marion Cook's enterprise that Colored Folks Day was conceived, a fact that did not resound in his favor in the midst of the controversy the event provoked. It appears Cook's opera fell victim to the poisonous racial environment surrounding the World's Columbian Exposition," according to two modern-day music scholars.[82]

Sissieretta did finally sing at the Columbian Exposition—a month later. She sang only one night, 25 September, in the Assembly Hall at the magnificently decorated Woman's Building, located north of the Horticulture Building and near the entrance to the Midway Plaisance.[83] The only publicity about her appearance was done at the fair on the day of her concert, but word spread quickly. About an hour before her scheduled performance, the hall was packed with both Americans and foreigners eager to hear her sing. The audience was enthusiastic, giving her an ovation following her song, "Ocean Thou Mighty Monster." Music critic Walt B. Hayson, writing a review of her concert for the *Cleveland Gazette,* compared her voice to that of Marie Selika, whom Hayson said held first place among music "connoisseurs." The critic thought Sissieretta's notes in the high register were thinner than Selika's, but this weakness was compensated by fuller and deeper tones in the lower register. Hayson said Sissieretta's voice is "always musical: there is present, too, that spirit, that musical taste and insight, that is found only in the born artist."[84]

Sissieretta's one-day appearance at the Columbian Exposition came between two extended appearances at the Pittsburgh Exposition, where she had been such a success the previous year. The 1893 Pittsburgh Exposition was held at the same time as the Columbian Exposition. Pittsburgh Exposition manager Johnson knew from previous experience that Sissieretta could draw large crowds and help the Pittsburgh Exposition compete with the Columbian Exposition in Chicago. Some had warned Johnson against holding the Pittsburgh Exposition that year because of competition from the Chicago event and a downturn in the economy, which might have kept merchants from spending money on displays and exhibits. Johnson decided to hold the annual event anyway and paid Pond handsomely for Sissieretta to appear the first ten days of the forty-day Pittsburgh Exposition—reportedly for two thousand dollars a week.[85] Sissieretta was a big hit, bringing in huge crowds to hear her afternoon and evening concerts with Ellis Brooks's band from New York. About ten thousand to twelve thousand people attended the first night of the Pittsburgh Exposition. Many of those fairgoers came to Sissieretta's opening night concert on 6 September 1893. Older people filled the three thousand seats surrounding the band platform, and younger folks congregated around the popcorn and lemonade stands and merry-go-round as Sissieretta made her entrance at 9:30 P.M.[86] She sang several selections, followed by an encore of "Swanee River" and "Killarney." For the next ten days, she entertained her audiences with classical selections and popular ballads, singing many encores. Her final day at the Pittsburgh Exposition was Saturday, 16 September. Nine days later, on 25 September, she sang her one concert at the Columbian Exposition in Chicago. About that time Pittsburgh Exposition manager Johnson began negotiations with Major Pond to bring Sissieretta back for the final six days of the Pittsburgh fair in mid-October. She would be singing with Gilmore's Band and would rotate concert appearances with the famous Italian tenor Italo Companini, who also had been hired for the last week of the Pittsburgh Exposition. The two singers alternated daily performance times, with him singing the 2 P.M. and 7:30 P.M. concerts the first day and her singing the 4 P.M. and 9:30 P.M. concerts and then reversing the concert times the following day. Calling "Black Patti" the "Exposition mascot," Johnson said he knew her return would be welcome news to fairgoers. "We have had great difficulty in closing this engagement; to do so necessitated our buying off two other places where she was booked to sing," he said.[87] A newspaper article published the day Sissieretta opened for the final week of the Pittsburgh Exposition said, "Black Patti is again in town, and you can no more judge her musical ability by her color than you can a book by its cover."[88] Another newspaper praised her willingness to sing popular, well-known songs requested by the audience, a practice that brought her great favor with the "hearts of music loving Pittsburghers."[89] On Saturday night, 21 October, the final concert of the exposition, Sissieretta sang "The Star-Spangled Banner" to an audience of four thousand to five thousand people. The huge crowd went wild when she sang that patriotic song, and "there was a demonstration the like of which has seldom been seen in Pittsburg [sic]."[90]

As the Pittsburgh Exposition closed, it appeared Sissieretta and Pond were back on track after all the unpleasantness the lawsuit had brought earlier in the year. The two thousand dollars a week that Pond reportedly received for Sissieretta's concert appearances guaranteed that Sissieretta would have been well paid. She had showed Pond she could attract large crowds and satisfy them with her voice and popular repertoire. Following her successful and lucrative performances in Pittsburgh, Pond had her join a new group of white entertainers—the Vilonas, three young musical sisters, and Della Thompson, an elocutionist. They toured through the end of 1893 and the beginning of 1894. The Vilona sisters, graduates of the University of Berlin, consisted of Emma and Nina, both violinists, and Lilly, a pianist.[91]

As the year came to a close, Sissieretta's career had reached new heights. Despite her legal efforts to be free of Pond's management, she would have had to recognize the numerous successes and triumphs she had accomplished under his direction. Pond had helped her become a household name. No longer only performing for African American audiences, Sissieretta was a favorite among many white concertgoers as well. She had done what many other black entertainers of her time had not yet done—share the same stage with white performers. Her appearances at the Pittsburgh Exposition showed that she was respected for her musical talent and ability and not just seen as a "curiosity." Critics, both black and white, had praised her training and natural ability as well as recognized the confident way she handled herself on stage. Sissieretta was famous and making lots of money, almost $8,000 a year (the equivalent of $197,000 in purchasing power in 2009),[92] not including expenses, making her one of the highest-paid African American entertainers, male or female, of her time. The talented soprano was becoming known as the greatest singer of her race, and she was not doing it by singing minstrel pieces or other coarse songs. As one scholar said, "She was a role model, a public representative of the progress and accomplishments of her generation of African Americans, born after the Civil War."[93] One of her African American contemporaries, lyricist, author, and later civil rights activist James Weldon Johnson, wrote that Sissieretta "had most of the qualities essential in a great singer: the natural voice, the physical figure, the grand air, and the engaging personality."[94] What could be ahead for her in the new year? In a partial newspaper clipping pasted in Sissieretta's scrapbook, the young prima donna, during an interview, revealed her dreams for the future: "My favorite music? Oh, operatic music, of course. I like ballads because they seem to please the public very much. I should like extremely well to sing an opera. My teacher wants me to study the part of Aida and Zelika [Selika] in 'L'Africaine.' I have no present plans, and can't tell what I will do until I have completed my contract with Major Pond. He is now talking of taking me to Europe next year. It is only during the past two years that I have sung for white people. I have found them very appreciative. Before that time I sung only in the presence of my own race. I should like very much to go abroad and study acting and become an opera singer."[95]

5

The Road to Europe
1894–1895

Shortly after Sissieretta's twenty-sixth birthday in early January 1894, she was invited to sing at a prestigious charity concert in New York directed by the famous Bohemian composer Antonin Dvořák, who had been teaching and coaching African American students since 1892 as director of the National Conservatory of Music in New York City. The conservatory, led by founder Jeanette M. Thurber, joined with the *New York Herald* to sponsor a charity concert on 23 January to raise money for the *Herald's* Free Clothing Fund. Thurber had opened her conservatory to anyone with musical ability, regardless of a student's race, color, or creed. She believed Emancipation had not gone far enough to free black people. "Bodies had been liberated, but the gates of the artistic world were still locked," said an article in the *New York Herald*.[1] The concert by the conservatory pupils, held at the Madison Square Garden Concert Hall, was billed as the "first public exhibition of the progress of musical experiment entered upon at the Conservatory in which the Afro-American is a factor."[2] All the concert participants were black, with the exception of one white student, Bertha Visanska, who played the piano. Sissieretta was the only soloist who was not a student at the conservatory.

Dvořák (1841–1904), an internationally renowned composer, was born in a village just north of the Czech capital of Prague. He came to New York in 1892 to direct the National Conservatory of Music, where he stayed until 1895. He composed his most famous work, Symphony No. 9 in E minor, better known as the *New World* Symphony, in 1893, while at the conservatory. Dvořák was particularly interested in the African American race, their songs and their folklore. He believed the music of African Americans was the foundation for a "truly national school of music."[3] After studying black music during his first year in the United States, Dvořák said, "I am now satisfied that the future music of this country must be founded upon what are called the Negro melodies. . . . These beautiful and varied themes are the product of the soil. They are American. These are the folk songs of America, and your composers must turn to them." He said such melodies are "pathetic, tender, passionate, melancholy, solemn, religious, bold, merry, gay or what you will. There is nothing in the whole range of composition that cannot be supplied with themes from this source. The American musician understands these tunes and they move sentiment in him. They appeal to his imagination because of their associations."[4] Dvořák sought to demonstrate his enthusiasm for African American musicians, singers, and their music with the musical program he chose for the *Herald*'s Free Clothing Fund concert.

As concertgoers entered the Madison Square Garden concert hall that evening, they saw a gallery at the back of the stage where a 130-member black student chorus sat. The sopranos and altos were dressed in white, pink, or blue, and the tenors and basses all wore dress suits. According to the *New York Herald*, "It was an interesting sight, and one not without its pathetic side, for there was a look of earnestness upon the faces of the members so intense as to cause a feeling of sadness."[5] The program opened with the overture to *A Midsummer Night's Dream* by Mendelssohn, played by the fifty students who made up the conservatory orchestra. Dvořák conducted. The *Herald* review said the young, inexperienced orchestra proved they had received excellent instruction at the conservatory. Next came Sissieretta, who sang the solo "Inflammatus" from Rossini's *Stabat Mater*. The male choir of St. Philip's Church sang the chorus. They were led by Edward B. Kinney Jr., the organist and choirmaster of the church and one of Dvořák's composition pupils. The audience loved Sissieretta, especially those hearing her for the first time. She sang with power and feeling and demonstrated her ability to sing high C's with little apparent effort. For an encore she sang "Robert, Toi Que J'aime." As much as the audience liked Sissieretta's solo, they could not help but take notice of the male choir accompanying her. The *New York Herald* described the choir's performance:

> As the shrill voices of the boys of St. Philips colored choir rose in Rossini's "Inflammatus," voices with the curious tonal color which is one of the characteristics of the colored race, you were compelled to admit that had the National Conservatory of Music done nothing more than to open wider to them music's unlimited resources of enjoyment it would have achieved a noble work.
>
> There was one little fellow who attracted everybody's attention. He had no sheet music, but he apparently needed none, singing with an evident enjoyment that showed how deeply he was interested in the work. He never took his eyes from the conductor's baton, and at every attack he made a funny little convulsive start as though he said, "Now for it!"

His ardor was shared by every individual in the choir. Their attention was riveted upon the affair in hand. The proof of this was found in the fact that every attack was as unanimous as though it were sung by one huge voice.[6]

Following Sissieretta's two selections, Bertha Visanska walked onto the stage, bowed timidly to the audience, and seated herself at the piano. The slim girl of about twelve or thirteen looked at Dvořák and nodded to let him know she was ready to begin. Dvořák began directing the orchestral accompaniment to Liszt's "Hungarian Fantasy." She played the piece's difficult passages with "breadth, authority, and clear, distinct technique." Because the audience had reacted so enthusiastically to Visanska's performance, Dvořák relaxed the rule of no encores for conservatory pupils so the young pianist could play one more number. Next on the program was a serenade for string instruments in two movements composed by Robert Volkmann. This was followed by Maurice Arnold, one of Dvořák's composition students, who conducted his own composition, *American Plantation Dances*—a series of four dances for full orchestra. These dances reportedly reflected many of Dvořák's thoughts and conclusions about the elements essential for the foundation of a national school of music. A reviewer for the *New York Herald* said, "The characteristic features of negro music have been closely studied and adapted for use in serious composition. Rhythms, harmonies, [and] melodic forms in these dances all originate in the folk music of the negroes. . . . The themes are all original, but they have about them a flavor of a music which we have been accustomed to associate with the negro race. The orchestration is praiseworthy, particularly in the second, though the third is bound to be the most popular. . . . There is such a gay swing about the last that nearly every boy in the choir marked time with his head."[7]

As the program moved toward the finish, the audience anticipated the grand finale—Dvořák's arrangement of Stephen Foster's popular folk song "Old Folks at Home," also known as "Swanee River." Sissieretta, who had become known for singing "Swanee River," sang the soprano solo, and Harry Burleigh, who studied under Dvořák, sang the baritone. They were accompanied by the orchestra and the black student chorus. In selecting this song for the program, Dvořák said, "American music is music that lives in the heart of the people, and therefore this air has every right to be regarded as purely national."[8]

When Dvořák came onto the stage to conduct the final number, the first violinist left his seat and approached the maestro, who began waving him back to his place. At this point, the violinist held out a gold-mounted ebony baton. He spoke briefly, explaining that this baton was a token of "loving esteem" from the orchestra. Dvořák was so overcome he could not reply. He

thanked the orchestra, using gestures rather than words, and then began con-
ducting with his beautiful new gift. A reviewer from the *Herald* called Dvořák's
arrangement of "Old Folks at Home" very effective, "with desolate character
being imparted to it by the flute in the prelude, with a very quiet and simple
accompaniment."[9] Another newspaper review said the song's simple theme,
with its great sound and melody, almost overwhelmed the listener.

One can imagine Sissieretta and Harry Burleigh, two powerful African
American singers, standing there poised and confident onstage in front of a
black chorus and black orchestra, singing the words Stephen Foster penned
in "Negro dialect" in 1851. The sentimental song about home had been written for blackface singers in minstrel shows, but it had moved beyond that and
become a popular song that "embodied longings that are shared by rich and
poor, by the weak as well as the strong."[10] The words to the song reverberated
around the concert hall as the performers sang their parts.

OLD FOLKS AT HOME[11]
Way down upon de Swanee ribber,
  Far, far away,
Dere's wha my heart is turning ebber,
  Dere's wha de old folks stay.
All up and down de whole creation
  Sadly I roam,
Still longing for de old plantation,
  And for de old folks at home

CHORUS
All de world am sad and dreary,
  Ebrywhere I roam;
Oh, darkeys, how my heart grows weary,
  Far from de old folks at home!

All round de little farm I wander'd
  When I was young;
Den many happy days I squander'd,
  Many de songs I sung.
When I was playing wid my brudder,
  Happy was I;
Oh, take me to my kind old mudder!
  Dere let me live and die
                              CHORUS

One little hut among de bushes,
  One dat I love,

Still sadly to my mem'ry rushes,
　No matter where I rove.
When will I see de bees a-humming
　All round de comb?
When will I hear de banjo tumming,
　Down in my good old home?

CHORUS

Sometime after her performance at the *Herald's* Free Clothing Fund concert, which raised $1,047 in contributions, Sissieretta was the star of another major New York fund-raising concert.[12] This one, called the Free Bread Fund, was sponsored by Joseph Pulitzer's newspaper, the *New York World,* and the Sons of New York, the leading black fraternal organization in the city. Members of the concert committee of the Sons of New York included Sissieretta's husband, David. The concert at the Standard Theatre was sold out. Most of the patrons were black. African Americans occupied more than half of the orchestra and balcony seats and all of the gallery. Several prominent white people attended, including the new state treasurer, Addison Colvin, his wife and friends, and Edward Harrigan, of the popular Broadway theatrical team of Ned Harrigan and Tony Hart.[13]

Sissieretta, the star of the evening, was joined by a number of talented black singers, musicians, and an elocutionist. The performers included the Creole Quartet, saxophonist Elzie Hoffman, singer Sidney Woodward, violinist J. H. Douglass, the Unique Quartet, and elocutionist Ednorah Nahar. Sissieretta's first selection was a waltz by Gounod, followed by an encore, "The Cows Are in the Corn." Her second selection was Gounod's "Ave Maria," accompanied by piano and violin obbligato. Although a reviewer praised her singing of "Ave Maria," he said it could not touch the way in which she sang "Swanee River." "Never was this gifted woman heard to better advantage. Never were her songs received with greater enthusiasm. Her rich, flexible voice with its marvelous range, power and sweetness, rang out superbly," said a review pasted in Sissieretta's scrapbook.[14] The concert raised $1,100 to help feed the thousands of poor people who came to the city's distribution bureaus and stood in line to get some bread. The country's deep economic recession had put many people out of work and left them desperate for help. This benefit concert was one of many held during 1894 by various groups in New York City to raise money to help the unemployed.

While Sissieretta was in New York, she reportedly visited the famous Australian opera soprano Madame Nellie Melba (1861–1931) at the Hotel Savoy, according to a small article in the *Cleveland Gazette* (31 March 1894), an African American newspaper. Melba was in New York in 1894 singing at the

Metropolitan Opera House. The *Gazette* said Sissieretta sang several selections for her, who "immediately told Mme. Jones that her voice was grand and also stated that Mme. Jones should go to Paris and finish under her instruction, and volunteered her services at the benefit for the same." The *Gazette* said that Sissieretta intended to take Melba's advice and that "in a short time one of the greatest concerts ever given in New York will take place. The main artist will be Mme. Melba and the proceeds will be to finish the musical education of Mme. Sissieretta Jones in Paris."[15] There is no evidence to date that this meeting between Melba and Sissieretta ever took place or that Melba gave any benefit concert to pay for Sissieretta to study abroad. Melba, although loved and admired by her audiences, was known to be demanding, temperamental, and competitive. She could also be quite generous and kind and was helpful to a few young singers early in their careers, making it possible that she could have been supportive of Sissieretta. It is difficult to know whether this alleged meeting between the two women might have taken place or whether it was just one of many legends surrounding Melba.

For the next five or six months, Sissieretta continued to give concerts, but little is known about her schedule. She spent part of April in numerous towns in Pennsylvania, such as York on 13 April, where the audience was "discouragingly small."[16] She canceled several concerts in Pennsylvania in late April[17] without any reason given in the press and then gave a concert in Wheeling, West Virginia, on 2 May. She apparently was giving concerts in smaller cites and towns along the eastern part of the United States. Perhaps the poor economy was affecting her travels. An interesting item appeared in the *New York Dramatic News,* one of the major newspapers devoted to the entertainment industry, which said that Sissieretta's manager, Major Pond, was "playing possum" this season. "In the Fall he came to the conclusion that this would be a bad time to venture much. Accordingly he is devoting his time and attention to mapping a campaign for next season."[18] This appears to indicate that Pond had given up on the current entertainment season, which began in the fall of 1893 and would end in early May 1894, and had instead decided to concentrate his efforts for the new season that would begin in August 1894. Perhaps by then business conditions would improve.

As for Sissieretta, after touring several small cities and towns along the East Coast, she likely wrapped up her touring season in early May, because many indoor venues in the days before air-conditioning closed for the summer. She and David returned to Rhode Island to spend most of the summer at Sissieretta's mother's home at 321 North Main Street in Providence. By the end of July, Sissieretta headed back to New York to get ready for the upcoming season. Between 12 August and 16 August, and again on 19 August, she sang concerts in Saratoga Springs, at Congress Spring Park, where she had attracted huge crowds in the past. On 12 August she sang before two thousand people gathered at the park.[19] Sometime during the month, she traveled to Milwaukee to perform and also sang at the Lake Monona assembly in Madison, Wisconsin, despite the objections from a white New York tenor, McKenzie Gordon, who refused to appear onstage with Sissieretta. "However the concert went on without the prejudiced fool. The 'Black Patti' is not only the better known and appreciated of the two but she can teach the jackass good manners, as well as how to become a conspicuous concert success thereafter," said the black newspaper the *Cleveland Gazette*.[20] This incident demonstrates once again the difficulties and indignities Sissieretta faced because she was black. On the one hand, she was a star, a singing sensation who was adored by her audiences, yet she had to contend with racial prejudice both on and off the stage, which must have hurt her and made her feel angry and humiliated. Toward the end of August, Sissieretta sang once again at Saratoga Springs. This time she performed with Guglielmo Ricci at a benefit concert for the Saratoga Home for Children on 24 August. Before the month closed, she appeared two more times at Congress Spring Park.[21]

Throughout the month of August, during Sissieretta's multiple appearances in Saratoga Springs, no mention was given in the press as to whom was managing these concerts. Although Pond had been responsible for booking her at Congress Spring Park in the past, there is nothing to indicate that he had arranged for her to be there in August 1894. Sissieretta's contract with Pond should have been in effect until mid-June 1895, but by the middle of 1894, he appears to have stopped being her manager. In an interview Sissieretta gave to the *New York Dramatic Mirror* in 1896, she said she stayed under Pond's management for two years, which would mean she ceased to be under his control in June 1894.[22]

By the beginning of November 1894, it was clear from press reports that Sissieretta had a new business manager, a white man named Rudolph Voelckel, who would, in time, become her manager for the remainder of her musical career. Voelckel, who was a year older than the twenty-six-year-old Sissieretta, was an associate of Morris Reno, president of the Carnegie Hall Music Association. Reno wanted Voelckel to manage a concert tour for Sissieretta in the United States and then in Europe.[23] The young, single manager, born in New York on 30 October 1867, was about five feet, seven inches tall, with gray eyes, light-colored hair, a fair complexion, and a long, narrow face.[24] Voelckel, whose office was at Carnegie Hall, took out a large advertisement in the *New York Dramatic Mirror* (10 November 1894) to announce a "Grand Transcontinental Tour" of the "Black Patti Concert Company." The company starred Sissieretta and included contralto Mathilde Walter, tenor Vincenzo Bielletto, basso Orme Darvall, German-born pianist Felix Heink, and a "marvelous child dancer" from England, Little Ruby.[25] Voelckel seemed to pattern the Black Patti Concert Company after Pond's winning formula of pairing Sissieretta with several white, European-born performers. The ad said that the fall and winter tour for the 1894–95 season was entirely booked and that the company would play the Palace Theatre in London in April, May, and June of 1895. The end of the ad said that Voelckel was currently booking summer engagements for Black Patti, with or without the company. In an item published in the same edition of the *Mirror,* Voelckel announced the thirty-week tour would include a trip to the Pacific coast, returning by way of the southern states. "The demand for this talented artiste is greater than ever before, and the time of the entire tour is all filled and presages a season of great success," said the press item, likely written by Voelckel himself.[26]

Sissieretta had talked about going to Europe before. Pond was supposed to have taken her there, but that never happened. Now it appeared that the young Voelckel would get her there. Sissieretta would be able to see how she was received in European countries, where there might be less racial prejudice toward black people. She also may have thought further vocal training might be available to her while she performed in Europe. If Sissieretta was successful in Europe, other singing opportunities might become available to her.

Sissieretta's first appearance as star of the Black Patti Concert Company was Sunday, 18 November 1894, at Carnegie Hall. Many patrons in the large audience were black. The concert, which began at 8:15 P.M., was entirely classical and included pieces such as a selection from Bruch's "Das Feuerkreuz" (op. 52), a duet from Gounod's *Faust,* and an aria from Halévy's *La Juive.* Little Ruby did not perform and was replaced by the Vilona sisters, the instrumentalists with whom Sissieretta had performed while under Pond's direction. Others on the program were Walter, pianist Orton Bradley, Bielletto, and Darvall. Sissieretta sang three numbers on the program: Gounod's "Valse-Ariette," an aria from Verdi's *La Traviata,* and Gounod's "Ave Maria," which included a violin obbligato played by Lilly Vilona.[27] Sissieretta also sang several encores, including "Swanee River."[28] The concert was a success. A short item in the *New York Dramatic Mirror* said, "If the enthusiasm with which Black Patti was received may be taken as an indication of her popularity there can be no doubt of the warmth of her reception while on the road."[29] The article said her upcoming tour would last twenty weeks (not the thirty weeks that was first announced), all of which was booked.

Sissieretta's company did not venture far after the concert at Carnegie Hall. One of the group's first stops was Ithaca, New York, where they played 22 November at the Music Hall. Next Sissieretta sang in Brooklyn at the Grand Opera House on Sunday, 25 November. An article in the *Brooklyn*

Eagle that day said that she had just signed a contract to sing for five weeks in London at the Palace Music Hall. The article also said a Colonel Maple-son had offered to book her at Covent Garden, "perhaps in the leading part in 'L'Africaine,'" but the article said she would only sing at the Palace Music Hall.[30] If the information in this news item is true, it seems odd that Sis-sieretta would not jump at the chance to sing the lead in this opera, unless Voelckel had an exclusive arrangement with the Palace Theatre. Sissieretta had expressed interest the year before in singing opera, but perhaps she did not feel ready to sing an entire role in *L'Africaine* and felt that it would take too long to prepare herself, given her other singing commitments.

Still in New York in early December, Sissieretta and her company were scheduled to give a classical concert 9 December at the Columbus Theatre in Harlem.[31] By late December she was finally touring away from New York, giving concerts in Ohio and Indiana.[32] Sissieretta's whereabouts in early Jan-uary 1895 are not recorded in the New York entertainment papers. Her name appears again in a one-line report in the *New York Dramatic Mirror* (9 Feb-ruary 1895). The item, from Atlanta, said, "Black Patti drew a tremendously topheavy house at DeGive's Grand Jan. 24."[33] She was scheduled to appear in Galveston, Texas, in mid-February, but she never made it there. Instead Sis-sieretta sailed on Tuesday, 11 February, for Europe, and a small newspaper item said that she would begin an eight-week engagement at the Wintergarten in Berlin on 17 February.[34] Originally Voelckel had announced that she would perform at the Palace Theatre in London and had not mentioned bookings in other countries prior to her London debut. Apparently the Wintergarten booking came up quickly, because Voelckel did not apply for a passport until 4 February 1895, just a week before he, Sissieretta, and David likely sailed together for Germany. (Voelckel's passport was issued two days later, on 6 February.)[35] Perhaps Voelckel managed to get Sissieretta the Berlin engage-ment and decided to drop the rest of the American tour in favor of going to Europe. Music scholar John Graziano has suggested the twenty-week Ameri-can tour, which would have lasted until 6 April, was not as well booked as Voelckel had indicated. Perhaps when theater managers around the country found out that the Black Patti Company performed more classical pieces than popular selections, they may have been afraid audiences would be small and canceled their bookings. Graziano said Sissieretta may have gone to Europe on her own rather than under Voelckel's direction.[36] The logistics involved in that scenario make it less likely to have been the case and more likely that Voelckel accompanied the Joneses to Germany. For one thing Sissieretta and David probably did not speak German, whereas Voelckel would have been familiar with the language, as both his parents were born in Germany and presumably spoke German in their home even after they arrived in New York. Also Voelckel's passport application coincided with Sissieretta's trip to Germany.

Sissieretta made her European debut at Berlin's Wintergarten on Tuesday, 19 February 1895. Thanks to English translations of her opening reviews published on the front page of the *Indianapolis Freeman* (4 May 1895),[37] it is possible to get a good idea of her opening night concert and how the German audience received the African American singer. Wearing little jewelry and a tasteful gown of salmon pink covered with jet trimmings, Sissieretta began her concert with the "Valse-Ariette," composed by Gounod for Adelina Patti. The large audience gave her an ovation. She followed with two American songs and closed with "The Last Rose of Summer," "apparently to allow the German audience opportunity" to compare her singing with that of the great Patti. "It turned out entirely to her favor, and the applause which greeted the close of each number was a tribute to a talent which is quite independent [*sic*] of color or nationality, a talent worthy of admiration for its own sake alone, and which can well appeal to an intelligent audience," said the critic for the *Borsen-Courier*.[38] Sissieretta was obviously giving her audiences plenty of opportunity to compare her singing with that of her famous namesake by singing many of the same pieces that were part of Adelina Patti's repertoire.

All six of the translated German reviews published in the *Indianapolis Freeman* sang Sissieretta's praises. The reviewers spoke of her natural talent and the evidence of her musical training. Quotes from several of the reviews provide a good picture of how Sissieretta was received:

"Her voice is clear and true up to the highest tones" (*Berliner Fremdenblatt*).

"Her voice has power and fire, and the florid passages remind one of the rapid flow of a mountain brook" (*Norddeutsche Allgemeine Zeitung*).

"Her well trained voice is of great range and fine carrying power. Her technical ability is admirable, she executes the most difficult florid passages with perfect ease, and the good taste of her delivery shows natural talent developed by careful and well directed study. A certain sharpness in the upper tones may have been the fault of the hall" (*Post*).

"It is not only the dusky complexion that is real about her, the clear, full-toned voice, a soprano with range of two octaves, has the true ring. The colored singer's voice has been well endowed by nature, it possesses agreeable tone color, flexibility; her singing shows sensible schooling— the delivery was in excellent taste. The florid passages earned enthusiastic applause" (Wilhelm Tappert, one of Berlin's chief music critics, *Das Kleine Journal*).[39]

Several reviewers discussed her nickname, "Black Patti," and took issue with the *Black* part of the name, calling her "mulatto" or bronze but not black. The *Borsen-Courier* said, "Our transatlantic-cousins have not exaggerated in comparing their country-woman with Patti, but the adjective 'black' seems to us unnecessarily impolite. Miss Jones is evidently of Negro blood, but not alone of Negro blood. She is a mulatto of bronzed complexion and pleasant expressive features with full lips and high forehead and the bearing of a lady, even to the choice of costume."[40]

Sissieretta apparently stayed in Germany until mid-April before leaving for London. An item in the *Cleveland Gazette* newspaper said that she had sung for the young emperor of Germany on 5 April 1895 and that he had ordered a diamond cross made for her.[41] Sissieretta debuted in London on 15 April 1895 at the Palace Theatre of Varieties, a music hall managed by Charles Morton. She was one of many performers on the music hall program. She shared the bill with entertainers that included several singers, comedians, a man with dancing dogs, someone who performed on ladders, a "serpentine globe-dancer," a male impersonator, and several dancers.[42] This variety-hall venue was a change for Sissieretta, who had previously sung concerts at churches, auditoriums, theaters, and small opera houses back in the United States. She was more accustomed to sharing the stage with classically trained musicians and singers than with vaudevillians or variety act performers. Sissieretta sang "Message d'Amour," "Valse-Ariette" by Gounod, and "The Last Rose of Summer." A review in the *London Daily Telegraph* said that the Black Patti, "if not of quite the same class as the divine Adelina, rejoices in a soprano voice with a range of two octaves, and can sing lyrics of all kinds and descriptions."[43]

A review in the *London Times* was fairly harsh. It said Sissieretta had a high soprano voice that was "not very pleasant in quality, but strong; and the singer made all possible use of its capabilities." The newspaper said the only way Sissieretta was like Adelina Patti was in her imitation of Adelina's virtuosity and her singing of "The Last Rose of Summer."[44] However, the *Era,* an entertainment weekly, reported that Sissieretta, "whose complexion is the burnished livery of the summer sun," showed herself to be "a mistress of the vocal art in her first selection, 'Sempre Libera,' an aria from *Traviata,* which is indissolubly associated with the Black Patti's namesake, and which demands exceptional capacity for its rendering. Her selection of 'The Last Rose of Summer' was justified by her artistic interpretation, and she further emphasized her undoubted success in two other items, Bishop's 'Bobolink' and a waltz song, 'The Idol of My Heart.'"[45] Again, as in Berlin, Sissieretta sang selections the great Patti was famous for performing throughout Europe. Her choice of music obviously invited the comparison to Patti, proving the young

Sissieretta was confident and secure in her own vocal abilities to withstand the comparison.

Another London journal, the *Entr'acte* (20 April 1895), also had positive things to say about Sissieretta's performance, although the reviewer noted she met some difficulties initially with some of those sitting in the gallery. She eventually won over her audience.

> The lady who is dubbed the "Black Patti," and who has made for herself a considerable reputation in America and in some of the capitals of Europe, made her first appearance at the Palace on Monday and prospered very well. As her sobriquet would denote, she is a lady of colour, and I may add—tone. Her first essay (this was from "Traviata") was of the bravura order, and was not apparently understood by some occupants of the gallery, in whom the spirit of ridicule lurked. The "Black Patti," however, lived this feeling down, and with subsequent contributions evidenced her capacity for phrasing cantabile schemes, which won for her considerable applause. She was thrice recalled, and it was evident that the impression she created was of a highly favorable kind.
>
> Negro singers are very often regarded more as curios than legitimate vocalists, but it should be said that the "Black Patti" is not only well endowed in the matter of voice, but that she takes her intervals and phrases so well as to show that she has been well trained. In my humble opinion, the lady shows to highest advantage in her bravura displays, for although the spirit of trickiness is sometimes asserted in these numbers, enough is done to show that the singer has subjected her voice to legitimate training, and that her method is the result of culture.[46]

Sissieretta performed at London's Palace Theatre until 25 May 1895. She sang at a special concert for the Duke of Cambridge on Thursday, 18 April, three days after her London debut,[47] and before the Prince of Wales (a great admirer of Adelina Patti) when he, accompanied by Colonel Clarke, attended the show at the Palace Theatre on Monday evening, 22 April.[48] One wonders how Sissieretta felt as she took the stage and began singing with the Prince of Wales sitting in the audience. She was a long way from being the little girl dressed in a stiff white dress singing her first concert at a church hall in Rhode Island. Life had presented her with many opportunities, which she readily seized. Those opportunities, along with hard work, training, persistence, and her natural ability, had brought her to this point—singing before European royalty.

While in London Sissieretta talked with a reporter from the *Era* and told him she did not like to be called "the Black Patti." She said a New York reporter had used the name "playfully," but it had stuck to her. The London reporter said Sissieretta was a "great deal more modest about her abilities than her description would suggest." She told the reporter that she had once heard Adelina Patti sing and that she had wept with both admiration and desire. She said she was born in the South but moved to Providence, which was more tolerant of its black population. After telling the reporter about her early marriage and her tour through the West Indies and South America, she talked about touring in the southern United States and about her reception in London. The London reporter wrote:

> Among her other exploits was a tour through the south, whereof she treasures the memory for two good reasons—the white folks came to hear her, more graciously, she supposes, than they had ever come to hear a coloured artist before, while her own people were frantic with delight at her success. Coloured people are passionately fond of music, and have produced some sweet singers. In the South, the coloured people are rigorously divided from the white folk in places of entertainment; but Miss Jones is overjoyed to think that her tour may have done something to soften racial prejudice.
>
> Her appearance at the Palace was preceded by two engagements on the Continent. She has been gratified by her reception in London, and charmed by the novelty of her surroundings. Miss Jones avows a passion for music, and says it is her ardent desire to have more opportunities for study under the direction of some really able and distinguished teacher.[49]

These comments show how Sissieretta thought her work may have lessened racial prejudice. Although against racial segregation, she was not one to use her fame and standing in the music world to speak out about the injustices of it. Rather she thought her singing was a way to gain acceptance for blacks in the white world by showing them that black people too were intelligent, talented, and educated. Sissieretta also found joy in the enthusiasm and admiration she received from her own race.

Although Sissieretta's run at the Wintergarten in Berlin and the Palace Theatre in London marked the first time she had sung as part of a variety show rather than at church or on the concert stage, she did not vary her repertoire that much from what she normally sang. She performed popular ballads, some operatic pieces, and classical selections. Her European debut came at a time when the world of entertainment was changing. Variety, burlesque, and vaudeville shows were becoming very popular both in Europe and in the United States, a trend that would affect Sissieretta in the months to come.

Sissieretta was in Europe from February until November 1895. Little is known about her itinerary. Based on the German articles reprinted in the *Indianapolis Freeman* and the articles in various London newspapers, she apparently spent February 1895 through mid-April in Germany and the last half of April and all of May in London. By the first week of July she was in Paris performing at the Pavillon de l'Horloge. Frederic Edward McCay, a special correspondent for the *New York Dramatic Mirror,* wrote in the 20 July 1895 issue, "The sensation of the week was the debut at L'Horloge of the Black Patti on July 1. She sang as well as I have ever heard her sing, and the audience was genuinely delighted."[50] New York's *Morning Advertiser* reprinted two translated reviews from Paris newspapers following Sissieretta's opening. *L'Echo de Paris* said that Sissieretta's performance "will be recorded as among the greatest artistic events of the season." *La Petite Republique* wrote, "It is said among the artistic Parisian world that the name of Mme. Jones, which last week was unknown in Paris , is to-day on everybody's tongue."[51] The remainder of Sissieretta's European tour has yet to be determined, and it is not known whether Voelckel continued to be her manager during the majority of her tour. Various American newspaper reports over the years said she also performed in Monte Carlo, Milan, and Munich. For example one newspaper said she was greeted by crowds in Italy, "where colored people are few," and that her five concerts in Monte Carlo Casino were the musical events of the season.[52] Sissieretta returned to Berlin in October 1895. While there, the *New York Times* reported, she was contacted by F. F. Proctor, who owned Proctor's Pleasure Palace, a high-class vaudeville house in New York City, and she agreed to come back to the states to sing a two-week engagement in November at his establishment before returning to Europe to sing for a long season in Paris.[53] A similar item in the *Cleveland Gazette* said that while singing in Berlin, Sissieretta was contacted by cable to appear at Proctor's Pleasure Palace for two weeks in November before going back to Europe. She was reportedly going to be paid a thousand dollars a week.[54]

Sissieretta gave a different account of her return from Europe. She said she came back to the United States and sang a number of concerts arranged by her new manager, Mary A. Rodman, whom she had met in Berlin. "One day I received a very fine offer from Mr. Proctor, which I accepted."[55] If this was the case—that she returned from Europe before the offer from Proctor—then it is unclear why she left Europe, where she reportedly was very successful. Perhaps her new manager had something to do with her decision. Little information has been found about Rodman, other than that she was from San Francisco and was described as "affable," "quiet," and "unaffected."[56] A newspaper article suggested another reason for Sissieretta's return. In an interview the singer said that although she had enjoyed being in Europe, "important business compelled us to come home." Her husband reportedly laughed and replied, "The important business was that she insisted on coming back to America to see her mother."[57] Sissieretta and her mother were quite close, so this may well have been part of the reason for her returning to the United States.

Sissieretta debuted at Proctor's Pleasure Palace on 25 November 1895. Proctor's, located in New York City on Fifty-Eighth Street between Third and Lexington Avenues, had opened a couple of months earlier, on Labor Day, 2 September 1895. The entertainment center combined a music hall, a concert hall, a garden area called the Garden of Palms, a roof garden, a German café, and an Oriental divan (a luxuriously furnished apartment with a library attached, in which visitors could lounge and wait for friends). The main theater featured continuous vaudeville from noon to midnight. Proctor was the first manager to introduce this style of entertainment to New York City, and it proved to be both popular and profitable. The building's architecture was of the Romanesque and Renaissance styles. The auditorium, which opened from a sixty-foot-long foyer, featured an orchestra section with seven hundred folding chairs upholstered in pale blue cloth and twenty-four private boxes. The rest of the auditorium had upholstered chairs as well. The building had four thousand electric lights, with six hundred of them on and around the stage.[58] An article in the *New York Times* prior to Sissieretta's first show at Proctor's said it would be her first appearance in vaudeville, though she had obviously sung in variety shows similar to vaudeville during her recent European tour.[59] Sissieretta would share the bill at Proctor's Pleasure Palace with a large group of vaudeville performers that included a comedienne, a ventriloquist, an elephant trainer, aerial artists, several comics, acrobats, and singers. They would take turns during the continuous vaudeville show, with Sissieretta singing twice a day.

An interesting article appeared in the *New York Dramatic Mirror* (30 November 1895) that said Proctor had encountered a "slight difficulty" in getting Sissieretta cleared to sing at the Pleasure Palace. "It seems that she returned from Europe under exclusive contract to Walter Damrosch, and some difficulties had to be overcome before Mr. Damrosch would consent to her appearance at Proctor's," the newspaper reported.[60] Another source, the *Afro-American Encyclopedia,* published in 1895, said Sissieretta had signed a contract with the Walter Damrosch Orchestra Company "for a three years' tour to Mexico and Europe, at a salary of $35,000 a year."[61] The encyclopedia entry likely referred to Damrosch's Opera Company, which included his New York Symphony Orchestra. Damrosch (1862–1950), a German American conductor who had been assistant conductor and assistant manager at the Metropolitan Opera and succeeded his father, Leopold, as director of the New York Symphony Society, founded the Damrosch Opera Company in 1894 to perform mostly German operas.[62] He organized an opera tour for the 1895–96 season that was to have been one of the largest the United States had ever seen. It included the New York Symphony Orchestra of seventy-five performers, a sixty-five-voice chorus, and the "leading Wagnerian singers of the world." The company was going to travel by special train with four carloads of scenery and baggage. Five preliminary concerts were to be given in Cincinnati beginning 11 November 1895, at the Walnut Street Theatre, to be followed by two weeks at the Chicago Auditorium. After this the company was to visit about twenty-nine cities.[63] For a few years, the Damrosch Opera Company became one of the Metropolitan Opera's strongest rivals. If reports about the contract with the opera/orchestra company were correct, this would mean that Sissieretta gave up a chance to sing opera with the Damrosch troupe in order to perform on the vaudeville stage at Proctor's Pleasure Palace. It is hard to understand why she would make that choice unless she was unsure about the new opera company's chances of succeeding or about her ability to perform in a full-fledged opera. Also unknown is what role, if any, Mary Rodman had in the Damrosch contract or with Sissieretta's engagement at Proctor's Pleasure Palace.

Shortly after Sissieretta opened at Proctor's, she became ill and had to postpone the rest of her appearance until Monday, 9 December 1895. She was reported to have had a "frog in her throat" that would not budge.[64] When she returned to the stage on 9 December, she sang an aria from *La Sonnambula*, "Bolero" by Arditi, and "Swanee River." A review in the *New York Dramatic Mirror* (21 December 1895) said her twice-daily performances greatly satisfied her admirers. The *Mirror* said that she did not sing "Swanee River" with the "depth of feeling one would naturally expect from one of her race, and she sang the last line of each verse in an entirely different way from that to which people are accustomed. It must be confessed that the change is not an improvement."[65]

Although Sissieretta met with great success while singing at Proctor's Pleasure Palace, she made it clear she preferred singing on the concert stage. "There are so many things in a vaudeville performance to distract the attention of the audience that they are not in a proper frame of mind to enjoy straight singing," she told a reporter for the *New York Dramatic Mirror*. She said she intended to go back to concert work when she finished her engagement with Proctor. "I may return to Europe in the Spring. I should like to live in Paris for a while, it is a most delightful city."[66] She would never step foot in Paris or any other European city again, because her career was about to take a very different turn.

6

A New Career

THE 1896–1897 THEATRICAL SEASON

On New Year's Day 1896, Sissieretta, who had been quite successful singing at Proctor's Pleasure Palace in December, made her first appearance at Proctor's Theatre on Twenty-Third Street in New York City. Once again she was singing in a vaudeville house rather than on a concert stage. Shortly after Sissieretta's opening, Mary Rodman took out ads in the *New York Dramatic Mirror* that said, "The Black Patti, just [returned] from her European triumphs, is available for a limited number of concert engagements, alone or with her Grand Concert Co." The advertisement, which had the word *vaudeville* twice at the top, said Sissieretta was "the largest drawing card in the country." No information was given about the other members of the Grand Concert Company.[1]

Sissieretta continued to sing at Proctor's lavish Pleasure Palace and Proctor's Theatre until mid-February while Rodman tried to book more concert engagements for her. Apparently she continued to appear more and more in vaudeville shows during the first part of the year. It is likely these kinds of venues were more available to her than concert opportunities, and these engagements probably paid better. American vaudeville, which arrived on the entertainment scene in the 1890s as minstrelsy was declining, was a descendant of variety shows. It differed, however, from variety shows, which tended to be coarse, rough, and risqué. Vaudeville was an inexpensive and popular form of entertainment that was clean, respectable, and suitable for the whole family. Usually there were eight acts, which might include an opening animal act, a comic or comedy sketch, a juggler, a magician, one or two acrobats, a dancing couple, a singer, and frequently a one-act play. All the acts had to avoid any off-color language. Vaudeville provided entertainment to the growing middle class, including women and children, up until the late 1920s and early 1930s.[2]

Rodman claimed Sissieretta's "great success" at Proctor's vaudeville houses had prompted contacts from vaudeville managers all over the country who were interested in having her perform. Rodman booked Sissieretta in places as far west as Kansas City and as far south as Atlanta.[3] Sissieretta sang in a variety of settings, such as a resort hotel in New Jersey and a social club in Chicago. She sang a benefit concert on 28 February at the Academy of Music in Philadelphia for the Frederick Douglass Hospital and Training School. At the end of the concert, she received many floral arrangements, but none as notable as the three-foot floral star given by Flora Batson and her husband, John Bergen. In presenting the arrangement to Sissieretta, the announcer said, "Ladies and gentlemen, above all the beautiful selections we have heard tonight and properly appreciated there is one little incident that will appeal to you greater than all else, and that is a tribute of one great artist to another. I hold in my hand a floral star; the gift of Flora Batson, Queen of Song, to Sissieretta Jones, the Black Patti." The audience showed its approval with "deafening" applause.[4] Apparently Batson and Bergen had mended their strained relationship with Sissieretta and her husband. Bergen had become upset with the Joneses in 1892 when David Jones was able to get Sissieretta a leading part in the "Grand Negro Jubilee" at Madison Square Garden.

Although Sissieretta preferred the concert stage to vaudeville, her future appeared to be in vaudeville rather than achieving new milestones in the concert or operatic world. She had to support her husband, who had no job of his own and was reportedly a big spender, gambler, and drinker. She also likely helped her mother financially. The singer found she was able to earn a good living (about three hundred dollars a week)[5] doing two vaudeville shows a day. Moreover concert and opera opportunities were becoming much more limited for African American concert singers (including Batson, Nellie Brown Mitchell, and Marie Selika as well as Sissieretta) near the end of the nineteenth century. Such vocalists were no longer a "curiosity" to white patrons, as music historian Eileen Southern explained in her 1983 book, *The Music of Black Americans: A History.* "The fickle public soon tired of black prima donnas. Although the singers were gifted, well trained, and fortunate in obtaining good management, their careers on the concert stage were relatively short, ranging from three to four years to a dozen or so in most instances. Their white impresarios staged concerts in the prestigious halls of the United States and Europe and arranged for command performances before important persons, but to no avail. By the mid-1890s the black prima donna had almost disappeared from the nation's concert halls because of lack of public interest. Some of the artists opened music studios and took over the direction of church and community choirs."[6]

Undoubtedly Sissieretta wanted to continue her singing career. She had achieved both fame and fortune and most likely would not have wanted to give that up to settle in Rhode Island to teach music. She was a talented, proud, and determined young woman who from childhood had shown a keen desire to sing and perform for others. She had made a name for herself, primarily singing before white concert audiences. But she probably realized there would be fewer concert opportunities available to her. Although she might have had more opera and concert prospects in Europe, she appeared reluctant to leave the country with her mother living in Rhode Island. Vaudeville presented her with an opportunity to keep working and to make a good living. She continued along this path with Rodman until mid-June 1896, when her former manager, Rudolph Voelckel, and his partner, John J. Nolan, an experienced operator in the dramatic and vaudeville field,[7] presented her with another choice—to star in her own troupe, Black Patti's Troubadours (later shortened to the Black Patti Troubadours).

Sissieretta was to be the "stellar attraction" of a company of "forty colored specialty, vaudeville, and lyric stars." Voelckel and Nolan had already lined up some talented company members—Tom and Hattie McIntosh, popular entertainers; Johnson and Shipp, "descriptive vocalists"; Bob Cole and his wife, Stella Wiley, "grotesque dancers"; Goggin and Davis, acrobats; Tom Brown, "protean artist"; and Marguerite Las Oros, "the Cuban nightingale." Sissieretta would have the support of a number of vocalists who would participate in an operatic act, which was to be one of the "chief features of the stage scheme."[8] This operatic part of the show would come to be called the "Operatic Kaleidoscope."

One biographer, Ann Charters—who wrote *Nobody*, a book about the life of black entertainer Bert Williams, a contemporary of Sissieretta's—claimed Sissieretta's husband, David, played a major role in the formation of the Black Patti Troubadours. Charters said he approached black entertainer and composer Cole to write and produce a show for Sissieretta. Charters said Cole not only wrote the hour-long skit, "At Jolly Coon-ey Island," which opened the three-hour show, but also brought along the vaudeville acts for the show's olio, or middle part.[9] Charters did not provide a source for this information, so it is difficult to know whether Jones contacted Voelckel and Nolan about creating the Black Patti Troubadours or whether the white managers came up with the idea first.

The Black Patti Troubadours would not be the only black touring company in the United States. There were at least three African American companies traveling around the country with this kind of show.[10] For example in the fall of 1895, white manager John W. Isham established the Octoroons company, which performed a three-part show. It began with a one-act farce with song and dance, followed by a number of vaudeville specialty acts, and finished with "Thirty Minutes around the Operas." It also included a female chorus and gave leading parts in the show to women. This show was so successful that Isham formed another show in 1896 called *Oriental America,* which was similar to the Octoroons but ended with "Forty Minutes of Grand and Comic Opera."[11] What the Black Patti Troubadours had that these shows did not was Black Patti—a well-known star whose name and reputation would draw large audiences and ensure the success of Voelckel and Nolan's venture.

With the Black Patti Troubadours, Sissieretta could look forward to steady employment, a good income, and dependable management. Her unemployed husband would certainly favor such an arrangement. Sissieretta could expect a forty-week season with an income of about five hundred dollars a week, or twenty thousand dollars annually, which would make her the highest-paid African American entertainer in her time.[12] She would be the star of the troupe, wear beautiful dresses and costumes, and sing concert and operatic selections of her choosing. In addition Voelckel and Nolan would eventually provide Sissieretta and the troupe with an elegant, well-equipped private railcar in which to travel. Sissieretta and the company would live in the railcar while touring, thus avoiding the difficulty of finding decent accommodations at a time when black people were routinely turned away from many white hotels and restaurants. Unlike most black women of her day, who were fairly limited in what jobs they could hold, Sissieretta would live quite comfortably, travel throughout the United States, and be well paid. She would continue to attract many white patrons while performing with the Black Patti Troubadours, but now she also would enjoy singing before many more African Americans as she traveled the country. Sissieretta, a role model for many African Americans, could continue to prove that black vocalists were capable of singing opera and concert selections. As leader of the Troubadours, she would be providing jobs for forty to fifty African American entertainers and giving them a chance to gain valuable show business experience. The Troubadours, with Sissieretta as star, were positioned to become one of the top African American music and comedy troupes in the country. For all these reasons and many more that will never be known because she left no diaries or letters discussing her decision, Sissieretta accepted Voelckel and Nolan's proposal.

Sissieretta could probably see what effects the emergence of ragtime music in the early 1890s and the growing popularity of vaudeville were having on the world of black entertainment. To understand the impact ragtime had on black entertainment, it is necessary to follow the path black performers had to take to gain access to the stage. Commercial blackface minstrelsy, where white performers blackened their faces and imitated blacks, had begun in New

York in 1843. Minstrelsy became American's first popular entertainment. After the Civil War, large numbers of African Americans eager to become entertainers began to perform in minstrel shows, and by the 1870s some formed their own companies.[13] As minstrels black performers had to make fun of themselves just as the white ones in blackface had done when they imitated black life. Although far from an ideal way to break into the entertainment field, at least African American actors were the ones getting paid to portray themselves. A generation of black performers got their training and experience performing in minstrel shows even though they had to "perpetuate the genre's derogatory stereotypes of black life." As one scholar noted, "Since the minstrel show was often the only outlet for black performers, they had no choice."[14] White audiences loved seeing "genuine Negroes" playing themselves. By the 1880s black minstrel companies had become so popular they took audiences away from white minstrel troupes and in the process employed hundreds of black musicians and performers. Then came ragtime in the early 1890s with its syncopated melodies. The music, created by and developed by black musicians such as Scott Joplin, appealed to both black and white audiences. It paved the way for African Americans to move away from nineteenth-century "Ethiopian minstrelsy" and encouraged creativity among black performers and musicians. As ragtime developed, audiences came to accept a wider range of black music and stage entertainment than just minstrelsy.[15]

Along with ragtime came the advent of "coon songs," which became synonymous with ragtime in the public's view. "Coon songs, with their ugly name, typically featured lyrics in Negro dialect, caricaturing African American life, set to the melodious strains of ragtime music," according to Lynn Abbott and Doug Seroff, two scholars who have studied these kinds of songs. The most famous coon song and the one that "was adopted as the slogan of a Jim Crow society that refused to acknowledge African Americans as individuals"[16] was "All Coons Look Alike to Me," written by black composer and performer Ernest Hogan in 1896. "The combination of the word *coon* and the new ragtime syncopation created a sensation. . . . It was a tremendous hit. Coon songs became the rage."[17] The song's lyrics, which told about a black woman forced to choose between two handsome young men, were not objectionable. The title of the song, however, is what people remembered and what many found offensive. Although Hogan's song was a financial success, "its title haunted him to the end of his days."[18] Syncopated coon songs became very popular and found their way into Broadway musicals, particularly through "coon shouters" such as May Irwin. Irwin was a white actress whose success singing a coon song in the show *Widow Jones* (1895) prompted her to add such songs to all her future Broadway musicals.[19] In fact Irwin was the first to

The Troubadours held buck-dancing contests, as depicted in this drawing.
Courtesy of the Museum of Performance and Design, San Francisco.

perform Hogan's "All Coons Look Alike to Me" in 1896 during the all-white farce-comedy *Courted into Court.* Black entertainers, both male and female, also became coon shouters and "established their superiority as 'portraying' themselves." Eventually the black middle class and the black press condemned coon songs and helped bring about their demise by about 1910.[20] In 1896, when the Black Patti Troubadours were being formed, coon songs, buck dancing, and cakewalks were popular and acceptable and would naturally have been included in the show.

While Voelckel and Nolan spent the summer of 1896 hiring black entertainers and getting ready to launch the Black Patti Troubadours, Sissieretta likely visited her mother in Rhode Island in June before heading to San Francisco for a singing engagement (4–11 July) at the Chutes and Casino. Tickets to the show were ten cents for adults and five cents for children; the children's admittance price included a ride on the merry-go-round. Sissieretta sang in the Casino twice a day, at 2 P.M. and again at 8 P.M. She shared the bill with the Russian Court Orchestra; Aragon, the queen of the wire walkers; the Marlo-Dunham Family, aerialists; Professor Fred Macart's Baboon, Dog, and Monkey Circus; and Captain Beach, "the fish man."[21]

Shortly after she arrived in San Francisco, she granted an interview to the *San Francisco Call,* during which she talked about her early musical career and her thoughts about singing opera. She said, "I can never remember the time when I did not sing. I used to sing to myself as a child because I loved music, but it was after singing a little solo at a Sunday-school concert at Providence that some people said to my mother, 'The child took a high C; you should let her learn music.' That was how I came to study." Later in the interview, the reporter asked Sissieretta whether she wanted to appear in operas. She said the lyric stage had always been one of her dreams, but many things prevented that from happening. "I am traveling most of the time, and it would be difficult to study the roles; so much study is necessary to do them well." After hesitating a moment, she told the reporter there was another major obstacle—her skin was not the color of most prima donnas. The reporter suggested that makeup and wigs could bring about "marvelous transformations" on the stage, to which Sissieretta replied, "Try to hide my race and deny my own people? Oh, I would never do that. I am proud of belonging to them and would not hide what I am even for an evening." The reporter reminded her that white prima donnas who played Selika and Aida had to assume an African nationality, Sissieretta replied, "Yes, but that is different. With me, if I made myself white, prejudiced people would say I was ashamed of being colored."[22] This interview shows that Sissieretta was proud of her race but quite aware of the limitations it placed on her musical career. It helps explain her decision to leave the concert stage, with its decreasing opportunities, for a more lucrative career as star of the Black Patti Troubadours, where she could sing some opera and concert selections along with popular ballads.

After leaving San Francisco, Sissieretta traveled to Los Angeles and opened 13 July at the Orpheum, where she spent two weeks. An article in the *Los Angeles Times* (12 July 1896) said the managers had been trying for two years to get her to sing at the Orpheum. The *Times* described Sissieretta's appearance and voice, as well as information about her recent European tour:

> This negro vocalist is tall, well formed, of good carriage. She is not of a jet black in color, but of a rich, deep brown. Her manners are said to be prepossessing and her face to show refinement and culture. Altogether she is an example of the best and highest type of the negro race.
>
> Mrs. Jones recently returned from a concert tour of England, Germany, France, and Italy. She scored a success everywhere. In Italy, where colored people are few, crowds of people gathered at the depots in towns through which she passed to see the "Black Patti." The series of five concerts she gave at The Monte Carlo Casino were the event of the season. She was feted in Paris, and in London the Prince of Wales, the Duke of Cambridge, and many other distinguished people went to hear her sing, and presented her with costly gifts and unbounded praise.[23]

Appearing at the Orpheum with Sissieretta were the Jackly-Roston troupe, "in its merry capers and monkeyshines"; the Fredricks, a troupe of acrobats "in some beautiful feats of pyramid-building and ladder climbing"; Lille Western, an instrumentalist; the Stewart sisters, who sang and danced as well as did comedy; and Billy Van, "a jolly black-face monologuist."[24] It appears from this list of performers that Sissieretta was one more novelty or "curiosity"—a black concert singer who performed serious music and some popular favorites. At least when she had her own troupe, she might have a say as to the kind of performers with whom she would share the bill.

By the time Sissieretta returned from California, Voelckel and Nolan had hired the forty-member cast of the Black Patti Troubadours and had booked a forty-week tour in what they described as "first class theatres." Voelckel said the company had some of the finest black specialty and operatic performers ever brought together. Sissieretta, of course, was the star singer, and Tom McIntosh the principal comedian.[25] Rehearsals began 17 August 1896 in New York City. The Troubadours show was scheduled to debut in Pittsfield, Massachusetts, on 10 September. Voelckel and Nolan were the proprietors of the Troubadours, with Nolan serving as the advance agent and Voelckel as treasurer. Bob Cole was stage manager, and J. W. Davidson was musical director. The cast included Sissieretta, Tom and Hattie McIntosh, Bob Cole, Stella Wiley, Billy Johnson, Goggin and Davis, Kingsbury and Cousins, the De Wolfe Sisters, May Bohee, Cravatt Simpson, Lloyd Gibbs, C. L. Moore, Hen Wise, C. H. Francis, Anthony D. Byrd, D. M. A. Frazier, W. A Underwood, Jesse Grant, T. C. Robinson, W. H. Jones, J. H. Barnet, Maud Clifford, Eva Swanson, Mollie Dill, Aida Overton, Lillian Daisy, Lena Wise, Hazel Belwood, Maude Johnson, Martha Morris, Anna Ring, Jennie Ship, Daisy Miller, and Leontine Russell.[26] Several of these performers— Cole, Wiley, Johnson, and Overton—later became famous in their own right as either singers, dancers, composers, comedians, or show producers and writers.

The Black Patti Troubadours show, which blended comedy, vaudeville, burlesque, spectacle, and opera, consisted of three parts, similar in its organizational format to a minstrel show. The first part was a comedy skit that included songs and dances. Next came a vaudeville olio during which the entertainers, actors, and singers performed a variety of specialty acts. The finale, which parted from the minstrel show format, was the Operatic Kaleidoscope, where Sissieretta sang arias in scenes from several operas. She was supported by a quartet of soloists and a chorus of thirty people, and it was the only section of the show in which she appeared.

A review in the *New York Dramatic Mirror* said the opening Troubadours' show in Pittsfield was a "distinctly creditable first performance and showed the effect of careful and frequent rehearsals."[27] The show began with a musical skit called "At Jolly Coney Island," which later came to be called "At Jolly Coon-ey Island." (The title of the show was a takeoff on a successful white musical comedy called *At Gay Coney Island*.[28]) The skit introduced several excellent singers. Cole, who wrote it, played a tramp, Willie Wayside, and was a big hit. The skit was set on the "Bowery" of Coney Island and featured all kinds of character types found there such as Cole's tramp figure, a bicycle woman, a "coon" singer, a bathing girl, a buck dancer and "Couchee Couchee" girls. The backdrop for the scene was painted on canvass by Harley Merry and his sons from sketches done at the actual spot.[29] The *Mirror's* review of the second part of the show, the vaudeville olio, said Davis and Goggins's tumbling act was "unusually clever," while Tom McIntosh's act was "too long by half, and needs pruning." As for the final act, the Operatic Kaleidoscope, Black Patti was said to have been "in fine voice" and was "enthusiastically received." Joining Sissieretta for this portion of the show were May Bohee, soprano; Madame Simpson, contralto; Lloyd Gibson, tenor; and C. L. Moore, baritone. The selections for the Kaleidoscope were from *The Bohemian Girl, Il Trovatore,* and other operas.[30] The Troubadours' opening performance showed great promise, and the show would certainly improve during September and early October with some fine-tuning as the company worked its way through New York, including stops in Saratoga Springs, Albany, Troy, and Rochester. Reviews of the Troubadours' shows in these cities were positive and supportive.

Voelckel and Nolan obviously believed in advertising and promoting their show. They took out a huge display advertisement in one of the key New York City entertainment newspapers, the *Dramatic Mirror* (26 September 1896), touting the new Black Patti Troubadours. They called the show a "royal hit," "the greatest colored show on earth," and the "hottest show of the age." The ad described the show and its fifty-member cast as "a revelation of MIRTH and MELODY. A laughing festival. A music jubilee, A joyous rendition of 'Coon Songs,' 'Buck Dances,' Cake Walks, Specialty Acts, and melodious Reminiscences of the Standard Grand and Comic Operas, embellished with elegant costumes and beautiful scenery." The ad called Sissieretta the "greatest singer of her race," and it highlighted several members of the cast, including Bob Cole, "comedian, dancer, author, and genius"; Stella Wiley, "the typical tough girl"; Billy Johnson, "vocalist and creator of coon songs"; and the De Wolfe Sisters, "duettists."[31] Sissieretta and the De Wolfe Sisters, from Providence, had worked together as early as 1888 when they sang in the Bergen Star Concerts.

Sissieretta took a one-night break from her new Troubadours on Monday, 12 October 1896, to sing a concert at Carnegie Hall with two other great

African American prima donnas, Marie Selika and Flora Batson Bergen. The event, the Zion Grand Centennial Jubilee Concert and Banquet, was advertised as the first public appearance of these three leading black concert singers.[32] New York mayor William L. Strong presided at this final meeting of the Zion Grand Centennial Jubilee, which had been a twelve-day celebration to mark the one hundredth anniversary of the founding of the Zion African Methodist Episcopal Church. The most fashionable African Americans in New York City were there, and they were elegantly dressed for the occasion, with many women wearing brightly colored, low-cut gowns and diamonds. Mayor Strong, whom the *New York Times* said was often "unfortunate" in how he expressed himself, was especially awkward that evening, although one newspaper said he meant no offense by his words. After Bishop Alexander Walters introduced him, Strong began his congratulatory remarks, which went smoothly for a time as he "enumerated the many great achievements of his colored brethren." The audience frequently interrupted his speech with applause and smiled at his comments until he said, "It gives me more than untold pleasure to congratulate you upon your remarkable achievements. Every citizen has reason to be proud of the African Methodist Episcopal Zion Church. Its achievements in the past 100 years are very pleasant to think of. To think that in the past century five hundred thousand—half a million—of you have lived and been connected with your organization and passed away is another pleasant thought."[33] At this point audience members looked at one another inquiringly as the mayor looked about for some positive audience response. Strong raised his eyebrows "quizzically" to Bishop Walters, who saved the day by starting to applaud, whereupon the smiling audience joined in. Another difficulty that evening was the way the chairs were arranged on the platform. Eleven chairs were placed in a semicircle with Mayor Strong in the middle chair and five African Americans seated to each side of him. The arrangement could not help but remind the audience of a minstrel show. The *New York Times* said, "Had the Mayor worn white cotton gloves, he would not have surprised any one by getting up and saying, "Mr. John Queen will now sing 'Sweet Evelina.'"[34] After Strong's speech and one by Bishop Walters, Strong introduced Sissieretta, who sang a cavatina from Gounod's opera *La Reine de Saba*. The audience loved her performance and applauded enthusiastically. Someone in the audience passed a bouquet of white roses up to the stage, which Mayor Strong retrieved and, bowing deeply, presented to Sissieretta. After a speech by Bishop George Clinton, Marie Selika sang "Ah, fors' è lui," from Verdi's *La Traviata*. Two speeches later mezzo soprano Flora Batson performed a waltz song by Arditi. Following Batson's selection, Booker T. Washington gave a speech on industrial education.[35] The event included a number of additional musical and vocal selections as well as speeches by other performers and dignitaries. Mayor Strong stayed the entire evening, and the *New York Times* said his "regrettable faux pas was forgotten, long before the end of the banquet, which took place after the entertainment."[36]

The night before Sissieretta sang at the Zion Grand Centennial Jubilee concert, she and the Black Patti Troubadours made their metropolitan debut 11 October in a sacred concert at the Standard Theatre in New York City. Despite inclement weather, the company drew a well-filled house. The Troubadours did not perform their regular show because it was Sunday but entertained the audience with various songs, stories, and music. The *New York Clipper,* a mainstream entertainment paper, said the opening number introduced the Troubadours in a "melodious hodge podge of darky songs." The *Clipper* said Cole was a "witty young man, who handles himself and his stories in commendable fashion." Sissieretta delighted the audience and performed in a "thoroughly artistic and praise-worthy manner."[37]

The tremendous success of the Black Patti Troubadours apparently got the attention of several other managers, who reportedly used "underhanded methods" to try and lure some of the principal company members away to join their own shows. A statement appeared in the two leading New York City entertainment newspapers that said, "It has been reported that several of the members were about to leave the company, and to correct this error a statement has been issued, signed by those most concerned, which states that they are entirely satisfied with their positions and give unqualified praise to Messrs. Voelckel and Nolan, the managers." The statement, signed by M. Sissieretta Jones, Tom and Hattie McIntosh, Billy Johnson, Bob Cole, Ed Goggin for Goggin and Davis, Lloyd G. Gibbs, and C. W. Moore, said the performers were so "satisfied" they were giving Voelckel and Nolan an option on their services for the next season.[38]

The show played in two New Jersey cities during mid-October and then spent a week in Brooklyn, 19–24 October, at the Hyde and Herman's Theater. After this stop the troupe was scheduled to perform in New Haven, Connecticut, from 26–30 October, and then in Hartford on 31 October and 1 November. Voelckel, however, was unable to find accommodations for the fifty black performers in Hartford, the *New York Times* claiming that every hotel "refused to take them on account of their color."[39] Voelckel threatened to cancel the shows if he was unable to get hotel rooms for his cast. He said he had successfully secured hotel accommodations in every other city of the state where the show had appeared. It is unknown whether Voelckel canceled the Hartford appearance.

With the growing success of the Black Patti Troubadours, Cole, who wrote the opening skit, "At Jolly Coon-ey Island," apparently wanted more recognition for his contribution to the popular show. He placed a large display advertisement in the *New York Clipper* (24 October 1896) a week before the show opened at the Star Theatre in New York City. The ad, which had Cole's name in big, bold letters, larger than "Black Patti's Troubadours," said, "Keep your eye on the dark horse. Character, comedian, and author. Bob Cole, stage manager, Black Patti's Troubadours. Staged and produced the entire production. En route. Best wishes to well wishers and others."[40] One can only wonder how managers Voelckel and Nolan, as well as Sissieretta, responded to Cole's attempt to get his share of recognition. This may have been the start of some friction between Cole and his bosses that would later lead to Cole's decision to leave the Troubadours in a rather dramatic fashion.

While Sissieretta and the Troubadours were entertaining nightly in New York City and nearby towns, Sissieretta had to attend to some private legal business. She was called to appear in city court before Justice John P. Schuchman on 7 November 1896, on a matter related to her 1893 lawsuit with her former manager, Maj. James B. Pond. Sissieretta and her husband, David, were examined in supplementary proceedings to discover whether she was financially capable of paying Job E. Hedges, now the private secretary to Mayor Strong, a judgment of $236 for legal services. Hedges, an attorney, had acted as counsel for the Joneses in the 1893 lawsuit they brought against Pond to recover $5,000 they believed Pond owed them. Hedges claimed that the Joneses had yet to pay him.[41]

Accompanied by her "stocky built and light colored" husband, Sissieretta arrived at court "resplendent" in a green silk gown covered with panels of roses in a darker color and a small, brimless, close-fitting hat. In a statement Sissieretta and David said Hedges had agreed to take their case for $100 and that Hedges had subsequently raised the fee to $236. They also claimed they lost their case with Pond when Hedges failed to show up on the day the case was called for trial. The Joneses said they had already paid Hedges $100.[42] In response to questions regarding her financial ability to pay Hedges more money, Sissieretta testified that as star of the Black Patti Troubadours she was under the management of Rudolph Voelckel and that her contract with him called for her to get one-third of all the profits. She said she did not have a bank account. Then David Jones testified that he acted as his wife's agent in the theatrical business. Hedge's lawyer asked David if he had any money, to which he replied with a laugh, "I wish to goodness I had. Oh yes, I have got money. I have 16 cents in my pocket." The hearing was adjourned until Tuesday, 17 November. After the hearing David told the press he did not believe Hedges had treated Sissieretta and him fairly. He said, "I live in Hedge's district, and I hope to get even with him in a political way."[43]

When the hearing resumed on 17 November, Sissieretta appeared in court with her lawyer but without her husband. Once again she took the stand and explained she was under contract with Voelckel to sing for one-third of the net receipts and was "under the impression" she was due about $5,000. She said her husband had paid Hedges $100, although he failed to get a receipt, and that they were surprised to receive a bill from Hedges for twice that amount. Neither Hedges nor his lawyer showed up for the 17 November hearing, so Justice Schuchman dismissed the proceedings. Sissieretta's attorney said the judge's actions barred Hedges from any further examination of Sissieretta or David.[44]

By the first week in November 1896, the Troubadours closed their engagement in New York City and took to the road for November and December for a series of one-night stands in cities and towns in Virginia, Delaware, and Pennsylvania, as well as some longer runs in big cities such as Washington, D.C., Philadelphia, and Cincinnati. According to the *New York Clipper*, Cole was working on a comic opera, "King Eat-'Em-All," to be produced by the Troubadours next fall, and Voelckel and Nolan were thinking about taking the troupe to Europe during the summer of 1897.[45] Shortly before Christmas the Troubadours entertained in Indianapolis at the Empire Theatre, the only theater in the city that did not discriminate against blacks. Black Patti's Troubadours played there 21–26 December to standing-room-only crowds and were said to have broken sales records for tickets sold at that point in the 1896–97 season.[46] The tour continued into the new year, with the Troubadours entertaining in Chicago as well as in Ohio, Minnesota, and Wisconsin.

On 18 January 1897 Sissieretta and her Black Patti Troubadours show helped open the new auditorium in Owatonna, Minnesota, a city in the southern part of the state. Manager John Nolan wrote a piece about the opening and sent it to the *New York Clipper*, which published it on 30 January. Nolan said the debut of the new opera house was one of the most important events in the city since its founding. "The opening of the house attracted one of the largest audiences that has ever assembled in a public building in Owatonna," he said. The auditorium, built at a cost of forty thousand dollars, was paid for by the Bohemian Slavonic Benevolent Society, one of the city's largest organizations. Located on the city's main thoroughfare and built of brownstone, the building, which seated about nine hundred people, was equipped with folding opera chairs and a large stage with excellent acoustic properties. Large dressing rooms were warmed by steam heat, and the building had all the conveniences usually found in metropolitan theaters. Nolan said the audience loved the Troubadours, especially Sissieretta. "Black Patti was the recipient of most of the applause, her vocalization in the operatic kaleidoscope creating a genuine furor," Nolan said. The rest of the Troubadours "covered themselves with glory," he added. After the evening performance closed, the Bohemian Slavonic Benevolent Society gave a banquet to celebrate the grand opening.

Managers Rudolph Voelckel and John Nolan used advertising flyers to publicize the Black Patti Troubadours. This same line drawing, from circa 1897, was used in numerous newspaper advertisements. Courtesy of the Museum of Performance and Design, San Francisco.

Members of the society and the Black Patti company "exchanged congratulations over the happy occasion which brought them together."[47]

The Troubadours continued their tour and found more success in cities and towns in Wisconsin during January. The show was so popular that some of the theaters and opera houses where they played could not accommodate all who wanted to see it. Voelckel and Nolan, who said the rest of the 1896–97 season schedule was filled, were already booking engagements for the upcoming season. The two managers hoped to book only week-long runs rather than one-night stands for the 1897–98 season.[48] In mid-January 1897 Sissieretta's managers took out huge advertisements in the two main New York City entertainment industry newspapers, the *Clipper* (16 January 1897) and the *Dramatic Mirror* (16 January 1897), that featured a large pen and ink drawing of Sissieretta, above which ran a headline in large, bold type that said, "Black Patti's Fifty Troubadours." The managers used the ads to publicize the company's availability during the next season for one-week stands and to brag about the show's success. The ads said the press and public of New York City, Chicago, Philadelphia, Boston, Buffalo, Washington, St. Paul, Milwaukee, and Cincinnati had proclaimed their show as "positively the greatest colored show on earth." Voelckel and Nolan called the Troubadours the "hit of the season," describing the show as a "revelation of comedy, burlesque, vaudeville and opera, embodying 'coon songs,' 'cakewalks,' 'buck dances,' and inspiring grand and comic opera melodies by the most talented and versatile singers, dancers, and comedians of the Sunny South, headed by the greatest singer of her race." When it came to describing Sissieretta in the advertisement, Voelckel and Nolan pulled out all the stops. After all she was their star, the main reason people flocked to the show. The ad said Sissieretta's "marvelous voice" and "lyric triumphs" were unparalleled. Further it said that Sissieretta, the most popular prima donna in the world "with people of all nations and races," had charmed "countless millions in every part of the civilization" with her phenomenal voice. The advertisement continued, "H. R. H. the Prince of Wales and the Duke of Cambridge and other members of the Royal Family of England have honored her with their distinguished patronage. Her first appearance in conjunction with her own great company, which is also without equal in the world."[49]

The huge advertisement, which was aimed at attracting theater managers from around the country to book the Troubadours, also listed the characters in the opening skit, "At Jolly Coon-ey Island," along with cast members who played each part. In addition the ad listed the songs in the opening skit, the performers in the vaudeville olio, and the selections sung in the Operatic Kaleidoscope. This information gave theater managers interested in booking the Troubadours a better idea of what to expect during the three-hour show.

At Jolly "Coon-ey" Island

Rube Green, an Alabama sport . . . . Mr. Henry Wise
Willie Wayside, a tramp . . . . Mr. Bob Cole
Jim Flimflammer, looking for the best of it . . . . Mr. Billy Johnson
Silas Kalsomine, the red hot man . . . . Mr. Billy Johnson
Rev. Sly, a reformer . . . . Mr. C. L. Moore
Michael McSweeney, the pride of the force . . . . Mr. David Rastus
Teddy, the handsome waiter . . . . Mr. C. J. Mahoney
Cheeky, a newsboy . . . . Mr. Coley Grant
Prof. Knowitall, a museum barker . . . . Mr. Anthony D. Byrd
Wm. Jackson, a photographer . . . . Mr. Ben Underwood
Sam Thomas, a cabman . . . . Mr. James Jones
Widow Dean, also a reformer . . . . Miss Jennie Reed
Liz Leary, the belle of Avenue A . . . . Miss Stella Wiley
Nancy, an adventuress . . . . Miss Sadie De Wolf
                    and a chorus of 40 trained voices.

Songs and Those Who Sang Them:

Opening Chorus, "At Jolly Cooney Isle"
    (original music) . . . . The company
"Bell of Avenue A" . . . . Stella Wiley
"The Three Little Kinkies"
    (original music) . . . . Misses Wise, Davis and Overton
Comic Song . . . . Bob Cole
"Black Four Hundred's Ball" (original) . . . . Billy Johnson
"Black Gal Mine" . . . . Henry Wise
Quintette Comique
"4-11-44" (original music) . . . . . Billy Johnson, Bob Cole, Henry Wise,
                                Sadie De Wolf and Aida Overton
"Honey, Does You Love
    Your Little Man?" . . . . Coley Grant, Anthony Byrd
                                and the Oriole Septette
"Red Hots, Red Hots" (original music) . . . . Billy Johnson
Finale, "Down to Cooney Isle" (original music) . . . . The company

Vaudeville Olio Performers

Sadie and Rosa, the DeWolf Sisters . . . . Vocal Duettists
Bob Cole, comedian and author,
    assisted by Stella Wiley . . . . a Terpsichorean Review
Billy Johnson singing descriptive songs, "The Baggage
    Coach Ahead" and "Through the Stages of Life"

A Spanish Review, conceived and arranged by Johnson and Cole
Lloyd Gibbs . . . . tenor solo
Coley Grant and David Rastus. . . . . comedy acrobats

The Operatic Kaleidoscope
(Starring Black Patti, assisted by Camille Casselle, contralto; Lloyd
    Gibbs, tenor; C. L. Moore, baritone; and a chorus of 40 voices.)

"Cavalleria Rusticana"—Intermezzo,
    "Ave Maria" (Mascagni) . . . . Chorus
"Faust"—Kirmess Scene (Gounod). Chorus
"The Bohemian Girl"—"The Heart
    Bowed Down" (Balfe) . . . . C. L. Moore
"Chimes of Normandy"—"Silent Heroes" . . . . Chorus
"Il Trovatore"—"The Anvil Chorus" (Verdi);
    "La Traviata" Grand Aria . . . . Black Patti
"Il Trovatore"—"Miserere" . . . . Black Patti & Lloyd Gibbs
"The Daughter of the Regiment"—
    "Rataplan" (Donizetti) . . . . Billy Johnson & Chorus
"All Hail the Queen" (Cole). . . . . Lloyd Gibbs & Chorus
"Grand Duchess"—"The Sabre Song"
    (Offenbach). . . . . Black Patti & Chorus
"Tar and Tartar"—Medley
    of National Airs . . . . Black Patti & Company[50]

While managers Voelckel and Nolan sought bookings for the 1897–98
season, the Troubadours continued touring. Their first stop in February was
a two-week engagement in Chicago, after which they spent the rest of the
month in Michigan, Kansas, and Toronto. During their travels a small item
published in the *Indianapolis Freeman* contained comments Sissieretta had
made that showed she was aware of the limitations racial discrimination had
placed on her singing career. She said, "In Europe there is no prejudice against
my race. It matters not to them in what garb an artist come [*sic*], so he be
an artist. If a man or a woman is a great actor, or a great musician, or a great
singer, they will extend a warm welcome, no matter whether he be a Jew or
Greek or Gentile. It is the artist [*sic*] soul they look at there, not the color of
his skin."[51] Sissieretta's comments show she longed for a world in which people would judge her by her singing ability and not the color of her skin.
    The Black Patti Troubadours spent the rest of the winter touring through-
out the Northeast and meeting with great success wherever they played. In
spring they toured Pennsylvania and New Jersey, as well as playing week-long

engagements in Brooklyn and Baltimore. Manager Nolan said the troupe's appearance 3–8 May at the Holliday Street Theatre in Baltimore brought in more business at the theater than any other attraction playing there that season. Nolan said the demand for tickets was so great that the box office could not keep up, so the doorkeepers had to take cash as well as tickets. Gross receipts for the week at the Holliday Street Theatre were more than four thousand dollars. An article in the *New York Dramatic Mirror* attributed the show's success "to their pleasing performances and the hustling ability of Voelckel and Nolan, the managers of the enterprise, who are great believers in advertising."[52] Advertisements about the Troubadours show that ran in the Sunday editions of the Baltimore newspapers were larger than those for the circus (which also was in town) as well as the four leading theaters in the city combined.

After the company played in Baltimore, it spent a week (10–15 May) in Washington, D.C., before heading back to New York City for an "indefinite" summer engagement at Proctor's Pleasure Palace beginning 17 May. While the troupe was at Proctor's, Voelckel and Nolan added new features and new entertainers to the show, bringing the troupe's size up to seventy-five.[53] Shortly after the show opened, Sissieretta received word that prima donna Flora Batson's estranged husband, John Bergen, had died suddenly on 18 May in New York City while taking a bath at Everad's Turkish Bath establishment on New York's West Eighth Street.[54] Bergen, a veteran concert manager, and Batson had been separated since December 1896, and Batson had announced her intentions to divorce him. Sissieretta certainly recalled her early days on the stage when Bergen and Batson had added the young singer to several concert programs Bergen arranged in 1888.

There was more bad news the following week, and this time the news hit closer to home. On Monday, 24 May 1897, Bob Cole was arrested at Proctor's Pleasure Palace and charged with stealing the orchestral music for the show. Manager Nolan told the *New York Clipper* that he had been seen "prowling around" the orchestra after the Sunday performance on 23 May. After Cole left the music could not be found. He was arrested and brought to police court, where he claimed the music he took was his own orchestration and that he took it after quitting the company. Bail was set at one thousand dollars, and Cole was held for trial.[55]

More information about the "theft" surfaced during the first week of June in the *Dramatic Mirror*. Voelckel and Nolan had tricked Cole into admitting he had taken the music on 23 May. The managers said Cole had requested a raise for the upcoming season that was three times larger than his current salary. They refused. Once the managers realized the music was gone, they set a trap for Cole. They told him that they could not run the show without him and asked if he would sign a contract for $150 a week for next season along with a clause stating he would not ask for another raise during the 1897–98 season. According to the managers, Cole agreed, and Voelckel and Nolan asked him to return the music at once. He said, "Certainly." Upon hearing his reply, a detective, who was within hearing distance, arrested him for larceny. With Cole in jail and the show without music, Nolan called the company together and hired a musician who could take down the notes as the company sang the music. New orchestrations were made, and "At Jolly Coon-ey Island" went on as before. Lloyd Gibbs and Billy Johnson also resigned, so Voelckel and Nolan hired cakewalkers Hodges and Launchmere as well as performers Billy McClain and his wife, Madame Cordelia.[56]

On 5 June, the same day Voelckel and Nolan's account of the incident appeared in the press, Cole's case was brought before the grand jury. He reportedly told the judge, "These men have amassed a fortune from the product of my brain; and now they call me a thief: I won't give up."[57] The grand jury refused to find a bill against him. The charges were dropped, and he was allowed to keep his music.[58] Cole wrote a letter to the *Dramatic Mirror* that was published the following week, 12 June 1897, explaining his side of the controversy with Voelckel and Nolan. He said his contract had expired on 15 May while the troupe was playing in Washington, D.C. He said he asked for a renewal, which the managers ignored, "leading me to believe that my services were no longer required." On 17 May, when the company was in New York City, Cole said he resigned as stage manager and performer and took the musical score of "At Jolly Coon-ey Island." He said the score was "my personal property, my own composition, in collaboration with Billy Johnson, and to which I hold the copyright." Once Voelckel and Nolan learned he had left and taken his music, they sought to renew the contract. Cole said he then asked for more money, "which they not only refused to accede to, but emphasized their refusal by sending me to prison, claiming I stole 'their music.'" As to the charge that he had incited others to leave the cast, Cole said that the "unprofessional" actions toward him by the two managers prompted Billy Johnson and Lloyd Gibbs to leave the cast voluntarily. Cole said he was working on a new show next season that would be one of his best creations.[59]

Cole and Johnson went on to write a new show, *A Trip to Coontown,* for the 1897–98 season and formed their own traveling company, which included Jesse Shipp, Tom Brown, Hen Wise, Stella Wiley, Lloyd Gibbs, and a chorus of twenty performers. Cole issued what came to be called the Negro Actor's Declaration of Independence: "We are going to write them ourselves, we are going to have our own stage manager, our own orchestra leader, and our own manager out front to count up. No divided houses—our race must be seated from boxes back."[60] Cole and the performers who chose to stay with him were "blacklisted" by Voelckel and Nolan, which meant that Cole's show was practically closed to every important theater in the country. They had to play small, second-rate houses to get any bookings. They opened their season in South Amboy, New Jersey, under the management of William Black.[61] Eventually the show went to Canada, where they had not been blacklisted. The show was successful in Ottawa and Toronto, and after rave reviews in Canada, New York's Klaw and Erlanger defied the lockout and booked them for a very successful run at Jacob's Third Avenue Theatre. *A Trip to Coontown* became the first all-black, full-length musical comedy organized, produced, and managed by African Americans.[62]

Despite Cole's departure the Black Patti Troubadours show continued to draw large crowds during the second and third week of the run at Proctor's Pleasure Palace, and there were indications the Troubadours might play there all summer. Comedian Billy McClain and Madame Cordelia, who had recently closed a very successful season with the show *Darkest Africa*, became part of the Troubadours' opening skit and vaudeville olio. One reviewer said McClain "was worth miles to go to see." Sissieretta continued to please audiences with her opera and concert selections, adding fresh selections each week. In addition to their daily shows at the Pleasure Palace, the company also performed Sunday concerts there as well.[63] By the third week the Troubadour show added a cakewalk featuring newcomers Hodges and Launchmere, sporting "gorgeous yellow suits," who provided the walk an "air of distinction." The *Dramatic Mirror* (12 June 1897) said, "It is participated in by the swells and belles of the colored four hundred." The newspaper said the cakewalk was the best ever seen in New York City: "Every one of the colored walkers had his or her eyes riveted on the cake, which is the real thing, and was made by the most prominent caterer in New York."[64] The cake contained six prizes, which were to be given to the six most popular couples in the walk during the next two weeks. As each couple pranced by, the man of the pair held a sign with the name of the city the couple represented. When the walk was over for each show, the audience voted for their favorite couple by shouting out the name of their particular city. The honors for the grand prize were about evenly divided between Brooklyn and Denver. The show staged a funny finish to the cakewalk each night by having a "bad" man arrive on the scene and ask why he had not been invited to the cakewalk. Razors and pistols were produced, and the walk ended in great confusion. The big cake involved in the cakewalk was finally cut up on Monday night, 14 June, and the prizes were given to the six couples who received the most applause during the two-week contest.[65]

After a four-week run at Proctor's Pleasure Palace, the Troubadours closed their season in mid-June. Nolan said the troupe had a number of offers to play various venues during the summer, but in light of the heavy fifty-week season ahead, he and Voelckel decided to give the company the summer to rest. Voelckel and Nolan said the 1897–98 season's tour would cover the entire United States, from ocean to ocean and from the St. Lawrence River to the Rio Grande, and would be "stronger and better than ever. The show, which would open 5 August 1897, at Asbury Park, New Jersey, would consist of new songs and acts to freshen it, along with a new program for Sissieretta's Operatic Kaleidoscope. Nolan said the cakewalk, which had become such a hit at Proctor's, would be featured in the new show. Nolan planned to relax for the rest of the summer at a cottage at Park Hill in Yonkers, New York, and Voelckel was thinking of taking a European trip to rest and prepare for the next season.[66] Sissieretta and David probably returned to Providence to spend the summer with her mother at 321 North Main, where Henrietta had moved in 1892 and had begun taking in boarders to help support herself.

The Black Patti Troubadours' first season had gone well despite the trouble between Cole and managers Voelckel and Nolan at the end of the tour. During the season the troupe had improved the pace and timing of the various acts and skits so that the three-hour show was more polished and moved along more quickly. Although Voelckel and Nolan had found it necessary to book many one-night stands while the Troubadours sought to establish themselves on the road, the two managers were successful in getting them some week-long bookings in major cities. They had promised to try and only book week-long engagements during the upcoming season. From all indications the show was a financial success as well. Certainly Sissieretta had to be pleased with the Troubadours' first season. As for herself, she was performing the operatic and concert music she wanted to sing, was earning lots of money, and was furthering her fame around the country. Although she had given up the concert stage, she could comfort herself with the fact that she had top billing in a well-managed show bearing her name. The future looked bright for the coming season of the Black Patti Troubadours.

7

The Black Patti Troubadours, Early Years
1897–1900

Sissieretta's triumph as star of the Black Patti Troubadours' opening season was the first of many successes she would experience over the next twelve years as star of the African American touring company owned and managed by Rudolph Voelckel and John Nolan. The shows would change from year to year, as would the music, the cast, the touring schedules, and the venues, but the two constants that made the Black Patti Troubadours one of the most successful black road shows for thirteen seasons were Sissieretta's singing and Voelckel and Nolan's business and management acumen. Sissieretta and her managers would spend the next twelve years traveling across the United States and Canada. Each touring season began in August and ended forty-two to forty-six weeks later in May or early June. Sissieretta and the Troubadours did about seven shows a week, including evening performances and matinees. During the months of June and July, Sissieretta stayed with her mother in Rhode Island. This was the pattern her life followed after the Black Patti Troubadours debuted in 1896. Other than the two months she spent with her mother each summer, her life was her work, and her "family" became the people she spent most of her days with—her fellow Troubadours. An examination of the Black Patti Troubadours show and its cast from 1897 until 1909 helps to reveal how Sissieretta lived between the ages of twenty-nine and forty-one.

The Black Patti Troubadours was the most successful of many African American road shows touring the country at the turn of the century and into the first decade of the 1900s, "whether judged by the fame of its star, the quality of the houses it played, or its sheer longevity," according to music scholar Thomas L. Riis.[1] Black musical comedy shows of the period employed ragtime music, coon songs, cakewalks, opera, comedy, song and dance, specialty acts, and musical farce to entertain both black and white audiences. Although many productions still employed elements of minstrelsy, the shows were moving away from that form of entertainment and more toward true musical comedies. During the years the Black Patti Troubadours toured, 1896 to 1909, many African American singers, dancers, comedians, and composers found great success in the entertainment field—Bob Cole, J. Rosamund Johnson, Ernest Hogan, Will Marion Cook, Aida Overton Walker, George Walker, Bert Williams, Ida Forsyne, Jolly John Larkins, J. Ed. Green, Homer Tutt, and Salem Tutt Whitney. These were Sissieretta's contemporaries, and many of them spent some period of their careers as a member of the Black Patti Troubadours.

One of the most famous black entertainers around the turn of the century was Hogan, who became Sissieretta's costar from 1897 until 1899. Voelckel and Nolan hired Hogan, a veteran minstrel man, comedian, singer, and songwriter, to serve as stage manager and principal comedian. Hogan, whose real name was Reuben Crowders, was born in 1865 in Bowling Green, Kentucky. His father was a bricklayer. Hogan, one of a number of children in the family, ran away at an early age and joined a traveling troupe. Although he experienced tough times during those early years, he kept working in jobs connected with the theatrical profession. "His face, black as the ace of spades, his cheery, sparkling eyes and heady wit, won for him many a helping hand in these early days of struggle," according to an 1897 article published in the *Indianapolis Freeman*.[2] Hogan, who had no formal education, was self-taught. He spent years in minstrel shows, although he did not use burnt cork to blacken his face or greasepaint to create large lips, as was the custom back then, even in black minstrel shows. Instead he wore old clothes and used his ability to distort his facial expressions to make people laugh. As an actor and singer, he could move people from laughter to tears.[3]

As the era of ragtime music took hold, Hogan began composing his own music and became famous for his 1896 coon song "All Coons Look Alike to Me." By 1897 Hogan claimed he earned about four hundred dollars a month in royalties from this song and other popular songs he had written.[4] When he wrote "All Coons Look Alike to Me," Hogan did not consider it an insult to his race but rather just popular ragtime music. In later years, however, he came to regret the song because it was used by white racists to insult African Americans and had become a popular racial joke. He apologized for the offensive title throughout his life. This one ragtime song launched the demand for more coon songs. In response to his critics, Hogan argued that his song and the coon song trend that followed helped provide money and jobs for many other songwriters. While reflecting on the song years later with his friend Tom Fletcher, who wrote *The Tom Fletcher Story: 100 Years of the*

Negro in Show Business, Hogan said, "With the publication of that song a new musical rhythm was given to the people. Its popularity grew and sold like wildfire all over the United States and abroad. . . . We came along in leaps and bounds after weighing the good with the abuse. With nothing but time on my hands now, I often wonder if I was right or wrong."[5]

1897–1898 SEASON

Ernest Hogan opened his first season with the Troubadours on 6 August 1897, in Asbury Park, New Jersey. The comedian led the opening farce, "At Jolly Coon-ey Island," which, like other black musical comedy shows of that time period, had a very thin story line. The sketch was used to introduce the cast, who sang popular songs, told jokes, and did dances such as the buck-and-wing. The three-hour show, which had the same name as the previous year's show but different characters and new music, toured the New England area for several weeks before traveling to Providence to play a week at the Providence Opera House beginning Monday, 30 August. An advertisement in the *Providence Evening Bulletin* (30 August 1897) called the Black Patti Troubadours a "phenomenal hit" but never mentioned that Sissieretta's home was in Providence.[6] The mainstream Providence newspaper did not carry any articles about Sissieretta or the Troubadours during the week. How disappointing it must have been for Sissieretta to have such little recognition in the city she had chosen to make her home.

A correspondent with the *Dramatic Mirror* reviewed the show in Providence and said the Troubadours "gave a very good entertainment, which consisted of coon comedy, vaudeville, and opera." Hogan pleased the fair-sized audience with his stump speech, "What Is Man?" and his songs and comedy. Sissieretta sang opera and concert selections in the Operatic Kaleidoscope accompanied by Louise Hyers, Alice Mackey, Mme. Cordilia, Pearl Meredith, Bessie King, Leola Harris, C. H. Francis, C. Moore, Anthony Byrd, Professor Will Coleman, H. S. Norten, and a chorus of forty voices.[7] After leaving Providence the Black Patti Troubadours spent the rest of 1897 touring New York, Canada, Michigan, Illinois, Ohio, Wisconsin, and Minnesota. Although Voelckel and Nolan had said they wanted mostly week-long engagements for the Troubadours, the troupe found themselves doing many one-night stands, one of which was a performance Sunday, 19 December 1897, at the state prison in Stillwater, Minnesota. The troupe did perform more week-long runs than the previous season with engagements in New York City, Chicago, Cincinnati, Montreal, and St. Paul.

Sometime during the middle of the 1897–98 season, the music company M. Witmark and Sons, with offices both in Chicago and New York, published a book of music called *Melodic Gems from Voelckel and Nolan's Black*

Patti's Troubadours. The eighteen-page songbook contained samples from ten songs with lyrics and melody (no accompaniment) and sixteen other songs with only words, no music. All the selections had copyright dates of 1896 or 1897. The words at the bottom of each sample sheet of music said "Complete Copies 50 cts. For sale at all Music Stores." In the days before sound recordings, the most likely purpose of the sample book was to encourage people to buy the complete sheet music at their local music stores so they could play the songs at home. The front cover of the book featured a photograph of Sissieretta with the caption "Black Patti." Also listed under her photograph were the words "The Sweet Singers of the Sunny South" and "Black Patti appeared before all the Crowned heads of Europe." Photographs at each of the four corners of the cover show Queen Victoria, the Prince of Wales, the King of Italy, and Emperor William of Germany, apparently confirming that Sissieretta had performed before these European leaders.[8] The fact that Witmark published the songbook indicates the popularity Sissieretta and her Troubadours were enjoying in their second season and suggests that sheet music of the Troubadours' songs were available around the country at local music stores.

The titles of the songs that have the melody included in the songbook are "I Love You in the Same Old Way," "Miss Modesty," "Sadie, My Lady," "My Gal Is a High Born Lady," "Can't Bring Him Back," "Mister Johnson," "All Coons Look Alike to Me," "Willie off the Yacht," "Black Annie," and "Oh! Susie (Dis Coon Has Got the Blues)." Although the songbook did not claim these tunes were sung in the Troubadour show, the title of the songbook certainly suggests that. If, indeed, they were sung in the show, the songs provide an idea of the kind of music performed on the stage—coon songs, a dance tune, and lots of songs about love and life, interspersed with comedy. Several of them were written in dialect. Here are two examples:

MY GAL IS A HIGH BORN LADY
(Words and Music by Barney Fagan)
Thar' is gwine to be a festival this evenin'
And a gatherin' of color mighty rare,
Thar'll be noted individuals of prominent distinctiveness,
To permeate the colored atmosphere,
Sunny Africa's Four Hundred's gwine to be thar,
To do honor to my lovely fiancee,
Thar' will be a grand ovation, of especial ostentation,
When the parson gives the dusky bride away.

CHORUS
My gal is a high born lady,
She's black, but not too shady,

Feathered like a peacock, just as gay,
She is not colored, she was born that way,
I'm proud of my black Venus,
No coon can come between us,
'Long the line they can't outshine,
This high born gal of mine!

ALL COONS LOOK ALIKE TO ME
(Words and Music by Ernest Hogan)
Talk about a coon a having trouble, I think I have enough of ma own.
It's all about my Lucy Janey Stubbles, and she has caused my heart
    to mourn.
Thar's another coon barber from Virginia. In society he's the leader
    of the day.
And now ma honey gal is gwine to quit me. Yes she's gone and drove
    this coon away.
She'd no excuse, to turn me loose. I've been abused. I'm all confused,
    cause these words she did say:

CHORUS
All coons look alike to me. I've got another beau, you see.
And he's just as good to me as you, nig! ever tried to be.
He spends his money free. I know we can't agree.
So I don't like you no how. All coons look alike to me.[9]

   The Black Patti Troubadours worked their way west during the beginning
of 1898, covering far more territory than the company had during its initial
tour, which had been confined mostly to northern states and those along the
East Coast as far south as Washington, D.C. The Troubadours arrived in San
Francisco in early February to play a scheduled two-week engagement (6–19
February) at the California Theatre. A large advertisement in the *San Francisco Call* (3 February 1898) announced the coming of the "world-famous and
unrivaled" Black Patti Troubadours. The ad said, "The Greatest Show on
Earth, and the biggest theatrical hit of the Century. Greeted everywhere by
applauding multitudes. Fifty ecstacies in Ebony who have set the entire world
singing their fascinating and melodious coon ballads. A joyous blending of
song, story, and dance, by the merriest people under the sun. A Veritable
Revelation! Coon Comedy. Coon Songs. Jubilee Shouts. Cake Walks. Buck
Dances. Vaudeville. Operatic Reviews." The last part of the advertisement
indicated that the show was clean: "Black Patti, and her Fifty Promoters of
Mirth and Melody are the features of this universally popular company. The
stage performance is the quintessence of refined fun and sweet melody, and is

*Sissieretta wearing a tiara, perhaps the one given her by the mayor of
Demerara during one of her tours of the West Indies and South America.
Photograph circa 1898. Courtesy of the University of Washington
Libraries, Special Collections, Negative Number UW 18730.*

intended for the ENJOYMENT OF ALL, especially ladies and children. Bring
the little ones to the matinee, they will enjoy it better than the circus. Everybody should bring their shouting voice, for it will be required during the
CAKE WALK!"[10] The advertisements clearly demonstrate the Troubadours show
was aimed at pleasing families and was not like some of the more bawdy and
risqué road shows. The ads also demonstrate the hype Voelckel and Nolan
used to attract an audience.

The show was a hit in San Francisco, which was celebrating its Golden
Jubilee commemorating the fiftieth anniversary of the discovery of gold in
California. Not only did Sissieretta earn rave reviews, but so did Hogan, who
was becoming more and more popular and a main attraction in the show.

A San Francisco review published in the *Dramatic Mirror* said the Troubadours had been a "pleasant surprise, for nobody expected such a stellar combination of rollicking farce-comedy artists as Black Patti collected around her."[11] The show was such a hit in San Francisco that it was extended to a third week, and nearly all the tickets sold out within forty-eight hours. The *Dramatic Mirror* said, "San Francisco has evidently gone wild over the Black Patti Troubadours. Reports received from that city indicate that this company have [*sic*] scored one of the biggest hits in the history of the California Theatre."[12]

Not everyone in San Francisco was impressed with Sissieretta and her Troubadours. In a scathing, racially charged column, writer Ashton Stevens questioned the musical ability of all black singers and said that Sissieretta could not measure up to white vocalists. His column, "The Good Coon Song, the Bad Coon Singer, and an Emotional Comedian," was published in the *San Francisco Call* (13 February 1898) during the Troubadours' run at the California Theatre. Stevens began his column saying he thought only white people could sing real coon songs but that he had changed his mind when he heard the Troubadours singing coon songs with "just as much flash-nigger swagger and crappy enterprise and emancipated move on, and ten times as much inspired ginger in the choruses." Stevens said he was surprised by this and added that there was no "constitutional reason" why a black person could not sing as well as a white one, "but did you ever hear a coon who could sing real music, who had in his or her voice a quality that, for all its occasional hints of sweetness and sympathy, did not suggest to you dark Darwinian thoughts on the origin of the species?" Then Stevens's column got even nastier: "There is still remotely extant a superstition that negroes are singers, but I have yet to hear the first of these nocturnal song birds, for whom the nation split and bled, warble in more than three removes from the crow. Take Sissieretta Jones, the prima donna soprano assoluta of the race, a woman whose voice is fairly educated, who phrases with some skill, who has a long range and no end of suppleness—take Sissieretta and paint her white and try her out somewhere seriously, and do you think she would pass muster? Never. It is not because Sissieretta is black—or I should say black and blue, since she will sprinkle cornstarch on that proud, onyx complexion of hers—that she is not a valuable vocalist: it is only because she is black that she should be encouraged to sing at all. A few more Black Pattis might eventually lift the hoodoo from the coon voice."[13]

A piece like this must have angered Sissieretta and the other Troubadours. Fortunately there were far more positive and complimentary reviews of their work than this prejudiced column. Although Sissieretta and her Troubadours were normally well received as they toured across the United States, this article demonstrates the kind of racial prejudice they sometimes encountered.

The Black Patti Troubadours left San Francisco and went to Los Angeles to perform at the Los Angles Theatre (7–12 May), where they were a hit. At one performance there was a large group of tourists from Georgia in the audience. When they heard Sissieretta sing "Dixie Land," the men and women from the South "leaped to their feet and shouted their appreciation. The enthusiasm became infectious, and reached an electrifying climax when the company began 'The Star-Spangled Banner.'" The curtain was lowered and raised six times. Women in the audience threw flowers onto the stage, and men began to shower the male performers with gold and silver coins.[14]

The Troubadours toured throughout California and Colorado, with a couple of stops in Utah. The show changed a little during the tour out West, most likely to give the audience more opportunities to enjoy Sissieretta. Previously she had only sung during the third act, the Operatic Kaleidoscope. Sissieretta added one selection—an aria from Verdi's *I Lombardi*—in the olio (second act) just before the cakewalk. She continued to star in the Operatic Kaleidoscope, which also featured contralto Alice Mackay, tenor Will Pierce, baritone C. L. Moore, basso Anthony Byrd, and a chorus of about twenty to thirty. During this third act, Sissieretta sang "The Sabre Song" from Offenbach's operetta *The Grand Duchess of Gérolstein* and a selection from Strauss's *The Queen's Lace Handkerchief.* For the grand finale, called "Tar and Tartar," Sissieretta and the entire company sang a medley of national airs, including "The Star-Spangled Banner," "Dixie," "Yankee Doodle," "The Campbells Are Coming," and "God Save the Queen."[15]

Voelckel and Nolan spared no expense when it came to costumes and scenery for the fifty-member company. The costumes were "magnificent and costly" and said to be among the "best examples of the costumer's art." The scenery, especially the scene that represented the Bowery at Coney Island, was described as "artistic and effective."[16] The show was truly a grand production, from the size of the troupe to the colorful and elegant costumes and scenery. The managers wanted the show to be successful and were willing to put their money and energy into making it so. They had expanded the show's reach to the West Coast and were rewarded with full houses and record-breaking receipts.

After leaving Colorado the company traveled to Nebraska and Iowa before spending a week in mid-April at Chicago's first-class Schiller Theatre, where the Troubadours scored another hit. J. Harry Jackson, a Chicago correspondent for the *Indianapolis Freeman,* wrote about a Chicago newspaper (unnamed) that said anyone who loved coon comedy, coon songs and dances, coon cakewalks, and every form of coon entertainment should go see the Black Patti Troubadours. "It is a great show they give, a fast and furious medley of everything laughable and melodious, and nothing but the genuine 'coon' article." Hogan was said to be the "life and spirit of the performance and whose rag-time songs set every foot to pattering." Sissieretta, whose voice was better than ever, according to the writer, was very popular with the audience. The hit of the evening was the cakewalk.[17] Voelckel and Nolan obviously capitalized on the coon aspect of the show and audiences' desire to see African Americans portray stereotypes of themselves, just as black entertainers had done when they played in minstrel shows. The show was moving away from the minstrel show format, but in its early years, like other black shows, it still had elements demeaning to African Americans. Hogan and the other Troubadours played silly roles such as Officer Ketchum, Percy-No-Brains, Miss Aflat Badnote, and Miss Eyewrite Coonsong, and sang songs such as "Captain of the Coon Town Guard" and "Who's Got Money in Dis Crowd."

After the show left Chicago, it played a week in Cleveland, Pittsburgh, and Baltimore, before closings its forty-four week tour with a week (16–21 May) in Washington, D.C. Voelckel and Nolan immediately began to focus on the next season's show. Pleased with Hogan's success on the road, the managers hired him to appear with the Troubadours for the next two years. Hogan had been earning rave reviews everywhere the Troubadours went. During the season he had almost become as big an attraction as Sissieretta. One wonders whether Sissieretta was pleased with his popularity and the increased success it meant for the show or whether she was the slightest bit jealous of his growing recognition. In May 1898 the *Dramatic Mirror* said of Hogan, "His clever comedy work as Jim Jollier, in the skit At Jolly Coon-ey Island, and his specialty, have established him the reputation of being the best colored comedian on the American stage. As a singer and composer of ragtime ballads Hogan stands absolutely alone and unequaled." Hogan, rather than resting during the summer like most of the troupe, wanted to book special engagements. He advertised his availability in the *Mirror* and listed Voelckel and Nolan as the contact for securing his services.[18]

Sissieretta returned to Providence. For some time trouble had been brewing between Sissieretta, now thirty years old, and her husband, David Richard Jones. On 4 June 1898, within days of arriving back in Rhode Island, she filed for divorce to end her fifteen-year marriage. Her divorce petition said her husband had "neglected and refused, being of sufficient ability, to provide necessaries for her support; that he had treated her with extreme cruelty: that he hath been guilty of continued drunkenness." In addition to seeking a divorce, she asked to be allowed to "rescue her maiden name of Matilda Sissie Joyner." She signed the petition, Matilda Sissie Joyner. The court set the date of 1 October 1898 for the divorce hearing.[19] There may have been another reason for the divorce. David reportedly fathered a child, Lawrence Smith Jones, who was born 25 January 1898,[20] about five months before Sissieretta filed for divorce. Years later, when Lawrence grew up, David apparently told him, falsely, that Sissieretta was his mother. It is unknown who Lawrence's mother was, as his birth certificate has not been located, but it could not have been Sissieretta, because she was performing in Seattle on that date.[21] If Sissieretta found out about the birth of David's son, that knowledge may have contributed to her decision to divorce him.

It is not known whether David fought the divorce or appeared in court, for no records exist to show how he dealt with the divorce proceedings. The Appellate Division of the Supreme Court in Providence granted the divorce on 27 June 1899. Sissieretta was allowed to resume her maiden name, Joyner, although she used Sissieretta Jones as her stage name throughout the rest of her career. A newspaper report published a few weeks after her divorce was granted said Sissieretta told the judge she had fed and clothed her husband ever since they were wed. She said Jones was constantly drunk and once struck her in the chest with a chair, "endangering her future ability to use her voice to best advantage. Another habit Jones had was of taking all the money and trinkets he could lay his hands on and exchanging them for liquor."[22] Although David had been helpful in the early years of Sissieretta's career, he had become a strain to her both financially and emotionally, and she was probably glad to be free of him. She was making plenty of money as the star of the Black Patti Troubadours to support herself—reportedly about five hundred dollars a week, or twenty-two thousand dollars a year[23]—and her career seemed secure.

1898–1899 SEASON

Despite "excessive heat" and a heavy thunderstorm, the Troubadours opened their third season on 24 August 1898 in Plainfield, New Jersey, with Sissieretta as the star and Hogan as stage director, principal comedian, and vocalist. The show opened with a new rendition of "At Jolly Coon-ey Island," as well as new specialty acts, a continuation of the popular cakewalk, new songs such as "When They Turn All the Black Folks White," and new selections for the Operatic Kaleidoscope. Voelckel and Nolan said the tour was booked solid and that after shows in New York, New England, and Canada, the troupe would again travel to the West Coast for five weeks before heading back east through Texas and into some of the southern states for the first time. The Troubadours expected to cover twenty thousand miles during the forty-four-week season.[24] Their September schedule provides an example of how they spent their months on the road, with one engagement following on the heels of another: 1–3 September, Syracuse; 5 September, Lyons, New York; 6 September, Geneva; 7 September, Penn Yan; 8 September, Canadaigua; 9–10 September, Utica; 11–17 September, Montreal; 19 September, Kingston, New

York; 20 September, Peekskill; 21 September, Newburg; 22 September, Port Jarvis; 23 September, Middletown; 24 September, Poughkeepsie; 26 September, Waterbury, Connecticut; 27 September, New Britain, Connecticut; 28 September, Danbury, Connecticut; 29 September, Pittsfield, Massachusetts; 30 September, North Adams, Massachusetts. This schedule meant the company had to set up, perform, and then repack everything eighteen times in thirty days. There were only three days in September that the Troubadours did not perform. Plans called for the Troubadours' season to end in early May 1899 and for the company to sail to Europe to play engagements in London, Paris, Berlin, and Vienna in the summer and fall.[25] An article in the *Dramatic Mirror* said that Voelckel and Nolan expected another successful and prosperous season. "These managers have demonstrated by their managerial skill and judgment that the public was ready to patronize a colored company of a high standard, and the Troubadours proved one of the leading money makers of last season. With a better company, and excellent bookings, and the public still interested in the 'coon craze,' there is every reason to believe that the success of last season will be duplicated."[26] Voelckel continued to travel with the show and manage it while Nolan acted as the advance man, working with theater managers, checking on bookings, handling advertising, and perhaps making hotel and travel arrangements for the forty-member troupe.

The Troubadours spent a lot of time together, away from their own families during the forty-four-week season. Night after night they performed on the stage, and during the day they traveled together and readied themselves for their next engagement. One of the ways in which road shows such as the Black Patti Troubadours communicated with their families and friends as well as with performers in other road shows was through reports written by a designated cast member who acted as a correspondent to the African American newspaper the *Indianapolis Freeman* and later, also, to the *New York Age*. These correspondents periodically sent information to the newspapers about the cast's activities and other noteworthy items about the show. The reports written about the Black Patti Troubadours provide some insight into the personalities of company members and help to describe what life was like on the road. Early in the 1898–99 season, Augustus "Gus" Hall served as the Troubadours' correspondent to the *Freeman*. His reports over the course of several months covered oddities such as the fact that Troubadour comedian James Bland, who played Dr. Parkhurst, was seven feet, five inches tall; gave notice of illnesses, mishaps, and marriages on the road; and told bits of gossip such as small pranks that cast members played on each other. Hall told how Hogan's mother and brothers came to visit Hogan and traveled with the troupe for several weeks so they could spend time with the comedy star. Sometimes Hall's reports also made note of unsavory incidents such as the one in which cast member Daisy Harris misled managers Voelckel and Nolan into believing her mother was ill so that Harris could invent an opportunity for herself to leave the Troubadours for another company. The correspondent said the "other members [of the Black Patti Troubadours' cast] were deeply chagrined at the unladylike and unprofessional way of doing business, and it is sincerely hoped that such actions will not ever occur again in the history of the colored profession." The reports were also a way to brag about the company, such as the time Hall said African American patrons could be proud of the Black Patti Troubadour show as it contained no scenes that were demeaning of black people.[27] On one occasion Hall made a surprising observation about race when he spoke of accommodations for the troupe: "On entering a city when you go to a hotel generally run by white people, you are seldom, if ever asked for your money first, but instead [they] seek to make you as comfortable as possible while you are there and then accept money for services, on the other hand when you wish to spend your money with a colored family, and eat the food you used to at home, why they will ask you, who will pay and when, before you have a chance to see whether you sleep on a bed or board. Read up my wise friends and treat us nice and you will be paid for all services rendered after, but not before."[28]

The Troubadours continued to tour the country, visiting many of the same cities as the season before. For the most part, they played to full houses, often having to post the "Standing Room Only" sign or to turn patrons away from the crowded venues. In Chicago and St. Paul, new performers joined the show—Will A. Cooke, Laura Meredith, and her daughters, Pearle and Carrie—while others left. It was not unusual for cast members to rotate in and out of shows while companies toured the country. Sissieretta and Hogan earned acclaim from most reviewers, despite the fact the show was similar to last year's show. One critic said Black Patti's voice was not as "fresh" as it had been, and another questioned her seemingly diminished role in the show. Sissieretta sang one selection ("In Days of Yore") during the second act and sometimes added a second ("My Old Kentucky Home"), and she performed three numbers in the Operatic Kaleidoscope, along with any encores she elected to sing. This was about the same number of selections she had sung the previous year. Hogan was featured prominently, both in the first and second acts, with one reviewer calling him the "life of the performance." He kept the audience entertained with his "refined" monologue and songs he had written, such as "Honey You've Made a Hit with Me" and "If They'd Only Fought with Razors in the War."[29]

The company headed north in early January 1899 to Minnesota, Wisconsin, and Canada, before turning westward to Montana, Idaho, Washington, and Oregon by early February. They spent two weeks in mid-February at the

California Theater in San Francisco, toured eight California cities, and played a week at the Los Angeles Theatre (13–18 March).[30] While the Troubadours were touring in California and then into Texas for the first time, Voelckel and Nolan sent an announcement regarding Hogan to the *Dramatic Mirror,* asking the entertainment weekly to publish it immediately. The announcement, published 18 March, disputed claims in earlier editions of the newspaper that said Hogan was going to star next season in a show managed by E. E. Rice and a "colored gentleman." Voelckel and Nolan said they had a contract with Hogan that would not expire until May 1900 and that no one had asked them for a release of Hogan's contract.[31] It is unknown whether Hogan had been negotiating with another manager in early spring of 1899. His fame and popularity had grown considerably during his time with the Black Patti Troubadours, and he was likely anxious to advance his career as a performer, composer, and playwright. He may have felt limited and confined with his role in the Black Patti Troubadours. About a month after Voelckel and Nolan's announcement appeared in the *Dramatic Mirror,* Hogan wrote to the newspaper and said he had "severed his connection" with the Black Patti Troubadours. He said he planned to write skits and songs during the spring and summer for a tour next season in which he would be the star. Hogan said he would collaborate with his "protégé," Tom Logan, author and character artist, and hoped to write several songs that would "eclipse" his famous "All Coons Look Alike to Me."[32]

According to one of Hogan's contemporaries, black entertainer Tom Fletcher, who wrote a book in 1954 about the first one hundred years of blacks in show business, a confrontation in New Orleans apparently hastened Hogan's departure from the Black Patti Troubadours. Hogan told Fletcher, years after leaving the Troubadours, that he left the show in New Orleans, which was the first place in the Deep South the show had ever played. Hogan said the custom back then allowed the leading man to get money by going to the box office and signing for it. In the theater in New Orleans, there were two box offices—one for black patrons and one for whites. Hogan said he went to the wrong box. He told Fletcher, "The man I met started cursing at me and raised his fist but I beat him to the punch and knocked him down. Before anything else could happen Mr. Nolan arrived and broke up the scrap. He hid me away until that night, then got me out of town. I didn't get myself together again until I was in Australia with my own company."[33] After leaving the Troubadours, Hogan went to New York City and starred in a show there. He went on to have a tremendous career in show business that took him from New York to Hawaii and Australia with his own company before returning to the United States and starring in several shows he wrote, as well as composing music. He contracted tuberculosis and died in New York City on 20 May 1909.[34]

With Hogan's departure from the Troubadours, the show was left without a principal comedian and stage manager just as it was beginning its first tour of cities in the Deep South, but the loss did not seem to hurt the company. For example Sissieretta's reputation as musical star of the Troubadours was enough to pack the McDonald Theatre to capacity—two thousand people, including many who had to stand—in Montgomery, Alabama. W. H. Parker, a patron from Montgomery, wrote to the *Indianapolis Freeman* to say that 4 April 1899 would never be forgotten in Montgomery "from the very fact that the Black Patti Troubadours made a big hit with both colored and white, of whom are capable of judging. . . . Black Patti is beyond contradiction the greatest character in this country, in her line of business."[35] Sometimes the Troubadours played to a "top heavy" crowd, according to published reviews, which was one way of saying the largest part of the audience was black and that these patrons were seated in the balcony, also known as the gallery—the only place black people were allowed to sit in the South. After leaving Alabama, the Troubadours traveled to Georgia, South Carolina, North Carolina, and Virginia. The mixed-race audiences who attended the show during its first tour of the South ranged from "large" to "good" to "fair." With their initial tour of the South behind them, the Troubadours took their medley of comedy, vaudeville, burlesque, and opera to Washington, D.C., for a week in late April, followed by a week in Baltimore. The company closed the 1898–99 season with extended engagements in Philadelphia (1–6 May), New York City (8–13 May at one theater and 15–20 May at another), and Boston (23–31 May).

At the beginning of the 1898–99 season, Voelckel and Nolan had said they planned to take the Troubadours to Europe for the summer and fall of 1899. By the end of the season, however, the managers had changed their minds, saying the European engagements had been postponed until June 1900 because of the "phenomenal success of the American transcontinental tour."[36] Apparently business had been so good that the two managers thought better about going to Europe, where they could not be certain how the Troubadours might be received. A short article in the *Dramatic Mirror* said, "Everywhere the big organization has appeared it has caused a sensation, and packed houses have been the rule during the entire season."[37] One press report said those with "intimate knowledge of theatricals" claimed the Black Patti Troubadours had made a net profit of twenty thousand dollars for the 1898–99 season.[38]

1899–1900 Season

As the opening of the Troubadours' 1899–1900 season approached, Voelckel and Nolan announced plans to take the company to the West Coast and to play all important points along the way. After touring California and the Rocky Mountain states, the Troubadours planned to head South again, this time playing in every large city in the region. An article in the *Dramatic Mirror* explained why the Troubadours would be spending more time in the South. "The phenomenal success this company enjoyed in Dixie Land last season will doubtless be repeated, for it is a matter of record that the company and performance created as big a sensation in that section as it has north of the Mason and Dixon line," the newspaper said.[39]

The fourth season of the Black Patti Troubadours opened in Asbury Park on 10 August 1899 to a packed house, despite warm weather that night. The two-and-a-half-hour show had a new opening skit, "A Rag-time Frolic at Rasbury Park," which consisted of "exaggerated comedy, plenty of character work, lightning dancing by both men and women, comic songs, and acrobatic fun." The skit's cast included a bull terrier "with invincible jaws and a death grip on everything that comes his way."[40] The cast was smaller than the first two seasons—down to about thirty entertainers—and there was no leading comedian. Sissieretta was still the star attraction, apparently singing only during the Operatic Kaleidoscope, which was "gorgeously costumed" and contained some of the "heaviest" selections from grand opera. The songs chosen for this part of the show included selections from *Chimes of Normandy, Faust, The Fortune Teller, Cavalleria Rusticana, Grand Duchess,* and *Tannhäuser.* The show kept its popular cakewalk and added a section by the Troubadour sextet sure to please the show's southern audiences—a selection of songs grouped around a theme called "Happy Ante-Bellum Melodic Memories of the Plantation and Levee."[41]

The Troubadours' route took them through New York, Montreal, Ottawa, Ohio, and Michigan by the end of September. They earned great reviews while in Detroit (24–30 September), with the *Detroit Free Press* saying the quality of the company's work had been "refined and in every way surprisingly improved." The newspaper singled out Sissieretta and the Operatic Kaleidoscope. "The chief figure here is Mrs. Sissieretta Jones, who has not inaptly been called the greatest singer of her race. She has a natural gift of song, and the art to exhibit it in a captivating manner; and she is sustained by several fine singers and a chorus of which any director of grand opera might well be proud," the newspaper said.[42] A large advertisement that ran in the newspaper just before the Troubadours opened in Detroit provides an idea about how the two-and-a-half-hour show moved from one song and dance to another because it showed the various selections and the time each began:

The Opening Skit:
8:15—"The Honolulu Dance"
8:20—"Ho-do-doo-Man"
8:35—"Roxy Ann Dooley"
8:45—"Thro' Out de Life Line"

8:50—"Happy at My Baby's Side"
9:00—"I Want a Real Coon"
9:05—"Hello My Baby"
9:10—"Babe from Boston Town"

The Olio:
9:15—The Rag-Time Buck Dance
9:20—The Troubadour Sextette
9:30—Jim Wilson, the Equilibrist
9:40—The Watts' Coon Eccentrics
9:50—Sisters Meredith, Senegambian Sylphs
10:00—The Grand Cakewalk
10:10—The Averys' "Ebony Ecstacies"

Operatic Kaleidoscope:
10:20–10:45—The Operatic Kaleidoscope
"Black Patti and the incomparable ensemble singing forces in a splendid presentation of operatic masterpieces, making a dignified musical climax to what is universally admitted to be one of the most delightful stage performances of modern times."[43]

After a four-day run in Toledo, Ohio, at the beginning of October, the show did a series of one-night stands in Indiana while working its way to Chicago, where the Troubadours played a week (8–14 October) at the Academy Theatre and a week (15–21 October) at the Alhambra Theatre. Reports written by a Troubadour cast member, most likely James Lightfoot, and sent to the *Indianapolis Freeman* described the Troubadours' Chicago experience both on and off the stage. Little about the Troubadours' two weeks in the Second City appeared in the mainstream white newspapers, other than a few small advertisements about the show. Lightfoot said that the Troubadours played to a standing room only audience when they opened at the Academy Theatre on 8 October. Madame Patti was in excellent voice, he said, and "sang exquisitely." The Troubadours also had a week of "big" business at the Alhambra Theatre. Two new cast members joined the group in Chicago—soprano soloist Julia Roan and "coon singer" and buck-and-wing dancer Ida Forcen. (Her actual surname, Forsyne, was always misspelled in press reports.) Cast member Leslie Triplett, playing his part as an Irish policeman, was a big hit and a large part of the fun in the first act, according to Lightfoot. Singer Mattie Phillips became seriously ill during the second week in Chicago and had to remain there under a doctor's care when the troupe moved on to the next stop. Florrie Wilson, the wife of juggler James Wilson, met up with the company in Detroit and traveled with the Troubadours for the next four weeks so she could visit her husband. Lightfoot said, "Although 'Jim' has been on the road for years and enjoyed any number of pleasant times, he claims to have enjoyed the four weeks his wife spent with him more than any during his experiences on the road." The final bit of news Lightfoot told the *Freeman* about was the marriage of cast members Mary Lange, of New Orleans, and Judson Hicks. The two were married in Chicago without telling the rest of the cast in advance. Members of the troupe had wanted to give the pair a "blow-out," but Judson preferred to keep the marriage quiet, "as it is the only quiet thing he ever did in his life."[44] These insights into life on the road show how the entertainers had to live their lives while constantly moving from one city or town to another. Wives had to travel with the troupe in order to visit with their husbands who were in the show. If someone was too sick to travel, they had to stay behind and catch up with the show once they recovered. Relationships often bloomed between cast members, as might be expected when they spent so much time together. Over the years there were several marriages between Troubadour cast members. Surely there were close friendships, as well as squabbles, jealousies, and misunderstandings between the thirty to forty people who worked and traveled together for nearly ten months every season. It is unknown how much Sissieretta interacted with other cast members, but it appears from newspaper reports over the years that she tended to keep mostly to herself or spent time with her maid, who was also a member of the cast.

After leaving Chicago the Troubadours did a number of one-night stands in the upper Midwest and traveled north into Minnesota, where they played a week (6–11 November) in Minneapolis. After closing in Minneapolis, the Troubadours began traveling in their own private railcar, which Voelckel and Nolan arranged. The cast dubbed their hotel car "Black Patti." A Troubadour cast member writing to the *Freeman* about the troupe's new method of traveling said the car was "very comfortable" and contained ten sections and two drawing rooms. Plans called for the Troubadours to continue traveling by private train car for the remainder of the season.[45] It would become Sissieretta's, Voelckel's, and the Troubadours' home away from home for many years to come. Several touring companies traveled and slept in private railcars attached to passenger trains rather than having to occupy the train's public cars. This method of traveling had to have been more relaxing for the black entertainers, especially with the increased amount of time they were spending in the South. Between the Troubadours closing in Minneapolis on 11 November 1899 and their opening 17 December in San Francisco for two weeks, the troupe entertained in twenty-one cities and towns in seven states—Wisconsin, Minnesota, North Dakota, Montana, Washington, Oregon, and California—as well as several parts of Canada.

Once again Sissieretta and the Troubadours were a big hit in San Francisco during their two-week engagement at the end of December. One newspaper, the *San Francisco Call,* said Sissieretta had surrounded herself with the "best and largest company she has ever brought to the coast, and the big performance is said to be far superior to anything she has ever given here."[46] A review in the *San Francisco Examiner* described the show as a "spasm of ragtime opera, cake-walk, and real coons." Sissieretta was said to "shine in the final olio in a series of operatic selections, assisted by a chorus equal to that of the average opera company." The review said the company had its own ragtime professor, "who keeps the piano quivering while the nimble colored folks wriggle about the stage, and they do some clever work." Dancer Ida Forsyne was described as a brunette who could not remain still "even when it is not her turn to oblige, and when Ida does get the center of the stage, the white folks yearn to keep her there." One number singled out in the review was performed by W. H. Stewart, who imitated the puffing of a locomotive with his feet in some sand scattered on the stage, all done to ragtime music. "When Mr. Stewart attains a speed of sixty miles an hour, they turn the lights out and [he] emits real sparks from his mouth."[47]

From January 1900 through early April, the Troubadours performed in sixteen states, including a series of one-night stands in Texas that covered sixteen cities and towns, while working their way south to New Orleans for a two-week run on 8–14 April. The company played to a "packed house" on opening night at the Crescent Theatre, but for the rest of their time in New Orleans, business was described as being only "fair."[48] The company stayed in the South until the end of April and experienced good audiences, although some audiences were described as top-heavy houses. In May the troupe began traveling up the East Coast toward New York City. While Sissieretta was singing operatic selections with the Black Patti Troubadours show in May, the *Dramatic Mirror* announced the formation of a black opera company created by Theodore Drury. The company, which planned to sing *Carmen* in English, was scheduled to perform 14 May at the Lexington Avenue Opera House in New York City. The newspaper said it would probably be the first performance of grand opera ever undertaken by a company of African Americans. Sissieretta's colleague from her concert days, Harry T. Burleigh, would conduct about thirty-six singers in the company.[49] One can only wonder whether thirty-two-year-old Sissieretta had any regrets that she was not part of this fledgling opera company or whether she was content with the direction her life had taken. Her years with the Troubadours had brought her widespread fame as well as a good income, and she was able to sing operatic selections of her choosing. In return she had to travel forty to forty-five weeks out of the year, often playing one-night engagements, and she starred in a musical comedy and vaudeville show rather than being part of a serious opera company.

Whatever her thoughts were, she continued with the Troubadours and pressed on to Washington, D.C., Baltimore, and finally to New York City, where the company gave its last performance of the season on 2 June at the Star Theatre. The forty-five-week tour, which extended from the Atlantic to the Pacific and from the St. Lawrence River to the Rio Grande, had been prosperous. The Troubadours had traveled between twenty-three thousand and twenty-five thousand miles and given nearly five hundred performances in almost every principal city in the United States and Canada, according to three newspaper reports. Estimates given in these reports were that more than one million people had attended a Troubadours performance during the season. The *Indianapolis Freeman* said, "This company is recognized as being the very best organization of its kind in the world. It was the first colored company to receive recognition from theatre patrons in the better class of houses. . . . Sissieretta Jones (the Black Patti) is the vocal star of the company who leads the singing forces in the operatic features of the program." The *New York Clipper* said the company was "universally admitted to be among the best of its kind in the world. Black Patti, the star of the organization, stands as a singer without equal among Afro-Americans." Because of the similarity of reports about the Troubadours's 1899–1900 season published in three newspapers, it appears the information for these articles must have come from a press release likely written by Voelckel or Nolan.[50] All three newspapers, the *Freeman,* the *Clipper,* and the *Dramatic Mirror,* saw fit to run the information and did not dispute the material provided, although the estimate of five hundred performances seems high.

With the season over, Sissieretta returned to Providence for the summer while Voelckel and Nolan began planning for the 1900–1901 season. Comedian Irving Jones (no relation to Sissieretta), who joined the Troubadours for the final four weeks of the 1899–1900 season, had been so successful that Voelckel and Nolan hired him to be the leading comedian for the upcoming tour. One entertainment newspaper said that he was the "best interpreter of the modern rag time ballad and one of the most accomplished composers of songs of that class. He's also a clever comedian." Although the terms of Jones's contract were not made public, the newspaper said he would probably receive one of the largest salaries paid to any "colored" comedian.[51] With the success of the Troubadours, Voelckel and Nolan could afford to pay for talented entertainers, and the two managers had shown a willingness to put money into their show to ensure its continued popularity and profit. During the summer of 1900, a short article in the *Dramatic Mirror* may have caught the attention of Voelckel and Nolan. It said that former Troubadour comedian

Ernest Hogan, who had just signed a contract to establish a first-class musical comedy company, believed the cakewalk and coon craze had "seen its day."[52] Perhaps Voelckel and Nolan, astute managers as they seemed to be, wondered whether Hogan was right and if black entertainment might be maturing and moving away from a steady bill of coon songs and comedy. Although that formula had worked well for the Troubadours' show for four seasons, it might grow stale to future audiences. The managers would have to watch patrons' reactions carefully during the next few years.

8

The Black Patti Troubadours
1900–1906

As the world adjusted to life in the twentieth century, Sissieretta and the Troubadours prepared for the opening of their fifth consecutive season, scheduled to run from August 1900 until May 1901. During this time President William McKinley, twenty-fifth president of the United States, was reelected for a second term (he was assassinated the following year, in September 1901); the first rigid dirigible (zeppelin) made its maiden voyage (2 July 1900) in Germany, carrying five people nearly four miles in seventeen minutes at a height of 1,300 feet; Picasso, Gauguin, Cezanne, Renoir, and Toulouse-Lautrec painted; and the cakewalk became the most fashionable dance in the United States.[1] For Sissieretta and the Black Patti Troubadours, this season would turn out to be pretty much the same as the last, except that they would not travel to the West Coast and would spend an additional twenty days in the South. The show had a fresh opening farcical skit, "A Darktown Frolic on the Rialto," which featured the company's new principal comedian and composer, Irving Jones. Sissieretta continued to star in the Operatic Kaleidoscope, with its grand scenery and expensive costumes.[2] The show's cakewalk, as always, was a big hit with audiences from Halifax, Nova Scotia, to Atlanta, Georgia.

Sissieretta and the Troubadours were largely well received throughout the 1900–1901 season, both in the far North into Canada and in the Deep South. Their travel schedule remained rigorous. The company played mostly one-night stands, with week-long performances in some major cities. Often the monotony of the tour was interspersed with social occasions, such as the first-class banquet hosted in Nashville by prominent black fireman William H. Oden and his wife. The guests included many of the South's most prominent black residents, including people from Tennessee, Kentucky, and Indiana.[3]

*Anonymous portrait of Sissieretta Jones, Providence, R.I.,
circa 1900. Ink on paper. Print. Courtesy of the
Rhode Island Historical Society, RH:X5 358.*

The Troubadour show, especially Sissieretta's Operatic Kaleidoscope, continued to earn high praise from black theater critic Sylvester Russell. In his
annual assessment of the state of black theater, published in the "Holiday"
issue of the *Indianapolis Freeman* (29 December 1900), Russell said, "There
has been nothing more encouraging to the black race of America than the
progress made upon the stage by black performers during the past six years."
He credited John W. Isham and his original Octoroon company for being the
first troupe to include opera and dramatic scenes in their show. The show
later declined, Russell said, when it dropped the opera selections. Russell said
black shows needed a prima donna and a star male soloist to succeed and that
shows could not just play all ragtime songs. Like Ernest Hogan, Russell predicted, "The days of all-coon comedy in a colored show are past and yet one
could not live without it, but white people in this day and time will not stand
for all rag-time—a little of everything will assure a happy return." Russell gave

his list of successful black entertainers, which included Bob Cole, Burt Williams, Irving Jones, Ernest Hogan, and Sissieretta, the only woman on the list. "The Black Patti (Mme. Sissieretta Jones), who has the envy of many of her race sisters, has not been surpassed by any of them yet," Russell said, adding that she could challenge "all comers" for a while.[4]

The Troubadours finished the 1900–1901 season at the end of May 1901, and Sissieretta returned to Rhode Island to spend the summer in the large nine-room house located at 7 Wheaton Street, on Providence's east side, that she had bought for her mother in 1899. As usual, while Sissieretta enjoyed visiting her mother and taking a break from her grueling travel schedule, Voelckel and Nolan were busy working on the 1901–2 season. The managers hired John Rucker, known as the "Alabama Blossom," to be the star comedian for the upcoming season. The new show opened with a musical farcical skit called "A Filipino Mis-Fit," followed by a number of vaudeville specialties. The second act of the show featured John Rucker singing and delivering a monologue, Mack Allen performing on the slack wire, the Troubadour Quartet singing several selections, a cakewalk, buck-and-wing dancing, and Sissieretta singing a series of songs called "Songs of Dixie," sure to please southern audiences. In the final act, the Operatic Kaleidoscope, Sissieretta and her fellow Troubadours, dressed in full costume, sang selections from *El Capitan, The Chimes of Normandy,* and *Martha.* Sissieretta closed the show by singing "Inflammatus," from *Stabat Mater,* supported by the chorus.[5]

The show, which opened 14 August 1901 in Newburg, New York, at the Academy of Music, spent the rest of August touring New York and New Jersey before heading south in September, where the company gave performances in twenty-two cities and towns in four southern states—Virginia, North Carolina, South Carolina, and Georgia. In early October the troupe traveled to Illinois, where they played three cities before arriving in Chicago for a short stop on 13 October. Ida Larkins and Janette Murphy-Green joined the company while it was in Chicago. One cast member filed a report with the *Indianapolis Freeman* that provided a good description of the show and its cast during the company's first three months on the road. The report said Sissieretta was in excellent health and singing well, "taking four and five encores at every performance." She and her chorus of twenty-five voices were satisfying audiences with the Operatic Kaleidoscope, which was the "supreme musical feature of the performance." According to the report, audiences were pleased with the performances of John Rucker and Al and Cecil Watts. The Ver Valins, musical specialists with the company this season, had a saxophone number that was "extraordinarily clever." Mack Alan, the "slack wire phenomenon" was a wonder and received rounds of applause every night. The report closed with kind words about Voelckel. "Mr. Voelckel, our genial manager, is enjoying good health and is indefatigable in his efforts to make the present tour successful."[6]

Between mid-October and the end of December, the Black Patti Troubadours performed in Wisconsin, Minnesota, North Dakota, Canada, Montana, Washington, Oregon, and California. The company played a week at Cordray's (8–14 December) in Portland. It was the third time the Troubadours had visited this city in its six years of touring, and the audiences there found much in the show to please them. Sissieretta was recalled to the stage five times when she sang during the show's finale.[7] An interesting review of the show, written by a cast member from another company (the Slayton Tennessean Jubilee Singers), appeared in the *Indianapolis Freeman,* which provided a critical look at the Troubadour show from the viewpoint of a fellow black entertainer. The entertainer's most notable observation came at the end of his review, when he wrote about Sissieretta singing more popular tunes rather than sticking to operatic selections and familiar ballads, which suited her better: "The show is a very good one. Their first act is furiously fast. Nothing drags; from the moment the curtain rolls up everything moves with plenty of snap and ginger. The surprises of the performance were the work of little Ida Forcen [*sic*] who is as clever a performer as ever faced a footlight; the Watts who left the audience screaming; and John Rucker who had an unparalleled up-to-datedness, so far as the colored profession is concerned, in his work. . . . The star [Sissieretta] acquitted herself in her usual manner although her rendition of 'Honey, Stay in Your Own Back Yard,' and songs of that kind are entirely out of her line and should be let severely alone."[8]

From 29 December 1901 until 4 January 1902, the Troubadours were in San Francisco at the California Theatre. A review in the *San Francisco Bulletin,* which Sissieretta pasted in her scrapbook, said the Troubadours' show was much better than the last time the company had visited San Francisco in December 1899. "They are better drilled, their work is more compact and there is less horseplay," the review said, adding that "not one of the principals is a bad actor." The review said comedian Rucker had a few clever gags, but "could not approach" Ernest Hogan. As for Sissieretta the reviewer said her singing of ballads was more pleasing than her operatic selections. "Black Patti grows no older or less imposing with the years. She has the dignity of an experienced prima donna, the poise and lovely gowns, and superb diamonds decorate her chocolate arms and fingers. Her voice is rich and strong, but has lost just a suspicion of the velvet quality that once distinguished it." Although this review suggested Sissieretta's voice had lost some of its rich smoothness, *Indianapolis Freeman* stage critic Sylvester Russell had nothing but praise for the prima donna's voice. In his annual year-end review, Russell said that the solos Sissieretta had selected to sing this year were the best ever and that "her voice is much better than in the past three seasons." He also said the Black Patti Troubadours "seem to be the best singing organization this season, the chorus being quite near to perfection."[9]

After leaving San Francisco on 4 January, the company continued its swing through California, Utah, and Colorado. The Troubadours spent a week in Denver at the Denver Theatre (16–22 February), where their three-hour show was a big success. A review from the *Denver Times* published in the *Indianapolis Freeman* said the Troubadour cast was above average and was as good as many first-class operas that had played before in Denver. The show had "clean bits of wit" without a single objectionable feature. As for Sissieretta, the review said, "She is as good as ever she was and there were not a few in the audience who insisted that she had improved. Be this as it may, Mrs. Jones to day [*sic*] possesses a voice of marvelous richness and volume that thoroughly delights and will continue to be the drawing card to the no less meritorious combination with which she is traveling."[10]

Ironically, on the same page of the *Freeman* that carried the Troubadours' review from the *Denver Times,* an article appeared about Flora Batson, who had recently returned from a tour in Australia and had just sung a concert 17 February in Savannah. Batson appeared in concert at a Savannah church with Gerard Millar, Australia's premier basso profundo, and she received a rave review. One could assume Sissieretta took note of this article when she read the *Freeman* and thought about her decision to leave the concert stage to star in the Black Patti Troubadours. She and Batson had followed the same career path during the late 1880s, but now their directions were very different. While Batson had been in Australia, Sissieretta had continued to earn a good living as star of the Troubadours and had become famous throughout the United States and parts of Canada. For example sometime during the 1901–2 season, Sissieretta was once again pictured on the cover of a book of sheet music from the Black Patti Troubadours published by M. Witmark and Sons, which was likely distributed throughout the United States. The twenty-five-cent songbook featured a photograph of Sissieretta, wearing a long gown with a train, seated in a chair. The words on the cover, written in large, bold type, read *Songs as Sung by the Black Patti Troubadours. The Greatest Colored Show on Earth.*[11] Sissieretta may have regretted not getting to tour in Europe again or to sing in far-off Australia, like Batson. Perhaps she thought about the new black Drury Opera Company and wished she had developed her operatic repertoire more so she could perform with the troupe in a full-length opera. However, given her fortune and fame, she may have been content with the career path she had chosen.

Despite any musings Sissieretta may have had about her life and career, she carried on with her demanding schedule, performing in the Oklahoma

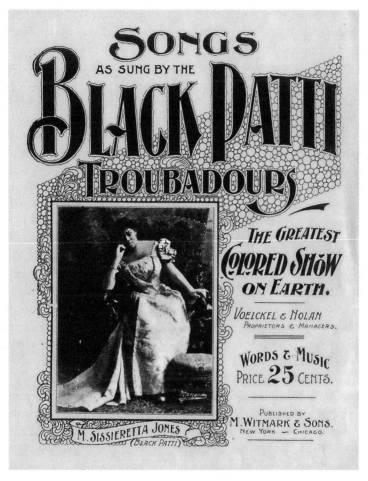

The Black Patti Troubadours had several songbooks published by M. Witmark and Sons. Courtesy of the Museum of Performance and Design, San Francisco.

Territory and fifteen states—Wyoming, Nebraska, Missouri, Kansas, Louisiana, Mississippi, Arkansas, Tennessee, Illinois, Indiana, Ohio, Pennsylvania, Maryland, Delaware, and New Jersey—between February and May. Normally the company finished its season in May, but this year the troupe worked until 7 June so it could play its final week of the season at the new Star Theatre in New York City.[12]

1902–1903 SEASON

"Darktown's Circus Day," the opening skit for the 1902–3 season, premiered 7 August 1902 at Asbury Park Auditorium. The book for the new show was written by none other than Bob Cole, the entertainer who wrote the first Troubadour show in 1896 and who left the following year after a bitter dispute with Troubadour managers Voelckel and Nolan. Since then Cole had become a highly regarded entertainer as well as playwright and composer of several black musical comedies. Several theater professionals attended the Troubadours' opening, and after the performance concluded, they told manager John Nolan that the show was good enough to run on Broadway in New York City. Nolan reportedly thanked them for their kind words but said the company did not have any plans to change their bookings, which he said were scheduled to last until 4 July 1903.[13]

A program from the 1902–3 season showed what the three-hour show was like. Part 1 was the skit, "Darktown's Circus Day." It had three scenes: scene 1, "Exterior of Darktown Circus"; scene 2, "Interior of Darktown Circus"; and scene 3, "Interior of Theatre." Part 1 closed with buck-and-wing dancing. The musical numbers in the skit included "When the Circus Comes to Town," "Castle on the Nile," "Ain't Going to Stay Here Any Longer," and "Under the Bamboo Tree." After an intermission came part 2, which consisted of specialty acts by some of the cast members. The final part of the show began after another intermission. It included selections from grand and comic operas. It starred Sissieretta and included Sarah Green, contralto; James E. Worles, tenor; J. Ed. Green, baritone; James P. Reed, bass; and a chorus. The selections included Sissieretta and Worles singing "Miserere" from *Il Trovatore,* the chorus performing "Behold the Queen," and Sissieretta and four others singing a quintet from *Martha.* The Troubadours show had its own musical director, who worked with local orchestras hired in the city or town where the show played. In addition to accompanying the vocalists, the orchestra played several selections, most likely during intermissions and before the show opened.[14]

The Troubadours' seventh season tour did not venture to the West Coast as in years past: the most western states on the company's schedule were Texas and Kansas. Instead the Troubadours spent more time in the South and Southwest—about 115 days in the South and 31 days in the Southwest—nearly double the amount of days the company spent in those parts of the country the previous year.[15] Over the last few years, the company's success in the South and Southwest (mostly Texas and Oklahoma Territory) had grown, which must have prompted the managers to spend more time there. The Troubadours toured New York and New Jersey in August; Washington, D.C., Maryland, West Virginia, North Carolina, South Carolina, and Georgia in September; Georgia, Alabama, and Mississippi in October; Tennessee, Kentucky, Indiana, Missouri, and Illinois in November; and Tennessee, Mississippi, Louisiana, and Texas in December. Most reviews of these engagements

praised the show and reported "good" to "large" audiences, like the two performances the Troubadours gave over Labor Day in Washington, D.C., where
nearly eight thousand people, both black and white, "packed the commodi-
ous Convention Hall to the doors."[16] Sometimes, however, there were reviews,
such as the one for the 2 October 1902 performance at the Academy of Music
in Charleston, South Carolina, which said that the audience was "top heavy"
and the show was "rather tiresome."[17] In several southern cities, there were
reports of "top heavy houses," although most newspaper reviews talked about
large audiences and made no distinction as to the racial makeup of the audiences. Mixed-race audiences with segregated seating were the norm for the
Troubadours when they played in the South.

As 1902 came to a close, Sissieretta found herself the subject of an article
in the *Indianapolis Freeman's* annual year-end stage review. In a portrait on the
front page, Sissieretta, seated in a chair, was shown wearing an elegant gown
and long gloves. Accompanying her portrait was a long article written by
critic I. McCorker titled "The 'Black Patti,' One of the World's Most Tuneful Cantatrices." McCorker, who had written about Sissieretta in the past,
recalled hearing her for the first time seven or eight years earlier when he was
working for a small weekly newspaper in Leavenworth, Kansas. He said he
went to the YMCA in Kansas City and spent seventy-five cents for a ticket to
see her perform. He was not disappointed. He said her voice was everything
newspaper reviews from New York and other cities had claimed.[18]

McCorker recalled how some white theater critics claimed blacks were
not prepared to handle classical music but instead excelled only in singing
plantation and camp-meeting songs, such as those written by Stephen Foster. These same critics said black singers "might" excel in "ragtime opera."
McCorker took these critics to task, saying Sissieretta exemplified the fact
that black people were as capable of high-grade music as anyone. "We believe,
as Mr. Dvorak, of New York, that music is an inherent quality of the Negro;
he comes by music as naturally as a duck takes to water. Comparisons are
said to be odious, but by comparison we do not think Mme. Jones would suffer any with any of the grand opera stars as Mmes. Calve, Melba, Nordica,
Eames, Miss Sybil Sanderson, Miss Suzanne Adams, or Fraulein Fritzi
Scheff."

The critic said audiences do not have to be "educated" to understand
music and distinguish between the good, the bad, and the indifferent. "We
recognize it as soon as we meet it in the road, the same as we are aware of the
fact when we stub our great toe." He said that when Sissieretta "loosens up,"
audiences know "she possesses the goods and is going to give us our money's
worth." McCorker continued, "She is a singer, every inch of her, with a well-
modulated and distinctive mezzo-soprano vocalness whose volubility is rich

Women loved seeing Sissieretta in her beautiful gowns, like this one she wore during a photography session. Photograph courtesy of the Dr. Carl R. Gross Collection, Moorland-Spingarn Research Center, Howard University.

Facing: Sissieretta looks confident and poised, almost regal. Photograph courtesy of the Dr. Carl R. Gross Collection, Moorland-Spingarn Research Center, Howard University.

and thrilling. In the less serious numbers for the softer and simpler ballads Mme. Jones is a pleasing person, and with an even temperament and other admirable graces that contribute so materially to her attractions of voice, she makes a figure that is away up in the rank of those whose dexterity and merit have forced them out of the ordinary file."[19]

McCorker's closing comments about Sissieretta demonstrate how proud African Americans were of her and her musical accomplishments. Her black audiences in the South must have been particularly proud when she presented herself elegantly on stage, dressed in all her finery and jewels, and sang music that touched the hearts of both white and black theater patrons. Sissieretta was graceful, intelligent, well-spoken, and professional, and she presented herself regally but was never haughty. She was a concert diva in the best sense of the word.

The Black Patti Troubadours opened 1903 in Waco, Texas, and spent the rest of January touring in Texas, Louisiana, Arkansas, Oklahoma Territory, and the Indian Territories. Most of February was spent doing one-night performances in Missouri, Kansas, Tennessee, Mississippi, and Alabama. The Troubadours performed in Tennessee, Kentucky, Ohio, and Indiana during March, playing Thursday evening, 19 March 2003, at Indianapolis's Park Theatre. A review in the *Indianapolis Freeman* said the Black Patti Troubadours was "full of stars," such as Black Patti, James Crosby, J. Ed. Green, Bobby Kemp, Leslie Triplett, and John Green. The show, which featured a circus skit, "was a departure from the stereotyped beach scene and boarding house gag, with its fast set of sports, etc." The reviewer, apparently familiar with Sissieretta's previous engagements in Indianapolis, gave her 1903 appearance lukewarm praise and suggested her repertoire had become stale: "M. Sissieretta Jones is holding her own, quite herself, singing with feeling. She has a fine stage appearance, makes up but very little, has a graceful tilt when she ambles off the stage, that is quite bewitching; it helps to get her back. She is becomingly modest and the barely discernible vein of 'swellery' makes her 'taky.' She has added nothing of note to her repertoire, still singing 'Miserere,' as the piece de resistance. Her Suwanee River was good and sweet, as well as good and old. The selection from 'Martha' and the waltz song, were prettily rendered, but seemed to lack the effectiveness of the finales of the past season."[20]

This description suggests Sissieretta may have stopped putting much energy into updating her repertoire and might be coasting on her star status. She may have become weary after seven seasons on the road and lost some of her energy. Or Sissieretta may have just had an off night in Indianapolis and failed to generate the excitement she had in previous performances there. Regardless of her somewhat tired repertoire, the theater critic still found the thirty-five-year-old singer attractive and her performance entertaining.

The Troubadours toured in Pennsylvania and Ohio during April and spent most of May doing extended runs in cities such as Philadelphia, Baltimore, Atlantic City, and Brooklyn. The company closed its seventh season in New York City the first week of June. Sissieretta once again returned to Providence for the summer. While there she probably read, with interest, an article in the *Indianapolis Freeman* (27 June 1903) by black theater critic Sylvester Russell, who gave her divorced husband, David, half the credit for her success. Russell's article, "Why the Great Singers Are Declining," was about "Negro" singers being unable to make a name for themselves and earn a decent wage for their singing abilities. He said that few if any managers were willing to promote good black singers. He used Sissieretta's rise to fame as an example of what it took to reach prominence.

In days when the Negro race was supporting its own female concert singers, not one of these women could get a reasonable hearing from combination managers. Sissieretta Jones, whose divorced husband must be given one-half the credit for her success, was untiring in his efforts to get her the altogether-to-be-desired hearing that would make her famous in her own country.

After they had toured the West Indies and found favor, on their return to America their chance came by accident. The New Yorkers wanted to see a big cakewalk at Madison Square Garden. They needed a prima donna. Dick Jones saw at once the opportunity of his life to bring his wife before the people. He succeeded. From the day of the Madison Square Garden jubilee Black Patti's name has been a household word throughout the entire world. After that memorial night, the great cantatrice was besieged by managers of every description. This is to illustrate that if there is no opportunity presented the best singer in the world of any race is shut out.[21]

Russell said good management opportunities for other African American singers, both men and women, were unavailable. He praised managers John W. Isham and Fred J. Piper, both of whom were dead, as having helped advance black women vocalists such as Mme. Flowers, Madah Hyer, Mattie Wilkes, Margaret Scott, and others. As for men, Russell said, Black Patti's managers, Voelckel and Nolan, helped champion Lloyd Gibbs, who later joined Bob Cole and Billy Johnson. Most managers of "colored shows," Russell said, paid black male singers poorly and did little or nothing to promote them.[22]

Sissieretta could indeed count herself lucky to have become a nationally known star who was earning a good living doing what she loved—singing. Whether she gave any credit to her ex-husband for that success is unknown. She was fortunate to have competent, steady managers such as Voelckel and Nolan who believed strongly in advertising and promoting the Troubadours as well as investing in talented entertainers, eye-catching costumes, and attractive scenery. Season after season the managers reaped the rewards for their efforts with excellent ticket sales and strong bookings to make for a full touring schedule.

1903–1904 Season

The eighth season (1903–4) of the Black Patti Troubadours began in Elizabeth, New Jersey, on 1 August. After five performances in cities and towns in New York and New Jersey, the Troubadours spent a week (8–15 August) in Harlem, where they opened the season for the New Star Theatre at 107th

Street and Lexington Avenue. This season's show, an updated version of the one Bob Cole had written during the last season, had the same name— "Darktown's Circus Day." The show was enhanced and expanded by J. Ed. Green, the stage manager and performer who had been with the Troubadours for one season. Many in the cast were holdovers as well. In addition to changes in the opening comedy sketch, the olio was updated to include Mack Allen on the slack wire performing ten new tricks; Billy Nichols as mimic; Nettie Goff, a lady trombonist; and Sissieretta, with Billy Ward and Georgia Dobbs, in a new sketch called "Life in the Philippines." This sketch, which came during the second part of the show, depicted a realistic tent scene "embellished by a ladies quartet of Red Cross nurses." The operatic third part of the show, with special new scenery and costumes, featured Sissieretta; Sarah Green, contralto; Ada Robinson, alto; James E. Worles, tenor; Anthony D. Byrd, baritone; James P. Reed, basso; and a chorus consisting of the rest of the company. Voelckel, once again, traveled with the company, and Nolan continued as advance agent. H. D. Collins served as assistant manager, and J. A. Raynes as musical director. Sarah Green, the contralto, acted as wardrobe mistress and assistant to Sissieretta, and J. Ed. Green directed the entire performance.[23] J. Ed. Green had successfully managed farce comedies in Memphis, where Voelckel and Nolan had first hired him. Before his work in Memphis, he had been vocal director with the show *South before the War* and interlocutor and stage manager with the Georgia Minstrels, and he had helped write and produce *Queen of the Jungle*, featuring Mamie Flowers. Green, also known as the "Bronze Chesterfield," was a composer as well.[24]

After the Troubadours closed their week's run at the New Star Theatre, they played in Albany, 17–19 August, at Harmanus Bleecker Hall, the largest theater in the city. On the final night of the three-day engagement, two thousand people attended, including theater critic Sylvester Russell, who wrote about the show in his 19 September column in the *Indianapolis Freeman*. Although the one-act farce comedy, "Darktown's Circus Day," was not Bob Cole's best piece of writing, Russell said, it did show that Cole understood "how to put a circus on a theater stage." The farce included Will A. Cooke, Billy Ward, and William Hallback, a newcomer from Mississippi. Leslie Triplett played an Irish policeman. Russell commended his dialect and the way he handled the part by not overdoing it but said it would have been better to have a "coon" cop. "White characters have no business in a Negro comedy, not if we desire to be genuine in our own work. A funny 'coon' cop would be quite as pleasant if anybody had wit enough to give such a character a breath of life."

Russell highlighted Georgia Dobbs's and Ida Forsyne's dancing and complemented Anthony Byrd's acting. When it came to describing Sissieretta's performance, he had high praise for the show's star. He said she appeared on stage dressed in a "costly pink cashmere gown, cut low," with a heavy diamond broach in the center and with small diamonds in her ears. She received her annual large reception from the Albany audience as she walked to the footlights and sang a very difficult "echo song to the responsive echos of a flute oblegato [*sic*]." Russell said Sissieretta's trills and "shakes were made with the same brilliancy and artistic methods that has marked her singing in the past." She was encored several times. "Mme. Jones having demonstrated to the world that she is the greatest singer of her race need not resort any longer to the most difficult class of music merely to show what she has already proven. She is still a young woman and her excellently cultivated voice should last for many years if not over taxed. In one scene in the opera she wore a startling white silk, printed at points with large pink roses and covered with the most expensive quality of delicate lace."

The chief criticism Russell had for the show that evening was the "distressingly bad" Bleecker Hall orchestra, which was "loud and mechanical." The critic said, "It is high time for managers to make a crusade on musicians and spoil the unions if necessary if they cannot succeed in supplying the public with real music." Russell said the company's musical director should not allow the various orchestras that would play with the Troubadours during the season to play loud during the opera or to hurry up this section of the show. Instead the audience should hear the four main voices of the operatic selections above the chorus and the orchestra. He urged musicians to remember that "a rare voice is a delicate human organ, and not a steam caliope [*sic*]." Russell said, "This cruel assault upon singers and a suffering public is a bleeding shame. That Grand Opera has at last been accepted and is now appreciated is one reason why its performances should be kept up to the standard by any organization that produces it. If this advice is not regarded, and especially in the rendition of the sextette, the opera may as well end in a camp meeting."[25]

Russell's complimentary comments about Forsyne's dancing were typical of the kind of notoriety she had been receiving in recent years. Born in 1883 in Chicago, she joined the Troubadours in October 1899 when she was sixteen and toured with them until 1905.[26] Her starting pay with the Troubadours was fifteen dollars a week, and her first role was to push a baby carriage across the stage and sing a lullaby, "You're Just a Little Nigger but You're Mine All Mine." During her years with the Troubadours, she learned how to dance by watching others and ultimately earned rave reviews for her dancing and her cakewalk performances. She also sang in the chorus during the opera section of the show. Years later, in the 1960s, she told authors Marshall and Jean Stearns (*Jazz Dance: A Story of American Vernacular Dance*) that no one in the Troubadour company had been trained to sing opera, but they had been told to sing loudly behind Black Patti. "We all stood in a row behind her and yelled our heads off, belting out our own version of how each opera should go, and I used to think the sound was wonderful," Forsyne said.[27] The young dancer went on to a successful career in Europe and then in Russia. She returned to the United States in 1914, toured some with singers Sophie Tucker and Bessie Smith in the 1920s, and had minor film roles in 1933 and 1936. Forsyne died on 19 August 1983 in Brooklyn.

Forsyne was not the only performer who gained fame while traveling with the Troubadour show or learned their trade and became famous after leaving the show for other show business opportunities. The list started with Bob Cole, who wrote and performed in the first Troubadour show before leaving in 1897. He eventually joined with J. Rosamund Johnson and his brother James Weldon Johnson to write songs and musical comedy shows. Later Cole and Rosamund Johnson left musical comedies and became a famous vaudeville act before Cole died from drowning, "which may have been a suicide," on 2 August 1941.[28] Another singer and dancer who started with the Troubadours in 1896 and went on to make a name for herself was Aida Overton, who married entertainer George Walker, of the famous Williams and Walker duet, sometime in 1899. She became the first black female choreographer and was regarded during her lifetime as the best black female dancer. She died in New York in 1914 at the age of thirty-four.[29] Then there was Ernest Hogan, already well known before he joined the Troubadours, who went on to a highly successful career in the theater after he left the Troubadours in 1899. The Black Patti Troubadours proved to be a training ground and stepping-stone for many talented performers and continued in that role for many years.

With a successful opening of their 1903–4 season behind them, the Troubadours headed south, where they planned to spend nearly 150 days that season—the longest amount of time the company had spent in the South. Business must have been good in this region for Voelckel and Nolan to spend so much time there. While in Atlanta during the Troubadours' 21–23 September engagement, two cast members were married—Allie T. Gilliam, who played the role of a tramp, Handy Andy, and Georgia Dobbs, part of the Ward and Dobbs dance team. Cast members Ida Forsyne and Lavinia Henderson were bridesmaids, and James Worles acted as best man. Sissieretta, Voelckel, Nolan, and music director J. A. Haynes "showered the young pair" with presents and congratulations at a reception held at the Vendome Hotel that went on into the late hours.[30]

While touring in the South, the Troubadours were successful and played to mostly large audiences, "not only receiving the patronage of the colored population but the whites as well," according to a report filed in the *Indianapolis Freeman* by a cast member serving as the troupe's correspondent to the newspaper. "This distinction is not enjoyed by all companies of this type," he added. The fifteen men in the company who were Elks enjoyed two events while in the South. The first was a "sumptuous repast" on 5 November in Selma, Alabama, hosted by the local Elks lodge, and the second was an Elk banquet two weeks later in Birmingham. But not all experiences were genial, such as the attack on Leslie Triplett on 11 November in West Point, Mississippi. Triplett, who played the Afro-Irish policeman in the show, was attacked and injured by a "mob of white hoodlums."[31]

As Sissieretta was performing in Mississippi, her mother, Henrietta Joyner, married Daniel Crenshaw, a cook, in Providence on 12 November 1903. He listed his age on their marriage certificate as thirty, and Sissieretta's mother said she was forty, which could not have been true, since Sissieretta was thirty-five years old at that time. Henrietta, who had reported in the 1870 federal census that she was twenty-two, in the 1880 federal census that she was thirty-five years old, and in the 1910 census that she was sixty, must have been somewhere in her mid-fifties when she married Crenshaw. The couple planned to live at the Wheaton Street home Sissieretta bought and shared with her mother during summers.

Sissieretta and the Troubadours spent December playing at least twenty-two one-night stands in the states of Illinois, Tennessee, Arkansas, Mississippi, Louisiana, and Texas, including a show at the Opera House in Lake Charles, Louisiana, on Christmas Day. Sometime during the month, J. Ed. Green, the Troubadours' stage manager, left the show and moved to St. Louis. No mention of his reasons for leaving appeared in the entertainment newspapers. Green would go on to have an impressive career in show business, writing songs and two unproduced plays before serving as managing director of the black-owned Pekin Theatre in Chicago. He died in February 1910 at the age of thirty-seven.[32]

As the Black Patti Troubadour railcar wound its way from Louisiana to Texas, the cast of the show likely read Russell's annual review of the stage in the *Indianapolis Freeman* (26 December 1903). The black theater critic lamented the lack of anything new on the stage, although he said several black playwrights had written unsuccessful melodramas. Russell said comedy was the only "class of negro plays that will ever be first in demand," but no new or original comedy plays had been produced. "There has been nothing funny to laugh at this season." Russell went on to mention opera among black performers, praising Theodore Drury's efforts in the field. He encouraged Drury to produce an "all-colored company" this season and make stage history. Turning his attention to the Black Patti Troubadours, Russell encouraged them to sing the best operatic choruses as often as they could. He praised Troubadour tenor Worles and predicted the singer would improve with careful training.

As for Sissieretta, Russell said she had the "distinction of being the first colored star who has ever succeeded in commanding a distinguished white audience in the lower portion of theaters in the Southern States." He went on to say, "this is no particular compliment to a woman who has sang [*sic*] in New York's most exclusive set and in Mrs. Astor's private parlor for one thousand dollars."[33] Although this may have been true, given the way African Americans were treated in the South in those days, Sissieretta's popularity with white theatergoers was noteworthy. Her prominence in the South among both black and white audiences was reflected in the Troubadours' 1903–4 touring schedule. The company spent most of September, October, November, and December of 1903 in southern or southwestern states and planned to spend part of January, most of March, and a good bit of April 1904 in those regions.

Voelckel and Nolan were fortunate to have a star such as Sissieretta who was well regarded in the South, because it was one of a few regions of the country where the theater business was healthy that season, according to a report in the *New York Dramatic Mirror*. Although the report focused mostly on the white theatrical business, the findings were likely true of black entertainment as well. The report said business had been "remarkably poor" in the East and "very bad" in New York City. Conditions were about the same in the Midwest, although it was improving in the Far West and good in the Pacific Coast region, the Northwest, the South, and the Southwest. One of the reasons given for poorer business in the East was the booking system that sent more one-night shows to small towns, which could not support that many attractions. Also the Theatrical Syndicate had a policy in large cities such as New York City of charging the same ticket prices for all shows that they charged for first-class shows even though all the shows were not first-class entertainment. Business was better in the West and South, the *Mirror* article said, because those two regions were "a year or two behind the general deterioration of theatre offerings, as the plays they usually see are one or two seasons old."[34]

Touring Texas in January turned out to be fun for the cast and quite lucrative for Sissieretta. Citizens of Houston, San Antonio, Greenville, Dallas, Gainesville, and Sherman, Texas, gave the cast receptions, Mexican dinners, and soirees to show their appreciation. Sissieretta received many costly gifts, including "one sable fox muff, one gold-handled umbrella, one cut glass powder box, one silver jewel case, one gold thimble, one silver sugar bowl, one handsome diamond ring set with thirty diamonds valued at $450, and others too numerous to mention."[35] If Sissieretta's admirers in other states she visited were as generous as those in Texas, the popular vocalist must have brought home many valuable treasures at the end of each season.

After leaving Texas the troupe moved on to the Indian Territories in mid-January, where they played to a "capacity house" in South McAlester on

19 January. Much to their surprise, the Troubadours experienced a "crush of women" at the show that evening, which one cast member described in a column in the *Indianapolis Freeman:* "At 6:30 P.M. S.R.O. [Standing Room Only] was being sold, and at 7 P.M. a women's riot occurred. No more S.R.O. tickets could be sold and an officer was called to clear the lobby, as the crowd continued to increase. Many speculators had exhausted their supply of tickets, and, regardless of the warning that no tickets would be honored, the purchasers of same swarmed to the doors and demanded admittance; force won and they succeeded in entering. The officers tried in vain to clear the lobby, the assistant treasurer called for the reserves, and only after a ten minute battle could the pressing crowd be induced to leave. For such a crush to occur after the heavy holiday business was a great surprise."[36]

The rest of the season was uneventful except for the four performances the Troubadours gave during their three-day stay in Havana on 19–21 March. This was the first time the troupe had traveled to Cuba. They played at the Great Tacón Theatre, which was later renamed the Grand Nacional Theatre. The company reportedly grossed about sixteen thousand dollars for their four performances at "one of the three grandest amusement temples in the world, taking rank with the grand opera houses in Paris and Seville."[37] The theater had 92 boxes, 552 orchestra chairs, 100 seats in both the first and second balconies, 500 seats in the first gallery, and 500 in the second, bringing the total seating capacity to about 2,000. In addition there was standing room for another 1,000 people.[38] Just how many people attended the four Troubadour performances is unknown; however, an article in the *Fort Collins (Colo.) Weekly Courier* said the gross receipts for the Troubadours' three-day run were "larger than that awarded to Adelina Patti, Sarah Bernhardt, and the Grand Italian Opera Company for the same number of performances."[39] Sissieretta and her Troubadours were likely awestruck by this magnificent venue, especially after having performed in some of the small theaters and auditoriums they had visited around the United States. This was the only time Sissieretta and the Troubadours went to Cuba. When their short Cuban tour concluded, the company sailed to Key West, Florida, where they performed for two days, 23–24 March.

The thirty-five-member Troubadour cast finished their 1903–4 season in New York City in late May. During their forty-two-week season, the company had visited 190 cities and towns and given 336 performances, with gross annual receipts of $255,200.[40] While they had been on the road, the world had changed in small and large ways. Orville and Wilbur Wright had their first successful flight in an engine-powered airplane on 17 December 1903. The longest movie to date, a twelve-minute silent film, *The Great Train Robbery*, debuted. The first coast-to-coast crossing of the United States in an automobile was completed in sixty-five days in 1903. Theodore Roosevelt won the November 1904 presidential election. In addition work began on the Panama Canal in 1904, author James Barrie published *Peter Pan,* and composer Antonin Dvořák died on 1 May 1904.[41] Sissieretta returned to Rhode Island to spend the summer with her mother and stepfather, while Voelckel and Nolan began planning for the Troubadours' ninth season.

1904–1905 SEASON

Rehearsals for the Troubadours' new show, "Looney Dreamland," began 11 July 1904, in Asbury Park. Dreamland, one of three amusement parks at New York's Coney Island, was the setting for the new farce. Once again Bob Cole wrote the new musical comedy and staged the entire show. John Rucker, who had been the chief comedian with the Troubadours during the 1901–2 season, was rehired. In his preview of the upcoming theatrical season, Sylvester Russell, "easily the most severe black theater critic of the era,"[42] said the Black Patti Troubadours were at the top of the entertainment list. He praised managers Voelckel and Nolan for "constancy, stability, and honesty of purpose" and predicted that Sissieretta would sing new and wonderful songs this season. She is the "picture of health and admiration, if one should judge by her latest photograph," Russell said.[43]

While the Troubadours were rehearsing for opening night, John J. Nolan visited the offices of the *New York Dramatic Mirror* to talk about contract jumpers while he was in New York City to institute legal proceedings against several performers who had violated their contracts. He said these performers "deserted us after we had gone to the expense of investing thousands of dollars in printing and other expenses in connections with our production." Nolan told the newspaper, which printed his comments on 30 July, that the company had suffered "serious losses through contracts made with performers who 'welched' at the last moment, leaving us at the time rehearsals start without a word of warning, to accept contracts or engagements with other managers." Nolan said he and Voelckel would have the law track down these contract jumpers (whom he did not name), regardless of where they went, whether to Europe or California. In addition, if they found other managers involved in getting these performers to violate their contracts, Voelckel and Nolan planned to prosecute them as well. "It is our intention to fulfill and live up to every contract that we enter into, and this has been our infallible purpose during all the years that we have been associated with the management of stage productions. The time has come now for us to act in self-defence and punish those who are unfaithful to their written and binding obligations."[44] Nolan's comments provide insight into the kind of businessmen he and Voelckel were—tough but fair, and committed to protecting their interests while making their show the best it could be.

After several weeks of rehearsals, the Black Patti Troubadours opened their new season on Friday night, 29 July 1904, to a crowd of seven thousand people at the Asbury Avenue Casino in Asbury Park. "Looney Dreamland" was reported to have cost more than ten thousand dollars. Every seat in the auditorium was sold hours before the performance, and many people were turned away at the doors. When the auditorium opened, the crowd was so large that the entire police force was called out to maintain order. "The crowded conditions of the vast auditorium and the spacious board walk approaches to the Casino at 8 o'clock was [sic] so serious that Mayor Tenbrook felt it incumbent to take personal command of the situation." The new show, which was deemed a "tremendous hit," reportedly brought in four thousand dollars in gross receipts for the evening.[45]

About a week later, the show opened for a week's run (8–13 August) at the New Star Theatre in New York City. The Troubadours earned a bundle of free publicity in the city's main entertainment newspaper, the *Dramatic Mirror*, when a white, female columnist with the paper, who went by the name of her column, "The Matinee Girl," decided to "drag" her Aunt Jane to see a Troubadours performance. She and her aunt boarded a Madison Avenue open car and rode northward "in a crowd so disposed as to color that it looked like a checker board. White jump black, black jump white, and no king row." Upon reaching the New Star Theatre, the Matinee Girl saw "elegant life-size posters, chiefly in red and yellow, of course, with black predominating." She said every woman, regardless of age, color, or marital status, "turned green at the sight of Black Patti's diamonds." Inside the theater the Matinee Girl reported seeing the same black-white checkerboard audience, with everyone happy. She said "Looney Dreamland" was "quite crazy" and "lively," with plenty of action and no chance of becoming bored. She praised the comedians, particularly John Rucker, for their ability to make everyone laugh. The Matinee Girl was also impressed with Sissieretta's performance of "Swanee River." "The song seems to be hers. I've heard nearly everyone sing it—Clara Louise Kellogg, Lilian Nordica, and the light complexioned Patti herself—but the song will always seem to me to belong exclusively to the stout negro woman in white who, her face grayish under the limelight, sang it with tears and longing and heartbreak in her voice."[46] Sissieretta's emotional delivery of "Swanee River" must have been something to witness, considering that someone as experienced as the Matinee Girl was so moved as to place Sissieretta's rendition of the song above the performances of the three famous prima donnas she mentioned in her column. This song had worked well for Sissieretta for many years and would remain a part of her repertoire for years to come.

The Matinee Girl wrote about her experiences in her 27 August 1904 column, where she posed two questions to her readers: "Wouldn't it be great fun

to have a negro theatre in New York? A theatre where negro companies produce negro plays, with negro music?" She went on to explain, "My motive is
purely one of pleasure. I decline to discuss color lines or race restrictions or
finances. Why do people go miles to see a negro camp-meeting or cross the
city to go to a negro church? Because the ardent temperament and childlike
enthusiasm of the black race amuse them—because over-civilization sighs for
the unveneered naturalism." The Matinee Girl invited Troubadours manager
Nolan to respond to her comments and included his remarks in her column.
Nolan told her that "colored people" would not support a theater for black
audiences alone because they want to go where white audiences go and see
what they enjoy. He said that someone had tried a black theater in New
Orleans and it had failed. The Matinee Girl said it may not have worked in
New Orleans, but New York was different. "A theatre where colored talent
plays to white and colored audiences, it seems to me, is worth experiment."
She said there was plenty of black talent to "furnish us talent enough for a
long and jolly season." She closed her column with an offensive, condescending, yet apparently well-meaning comment. "Whatever may be the shortcom-
ings of the colored race, it has the chief element of fascination. It is intensely
alive."47 It would not be many years before black-owned and black-managed
theaters were established successfully in many cities around the country such
as Chicago, Memphis, and New Orleans.

The Troubadours' next stop was a three-day engagement (15–17 August) at
Harmanus Bleecker Hall in Albany. Once again the troupe earned more press
notoriety—this time from Russell's lengthy and detailed review of the Troubadour show, which he described as combination of opera, comedy, and
vaudeville. Russell said Cole's opening skit, "Looney Dreamland," introduced
the "strongest set of colored comedians ever brought together in one performance." The skit featured Rucker, a former minstrel man, who demonstrated
his ability to play a legitimate comedy part. Anthony Byrd played Dinah Jones,
Rucker's wife in the skit, and wore a dress for the part. Russell said the most
interesting feature of the skit was the "Big Indian Chief," the "first original
development of Indian song music, not in rag-time, by Cole and Rosamond
Johnson. Negro actors make elegant Indians so everything in that line was
perfection." As for the second part of the show, the olio, where the specialty
acts performed, Russell said it was much stronger than in the past. One
number in the olio was called "Plantation Pastimes," which featured "cotton
picking, singing, and dancing." One wonders how the African American performers felt about enacting cotton-picking scenes and singing southern songs
associated with plantation days and slavery. Voelckel and Nolan apparently
employed these themes to appeal to white southern audiences. Russell said
Ida Forsyne, "the greatest dancer of her race," performed a number in the olio

that showed she "cannot be excelled by any dancer of the same style in America." She was followed by two expert roller skaters, one of whom skated between a set of electric lights on toe wheels, and then by Harry Kraton, a "hoop controller." Russell was most impressed with Sissieretta's performance of operatic songs and popular ballads during the olio: "Black Patti, who has taken off weight and thereby added youthfulness, appeared and sang a cavatina so full of thrills and shakes as to render only the most exacting technical skill invaluable to perfection. Her voice is better than last season and in view of new contestants, she is showing us what she really can do in sustaining the reputation of being the greatest female singer of her race. She was attired in a very handsome well-fitted white satin, embroidered with Iris pointed lace and beaded spangles, and wore her favorite large diamond brooch. For encores she sang 'You Can't Pick Plums From My Plum Tree,' and 'Swanee River' with an invisible chorus."

Russell praised the third part of the Troubadour show—the opera selections. He said it "surpassed anything presented within the past five years" and included selections from *Orpheus in the Underworld* and Sissieretta singing, "Say to Him" from *The Grand Duchess*. Russell said Sissieretta "wore a pale blue silk dress of startling beauty without diamonds. Her obligato [*sic*] airs in these final scenes blended harmoniously with a chorus that was well balanced. All her high and higher notes were heard distinctly above both chorus and orchestra just as they should be and reflected great credit upon Trevor L. Corwell, a very promising young conductor indeed."

Russell closed his review with a comment on the racial makeup of the audience and questioned why managers in other theaters in the North did not allow mixed race seating. He also predicted great success for the Troubadour show this season. "The aristocracy turned out each night and filled several of the best boxes and some of the elite of the colored race of Albany sat in the most desirable orchestra seats unnoticed," he said. "If this is the case in Albany there would be no objections in New York or anywhere else in the North except the managers, themselves, draw the line. This show could easily run on Broadway in New York. It is the best company Voelckel and Nolan ever had, and may not be excelled by any of the all-comedy companies this season."[48]

The Troubadours spent the rest of August and first part of September touring cities and towns in New York, Pennsylvania, and Ohio before arriving for their annual engagement at the Park Theatre (19–21 September) in Indianapolis. During the Troubadours' three-day stay, the *Indianapolis Freeman* published several articles about the show and Sissieretta. Critic J. D. Howard commended Voelckel and Nolan for providing a "clean" and entertaining show and spending their money to hire the "best available people who interpret almost faultlessly the bunch of nonsense and horse play Bob Cole has spliced together for them." He highlighted the comedy work of Rucker, the dancing of Forsyne and Mattie Phillips, the singing of Sarah Green, and the hoop work of Kraton. He saved his most enthusiastic words for Sissieretta. "The Madame is still the wonder of the musical world. It is simply marvelous how this woman, practically 'barn storming' as she holds up singing two performances a day. But she does and strange to relate maintains her same sweet intonations and flexibility of range," Howard said. "I do not think this century will ever know her like again. Her 'passing out' will record the adieu of one of the greatest singers of her time."[49]

While the Troubadours were in Indianapolis, a friend of Rucker's, W. Milton Lewis, got the comedian to introduce him to Sissieretta so he could interview her and write a piece about the star for the *Freeman* (8 October 1904). When he arrived Sissieretta was dressed for the stage and looked "splendid and pomp" as Madame Pompadour. "But allow me to correct the impression that she was in any way haughty. She was most genial and pleasing, received me with the kindliest attention," Lewis said. Sissieretta told him she was suffering from a cold and was waiting for a carriage to take her to the doctor's office. "Manager Voelckel showed his appreciation of the singer by the attention he paid her in seeing to her physical welfare," Lewis said. Sissieretta told Lewis that singing twice a day was "exacting" and that she had decided not to appear in the olio section of the show during the afternoon performance but only in the operatic section at the end. Ultimately she did not sing at all for the evening performance. During his talk with Sissieretta, the subject of her age (then thirty-seven) came up: "In the conversation it was brought out that many people thought the madam was well along in years, something like 50 or 60. She plainly asked with her eyes, 'What think ye my pencil shover?' I evaded the question as too direct and told her in a burst of enthusiasm that she was a good looking woman. And what would she care about the doubtful thing age, if she were good looking? I told her so because it was the truth and because I knew she would like to hear it. And while I honestly thought her a woman of from 35 to 45 she appeared that afternoon from 28 to 35. I was afraid to give out a verdict since she may have hoped to have appeared from 20 to 30."

Lewis described Sissieretta as being in her "physical zenith." He said she was a "comely looking brown woman of the robust order, but not stout. She is thoroughly feminine in her actions moving with the agility, ease, and grace of a tiger." Lewis said she was "regal" both on and off the stage and full of "dignity and grace," adding that she was a "charming woman of fine physical proportionment." As for her singing, Lewis said she was a "warm, heartfelt" singer rather than a "scholarly" vocalist: "Her voice fits her for opera owing to quality but she must have straight parts to be eminently successful; she needs time to throw soul into music; rapid passages are generally too fleet for her; it takes the coldly classical to do that and that class is generally feelingless and hence not popular. When the two or three qualities are found in the same individual, soul, tuneful voice and 'mechanical' ability then the great singer is achieved—such was Adelina Patti."[50]

The Troubadours spent October through December performing in Kentucky, Arkansas, Mississippi, Louisiana, Texas, Oklahoma Territory, Colorado, Wyoming, Washington, Oregon, British Columbia, and California. While they were playing in Portland at the Empire Theatre, Russell published his annual stage review of all the black shows, comedians, singers, and composers of the day. This year's article brought a plea from Russell for a return to old-time jubilee music. "It is the only savior of a music that must be developed into a higher grade of schooling than rag-time," he said, adding that although no white person can sing it, they will be trying to do it if blacks do not reclaim it. Russell suggested that Voelckel and Nolan could introduce some jubilee singing into their Troubadour show and that it could be incorporated into vaudeville. "It could even play havoc with rag-time," he said. In modernizing jubilee singing, he said, the "use of smutty words like 'nigger' and the sacred name of the Deity in comics should be abolished." Russell, like other prominent African Americans in the theatrical world, had begun campaigning for black entertainers to stop using the word *nigger* on the stage and in songs. The black theater critic then focused on the various black shows playing that season. He said the Black Patti Troubadours held second place in the world of comedy and "first honors" as singers. "Mme. Sissieretta Jones (Black Patti) who has acquired the art of perfect singing by practical service still heads the list of great sopranos. When we hear another woman who can sing as she did in Madison Square Garden, New York, to make her present enviable reputation then we will be willing to give over the laurels, but we haven't heard one yet," Russell said. "I here deny that Mme. Jones has ever sang [*sic*] a ragtime coon song. She once sang a Negro ballad and can add it to her credit."[51]

By the time the Troubadours left California on 15 February 1905, the company had played in twenty-two cities and towns in that state. Most of their appearances had been one-night stands, with week-long runs in Los Angeles and San Francisco. Once they left California, the troupe went to Nevada, Utah, Wyoming, and then back to Texas at the end of February. The Troubadours spent most of the rest of the 1904–5 season touring the South, where they played to many top-heavy audiences. In all they spent about seventy-nine days in the South. One of these appearances, in Charleston, South Carolina, at the Academy of Music (11 April 1905), demonstrates the kind of reception the Troubadours often experienced in southern cities and towns. The local newspaper, the *News and Courier*, previewed the upcoming show and said, "Their happy revival of the sweet melodies of the South, reminiscent of antebellum days, the plantation, the cotton fields and the levee has been very popular." The day after the show played, the newspaper review said the audience had consisted mostly of "colored people" who enjoyed the comedy and music "immensely." The black audience probably appreciated seeing black entertainers making good in their profession and admired the ever-popular Sissieretta, but they likely did not have fond thoughts about plantation days. The newspaper said, "The company is one of the best of the kind and the performance given is entirely satisfactory."[52]

At the close of the 1904–5 season, Russell wrote about the successful and prosperous season the Troubadours had just completed. He singled out Rucker and Forsyne as "prime favorites" with audiences during the year. Russell took special note of the troupe's success in the South: "It is no vain glory to say that to win the people of the south with a modern band of colored Thespians is something. It is something which has not yet been achieved by any other style of colored performances except minstrelsy. But southern society must understand that when Black Patti (Madame Sissieretta Jones) sings to them, it is nothing more than a common thing in her history as she has been heard in the richest and most exclusive circles in America and Europe."[53]

1905–1906 Season

The 1905–6 tour marked the tenth season the Black Patti Troubadours had toured since their debut performance on 10 September 1896 in Pittsfield, Massachusetts. Since then the company had crisscrossed the United States and Canada, bringing their music and comedy to hundreds of cities and towns. The Troubadours had become regular visitors in the southern states and had played a number of times to large audiences in western states, including those along the Pacific Coast. Other shows had come and gone, but the Troubadours, starring Sissieretta, remained a staple each season. The Troubadour show reflected the times in that it evolved from a musical farce and three-part show patterned after minstrel shows into more of a musical comedy and variety show. Black show business had changed during the ten seasons the Troubadours had been on the road. It had become more professional as African Americans who aspired to the stage had more opportunities to learn their trade while working in well-run shows such as the Troubadours. Also many black shows were beginning to employ opening comedy sketches with stronger story lines rather than relying on a farce with a thin story line whose main purpose was to introduce the cast and support various musical numbers. Another change was a crusade by black theater critics and some black entertainers and playwrights to eliminate racial epithets on the stage.

When the Troubadours first came on the scene, the words *coon* and *nigger* were freely used in both black and white speech. These words were a holdover from minstrel days, when white actors used blackface to imitate African Americans. As black entertainers began to portray themselves on the stage, they continued to use these derogatory terms. By 1905, however, Russell was calling for an end to the use of insulting racial terms, particularly *nigger*. That same year he interviewed entertainer and composer Bob Cole, who told Russell he was going to push to see the term *coon* eliminated when describing African Americans. "The word 'coon' is very insinuating and must soon be eliminated," Cole said. "The best class of white people in America abhor the word 'coon' and feel ashamed whenever they hear it used. In London we had found it used in a common slander."[54] When Russell asked Cole why, years ago, he had named his first show "A Trip to Coontown," Cole said softly that the time for that kind of name had passed. He said it was important to eliminate these derogatory and hurtful terms.

At some point during the first part of 1906, the New York music company M. Witmark and Sons published another *Songs as Sung by the Black Patti Troubadours,* this time containing songs likely performed during the 1905–6 season. Most of the music in the sixteen-page book was copyrighted in 1906, although some songs were dated 1905 and 1903. Of the twenty-two songs included in the 1906 music book, only one had lyrics written in dialect, whereas the previous Black Patti Troubadours' songbook, published in 1897 at the beginning of the coon song craze, had three songs written in dialect. Also the new songbook had only one song with the word *nigger* in it and three that contained *coon,* while the 1897 songbook, which contained Ernest Hogan's "All Coons Look Alike to Me," used these derogatory words in six songs. One of the songs, "Ole Man Moon," which Sissieretta sang during the "Scenes from the Southland" section of the show, contained *coon* in one line of the song's refrain. The word was used to refer to the moon. The line said, "Ole Man Moon! He is a great big coon. He'll pull yo' by de pigtail—make you holler—Ole Man Moon."[55] Voelckel and Nolan, aware of the push by Russell, Cole, and other prominent blacks to eliminate *coon* and *nigger* from songs and shows, likely realized they should refrain from using these racial epithets in the future. However, change came slowly. It would take several years before these words disappeared from Troubadour shows.

The Black Patti Troubadours opened the 1905–6 season to a standing-room-only crowd at the Casino Pier Theatre in Asbury Park on 2 August 1905. The show's opening skit had the same name as the year before, "Looney Dreamland," with some new musical numbers. Once again the show starred Sissieretta and featured Rucker. Sissieretta had a prominent part in the olio section of the show called "Scenes from the Southland," in which she sang "sweet old time melodies of the South." Her other major role in the show was to enact the role of Josephine in the "Pinafore Review," a condensed version of Gilbert and Sullivan's comic opera *H.M.S. Pinafore,* which had replaced the Operatic Kaleidoscope.[56]

The Troubadours headed south in early September, where they played for the opening of a new black-owned and black-operated theater in Jackson, Mississippi. The theater, which seated about two thousand people, opened in the same building that housed the African American–owned American Trust and Savings Bank. The American Theatre was established after the white-owned Century Theatre refused to book black troupes and made African American patrons use the fire escape to reach the gallery.[57] The American Theatre was one of a growing number of black-owned theaters becoming available to black entertainers. Sissieretta and the Troubadours must have been proud to be the first company to play in the new venue, where blacks could sit anywhere in the theater and were not confined to the balcony.

Seating African American theater patrons in the balcony, or "peanut gallery," in white-owned theaters was a well-established practice in the South—a practice that aroused the ire of a black newspaper editor in Atlanta, who wrote about it in the *New York Age* (12 October 1905). His article showed the conditions black theater patrons had to endure to attend shows. Black citizens had to walk through dark back alleys and doors to reach the balcony reserved for them. Even after reaching the balcony where they were supposed to sit, black theater patrons might find their seats taken by white theatergoers, and they would have to sit on the tobacco-stained aisle steps and sometimes on the floor. "Afro-American women in fine raiment and gaudy feathers were forced to sit bolt upright on the dirty floor because a few white men had taken seats in the place usually reserved for Afro-American patrons," the editor said. The editor could not believe African American women would do this. He said black people, who ought to know better and who should make a great show of race pride, "cheerfully enter the theaters by the alley route to hobnob with the denizens of the red light district and other undesirable characters. . . . It is a little funny that people will pay their good money to be treated this way." The editor said he understood black citizens were forced to ride in streetcars that enforced "Jim Crow" laws, but "for milady deliberately to dress up in her finest toggery and laces and to crown her head with that picture hat and adorn her feet with snow white shoes, knowing that she must push her way through a foul smelling back alley and up dingy stairs to find a resting place on tobacco smeared steps, is one of the inexplicable things of the period." The editor said there should be some "decent provision" for African Americans at southern theaters as blacks were generally "show-going" citizens and deserved better treatment.[58] He threatened to publish the names of

African Americans who continued to attend shows in this demeaning manner. His description of the balcony provides a clearer picture of what black audiences had to suffer to see shows such as the Black Patti Troubadours.

The Troubadours spent about eighty-six days in the South during the 1905–6 season. The majority of their southern performances occurred between the beginning of November 1905 and the first half of January 1906. By mid-January the troupe moved into Illinois and then on to Indiana, where they gave their annual performance in Indianapolis (12–14 February). As usual the *Indianapolis Freeman* gave the Troubadours' visit lots of coverage. Prior to the company's arrival, the newspaper announced their upcoming engagement and ran a large pen and ink drawing of Sissieretta seated in a chair as she held a long-stemmed rose and looked regal in a fancy gown adorned with lace. The caption under the drawing said the Troubadours, now in their tenth season, would perform at the Park Theatre.[59] A large advertisement about the show ran on the same page.

The Troubadours met with great success during their three-day engagement in Indianapolis, where they attracted many of the city's black citizens. W. Milton Lewis wrote a glowing review of the show for the *Freeman*. He said changes to the show from the previous season had greatly improved the performance. He particularly liked the way the show interspersed high and low comedy in the plantation scenes, and he thought the "Pinafore Review" provided another good opportunity for the players to show off their "individual work." Lewis said Sissieretta, who wore an elegant costume along with diamonds and pearls, sang ballads, plantation songs, and operatic selections and showed herself to be "the all around artist that she is." The show was "notably good" from start to finish, he said. "The management apparently has in mind the steady elevation of the Negro show to the point of individualism and merit that will simply characterize it as others of the same class."[60]

The Troubadours continued to earn high praise in the press as they traveled throughout Ohio and Pennsylvania in February and March. For example when the troupe played at the Empire Theatre in Pittsburgh (5–10 March), the *Pittsburgh Post* wrote, "Nothing seen in that house this season has surpassed this performance for genuine amusement. It is all music, singing and dancing, and of the best, too."[61] While the Troubadours were in Pittsburgh, the city where the world's first regular movie theater had opened in June 1905, a reporter for the *Pittsburgh Post* interviewed Sissieretta and wrote two articles about his talk with the famous singer. His first article concentrated on her voice and how it had retained its strength and "purity" during nearly twenty years on the stage. Asked how she preserved her "vocal organs," Sissieretta told the reporter she attributed "regular habits and general good health" to helping her maintain her vocal strength. The reporter said he found Sissieretta

*Sissieretta wearing a dark robe. Photograph courtesy of
the Dr. Carl R. Gross Collection, Moorland-Spingarn
Research Center, Howard University.*

most interesting to talk with because she was a woman "of wide experience,
thorough cultivation and a pleasing personality."[62]

The reporter's second article, titled "Has Sung around the World," discussed places where Sissieretta had sung and countries she would like to visit.
The writer wrongly stated Sissieretta had toured "entirely around the world"
three times, rather than describing her two tours of the West Indies and South
America in the late 1880s and her visit to Europe in 1895. The article included
Sissieretta's comments about the lack of racism in England and its colonies
and listed several countries where she would like to sing. She also spoke about
her appearance in London's Covent Garden during the early days of her career
in 1895:

> My life having been spent mostly in America and my greatest success
> having been achieved here, I of course enjoy singing in this country

more than any other. But outside of America I think England and the English provinces of India, and Australia and South Africa are the places I would prefer visiting were I to start on another world-girdling tour. There is not the slightest antipathy in the matter of color in England or its provinces.

My appearance in Covent Garden, London, was one of the most exalted triumphs of my career. There was a fine audience and women took bouquets from their corsages to throw upon the stage. And the curious thing about it all is that "Suwanee River" and the various Foster melodies were received with great enthusiasm.[63]

In March the Troubadours traveled throughout the eastern portion of Canada, performing in Toronto at the Majestic Theatre, 16–21 April. While there they learned of the catastrophic earthquake and devastating fire in San Francisco. The earthquake came at 5:13 A.M. on 18 April 1906 and was followed by a fire that lasted three days. The official death toll was seven hundred people, but some said the number of deaths was more likely in the thousands. A large part of the city was destroyed, including two theaters where Sissieretta and the Troubadours had performed over the years. It would be three years before the Troubadours returned to San Francisco.

After touring eastern Canada, the Troubadours worked their way through New York and Connecticut in May before their engagement at the American Theatre in New York City on 21–26 May. Sylvester Russell attended the 21 May performance to write about the close of the Troubadours' tenth season. The night he attended the show, the theater was crowded, with all the lower boxes and orchestra seats filled, and African Americans filling more than two-thirds of the balcony. Russell said John Rucker was wonderful, as was singer and dancer Mattie Phillips. The critic enjoyed the olio act of musicians Harry and Laura Prampin. Prampin played a horn while balancing it on his lips, and Laura performed several cornet solos. After the Prampins came the "Scenes from the Southland," staged by Al F. Watts. The solos and the choruses in this section "served to introduce" Sissieretta, Richard Barrett, and James P. Reed. Russell described this part of the show as well as the audience's reaction to Sissieretta on the anniversary celebration of her tenth year heading up the Black Patti Troubadours: "'Old Black Joe,' rendered by Mr. Reed, gratified the audience immensely because of the beauty of tone and depth of compass of his excellent bass voice, while Richard Barrett, a high baritone, displayed a voice of melody and sweetness and a method of using his voice that served him well in a serenade which brought Madam Jones to a cabin window in the garden spot of Virginia. Here Madam Jones sang, 'My Dear Southern Home,' and for encores she gave 'Old Man Moon,' as the moon arose in the garden, and

'Suwanee River' at the conclusion of which two beds of flowers were passed over the footlights to her as an anniversary gift. For the deafening applause which followed she sent out kisses, but would not sing any more, preferring to save her voice for the opera."[64]

For the final part of the show, the Troubadours presented a condensed version of *H.M.S. Pinafore.* The backdrop of the stage was made to look like the top deck of a ship with the lower part of a large sail hanging just above it. The women on the stage were dressed in long white or light-colored dresses and all wore large hats. Some of the men were dressed as officers, and others wore simple sailor suits.[65] Tenor Charles Bougia played Ralph, the lover, and contralto Jeanette Murphy Green played Hebe. Mamie Carter played a "fair" Buttercup, and John Green, as Dick Deadeye, was "quite entertaining," according to Russell. The theater critic saved most of his comments for Sissieretta's performance as Josephine, describing how she had finally become more comfortable playing a part while singing rather than just delivering a song as she stood on the stage: "Madam Sissieretta Jones (Black Patti), as Josephine, surprised everybody beyond expectations in having at last acquired the 'chic' of an operatic prima donna, and where her gestures were once awkward, she now indulges in real dramatic art. After she had rendered her principal solo, 'Sorry Her Lot, She Loved So Well,' to the few who are advanced in the language of music it was easy to discern why Black Patti is still the supreme cantatrice of her race. So perfect was she in her articulation that her diphthong enunciation carried the day in vocal significance. 'Farewell, My Own,' was also delivered with much sympathy and pathos. Singing in a role in 'Pinafore,' which has been heard so often by white prima donnas, shows how superior Black Patti's voice is to those who are really capable of judging. The maturity of this voice of continual sweetness, methodically schooled, means years to its preservation."[66]

Obviously Sissieretta's ten years performing operatic selections with the Troubadours had taught her more about acting and how to move about the stage while she was performing. It is interesting, however, that it took her ten years to perfect her acting ability to the point where Russell, who had watched her performances for many years, finally commented on her successful transition to "real dramatic art." Perhaps it was the staging of a single, although condensed, opera rather than the performance of various selections from a number of operas that helped Sissieretta get the feel for her character, Josephine, and inspired her to play this role more dramatically.

After the show Russell, by arrangement with Voelckel, went to Sissieretta's dressing room to interview her. Russell had known Sissieretta since her early concert years, and he had sung on stage during the jubilee at Madison Square Gardens "on the evening she made her New York–American reputation, when the critics hailed her as the greatest singer her race had produced." When Russell arrived at her dressing room door, Sissieretta, wearing a loose blue gown with designs in a darker color, said, "Why, Mr. Russell, how do you do? Are you never going to get old?" The critic said Sissieretta thanked him when he told her how superbly she had sung in the opera. "She spoke of the nervous strain of singing before so exacting a critic. I smiled approvingly and nodded yes," Russell wrote. He asked Sissieretta about the diamond brooch she wore in the opening scene of "Scenes from the Southland," which Russell described as a solid gold throat necklace studded with diamonds, clustered in a star that fitted close to her throat. Sissieretta said the necklace was a gift, but she did not identify who gave it to her. She told Russell her age, but he said he did not believe in revealing it to the public. Russell said Sissieretta was still young (thirty-eight at the time) and had kept her wonderful voice. "This fair daughter of Virginia actually grows handsomer every year," he said. Aware that Sissieretta's carriage driver was ready to take her away from the theater, Russell ended the interview, but not before Sissieretta had a chance to say to him, "Mr. Russell, don't be too hard on the actors in your criticism, will you?"

> It was one soft side of a good woman's nature that can reach the stony
> heart of any mean old sage critic living. So I promised her that hereafter
> I would not be quite so hard on the diminishing faults of Thespians.
> This of course means a great deal to actors in her class who have boldly
> walked right into the sharpest edges of the critic's sword. So this sweet
> woman whom Ernest Hogan speaks of as a Christian, has broken the
> soil that will bury much sharp criticism, with all its roots and branches.
> But if actors continue to act like children, who never had a father to
> chide them, what can we do? We must scold them a little of course. As
> we parted and signaled goodnight the Madam told me to be sure and
> visit her again.[67]

Sissieretta and the Troubadours played their final show of the season at Coney Island's Manhattan Beach Theatre on 30 May 1906. Sissieretta retired to Providence, while some of the Troubadour cast members spent part of their summer performing in a new company, the Dandy Dixie Minstrels, which Voelckel and Nolan had formed toward the end of the season. Plans called for Nolan to travel with the Dandy Dixie Minstrels next season while Voelckel would remain with the Black Patti Troubadours.

9

The Final Troubadour Years
1906–1909

1906–1907 Season

As the owners and managers of two shows—the Black Patti Troubadours and the new Dandy Dixie Minstrels—Voelckel and Nolan had their hands full as they began rehearsals for the 1906–7 season. Nolan began practice for the Dandy Dixie Minstrels on 23 July 1906 in Washington, D.C., at the black-owned Majestic Theater, while Voelckel started rehearsals for the Troubadours' eleventh season on the same day in Liberty, New York, at the Opera House. The Minstrels, a smaller company of black performers than the Troubadours, was a traditional minstrel show with an olio that included singing, dancing, a slack-wire performance, a comedy sketch, and an acrobatic number. John Rucker, the chief comedian of the Troubadours during the previous season, joined the Minstrels, and "Jolly" John Larkins, a vaudeville performer and actor, was hired as the comedy star of the Troubadours. Larkins played "King Jasper," the "Negro" king of Zululand, in the opening comedy sketch, "A Royal Coon." This season the final part of the Troubadours' show featured Sissieretta playing Germaine, the Lost Marchioness, in the chateau scene from the 1877 comic opera by Robert Jean Planquette, *The Chimes of Normandy*.[1]

The Troubadours, which Sylvester Russell described as "the leading attraction" traveling through the South,[2] planned to spend about ninety-six days in southern states, fifty-four days in the Southwest, and about thirty-five days in the West and Pacific Coast states. Between September and December, the Troubadours performed in Arkansas, Louisiana, Texas, Oklahoma Territory, the Indian Territories, and in several states in the Deep South. In early December, Sissieretta and the Troubadours received word of the sudden death of world-renowned singer Flora Batson. Batson, forty-six, died at her home in Philadelphia after a brief illness. She was born in Washington, D.C., and, like Sissieretta, moved to Rhode Island as a child. A long, front-page article in the *Indianapolis Freeman* (15 December 1906) published after her death said that Batson had first attracted attention singing in the Meeting Street A.M.E. church choir in Providence. Russell, who wrote the article, said that after Batson left the choir, Sissieretta and Marion Adams Harris succeeded her as soloists at the church. Russell said that Batson had been married twice. Her second marriage, in December 1887, was to her white manager, John C. Bergen, who made his living giving concerts for colored churches and offering prizes to the largest ticket sellers. "Despite what happened in after years, it was a case of true love, for they were devoted to each other," Russell said. The Bergen concerts in which Batson starred were always "the greatest social events in colored musical circles everywhere." Some sources claimed Batson divorced Bergen and that he died of a broken heart, but Russell had a different story. He said Bergen moved Batson and her mother from Providence to Philadelphia shortly after Sissieretta got the leading part in the 1892 Madison Square Garden "Negro Jubilee." When Bergen's health failed, Batson and her mother learned he had not purchased the Philadelphia house as they had thought but instead had leased it. Bergen, to whom Batson had entrusted her money against her mother's advice, had used her money to pay for his grown son from a previous marriage to attend college. Bergen had intended to pay back the money with future concert ventures, but his health prevented him from doing that. Russell said Bergen spent some time recuperating at the Soldier's Home but eventually went back to live with his wife, "whose love had chilled." After Bergen died Batson continued to sing under a manager who was not popular with people, and many of her concerts failed, according to Russell. The manager persuaded her to join the show *South before the War,* in which she did scenes and selections from *Il Trovatore.*[3] Other sources said that Batson twice traveled the world, including Europe, South Africa, India, China, and Japan, and sang before the crowned heads of Europe and leaders of countries in the Far East.[4] Russell said that Batson went to Australia as the star of the McAdoo Concert Company and was successful there. When McAdoo died she returned to the United States and toured. Her final appearance on the stage was a concert at Bethel A.M.E. church in Philadelphia on Thanksgiving evening, 29 November 1906. She died the following Saturday.[5] Shortly after Batson's death, press reports appeared saying that "Black Patti" was dead, which many people mistakenly assumed was Sissieretta.[6] The confusion stemmed from Batson's husband's use of the nickname the "Real Patti" for his wife even though everyone associated the Patti name with Sissieretta. The misleading press reports, although corrected quickly, were likely upsetting to Sissieretta.

Despite the separate paths their lives had followed since their early days on the stage together, Sissieretta must have been saddened by Batson's death. Not only had Batson been one of the great black concert singers, she had helped Sissieretta in the early days of her career back when the two lived in Rhode Island. Sissieretta likely had time to think about their relationship as she traveled by rail from state to state to give performances. The Troubadours reached California by mid-February, Oregon by mid-March, and North Dakota by early April. They made their annual stop in Indianapolis at the Park Theatre (2–4 May), where they were warmly received, as usual. A review in the *Indianapolis Freeman* said that Sissieretta's special numbers were "beautifully rendered" and that she was doing more acting when she sang the role of Germaine in the opera section of the show. The reviewer said the scene from *The Chimes of Normandy* was "more pretentious than anything heretofore attempted by a traveling company."[7] Clearly Voelckel and Nolan were willing to invest their money and energy to see that Sissieretta's section of the show was successful.

While in Indianapolis lead comedian John Larkins, who had been earning rave reviews all season, was highlighted in an article by J. D. Howard published in the *Freeman* (18 May 1907). Howard said that Voelckel and Nolan had taken Larkins from high-class vaudeville houses and given him his first opportunity to play in a real musical comedy. In addition to his comic ability, Larkins, according to Howard, was a good songwriter who composed "catchy songs that are materially different in style and selection from the usual stuff of the day. Most of them tell consistent stories." For example Larkins wrote the song "Royal Coon" to fit in with the text and story line of the comic skit. Howard said that Larkins, in his role as the king of Zululand, provided "the first glimpse of just how colored actors will look as costumed comedians in the distant day when Negroes will be called upon to take their place in the higher atmosphere of legitimate comic opera."[8]

A couple of weeks after the Troubadours left Indianapolis, a lengthy article about the women in the Black Patti Troubadours, written by someone named "Dorothy," appeared in the *Freeman* (18 May 1907). The article, "Black Patti Troubadour Girls," accompanied by several photographs, focused on Sissieretta and the twelve women in the Troubadours' company. Here is how Dorothy described Sissieretta:

Madame Jones, the star, has been before the public for many years as an artist and has met with unlimited and unquestioned success, having sung from [*sic*] crowned heads abroad and to newsboys in the gallery in America. She is the highest salaries [*sic*] colored woman in the business, and the possessor of a fortune in jewels, besides costly gowns and everything else that makes life worth the living to any woman. She is honored everywhere as a positive exponent of the profession she represents and also a lady of refinement and culture.

Her ideals are high and her manner worthy of imitation. Her form is good and she wears her gowns with that queenly air that characterizes aristocratic heredity. She is as dear as she can be and makes you feel that you have always known her. There is not a trace of self conceit and very prominent in her make-up is her general interest in her friends. She is the only child of her family and her mother lives at Providence, R.I., and Madame spends her short vacation there.[9]

Dorothy described the rest of the women in the cast. Mabel Gant, a "coon song" singer, buck-and-wing dancer, and fancy dancer, who performed with Al F. Watts, was "pleasant, but reserved." Elizabeth Wallace was quite lively both on and off the stage and was anxious to be a "real top notcher." Wardrobe mistress and singer Lizzie Taylor was from Chicago, where her husband and mother were living. Lizzie planned to stay home next season and keep house. Her sister, Helen, also with the Troubadours, liked to tease everyone. Helen would often visit the women's dressing rooms, amusing them and giving them her opinions on things. There were two other sisters in the show—Marie and Cora Lacale. Marie, called "Cuppie," had been on the stage for some time, but never in big parts. Her sister, Cora, was quite young and appeared almost childlike, but she worked hard. The Lacale sisters supported their mother, who lived in New York. Emma Baynard Whitney, who had to leave the Smart Set show at the beginning of the season when her mother became seriously ill, joined the Troubadours after her mother recovered. She planned to rejoin her husband, Salem Tutt Whitney, for the summer season of the Smart Set. Dorothy said Mrs. Montrose Douglas was the only woman in the show traveling with her husband.[10]

Dorothy also wrote about Jeanette Murphy Green, the wife of J. Ed. Green, who himself had been a Troubadour in 1902 and 1903 and was currently a playwright and producer at the Pekin Theatre in Chicago. Married for more than nine years, the couple had a son, James Ernest, born four years after they married. Their son was named James after a friend of J. Ed. Green's and Ernest after Green's former associate, Ernest Hogan. It appeared that James Ernest lived on the road with his mother, although Dorothy did not make that clear in her article. There is a photograph in the newspaper accompanying Dorothy's article of James Ernest standing on a chair. Jeanette Green, a Troubadour since October 1901, had been Sissieretta's "devoted companion" for the last five years. Dorothy described Jeanette and her relationship with Sissieretta: "She [Jeanette] is of a quiet and retiring disposition and is Madame's 'jewel.' She looks after everything for her and accompanies her everywhere. The sight of Jeanette is all sufficient to allay most any worry that the great singer may have and the thought that perhaps Jeanette and J. Ed., together with the baby, may settle down to housekeeping next season and that she may lose her Jeanette is causing Madame Jones to lay awake nights and wonder what she will do without her. She thinks that J. Ed. and baby James may need her [Jeanette], and then she says to herself: 'I can't give her up now, for I need her most.'"[11]

The Troubadour season ended on 28 May in Yonkers, New York. At the close of the season, the *New York Age*'s new black theater critic, Lester Walton, said that the Black Patti Troubadours' tour, which traveled from the Atlantic to the Pacific, had covered more territory and earned more money than any other African American company. Walton said that the Troubadours also played more one-night stands than any other black show.[12]

Russell used his end-of-the-season article to continue his crusade to elevate and improve the quality of African American shows and songs by eliminating coon songs and songs with the word *nigger* in them. Russell recalled three songs that helped start the coon song craze—"All Coons Look Alike to Me," "Coon, Coon, Coon," and "Nigger, Nigger, Never Die." Ernest Hogan had written the first song, and Raymond Brown, a white poet and songwriter, wrote, "Coon, Coon, Coon." Russell said these "two gentlemen" had no idea when they wrote these songs what a bad effect this music would have on the "minds of new native-born and foreign races of the common people." They were simply writing songs that suited the popular sentiment of that time, Russell said, and they were trying to make money. Soon other songs of this type followed, which were sung by both black and white entertainers. The black critic implored "intelligent colored actors" to chide the ignorant ones not to sing these songs as well as to express their disapproval, "in a nice way," to white singers and song publishers so there might be fewer of those kind of songs performed and published. "Now, if the stubborn, ignorant class of the colored actors will please cut all self-ridicule out and if song publishers will please kindly oblige the respectable element of the colored race by restricting race insult from comic songs, they will be doing a heap of good to a badly demoralized country," Russell said.[13]

The *Freeman* published an article in May, near the end of the 1906–7 season, that showed how one African American show was advancing the realm of black entertainment and inspiring race pride. The article was written by someone in Louisville who saw Bob Cole and Rosamund Johnson's show *The Shoo-Fly Regiment* when it played there in May. The article praised the production for showing black progress and helping audiences to see the intelligent African American. The article said minstrel shows starring black actors gave audiences a poor view of the race by highlighting horseplay and chicken thefts, leaving audiences to laugh at the "singular discomfiture of the Negro" rather than at constructive humor. "Really, there should be some ethical distinction in humor, and the disabilities and failures of an oppressed people should always be tragedy, indeed, never farce," the article said. Cole and Johnson's play barely mentioned "chicken, which is the Magna Charta of most Negro stage business." The entire play was of a "high class order." The story showed black youth as brave soldiers serving in the Philippines. The music was very melodic and incorporated plenty of harmony, the acting was "superb," and the staging "magnificent." The newspaper called the show "elevating and inspiring."[14]

Although Voelckel and Nolan probably continued to feel some pressure to stop using coon songs in the Troubadours' show, they were apparently reluctant to take them all out. The show continued to feature ragtime music and use coon songs, although fewer than in the past.

1907–1908 Season

Shortly before rehearsals began in late July for the Troubadours' twelfth season, Voelckel and Nolan announced a change in the leading comedy role after "Jolly" John Larkins ignored his contract with the Troubadours and left the show to star in *A Trip to Africa,* a three-act musical comedy managed by Myers and Free. Voelckel and Nolan reportedly were not sorry to see Larkins leave. They hired "Tutt" Whitney to play the leading comedian, and his brother, Homer Tutt, to be the straight man. Whitney had produced the Smart Set show the previous season, and Homer had been a cast member of that same show. Whitney was married to Troubadours' cast member Emma Baynard Whitney, who had joined the company during the previous season.[15] A report in the *Indianapolis Freeman* said that Whitney would be great with the Troubadours, not only because he was talented but because he had great patience, "a virtue to him in dealing with a fussy, fretful manager like Mr. Voelckel, a man who beats the record in discipline and regularity."[16]

An erroneous report in a Philadelphia newspaper must have had everyone in the Troubadours cast talking while they were in rehearsals for the new season. The report said Sissieretta was severing her relationship with Voelckel and Nolan and would be under the Shubert management this season. She reportedly would be the first to sing at the opening of a new Shubert theater in Paris.[17] Although she might have liked to sing in Paris, she instead opened her twelfth season as star of the Black Patti Troubadours on 20 August 1907, in Liberty, New York. She was surrounded by many of the same cast members who had been with her for years, including her beloved assistant, Jeanette, who did not move to Chicago to be with her husband. Manager Rudolph

Voelckel continued traveling with the Troubadours, and John Nolan accompanied the duo's other show, the Dandy Dixie Minstrels, which opened its season out west in early August. The new leading comedian, Whitney, played the title character, Prince Bungaboo, in the show's new opening skit. He also served as stage manager for the entire Troubadours' show.[18] Sissieretta sang three numbers in the olio section, including one the Tutt brothers wrote for her, "Good Night, Marie," in which she was assisted by the Troubadours' male sextet. The operatic finale included selections from Michael William Balfe's 1843 opera, *The Bohemian Girl*. Sissieretta sang the opera's best-known aria, "I Dreamt I Dwelt in Marble Halls," as well as "The Wound upon Thine Arm."[19]

The Troubadours began September in Pennsylvania before heading to Maryland, Virginia, North Carolina, South Carolina, Georgia, and Florida. The company did twenty-five one-night stands that month. In October they performed in twenty-six southern cities—all of them one-night stands except a two-day performance, 2–3 October, in Atlanta. The Troubadours' September and October schedules were indicative of their ten months on the road that season. Sometimes they had week-long engagements in several major cities, but by and large they spent most of the time traveling in their private railcar, going from town to town, setting up the scenery each night and unpacking and repacking their costumes, all to perform for one night or, at most, a matinee and an evening performance. Someone who knew Sissieretta well, perhaps a cast member, or maybe even Sylvester Russell, wrote an unsigned column in the *Freeman* in early November that described Sissieretta's life on the road and how well she coped with her rigorous schedule:

> This is the record of the greatest singer of her race—Sissieretta Jones. Twelve seasons of forty to forty-five weeks duration. Twelve seasons of one-night stands, covering a territory including the United States, Canada, Mexico, and Cuba. Twelve seasons of car life, monotonous at its best. Contemplate this and the grinding, heart-rendering effort to appear at one's best, night after night, sick or well, cold or hot, wet or dry. Contemplate this and you will have some idea of the wonderful vitality, the indefatigable courage and indomitable will of the woman whom Messrs. Voelckel & Nolan have been successfully starring for twelve years.
>
> If this continual strain had detracted from the exquisite beauty of her voice, critics have failed to detect the fact. Those who have had the honor to become personally acquainted with Mrs. Jones are bewitched by her charming personality, at all times dignified, but never arrogant. She is a delightful conversationist, showing culture and refinement. She

enjoys a good joke and laughs with the hilarious abandon of a school girl. She is devoted to her home ties and is never so happy as when talking of her mother and father in her beautiful home in Providence, R.I.[20]

About two weeks after the piece about Sissieretta appeared in the *Freeman,* an unsigned article about Rudolph Voelckel was published, which appeared to have been written by a cast member. The writer described how Voelckel, "our general manager," early in his business career had adopted the axiom "Nothing succeeds like success." In the years that followed, Voelckel added one more axiom: "Be sure you are right, then go ahead." The writer said that living by these axioms had netted Voelckel and the Troubadours twelve years of "unqualified success." The Black Patti Troubadours had become a household name in the South, and their appearance was often considered the "theatrical event" of the season. The troupe may have traveled to many small cities and towns and played to many unsophisticated audiences, but they met with financial and theatrical success each season. The writer said although some might think the Troubadours spent a lot of time in the "woods," the Troubadours "bring back the money." It seems, the writer added, that "Mr. Voelckel is an expert woodsman." The writer noted how nearly all black performers "of any repute" other than Bert Williams and S. H. Dudley had been members of the Troubadour company: "Mr. Voelckel is, without doubt, the most successful manager of colored performers. Aside from being an ethnologist Mr. Voelckel is a diplomat, remarkable for his display of tact, a profound student of human nature and an observant observer. He never bullies, never nags, never makes the mistake of speaking imperatively when persuasion would be better. He has his people's interest at heart at all times. A letter from home, telling of sickness or death, always meets his ready sympathy. 'Do you need money?' is his first question. 'You can have what you need'; and he means it. Twelve years of intimate association with all kinds of colored performers has failed to place a single wrinkle in his jolly countenance."[21]

It appears Voelckel treated his cast members well and, in return, earned their loyalty and respect. What little is known about him comes from newspaper clippings, which described him as "fussy" but fair, a good businessman, and a stickler for discipline and order. He believed in keeping his entertainers prepared to play one another's parts in the show so that he could replace an ill or absent cast member with an understudy at a moment's notice. He and Nolan put plenty of money into the Troubadour shows to ensure they had top-notch scenery and costumes as well as talented performers. The managers also tried to make the performers comfortable on the road by providing a well-appointed private railcar in which the cast traveled and resided and hiring a cook to keep them adequately fed while working around their strenuous performance schedule. The private railcar reportedly cost about thirty thousand dollars and was "fitted with gold plush upholstery and hand-carved pianos."[22] It had ten sections and two public rooms, where the cast passed endless travel time playing cards, sewing, reading, telling stories, and celebrating special events. Most likely Voelckel had a special relationship with Sissieretta, who was the key reason the Troubadours were successful all these years. The two, who were about the same age, had known one another since 1895, when Voelckel approached Sissieretta about managing her on a European tour. They had traveled together, day after day, about ten months each year for thirteen years. They likely had developed mutual respect for one another and a lasting friendship. It is unknown whether their friendship ever developed any romantic overtones.[23]

The day after the glowing article about Voelckel was published in the *Freeman,* the Troubadours opened a seven-day run, 17–23 November, at the Elysium Theatre, 900 Elysian Fields Avenue, in New Orleans. This 1,500-seat theater, first opened in 1903, was reopened in September 1907 under the management of the New Orleans Amusement and Investment Company, a group made up of leading black citizens of New Orleans and capitalized with thirty thousand dollars. The theater, which catered to black patrons, had booked the Black Patti Troubadours and the Dandy Dixie Minstrels, and negotiations were under way to get Cole and Johnson's and Ernest Hogan's shows to play there. Plans called for the greater part of the season to be devoted to a stock company of African American actors as well as vaudeville and specialty performers from the North.[24]

Sissieretta and the Troubadours played to "immense crowds" during their afternoon and evening performances. A review said, "No finer troupe has ever been seen at the Elysium, and the display of costumes alone was worth the admission." During the opening skit, "Prince Bungaboo," Charles Bougia captured the audience with his song, "Dagone, I'm Happy Now." Homer Tutt brought "paroxysms of laughter" by singing "The Swellest Coon from Dixie Land." His brother, Tutt Whitney, earned lots of applause for his rendition of "Prince Bungaboo," and he was called on to sing multiple encores. The olio included hoop work by the "Great English," a fire dance by Queen Dora, and a comedy act by King and Baily. The review mentioned New Orleans native Andy Pellebon, also known as the "New Orleans Honeysuckle," who had joined the Troubadours the previous January and had worked his way up in the company. Sissieretta charmed the New Orleans audiences. The review said, "Last night she gave an exhibition of vocal powers which showed that she has lost none of her strength or art."[25]

In addition to a week of matinee and evening performances, the Troubadours kept a whirlwind social calendar while in the Crescent City. After the

Monday night performance, Paul Steele, a member of the popular Tramp Club, escorted the Troubadours to a hall decorated with flowers and lights, where the club was holding a ball in honor of the Troubadours. Music filled the air and got everyone dancing until the wee hours of the morning. One who attended the ball said that everyone went home feeling that "life is worth living after all." The next social event was a banquet following the Troubadours' Thursday night performance. Hosted by Mr. Winston, proprietor of the Astoria Hotel, 235 South Rampart Street, the event, held at the hotel's spacious dining hall, featured a full-course meal with a "copious flow of wine." The Troubadours also were invited to another reception, sponsored the Allegro Club, given in honor of the hometown Troubadour favorite Pellebon.[26] The degree to which Sissieretta participated in these parties is unknown, but these events in New Orleans exemplify many of the social rewards the Troubadours experienced as they traveled the country.

After the Troubadours left New Orleans, they played in other Louisiana towns and then headed to Texas, Oklahoma, Arkansas, Kentucky, Illinois, Missouri and Kansas during December, January, and early February. The company returned to New Orleans, 16–23 February, for an eight-day run at the Elysium. In addition to their nightly shows at 8:15, the Troubadours did matinees on Tuesday, Thursday, and Saturday. In all they gave twelve or thirteen performances within those eight days. A review in the *Times Picayune* praised Sissieretta and those who sang with her during the operatic act featuring gems from *The Bohemian Girl.* "The singing rises at times to high art, and reflects credit upon the singers who interpret the masterpieces. The show is a tribute to the people of the cast and to the management of the pretty theatre, which is said to be the best colored theatre in the United States."[27]

While the Troubadours were in New Orleans, a juggler and acrobatic dancer, Pewee Williams, joined the company, and Pellebon left the troupe because his wife had a serious accident. Voelckel, who had taken some time off, rejoined the Troubadours after a month's vacation. Once again the Troubadours had a busy social life while they were in New Orleans. The Tramps Social Club hosted a special event for the troupe. This club, whose members were entertainers in New Orleans, gave balls and shows to raise money "to assist in caring for the sick and burying the dead." In addition to the party sponsored by the Tramps Club, the organization's Ladies Auxiliary gave their Pink Domino Ball in nearby Biloxi, Mississippi, 17 February, to honor the Black Patti Troubadours. The ladies wore pink costumes, and the men wore pink ties.[28]

With New Orleans behind them, the Troubadours worked their way through Mississippi, Alabama, Florida, Georgia, and the two Carolinas during February and March, often playing to large, mostly black audiences but sometimes performing before only fair-sized crowds. In fact they were scheduled to perform in Vicksburg, Mississippi; Monroe and Shreveport, Louisiana; and Galveston, Houston, and San Antonio at the end of March and beginning of April, but the Troubadours canceled the shows because of low attendance during Lent and instead took some time off.[29] Although the troupe did not stick to their original schedule, they did keep their 1 April 1908 engagement at the opera house in Chattanooga, where they delighted a "large and dusky audience." The balcony was filled with African American patrons eager to see the show. "An unbroken row of gleaming ivories shone from the gallery and the plaudits from both regions were unrestrained. The body of the house contained only a sprinkling of white people, which taking the real excellence of the production into consideration was somewhat strange," said the city's mainstream, white newspaper, the *Daily Times*. Sissieretta held her audience "spellbound" when she sang old-time songs, including "The Old Folks at Home." "The notes of pathos in the song rang true, as they came from the throat of the dusky singer like an echo from the old South," the newspaper said. The reviewer, obviously white, wrote about witnessing the black audience's joy and delight with Tutt Whitney's performance: "His blackface comedy is the genuine article, while the comedy is at best only an imitation. It was worth while being present to see the colored comedian if only to hear the uncontrolled shouts of the galleries. For with comedians of his own race upon the stage and only a few of the 'white folks' below stairs, the Negro literally takes the check-rain [*sic*] off his emotions and demonstrates his approval by ecstatic roars of laughter."[30]

In April the Troubadours had three week-long engagements, one of which was at the Avenue Theatre in Louisville, 12–18 April. On opening night, Sunday, the company played to a large and appreciative, mostly white audience, which gave Sissieretta a rousing applause after she sang "My Old Kentucky Home." When she finished she was given a bouquet of flowers, "the first colored performer" ever to receive a bouquet at the Avenue Theatre.[31] In between their Louisville engagement and their upcoming week in Chicago at month's end, the Troubadours played several one-night stands in Indiana, including a very special performance in Logansport, the birthplace of the Tutt brothers. Voelckel and Nolan made special arrangements for the Troubadours to perform 23 April in this northern Indiana town after the managers discovered the brothers had never played in their hometown. Family and friends filled the audience on the night of the performance to watch the native comedy stars perform with the famous Black Patti Troubadours. After the show the Elite Social Club, schoolmates of the Tutt brothers, gave a banquet for the entire company. The evening began with a reception from 11:00 P.M. until midnight, followed by a banquet from midnight until 1:00 A.M., and then came dancing that lasted until 4:00 A.M. It was a major social event in Logansport's African American community. "The brothers were almost overwhelmed with congratulations, and the unbounded hospitality shown to the Black Patti Company made an indelible impression upon their hearts that time will fail to erase," said one Troubadour.[32]

As the 1907–8 season edged toward its close, the Troubadours played to "fair" business during a week's run in Chicago at the Columbus Theatre and good crowds during a week in Pittsburgh (4–9 May) and Baltimore (11–16 May). The Troubadours finished their twelfth season in late May in New Jersey.

1908–1909 Season

After spending the summer with her mother in Rhode Island, Sissieretta went to Boonton, New Jersey, to begin rehearsals on 24 August 1908 for the thirteenth season of the Black Patti Troubadours. Little did Sissieretta or the cast know that it would be their last season together as the Troubadours. Salem Tutt Whitney returned as the principal comedian and his brother, Homer, also remained with the show. Whitney wrote the opening one-act musical comedy, which he first called the "Barnstormers" but later changed to "The Blackville Strollers." His wife, Emma Baynard Whitney, one of the Troubadours' sopranos the previous season, was too ill to travel with the troupe this time. Another singer, former Troubadour Sarah Green, rejoined the company after a three-year absence. She had spent two seasons with Ernest Hogan's Rufus Rastus company and a year in Europe with the Creole Bells. Several longtime cast members were still with the show—Will A. Cooke, Gus Hall, Charles Bougia, and Jeanette Murphy Green. Green, a leading soprano in the show and Sissieretta's companion, also made and maintained costumes for the troupe. Cooke, one of the longest-serving members of the Troubadours, helped Whitney stage the new show as well as play the difficult role of Count-de-no-Count, a dusty knight of the road. Hall, a baritone, sang with Sissieretta. He became the Troubadours' correspondent to the *New York Age* for the entire season, providing readers with news about the show and information about the Troubadours' reception around the country.[33]

The 1908–9 Troubadours season opened 5 September to a packed house at the Harris Lyceum in Boonton. Plans called for the Troubadours to head south first and then, midway through the season, go west to California and Washington. The new show started with the opening skit, "The Blackville Strollers," which the *Freeman* described as "uproariously funny, pure, and well acted by the cast." Later in the show, the Tutt brothers did an original sketch called "Soldiers of Fortune" and sang their latest song, "I Ain't Goin' to Let Nobody Make a Fool Out of Me," which promised to be the "coon song" hit of the season.[34] The olio included the Woodens, bicyclists and hoop jugglers; Slim Henderson singing "The Right Church, but the Wrong Pew"; and James Goodman, a musical monologist with a novelty act. After the season opener in New Jersey, a writer for the *Freeman* who signed his name as "Hoosier" said that the olio, with the exception of Goodman's musical act, "could well be dispensed with." Hoosier had kind words for Sissieretta and predicted her rendition of "Red, Red Rose," accompanied by eight male singers, would be a hit this season. In addition she sang "operatic gems" in the third act of the show. Hoosier commended Voelckel and Nolan for sparing "neither money nor pains" to provide the show with the best scenery and costumes.[35]

As the Troubadours traveled through Pennsylvania, West Virginia, and Virginia in September, baritone Gus Hall, in his report to the *New York Age,* said stage manager Cooke was diplomatic and had earned the company's respect. Hall also commended the Troubadours' "genial" chef, Judge Milton, who "makes the company feel as guests of any first-class hotel when he distributes his viands daily and too much praise cannot be given to the care and wholesomeness of the food he prepares." Hall added the show's musical director, Trevor Corwell, a white Englishman, to his list of acknowledgments. Corwell had quickly earned the company's respect and rapport. "Having been introduced to the company at 10:45 A.M. and by 10:46 he treated all the ladies in the entire show to ice cream and cake—an instant hit, and the men to wet goods and cigars. His slightest wish is the company's musical command," Hall said. As the Troubadours traveled into North Carolina in early October, Hall said business was good despite some warm southern weather. He said the Woodens, the bicyclists, left the company in late September. Hall also provided a brief bit of information about the Pullman car that housed the company during its tour. He said that the women in the cast had tastefully decorated it with "bric-a-brac" and that everyone in the company worked hard to keep it neat and comfortable. Hall added that Cooke had decided to form an athletic club for the cast, both men and women, and that baseball fever had struck the company.[36]

During the middle of October, while the troupe was traveling in the Deep South, Voelckel and Nolan asked Whitney to rewrite "The Blackville Strollers" by making it a two-act musical comedy with the second act written around Sissieretta, so that it featured "the greatest of colored singers to best advantage." Plans called for the olio and popular grand opera finale to be dropped. Corwell and the Tutt brothers were asked to compose original music for the new show, which was scheduled to debut 2 November 1908 at the Grand Theatre in Macon, Georgia. A news item in the *Indianapolis Freeman* predicted the new format would be a success. "Notwithstanding the fact that the Troubadour chorus at present is the strongest they have had for years, it will be strengthened and the entire show bids fair to outrival anything seen in the Sunny Southland," the newspaper said.[37] The change in the show was a radical departure for Sissieretta, who had sung operatic selections in the Troubadours' third act for thirteen seasons. In recent years she had become more comfortable acting and playing a role during the opera scenes, and she had been performing more popular music during the olio for several years. But this new change would take her completely out of her traditional operatic role and make her part of the musical comedy, a place where she had never before appeared. Although she was likely ready for some new challenges after thirteen seasons on the road, she was probably apprehensive as well. It remained to be seen how audiences would react to the change.

Sissieretta and her fellow Troubadours had a busy October, because they had to rehearse the new show during the day while they continued to perform the original show at night at their scheduled engagements throughout the South. They met with great success and "rousing receptions" in Charleston and Savannah in October. The company broke attendance records in the two cities even though the large traveling show the Smart Set had preceded them. En route from Tampa to Quincy, Florida, where the Troubadours were scheduled to perform 26 October, Whitney prepared a banquet for some of the female members of the troupe who called themselves the "None Such Girls Social Club." Led by their president, Ruby Taylor, the women dressed in their finest and wore their club colors across their shoulders. Music, laughter, and song filled the railcar. A female quartet sang several selections, and the evening concluded when all members of the None Such Girls Social Club sang the "Good Night Song."[38] Sissieretta was not among the "girls," but surely she could hear their merriment from her private room in the railcar.

Three days later the Troubadours reached Moultrie, Georgia, where Voelckel learned his sixty-seven-year-old mother, Margaret, had died suddenly the day before, 28 October 1908, in New York City. Voelckel, who "cherished his mother above all else," was "prostrated by the shock."[39] He left immediately for New York City. The whole cast was in a "deep gloom" over Mrs. Voelckel's death. Sissieretta and the cast forwarded a beautiful floral arrangement to New York in memory of Voelckel's German-born mother. With Voelckel in New York City attending to his mother's funeral, the company moved on to Columbus, Georgia, where they performed 31 October at the Springer Opera House. While in Columbus, Sissieretta, who loved "first-class dogs," purchased a fine French poodle, which she said she would keep with her until she returned to her home in Providence at the end of the season. Next season she planned to leave the dog in her mother's care.[40]

About mid-November Voelckel rejoined the Troubadours, who were still traveling in the South and working their way toward Texas and Oklahoma.

At some point during November, the Troubadours debuted the new two-act musical comedy, which was quite successful, according to a cast member (likely Gus Hall) whose Troubadours' report was published in the *New York Age*. "Since the show has changed to a two-act musical comedy, praise unstinted has been showered on us by the press and public and the management is all smiles in consequence. Mme. Jones is seen at her best in the new show and a rare treat is in store for the music-loving public of all large cities and towns on our way back from California," the report said.[41]

The Troubadours experienced another death that cast a "deep gloom" over the entire troupe. Whitney's wife, Emma, died in Philadelphia in November. "She was a most loveable and respected woman and a gifted soprano and had a host of friends," said the Troubadours' correspondent to the *Age*. Whitney left the Troubadours upon his wife's death. Toward year's end he became the manager, comedian, producer, and amusement director of the New Lincoln Theatre in Knoxville.[42] The Tutt family had already been troubled earlier in the month when Homer Tutt's wife, Marie Belle, took ill 16 November while the Troubadours were in Pine Bluff, Arkansas. Belle had to leave the troupe and return to Knoxville, where she planned to rest for two weeks. Tutt also left the Troubadours at some point during November. One good piece of news for the Troubadours in November was the return of former cast member Andrew Pellebon and his wife. Pellebon had left the company in February after his wife had a serious accident. An interesting item in the Troubadour correspondent's report provided some information about how much the cast knew about their schedule during their forty to forty-five weeks on the road each season. They probably had a general idea of where they would be traveling for the season, but they apparently learned specifics along the way. The report in the *Age* said the cast had just received their new route cards, which gave them all the performance dates ahead until 21–27 February 1909, when they were scheduled to be in San Francisco.[43] It is unknown whether bookings were fluid and subject to change or whether the managers did not want to give the cast too much information ahead of time or wanted to keep the competition in the dark regarding the troupe's future destinations.

After the recent death of Voelckel's mother and Whitney's wife, the Troubadours were ready for something to cheer them. During their travels throughout Oklahoma in late November and early December 1908, prominent black citizens in towns such as South McAlister, Oklahoma City, Shawnee, Ardmore, Tulsa, and Muskogee entertained the cast in "grand style." One Troubadour said it was the "treat of a life time" to see so many wealthy and influential black men and women in these towns. "No pains were spared to make each affair most enjoyable and interesting as well," the cast member said. As December began talk turned to the annual Christmas party the Troubadours held for themselves each year after their evening performance on 25 December. This year the troupe would be in Jackson, Mississippi, for Christmas. Someone in the troupe made arrangements by wire for a Christmas tree and a large "spread" of food and drinks. "Many suspicious and large packages are being brought to the car and hidden away daily, so many surprises are in store for the popular members and sweethearts," one cast member said.[44]

With the departure of the Tutt brothers, Voelckel had to make cast adjustments. He called on Slim Henderson to play Whitney's part and Will Cooke to serve as stage manager. Charles Bougia had to step in and play Tutt's role, and newcomer George Day took another Troubadour's part. Voelckel's practice of keeping his understudies in constant readiness paid off when he lost two of his top stars.[45] The Troubadours continued their tour through Texas until 21 December, when they went into Mississippi. While they were on the road in December, the *New York Age's* theater critic, Lester Walton, published a column about the seating situation for black patrons attending the theater. He said seating arrangements should be left up to local theater managers, and he cited two examples. Theater managers in Cleveland had begun to ban "colonization" of black theater patrons, a practice that relegated all people of color to one section of the theater, usually the balcony. Instead many theater managers were treating ticket purchasers equally, regardless of color, by giving them seats based on the price of their ticket. Walton said that Cleveland theater managers realized that cleanly dressed black patrons objected to sitting next to dirty, whiskey-breathing black patrons just as much as white theatergoers would. The managers thought blacks should be able to purchase tickets anywhere in the house just like whites. In contrast Walton described a case in Nashville where a "certain class of Negroes" had disgraced the local theater with their offensive conduct to the point that the manager stopped the production and pleaded with those in the balcony (which the *Nashville Clarion* called the "buzzard roost") to quiet down and behave themselves. Local black newspapers denounced the misconduct of these black theatergoers. Walton said he believed black citizens in each city would have to fight their own battles for proper seating accommodations. He said eastern and western businessmen were more anxious to make money and have successful theaters than to "bother to any extent about race prejudice, and it is, as a rule, noticeably true that the larger the community and the more business that is transacted, the less prejudice is evident."[46]

The day before the Troubadours' big Christmas party in Jackson, the *New York Age* published its annual Christmas edition, which featured lots of news about Sissieretta and the Troubadours. One extensive article recapped her career and described her early years as a singer. It was accompanied by a large photograph of Sissieretta dressed in an elegant gown and seated majestically in a chair. But the most interesting Troubadour-related article, "Negro Folk Song," was written by Sissieretta herself.[47] She said that black folk songs were distinctly American and should be embraced by everyone. Her love for this kind of music and the importance she placed upon it explained why she continued to sing songs such as "My Old Kentucky Home" and her signature song, "Swanee River." Sissieretta's article provided a glimpse into her thoughts and feelings for the black race and described the emotions she felt when singing these songs:

> The Indian has given us no music. The European settlers brought their "folk song" with them. So it was left to the poor enslaved ignorant Negro to open his mouth and pour out his soul in melody so sweet that the whole world listened enraptured. David tells us that when the Israelites were enslaved they hung their harps upon the willows and filled the air with lamentations. But as the crushed rose emits the sweetest perfume, so the Negro, bruised and beaten, sung [sic] the sweetest songs.
>
> Is there a soul so insensible that it cannot be stirred to the very depths by the heartbroken cry of the poor old homesick darky longing for "The Old Folks at Home?" Is there a heart so dead to human feeling that it cannot be touched by the tender, "To My Old Kentucky Home?" Their very vocabulary inadequate, and their freedom of speech denied, the Negroes very naturally fell to expressing themselves in song. Thus we have the "Negro folk song" running the entire gamut of human emotions.
>
> To my mind no artist should omit one of these beautiful songs from his or her repertoire. Every school, college or university should include one of these songs in their musical program. Let the "Negro folk song" become universally popular and their sweet dolorous melodies will proclaim to the world that the Negro is a people of sorrows who has made companionship with grief. A people that will yet come through the furnaces of affliction and persecution and become as gold, tried in the fire.[48]

The 1908 Christmas issue of the *New York Age* also heralded its new dramatic editor, Lester A. Walton, by having longtime *Indianapolis Freeman* theater critic Sylvester Russell write an introductory article about Walton. Russell said Walton was the third black theater critic produced in the United States. The first had been Benjamin F. Lightfoot of Providence, who had died several years earlier. Sissieretta had performed with Lightfoot during her early years on the concert stage. The second black critic was Russell, and now the third and newest member of this exclusive group was the "amiable" Walton. Russell said New York had been deprived of dramatic news in past years during the reign of *New York Age* editor Thomas Fortune. Russell said that the newspaper's new editor, Fred R. Moore, recognized the trend to record stage history and hired Walton as the *Age*'s dramatic editor.[49]

The *Freeman* had its own share of theatrical news about Sissieretta and the Troubadours. Russell said the Troubadours had a new principal comedian, Tim Owsley, who was also a comedy playwright. Owsley had announced he was preparing a new comedy for next season in which Sissieretta would have a speaking role. "Sissieretta Jones has now had years of experience in which she has developed most excellently as an actress, and if she can essay a speaking part, there will be nothing left to be deserved and her entrance into the big comedy contest would be quite or even more important, in a complete comedy production, than the advent of any colored company on the road," Russell said.[50] This new role would mean major changes for Sissieretta, who had never before had a speaking part in any show and had only recently begun to sing during the musical comedy part of the show.

Russell, who since Walton's hiring now billed himself as "America's Greatest Colored Stage Critic," also weighed in on the issue of seating for black theater patrons, particularly the push by black entertainer Bert Williams, of the Williams and Walker duo, to force first-class theater managers to mix the races in all sections of seating in their theaters. Russell said, "This effort, even if justifiable, is ill-advisable, and, therefore, cannot be approved of at the present state of race problems. The possibility of forcing the race issue in theaters in the North, where conditions are, and have constantly been growing more favorable, is impropriety on the parts of Mr. Walker and the Shubert brothers." Seating practices among the races should be determined by local managers according to sectional conditions around the county, Russell said. Williams and Walker did not play in the South "for these very race reasons," the critic said. "Surely America must be very sectional when the elite of the South turns out to see Sissieretta Jones (Black Patti) and refuses to entertain Williams and Walker or the Smart Set," he added.

Russell said Williams and Walker should confine their efforts for the moment to some of the seating in New York's first-class theaters. The theater critic said he believed anyone with the money to purchase an orchestra seat, despite the color of their skin, should be seated there. He suggested having a couple of rows across the orchestra section for white patrons and then a row for black patrons, and then resume the white rows and black rows for the remainder of the section. By doing the seating that way, black patrons would not be confined to seats along the back or the sides of the orchestra section, he said. This arrangement would give both races a chance at center seats on the first floor.[51]

As the new year was about to begin, the Troubadours remained in a festive mood. The company performed New Year's Eve in Columbus, Mississippi, and then after the show celebrated together at a banquet hosted by several Troubadour ladies, led by their president, Ruby Taylor. The men in the cast were most appreciative of the multiple-course meal prepared by "master hands." Voelckel donated a claret punch large enough to serve fifty people, and Professor Richards, the new musical director from Boston, supplied "other kinds of wet goods" for the celebration. "After all had 'sumped dinously' and speeches were made cementing the bonds of friendship and professional courtesy, cigars were passed to the men by the president, Miss Ruby Taylor, and then good nights to greet the dawn of 1909," said one cast member. The ladies promised to hold more banquets in the future to help pass "some of the monotonous hours" while on the transcontinental tour.[52]

Between mid-January and mid-March, the Troubadours traveled through Louisiana, Texas, Colorado, New Mexico, and Arizona before reaching California. Singer Gus Hall sent frequent reports about the Troubadours to the *New York Age*. During this time Voelckel left the troupe for a short time to go hire new talent and to purchase $3,300 in railroad tickets to take the cast to California and then into Canada. Hall said the new lead comedian, Tim Owsley, was doing "very creditably" playing the role of Silas Green, and Sissieretta was thrilling audiences with the song "Red, Red Rose," which she was using as her second encore selection. In most cities and towns they visited, people presented Sissieretta with some "token of their esteem" such as roses, candy, and perfume. Hall said the company had experienced delays in getting their mail because the tour had changed so much from its original route. He also said many in the company were collecting postcards. "It is safe to say that any such collection bids fair to eclipse that of any members of any other show, white or black, as this show covers more ground than any other extant." When the Troubadours got to the Panhandle section of Texas in mid-February, Hall noted the absence of any "colored person" in the crowded houses that greeted the company in the seven or eight towns they played. Toward the end of February, despite a blizzard, the Troubadours did "phenomenal" business on opening night in Denver at the Curtis Theatre. The audience there loved Sissieretta's renditions of "Gay Butterfly Waltz," "Red, Red Rose," and "Swanee River." While the troupe was in Denver for the week, the Troubadours' railcar was overhauled and painted.[53]

The Black Patti railcar pulled into Los Angeles in mid-March for its week-long engagement, 14–20 March, at the Majestic Theater. Hall said the railcar had been "dressed up" in the Southern Pacific Railroad yards to make it ready for the company's California tour. "We should be seen on the end of these fine California trains, as we can sit at the windows or stand on the platform with as much gusto as anybody and feel proud," Hall said. Tom Floyd, the company's porter, had overseen renovations to the car's interior to ensure it would be one of the "best equipped cars ever used by any show of its kind," Hall added. Los Angeles proved to be a profitable engagement for the Troubadours, with business 30 percent better than the management expected. Despite competition from several other attractions in the city, the Troubadours enjoyed audiences filled to overflowing, "with all the boxes filled and the galleries as jolly as ever," Hall said. Owsley, a native of Los Angeles, was a hit at the Majestic, and he enjoyed being among his family and friends. "He is a performer of merit and one who will make the East hear from him before long, probably next season," Hall said.[54]

The Troubadours earned good reviews while in Los Angeles. The company had not visited this city since February 1907, when the Troubadours played 10–16 February at the Grand Theatre. The *Los Angeles Times* (15 March 1909) said, "The black Patti easily makes good her claim of being the best singer of her race. Like rare wine her voice has mellowed with age." Sissieretta's opening numbers, "Gay Butterfly Waltz" and "Red, Red Rose," were less familiar to the audience than her well-loved "Swanee River," which the *Times* said she sang with a "sympathetic quality in her voice that aroused her audience to enthusiasm." The *Times* said Sissieretta did not play a role in the two-act comedy other than to "interpolate" her song numbers. At the end of the comedy show, she appeared again, with the chorus accompanying her, and sang the "Dream Song" (from the comic opera *Fatinitza*) "as well as it has been sung on a Los Angeles stage," the *Times* reported. When Sissieretta had finished her selections, ushers carried large bouquets of flowers to her from admirers, both black and white.[55]

Following their successful week in Los Angeles, the Troubadours gave one-night performances in March and early April in sixteen California cities and towns, including Oxnard, Ventura, Santa Barbara, San Luis Obispo, Salinas, Santa Maria, Monterey, Hollister, Watsonville, San Jose, Santa Cruz, Palo Alto, Vallejo, Napa, Santa Rosa, and Petaluma. The company arrived in San Francisco for a week-long engagement (4–10 April) at the American Theatre. The Troubadours' last visit to San Francisco had been in 1905, the year before the destructive earthquake and fire. The *San Francisco Call* said Sissieretta could "not be excelled by many sopranos of lighter shade in the interpretation of those songs which appeal directly to the heart." The newspaper said her rendition of "Swanee River" was worth the price of a ticket. "She invites the tribute of tears."[56]

The Troubadours next week-long engagement was 18–24 April at the Baker Theatre in Portland. A review in the *Morning Oregonian* (19 April 1909) following the Troubadours' opening night performance said there was not much music in the first act of the "Blackville Strollers," but the music picked up considerably once Sissieretta appeared in the second act. "Black Patti, like the original Adelina, seems to have learned the secret of voice preservation, for she trills and warbles and skips around on the high notes with ease, as in the old days. She can sing a ballad in true, prima donna style." Although the review said the show lagged some, it praised Owsley's portrayal of Silas Green. The newspaper described the thin story line of the two-act comedy: "Silas and Kitty Green fall heir to a large tobacco plantation and a fortune. Silas starts north in search of his sister Kitty, who ran away nine years ago with a theatrical company. At Blackville, Silas falls in with the Blackville Strollers and is induced by manager, Ned Walkback, to become the company's angel. Through the aid of a tramp detective, 'Shoo Fly,' Green finds his sister and everything ends with everybody happy."[57]

During their Portland engagement, the Troubadours learned that comedy star, composer, actor, and former Troubadour Ernest Hogan was seriously ill. Hogan had been ill for some time but had planned recently to return to the stage. He took a turn for the worse, however, in late April and was in serious condition. The Troubadours, particularly Sissieretta, were saddened to receive the news. Hogan, who worked with the Troubadours between 1897 and 1899, had always held Sissieretta in high esteem, and they had a good relationship. He reportedly said of her: "Without any doubt the greatest of them all was Madam Sissieretta Jones (Black Patti). I claim that her equal has never been produced. Ask Emma Eames or Marcella Sembrich to tour the road and sing every night for forty weeks and see how long they would last. This great artist is simply divine. She doesn't get the credit due her. She is not the greatest singer of her 'race,' but the greatest singer of the world. God bless her."[58]

Although word of Hogan's illness surely dismayed the Troubadours, they had much more pressing news to deal with while they were in Portland. The company's two longtime managers, Voelckel and Nolan, had decided to stop doing business together after nearly fourteen years. Undoubtedly the troupe knew things were not right between the two managers for some time before the news broke on 29 April in Lester Walton's column in the *New York Age*. Walton announced that Voelckel was now the sole manager of the Black Patti Troubadours. "For the last two or three seasons rumors have reached New York that the members of the firm were not getting along amicably, but as so many unattended reports are daily circulated about managers and members of the profession not much credence was put in them. The Black Patti Troubadours had not been on the road more than two months last fall when word reached New York City that Voelckel and Nolan had had a parting of the ways," Walton said.[59] At the beginning of the 1907–8 season, Nolan left the Troubadours and took over management of the pair's new show, the Dandy

Dixie Minstrels. Walton said the Dandy Dixie Minstrels closed for the season in April 1909 and reportedly would not continue next season. Walton did not know why the partnership had been dissolved.

With news of the breakup finally made public, Voelckel and the Troubadours continued their tour, doing several one-night stands in Oregon and Washington during the last week of April, a week-long engagement in Seattle in early May, and then back to one-night stands in Washington, Idaho, Montana, and North Dakota for the rest of May. When the troupe reached Bozeman, Montana, on 25 May, they learned Hogan had died in New York on 20 May 1909, after a seventeen-month illness. Funeral services were held in New York, and his body was shipped to Bowling Green, Kentucky, his birthplace, for burial. Hundreds of admirers, both black and white, turned out for his funeral, including many notables in the theatrical business. Walton wrote that the theatrical profession had "sustained a great loss" and that there was no one at this time to replace Hogan. He said Hogan had "accomplished great good for his race, and advanced the standing of the colored members of the theatrical profession."[60] Sissieretta sent a telegram of sympathy to the *New York Age* and asked that it be published in the black newspaper. It said:

Through your valuable paper kindly express to the relatives of the late Ernest Hogan my heartfelt sympathy in the loss of America's foremost comedian, and my personal friend. God have mercy. My entire company joins in expressing sympathy.

Sissieretta Jones
Bozeman, Montana[61]

After the Troubadours left Bozeman, they did several other one-night engagements in Montana. When they were traveling 30 May from Miles City, Montana, toward their next stop, Glendive, Montana, the company was involved in a train wreck on the Northern Pacific line eight miles out of Miles City. The Black Patti railcar was the only car that did not derail. Voelckel said, "It was a pretty close call for all of us."[62] The Troubadours continued their tour into North Dakota in early June. Normally the company wrapped up its tour in late May, but this year the troupe continued until mid-June. The Troubadours left North Dakota and finished the season 17 June in Menominee, Michigan, after a week of one-night stands throughout the state. As soon as the show closed, Sissieretta headed back to New York City and then on to Providence to spend the summer with her mother and stepfather. Voelckel decided to take many of the Troubadours' cast on the road for the summer in a show he was calling the Dixie Troubadours. This summer troupe presented a two-act musical comedy called *A Trip to New Orleans* and featured Trouba-dour singer Sarah Green Byrd as the prima donna. Voelckel planned to tour the summer show throughout Canada. He also announced some preliminary plans for the next season of the Black Patti Troubadours. He signed a three-year contract with former Troubadour comedian "Jolly" John Larkins and planned to feature Larkins and Sissieretta in a three-act musical comedy, *A Trip to Zululand.* Voelckel said that Larkins would write the book and lyrics for the show and Joe Jordan would compose the music.[63]

During the summer an article appeared in the *New York Age* (19 August 1909) that summarized Sissieretta's record for the thirteen seasons she had headed up the Black Patti Troubadours. In all those seasons, she had missed only two performances, both of them matinees. This record was more amaz-ing because three-fourths of the shows in those thirteen seasons were one-night stands. "Now if you want to know the difference between playing one-night stands and one-week stands, ask any performer with whom you are personally acquainted," the *Age* said. The newspaper calculated that Sissie-retta had appeared in 3,820 of the 3,822 shows the Troubadours had per-formed. To reach this number, the newspaper estimated that the company averaged forty-two weeks in a season and gave seven performances each week, thus the 3,822 performances in thirteen seasons. The newspaper continued, "Manager Rudolph Voelckel is very proud of the record held by his star, and asserts that there is not another performer in the business who can claim such distinction. Despite the strenuous life which necessarily goes with playing one-night stands, 'Black Patti' enjoys the best of health, owing to the excel-lent care she takes of herself while on the road. Her example could be emu-lated by many of our performers—male and female—who are not compelled to play more than a dozen one-night stands during a season.[64] The forty-one-year-old Sissieretta had achieved a remarkable record.

10

The Black Patti Musical Comedy Company
1909–1914

As the summer of 1909 came to a close, Rudolph Voelckel began making arrangements for the 1909–10 theatrical season. Voelckel, now sole manager of the Black Patti Company, signaled that fact by changing the name of the Black Patti Troubadours to the Black Patti Musical Comedy Company. More information about the split between Voelckel and Nolan surfaced in the black press. Apparently toward the middle of the previous season, the two managers disagreed over the company's route. Voelckel had wanted the Troubadours to tour California and the West, while Nolan wanted the company to play in Kansas, Oklahoma, and other nearby states. Voelckel got his way, prompting Nolan to "sever his connections" with the Troubadours and take over management of the duo's other company, the Dandy Dixie Minstrels, who finished their 1908–9 season in May and then disbanded. Nolan then signed on as business manager for the 1909–10 season of the Southern Smart Set headed by former Troubadour Salem Tutt Whitney. Initially the two managers agreed to have the National Association of Producing Managers settle ownership and partnership issues related to their breakup, but later they decided to take their case to the New York Supreme Court.[1] Voelckel ultimately became sole proprietor and manager of the Black Patti Company.

Along with the company's new name, Voelckel decided to change the show's format to a three-act musical comedy and, for the first time, give Sissieretta a speaking part in the production. She would star, along with former Troubadour lead comedian "Jolly" John Larkins, in *A Trip to Africa,* reportedly written by Larkins and former Troubadour J. Ed. Green, with Joe Jordan furnishing some of the music. The *New York Age* praised the new format as being suitable to showcase Sissieretta's talents. In the thirteen years the Black

Patti Company had been on the road, it had "exerted no little influence over the musical minds of hundreds in the South," the *Age* said. With the new format, the "antiquated policies of the oldest colored show in the business will be no more." The article noted, "For years an effort has been made by many of our prominent colored performers to induce the managers of the famous singer to put her out in a show that would do her credit. . . . [We] all rejoice that 'Black Patti' is to have a vehicle which will not consist of a first part, an olio, and an afterpiece. There is no more conclusive evidence of the signs of the times than the capitulation of Manager Voelckel to up-to-date stage methods. It also means that theatregoers in the South and West who are not favored with visits by the large colored shows will be more enlightened as to what is going on in the theatrical world. In the past it has been a source of deep regret that the large colored companies have been unable to go south of Louisville."[2]

In early September, shortly before rehearsals began for the Black Patti Company, Lester Walton of the *Age* interviewed Sissieretta for an hour while sitting in her private railcar at Union Station in St. Louis. She told him how excited she was with her new speaking role. "Yes, I am to be a sure enough actress this season. Heretofore I have never had lines, but in my new show I will have quite an amount of talking to do, and I certainly feel elated over the part I have been given," Sissieretta said. "Heretofore, I have never had a speaking part, as all my other shows did not call for such. I sang my songs and then I was through. This year I am to do considerable talking and am anxious to begin my work."[3]

Sissieretta played two roles in the show—Lucinda Lee and Princess Lulu. The plot of *A Trip to Africa* was "somewhat deeper" than the average show of this kind. The story began with the kidnaping of a favorite teacher, Lucinda Lee, from Long Creek College. She is taken to the heart of the African jungle by members of the Zamboo tribe, who make her their Princess Lulu. Lucinda Lee's friends follow her and attempt to rescue her. The play centers on these rescue adventures. The show did not have any "horse-play" or "coon songs" as were previously present in many of the Black Patti Troubadours' productions. Some of the biggest musical hits in the show were "The Beaming Sun," "In Zulu Land," "I Wish I Was in Heaven," "All Hail the King," and "Rag Time Baseball."[4]

The Black Patti Musical Comedy Company first performed their new show when they opened the season to a packed house at the Auditorium in Hot Springs, Arkansas, on 23 September 1909. The cast had spent seven days and nights rehearsing the new show while continuing to do nightly performances of the old summer show, "Dixie Troubadours," in places such as Fort Smith, Arkansas, on 20 September and Little Rock on 22 September.

Sissieretta garnered a "grand ovation" for her roles as Lucinda Lee and Princess Lulu, and she received "repeated encores" for her singing of "Dixie Land Is Good Enough for Me." Larkins kept the audience laughing and "created pandemonium" when he appeared on the stage. The "bright and smart" costumes and the elaborate scenery also added to the audience's enjoyment. Frank Head, manager of the Hot Springs Auditorium, wired a report about the show's debut to the *New York Age* praising Sissieretta's new role and Larkins's comedy. "The performance was unquestionably the best 'Black Patti' has ever brought to the Vapor City," Head said.[5]

The Black Patti Musical Comedy Company spent the rest of 1909 touring throughout the Southwest and the South, often playing to predominantly African American audiences. Sissieretta and the company earned great reviews, and the show, according to cast member Anthony Byrd, was doing "record-breaking" business in the South. Byrd, the company's correspondent to the *New York Age,* reported that Sissieretta, in her new speaking role, "shows exceptional ability and that she has had in reserve [a] wonderful conception of dramatic art in her store house of knowledge. Her speeches receive rounds of applause at each performance."[6] Although audiences enjoyed hearing Sissieretta speak her lines, it was still her singing that attracted them the most.

Shortly before Christmas the company played in Macon, Georgia, a city the Black Patti Troubadours had visited often. The Macon audience loved the new show, and the 13 December performance earned a glowing review in the *Macon Daily Telegraph:*

> The show as given by Sissieretta Jones and her company last night
> pleased those who love the Negro voice. There is melody in his voice,
> whether on wharves rolling the cotton into the holds of steamboats,
> or on the stage in an opera house. There is a certain sweetness in it that
> falls softly on some ears, and feels like music. The Black Patti, seen here
> often, retains her voice, and be it said that last night when she had given
> as an encore after singing a selection from Lucia di Lammermoor, that
> southern favorite, "Way Down Upon the Sewanee [*sic*] River," one shut
> eyes and listened and thought it sweet, as it was.
>
> The company is better than she usually brings. John Larkins, he of
> the coal black face, the crimson lips and as white a set of teeth as ever
> shone in man's mouth, was excruciatingly funny in all that he did, and
> one could not help laughing at him. But there were others, and on the
> whole the audience, which was top-heavy enough to topple, the galleries
> being full, was tickled to death at the funny business and delighted at
> the singing. Between the fun and the music, as well rendered, the show
> was well worth going out on a cold night to see.[7]

By the start of 1910, the Black Patti Company began touring in Florida. Several of the cast members had left the show for various reasons, bringing the cast size down to about seventeen people. The smaller cast, however, reportedly did not appear to negatively affect the quality of the show. After the company played Tampa, the *Tampa Morning Tribune* said that the small company had "strong and well-balanced voices" and was "sufficiently large to produce the comedy satisfactorily."[8]

When the Black Patti Company arrived in St. Augustine for their two-night performance, 13–14 January, at the Jefferson Theatre, they were in for a surprise. The company was to be the first black show to play in the new $100,000 theater, the best in St. Augustine. The management decided to change its usual seating policy for the Black Patti show by allotting the orchestra and first balcony seats to black patrons. But in doing so the management failed to consider how the white ushers would react to this change. They did not take it well. "When these knights of the seat check learned that colored people would occupy the first floor they turned so many colors that their faces, for a few minutes, rivaled the rainbow for diversity." They told the management that seating blacks in the orchestra "would mean the degeneracy of Southern traditions." When opening night arrived, none of the ushers showed up, leaving the management with a problem. Managers asked members of the theater's board of directors to come to the theater to find a solution to the situation. Someone in the group said the only thing to do was to serve as ushers themselves, and after some discussion they all agreed. Although both the new ushers and the black patrons showed some embarrassment, everything went smoothly. The directors served as ushers until all the seats on the first floor were filled. That night the house did the largest business it had done since the theater had opened a few months earlier. The striking ushers found themselves looking for new jobs after refusing to serve black theatergoers. The *New York Age,* which published an account of the seating incident, began its article with "Southern ethics and customs were given a solar plexus during the engagement of the Black Patti Musical Company at the Jefferson Theatre." The *Age* said that the *St. Augustine Evening Record,* in its review of *A Trip to Africa,* also mentioned the unusual seating arrangements. "Ever pleasing, especially to the members of her race, Black Patti and her musical comedy company delighted a colored audience that packed the Jefferson Theatre last night," the newspaper said. "The orchestra was given up to the colored people, and both it and the gallery were crowded. The balcony was filled with white people. It was an appreciative audience as will ever be seen in the Jefferson, for to the members of her race Black Patti stands at the very head of her profession."[9]

While the Black Patti Company entertained audiences in Florida, an interesting article appeared in the *Indianapolis Freeman* in mid-January warning about the future for black road shows in the South and Southwest. The article, "The Outlook for Colored Road Shows; The Moving Picture House Is Taking the Day," likely had tongues wagging in the Black Patti railcar. The unidentified writer from Chicago said that the public in big cities would no longer pay high prices to see "ordinary" black road shows when they could go instead to ten-cent vaudeville houses and moving-picture houses for their entertainment. The writer predicted the same thing would happen soon in smaller cities and towns. "Once upon a time the dramatic papers were filled with ads for attractions to play the many different small cities. To-day it is different. Every one of the small houses is playing quick vaudeville at small prices and pictures. This latest craze has come to stay: the managers are making money out of it; the public is satisfied. This fad has spread all over the country." The writer said that southern theater managers were maintaining stock companies to attract audiences, but the public wanted "moving attractions; they tire of looking at the same old faces. No matter whether big or little acts, they want quick changes." He said that this change in the public's entertainment preferences offered blacks in the South and Midwest an opportunity. The writer suggested African Americans form their own circuit by opening venues in every city that had two thousand or more black citizens and provide changing shows of vaudeville acts and moving pictures. There would be more opportunities for black vaudeville acts and more money for black theater owners. The article closed with the words, "The writer is looking to the South and Southwest as the future field for the Negro in vaudeville."[10] It would be interesting to know how Voelckel, Sissieretta, and various members of the Black Patti cast reacted to this article and whether they realized that the growing popularity of moving pictures and vaudeville shows ultimately had serious implications for their own future.

By the end of January 1910, the company was touring in North Carolina and had a date (27 January) to play at the Academy in John Larkins's hometown of Wilmington. When the company pulled into town, Larkins's childhood friends spent half the day with him. Larkins reminisced about his attempt as a youngster to "steal" his way into the gallery of the Academy and how he fell into a tank in the process and had to call for help. He also recalled, sadly, how his brother had fallen from the winding stairway of the theater and had died from his injuries. While Larkins was in Wilmington, his aunt, whom he had not seen in twenty years, visited him and brought him sad news that his mother had died late last year, on 26 November in Norfolk, Virginia.[11] In a report published in the *New York Age,* cast member Anthony Byrd described how Larkins, saddened by news of his mother's death, still went on with the show that evening: "That night he proved himself 'true blue' and a man of fortitude, combined with great will power. One who witnessed the show could have seen that pathos and comedy went hand in hand throughout the performance. While singing, 'That Wont [*sic*] Do for Mother's Chile,' in the jungle scene, with tears rolling down his cheeks, in a twinkling of an eye a broad smile flashed over his face. His support was watching every movement for fear he would break down, and he was praised in the highest terms for the display of courage and iron nerve."[12]

By mid-February the company made its annual appearance in Indianapolis at the Park Theatre. Despite unusually severe weather during its three days there, the show played to good houses. Sissieretta, suffering from a cold and hoarseness, still managed to impress the audiences, as did the other sixteen members of the company. While appearing in Indianapolis, members of the Black Patti Company learned of the death of J. Ed. Green, former stage manager and comedy star of the Black Patti Troubadours. Green died on 19 February 1910 in Chicago at the age of thirty-seven, after a three-month illness.[13] He had been married to current Black Patti Company cast member Jeanette Murphy Green, who had performed with the Black Patti show for years and also served as Sissieretta's personal assistant. It is unknown whether Jeanette was still married to Green at the time of his death or whether they had separated, as she had been traveling with the Black Patti troupe for several years while he was living in Chicago.

In March and throughout the remainder of the season, the Black Patti Musical Comedy Company played many more three-day runs and week-long performances in major cities such as Detroit; Dayton and Columbus, Ohio; Pittsburgh; Baltimore, Washington, D.C.; Jersey City and Newark, New Jersey; Brooklyn; and Boston. When the company played at the Columbia Theatre in Newark, 18–24 April, Walton traveled from New York City to see the show. He said the company was small enough to appear more like a large vaudeville act, but from this "diminutive parcel is produced the greatest singer of her race—Mme. Sissieretta Jones."

> Mme. Jones is without a doubt just as strong an attraction to-day as she was some years ago, and she is every bit as great an artist. After listening to one or two vocal selections you feel fully repaid for going as far as Newark to hear her sing. Theatre-goers of the South and Southwest are to be envied for being favored with a visit by Mme. Jones each year. It is too bad that the theatrical situation is such at this time that the Black Patti Musical Company is unable to grace New York City with a week's stay.

Five songs are rendered by Mme. Jones during the performance, and each is enthusiastically received. It is her singing of "Suwanee River" in the third act when she appears to best advantage, having an opportunity to show her range of voice. Her notes are clear and bell-like as of old, which is particularly true of her middle register. Aside from Mme. Jones' pleasing voice she works with sprightliness of manner that commands admiration. There are many chorus girls who could take lessons from Mme. Jones for vivacity, and it must be remembered that the celebrated singer carries herself about the stage like a "two-year-old," despite the fact that this is her thirteenth [actually her fourteenth] season on the road, and it should not be overlooked that three-fourths of the time has been consumed in playing one-night stands.

This is Mme. Jones' first season to have a speaking part, and she now aspires to appear in more pretentious roles. While in conversation with the dramatic editor of THE AGE the gifted songstress declared that she has become so carried away with her lines that she is ambitious to be taken in the future as seriously in speaking parts as she is in her vocal selections.[14]

Sissieretta evidently embraced her new role in the show. Based on reviews around the country during the season, it appeared her audiences were pleased with the change as well. Walton's words about the "theatrical situation" in New York City that kept the Black Patti show from playing there for a week's run may have referred to the control white theatrical syndicates had over what played at the city's theaters.

As the first season of the Black Patti Company came to a close, the troupe was likely pleased with the success of the new format. Every member of the cast had had to work hard, especially with the troupe being the smallest it had ever been. Voelckel may have kept the cast small to hold down costs now that he was sole owner of the company. Also the troupe did not travel any further west than Texas and Oklahoma, and this would be the case for the remaining years the company was in business. They would never again visit the West Coast. Voelckel may have found it too expensive to get profitable bookings in the West. Also railroad fees, in addition to production expenses, had increased in recent years, probably making it necessary for him to trim travel and production costs to keep the company profitable. But they were still in business, and Voelckel planned to take the show on the road again for the upcoming 1910–11 season. The *New York Age* called the "colored" theatrical scene "cloudy and unsettled." Three seasons before there had been four large black shows touring throughout the East and Midwest as well as several "colored productions of merit" playing the South and West. Black musical companies that had played week-long engagements were the Williams and Walker Company, the Ernest Hogan Company, the Cole and Johnson Company, and the Smart Set Company, headed by Sherman H. Dudley, the newspaper said. Of those companies three were no longer active at the start of the 1910–11 season. Hogan had closed his company in 1908 because of illness; he died fifteen months later. George Walker suffered a breakdown at the close of the 1907–8 season, which broke up the Williams and Walker team. Walker was in a sanitarium, and Bert Williams had joined the white Ziegfeld Follies in 1910. Bob Cole and Rosamond Johnson had decided to leave the musical comedy business and return to vaudeville. That left two large African American shows on the scene in addition to the Black Patti Company, according to the *Age:* the Southern Smart Set Company, starring Salem Tutt Whitney, and the Down in Dixie Minstrels, featuring John Rucker. The newspaper described the Black Patti Musical Comedy Company as the "principal attraction in the South" and the "most successful of all colored shows touring the South."[15] Voelckel was taking the traveling troupe on the road for a fifteenth season.

Rehearsals for the 1910–11 season of the Black Patti Musical Comedy Company began on 4 August at Passaic, New Jersey, and the company opened to an "overflowing house" at the Passaic Opera House on 11 August 1910. The show, *A Trip to Africa,* the same as the previous year's show, starred Sissieretta and Larkins. Larkins's wife, Jennie Pearl Larkins, played the role of Dinah Green, replacing Sarah Green Byrd who left the company with her husband, Anthony, at the close of the 1909–10 season. Jennie Pearl had played four seasons as the leading soubrette of the Smart Set Company. The cast this year was much larger. It had about twenty-eight performers, including Sissieretta and Larkins, plus a music director (D. L. Richards), two cooks, and a master mechanic. Al F. Watts, who had left the company several seasons ago, returned as stage manager and general understudy, as well as playing the role of Secret Service Bill, a detective. Baritone soloist James H. Gray became the troupe's correspondent to the *New York Age.*[16]

The *Indianapolis Freeman,* which reviewed the show's opening night performance, noted the updated scenery and stage effects, the "new and catchy" songs, and the "bright and gorgeous" costumes. It also had high praise for Sissieretta and Voelckel:

> Black Patti, Madam Sissieretta Jones, thrilled the audiences as only an artist can and was forced to respond to deafening encores and easily reestablished herself as the queen of song. Her costumes this season outshine all previous gowns that she has worn and excites [*sic*] no little admiration each time she appears on stage.

Mr. R. Voelckel, owner and manager, has spared neither pains nor money to assemble one of the strongest singing aggregations in the history of colored theatricals, and as his business methods are of the highest order and looking for the welfare of his people is his motto, too much praise cannot be given him both as a manager and a gentleman. This is the beginning of the usual trans-continental tour.[17]

About mid-September, after the company had been on the road for over a month, Gray reported to the *New York Age* that business had been good, despite some hot weather. He complimented Watts, who had returned to the Black Patti Company, by saying the "genial" stage manager was able to keep everyone happy—management, performers, and southern stagehands. Gray told the *Indianapolis Freeman* that the company would soon be heading to Oklahoma, and some in the cast wondered how the show would fare there, as many African Americans had been leaving Oklahoma because of race prejudice. He also said that some cast members had left the show but that others were hired to replace them, making daily rehearsals necessary for several weeks. Gray noted a program change—the sextet, led by Sissieretta, that had been singing the sextet from *Lucia di Lammermoor* was replaced with a quartet, also led by Sissieretta, performing a difficult operatic quartet from *Rigoletto*. He also told about Sissieretta's reception in the South. "Mme. Jones' voice is heard to great advantage in solo and operatic numbers, coupled with beautiful gowns, magnificent jewelry and commanding presence the Southland people sit agape with astonishment," he said.[18] He did not elaborate whether he was talking about white people or black people in the audiences, but it was most likely true for people from both races. White theatergoers seeing Sissieretta probably could not believe that a black woman had achieved the training, polish, presence, and wealth that she displayed, and the black patrons were probably awestruck that one of their own race had achieved such visible signs of success.

The Black Patti Company played Kempner's Theatre in Little Rock on 26 September. As was more and more the case, the audience was predominately black, with a "scattering" of white patrons downstairs and the balcony filled to capacity with black patrons. Gray sent a review of the show from the white newspaper the *Arkansas Gazette* to the *Age,* which published it in its 6 October 1910 edition. "And yet the show is well worthy of patronage in all parts of the house. It is the most pretentious production the black prima donna has yet had, being a full-fledged musical comedy with scenic and electrical effects and fine costumes," the review said. "To tell the unprejudiced truth, in comedy and good singing, 'A Trip to Africa' is a better show than many of the high-priced musical comedies, for few of them can boast a prima donna with a voice equal to that of the Black Patti and few have a leading comedian as genuinely and irresistibly funny as John Larkins."[19]

In that same issue of the *Age,* Lester Walton wrote about how Cole and Johnson's return to vaudeville after a four-year hiatus demonstrated what black entertainers were up against when they tried to step out of comedic, stereotypical roles white audiences expected from them. Walton attended the duo's debut performance in New York City at the Fifth Avenue Theater in early October. That night Cole and Johnson, as they had done in their original vaudeville act years ago, dressed in evening wear, used excellent English, and often sang extremely sentimental songs. Prior to leaving vaudeville four years earlier to concentrate on musical comedies, the two songwriters had been the most refined black vaudeville act in the business, but conditions in vaudeville had changed "greatly" in the theatrical world, and white audiences were no longer open to this kind of performance, Walton said. Cole and Johnson quickly learned that the average present-day white theatergoer was "not disposed to enthuse to any extent over the work of a performer of ebony hue unless he resorts to low comedy and comes up to the playgoer's idea of how a colored performer should dress, talk and act." The duo concluded, Walton said, "that the majority of white patrons do not highly appreciate a refined colored act." Black performers were no longer presenting refined acts in vaudeville. Instead most black acts had resorted to "low comedy and wearing grotesque costumes." Walton said, "The white public in particular seems inclined to view the race on and off the stage in a humorous vein. To depict the intelligent and cultured Negro on the stage as he exists to-day fails to evoke generous applause. Such a picture seems to be repulsive to three-fourths of the whites who patronize vaudeville houses."

Walton offered three reasons why white audiences did not want to see black performers in a polite and refined act. The first reason was ignorance. The second was race prejudice, and the third reason was the large number of white vaudeville acts performing in blackface. Walton said that there were "three times as many white performers appearing over the large vaudeville circuits doing blackface acts than there are colored artists." He said managers favored booking these white acts rather than the colored acts. "They do not seem to want the real thing nowadays—only an imitation. . . . The white vaudevillian in cork has taught the white audience to appreciate imitations and regard with disdain many types of the Negro race true to life," the critic said. Cole and Johnson made some changes in their act after their debut, Walton said, and they would likely "size up conditions and act accordingly." He predicted they would become successful despite the current state of affairs.[20]

But Cole and Johnson would not get a chance to rework their vaudeville act. A week after the article ran in the *Age* about the pair's debut, the newspaper

carried sad news about Cole. The famous composer, playwright, and entertainer had suffered a "slight mental breakdown" and was being treated for
"nervous trouble" in a private sanitarium in New Jersey. "His case is not considered serious by his attending physicians, who think he will be able to
resume his vaudeville engagements after a short rest," the newspaper reported.
The breakdown was attributed to overwork. He had been working day and
night for four weeks on several vaudeville acts as well as his own, writing songs
and also helping to stage several numbers in another show. But Cole did not
return to vaudeville after a week of rest. Instead he was transferred to the
Manhattan State Hospital, where doctors predicted it would take a year
before he recovered.[21]

With the death of Hogan and the illnesses of Walker and Cole, Sissieretta
remained one of the few well-known, longtime African American entertainers still performing. She had been on the stage for twenty-two years—eight
years on the concert stage and fourteen years as singing star of her own musical comedy company. While Hogan, Walker, and Cole had concentrated on
longer runs in eastern cities, particularly in New York City, Sissieretta traveled
around the United States, particularly in the South, Southwest, and West,
playing mostly one-night stands in smaller cities and towns. She had logged
thousands of miles in her twenty-two years in front of the lights and most
likely held the record for the most single-night performances. At forty-two
years old, the singing star continued to be blessed with good health and
showed no signs of retiring.

The Black Patti Musical Comedy Company toured Texas and Louisiana
in October and November 1910, playing a two-day engagement, 14–15 October, in Dallas. The *Age* reprinted comments a Dallas theater critic made after
seeing the show. Before printing the comments, the newspaper apologized to
its readers for the critic's use of the word *nigger*. The review, although likely
meant to compliment black shows and black performers, nevertheless provides
a good example of the deep racism and negative stereotypes that Sissieretta
and other black entertainers faced from many white theatergoers and critics.

Did you ever watch an audience that was three parts animated, joyous,
eager, squirmy colored folks and one part languid, rather uncomfortable
and mostly disdainful members of the Caucasian race at a show that was
frankly and solely altogether nigger? Don't look disgusted—they're pretty
good stuff those coon shows—and it's a revelation to watch the people
in the balconies, an education in plain human nature, to observe those
in the pit.
    And don't think for a minute that these colored aggregations are lack-
ing in talent. There's as much downright funniness to the square inch in

such musical comedy as can be discovered in the ordinary production. A nigger that is willing to come right out and be pure nigger, to avail himself of the delicious peculiarities of his race, can be quite the funniest thing going; and the one who pompously apes the mannerisms of his brother in white can be just a tiny bit funnier; and the combination is positively hilarious.

Then, too, there's music in the soul of every true son of Ham and a big bunch of darkies can always manage to coax a lot of tunefulness out of any melodious music with the throaty gurgle and the sort of vocal somersault that comes in between, that can be approached by no other human; and there's a plaintive note that is purely African and wholly delightful.[22]

As the troupe continued its tour through Texas, Sissieretta made plans to increase her operatic repertoire in the show with a "new, specially prepared" selection she intended to sing when touring in larger cities in the South. Voelckel, who had been in Tulsa on business related to another show he was managing, the Kersands Minstrels, returned to the Black Patti Company as it toured the Texas panhandle on its way to the Gulf. Music director D. L. Richards had been acting as manager in Voelckel's absence. Gray, the company's correspondent to the *Age,* said the troupe was looking forward to playing 30–31 October at the Opera House in San Antonio, "a city which is to us this time of year what Broadway is to other big shows." Sissieretta and the show earned good reviews from the San Antonio press, according to Gray. The audiences loved Sissieretta's singing and the beautiful gowns she wore and praised Larkins's comedic work.[23]

In late November, Larkins and Voelckel decided to part ways beginning 3 December when the troupe reached Donaldsonville, Louisiana. Rumors had surfaced for several weeks that the two were not getting along. Apparently the disagreement came to a head, and Larkins and his wife, Jennie, planned to leave the Black Patti troupe and head east to do vaudeville. In preparation for the upcoming departure, other cast members began learning new parts. However several weeks after Larkins's announced departure, Voelckel and the comedian "patched up their differences," and all was right with the company once again, the *Age* reported. Larkins and his wife planned to stay with the Black Patti show for the rest the season.[24]

The company spent Thanksgiving, 26 November, in Crowley, Louisiana. After the cool temperatures they had experienced while touring in Texas, the troupe encountered hot, humid weather in Louisiana. Gray reported that despite "the torrid atmosphere, full justice was done to an elaborate dinner prepared by our chef, William K. Carson, who is an artist in the culinary department." Sometime between the show's appearance in Crowley and before it reached New Orleans in early December, Sissieretta was the victim of a painful accident. "While singing, a bug lodged in her throat, causing a severe nausea and hoarseness. Mme. heroically persevered despite the inconvenience," Gray reported. Sissieretta was fine by the time she opened at the Temple Theatre in New Orleans on 7 December. As usual the show was well received and the cast enjoyed a variety of social activities during their week's stay.[25]

After the company left New Orleans, it headed for several one-night engagements in Mississippi. The cast likely read with interest an article in the *New York Age* (22 December 1910) by former comedy star of the Black Patti Troubadours Salem Tutt Whitney. The opening of the article, "The Negro on the Stage," addressed the question of whether black performers on the stage helped elevate the race in the South. Whitney, who had been touring the South with the Smart Set show, did not claim to be an authority on this issue, but he offered his thoughts: "The Southern Negro is intensely interested, and reasonably so, in anything appertaining to the ultimate mental, moral, physical and spiritual redemption of the colored race. It has been our good fortune to please most of our Southern audiences, and in every town of any consequence, people have remained after the show to thank us for the influence for good any first-class colored company exercises on a Southern community: not only does it stimulate race pride and ambition, but it increases the respect for Negro ability—a fact the Southern white man is forced to concede."[26]

Perhaps Sissieretta and the rest of the Black Patti cast felt the same way. For years Sissieretta and the Black Patti Troubadours had toured the South, visiting many small towns and larger cities. They had been well received by both blacks and whites but especially among black patrons, who filled the balconies in southern theaters. Sissieretta, with her beautiful voice, gorgeous gowns, expensive jewelry, and stately manner, was a source of pride to African American theatergoers, especially in the segregated South. Year after year her show helped bring professional musical comedy productions to those who could not travel to New York City to see the big shows, and her operatic and classical music selections made those types of music more accessible to people of both races in the rural South and Southwest.

The company spent Christmas in Mobile, Alabama, where they played to "fair" houses 22–24 December at the Mobile Theatre. The weather was so hot it felt more like the Fourth of July than Christmas, according to Gray. Sissieretta and Larkins gave small gifts to each cast member. Larkins surprised his wife, Jennie, with a gold watch decorated with a large diamond, and she gave him a pair of gold cuff buttons. Voelckel gave Sissieretta a silver manicure set. Gray said business in the South had been good. While traveling in that region, company members had noticed how the entertainment field had opened up for black performers at a time when "the door appears to be against him in the North." Almost every city in the South was starting a small theater, Gray noted.[27] The company gave a New Year's Eve performance in Selma to a "top-heavy house" at the Academy of Music.

Several days later, while in Florence, Alabama, Sissieretta, who had wisely used some of her earnings over the years to invest in real estate in Rhode Island, sent a letter to her attorney, Charles H. Page, in Rhode Island, with questions about her rental property. The letter was written on special Black Patti Musical Comedy Company letterhead, which featured an oval-shaped, head-and-shoulder photograph of Sissieretta. The top of the letterhead said "America's Foremost Negro Organization" and then "R. Voelckel presents the New Black Patti Musical Comedy Company." Further down on the letterhead it said, "with Sissieretta Jones, the Original 'Black Patti' and 40 others of exceptional merit. Home office 601 Times Bldg., New York City."

In the letter Sissieretta asked her attorney for an updated statement of receipts and disbursements regarding her rental property in Rhode Island and a check for the balance due her. Apparently her tenants owed her money, and she wanted to know the extent of their debt and the reason for it. She asked, "Would it be possible to embody this in next statement, also show what amount each and every tenant is supposed to pay monthly?" She said her mother had told her that Mr. Page had been quite ill, and she expressed hope for his early recovery. She told him to send the statement and her check to her home at 7 Wheaton Street, from which it would be forwarded to her on the road.[28] In addition to the Wheaton Street property, she owned two pieces of rental property on Benefit Street near Church and Howland Streets and reportedly two others on Wheaton.[29]

While the Black Patti Company was traveling from Alabama through Georgia and on its way to Florida, the cast learned of the 7 January death of the famous black comedian George Walker, who for years had been the other half of the Walker and Williams team. Walker died quietly, with his mother at his side, in a private sanatorium in Islip, New York. His wife, Aida Overton Walker, was appearing in Cincinnati at the time with Dudley's Smart Set Company. She had been a member of the Black Patti Troubadours during its first season, 1896–97. Sissieretta and the cast heard about Walker's death too late to send flowers, but through words published by the *New York Age,* company members were able to express their sympathy to Walker's mother and wife for the loss of "an illustrious son and husband."[30]

The Black Patti Company reached Florida in mid-January 1911 and played ten days in the state's winter resort towns. Business was "brisk," with audiences consisting mostly of northern tourists. Members of the cast spent their free time visiting ostrich and alligator farms, orange and grapefruit groves, and also fishing in the tropical climate. They had such a good time that they hated to leave the state. The troupe's last Florida engagement during this tour was at the Duvall Theatre in Jacksonville, where they performed for two days, 30–31 January, doing both afternoon and evening shows. Both black and white patrons filled the theater at all the performances, and people reportedly stood in every vacant space to see Sissieretta and Larkins in a revised *A Trip to Africa.* Tim Owsley, in an article published by the *Indianapolis Freeman* (11 February 1911), said, "Madame Patti (Sissieretta Jones) sang as well as ever and just as sweet, not only did she sing, but we find she can act as well. And her every effort was highly appreciated by both races. Her songs brought encore after encore. Her gowns were of the latest style and fashion, and in each act that she appeared she received a hearty welcome, made known by the applause she received by which one can see she will never be forgotten by the people of the Southland."[31]

As the company continued its tour of the South, Larkins, anxious to see how he would fare with audiences in larger, eastern cities, announced in mid-February that he planned to leave the Black Patti Company at the end of the season to star in *A Royal Coon.* The show was supposed to be a "gorgeous" musical comedy in three acts, supported by a chorus and an all-star cast, which would also include Larkins's wife, Jennie Pearl.[32] Meanwhile things were happening on the entertainment scene in New York that did not bode well for black musical comedies. The Court Theatre in Brooklyn announced that it would switch from theater productions, most notably black musical shows, to vaudeville and motion pictures. The change signified the "meteoric career of the motion picture business" over the last several years, which had produced a marked change in the theater business. The Court Theatre announcement had an even greater significance to black musical shows because, for the last two years, it had been an "oasis of the local theatrical desert and the only popular-priced house in Greater New York that furnished financial encouragement to colored productions."[33] Vaudeville and the motion pictures were taking over more of the popular-priced venues where black shows played. Although Sissieretta and her company were not involved directly in the situation in Brooklyn, the change there symbolized what was happening more and more in other cities. The entertainment field was changing.

After six and a half months touring the Southwest, South, and Gulf states, the Black Patti Company arrived at the beautiful new 1,200-seat Howard Theatre in Washington, D.C., to open a week-long run that began 13 March 1911. The theater, which had opened the previous year, was owned by white men but managed by blacks. It was located near Howard University and was so large that it "occupied an entire city block."[34] Gray reported to the *New*

York Age that manager Voelckel had spared no expense to present the company in top form for its run in Washington, D.C. Cassie Jackson, the wardrobe mistress, had been busy fitting outfits for the cast. "The handsome evening gowns worn in the last act are the latest design, from a New York establishment," Gray wrote. At the end of the opening night performance, Sissieretta received a beautiful basket of flowers. Her encore that evening— her famous rendition of "Swanee River"—set the "house wild," according to Gray. Larkins also had the Washington audiences excited with his new song, "The Great I Am," and he was called on to give several encores. Former cast members Jeanette Murphy and Estelle Cash rejoined the company in Washington. On Tuesday night, during the society scene near the end of the third act, Cash married former stage manager Al F. Watts onstage before a large audience. "An exceptionally large aggregation of romantic folks were out to do the occasion honor," Gray said. Jerry Mill, the show's new stage manager, had been working with the cast since joining them in Norfolk after taking over the job from Watts earlier in March. Mill had "completely rearranged" the show, and it was so good that it could be given on Broadway, Gray said.[35]

A review of the show by W. P. Bayless published in the *Indianapolis Freeman* (1 April 1911) credited Larkins for writing the show and playing the starring comedic role. Bayless also praised Sissieretta. "Madame Sissieretta Jones, of world wide fame, is a solo artist who has sustained a reputation second to none for many years and today she is a star and a drawing card wherever she goes." It appears that Voelckel's company, after a somewhat rocky start the previous season when he first took over as sole proprietor, was back up to full strength and dazzling the Washington audiences. Bayless found the show attractive and professional: "On the whole the production was brilliant and tasteful. The stage pictures had every advantage that light and color could bestow, yet there was not a single touch of garishness. The young women of the company wore beautiful gowns with an air of accustomed ease that made them more alluring to the eye than all the tricks and fantasies a stage milliner could invent. It was a company of actors who drift up and down, around and about, in and off the stage with such steady and varied supply of song, action, and smartness that one could easily see that the company was well drilled from 'star' to 'supers.'"[36]

Because many theatergoers could not get tickets to see the Black Patti show during its week-long engagement in Washington, the management of the Howard Theatre arranged with Voelckel to cancel a week of one-nighters so the company could play a second week in Washington beginning 20 March. During the second week's performance, the sextet from *Lucia di Lammermoor*, led by Sissieretta, was included in the program. The *Indianapolis Freeman* ran another review of the show during its run at the Howard Theatre.

*An older Sissieretta wearing a hat while having her
picture made at a photography studio. Photograph courtesy
of the Dr. Carl R. Gross Collection, Moorland-Spingarn
Research Center, Howard University.*

The review said Sissieretta was singing better than ever before and making "a host" of new friends in the capital city. "Her reception to the ladies, following each matinee, has proven a popular feature. The Madame's 'Suwanee River' brings down the house as of yore, and her stunning gowns and $15,000 worth of diamonds, worn at each performance, are revelations to the fair sex."[37]

After a two-week run in Washington, the Black Patti Company did a series of one-nighters in March and early April as they moved northward into New

Jersey and Maryland on their way to Boston, where they played at the Grand Opera House from 17–22 April 1911. Sissieretta's troupe had not been to Boston in years. After a successful engagement there, the company went to Newark, where they played a week, 24–29 April, at the Columbia Theatre. Voelckel ran a large advertisement in the *New York Age* while the show was in Newark. His ad, which featured photographs of Sissieretta and Larkins, was designed to draw audiences from New York as well as New Jersey by reminding theatergoers that the Columbia Theatre was only twenty-three minutes from the Hudson Terminal Station and thirty-four minutes from Pennsylvania Station. The ad also said there were frequent trains to New York after the performance. Voelckel ran another ad in the same edition of the *Age*. This advertisement sought black performers to audition for his minstrel show, Dandy Dixie Minstrels, which was scheduled to open its season on 23 August 1911 in Washington, D.C. The ad indicated he owned this minstrel troupe with a man named Walter Forbish.[38] Apparently Voelckel once again was going to have two shows in the upcoming season, the Black Patti Musical Comedy Company and the Dandy Dixie Minstrels. It appears that he remained sole proprietor of the Black Patti show but shared ownership and responsibilities for the Dandy Dixie Minstrels.

One of those who attended the Black Patti show when it played in Newark was Lester Walton, who wrote a lengthy review for the *Age*. Although he highlighted the work of Larkins, Jennie Pearl, Jerry Mills, Alice Ramsey, and other cast members, he devoted most of his review to Sissieretta—her voice, her signature song, and her grueling forty to forty-five weeks on the road.

> While the song "Suwanee River" was not especially written for Mme. Sissieretta Jones (Black Patti), yet no singer has become so closely identified with this well-known composition so suggestive of Southern environment as the race's leading soprano. For fifteen years Mme. Jones has delighted audiences with her artistic rendition of "Suwanee River," and judging from the agreeable manner in which she dispensed dulcet tones over the footlights at the Columbia Theatre, Newark, last week, she will be winning applause with "Suwanee River" for some time to come.
>
> Mme. Sissieretta Jones is really a remarkable woman—an artist whom biographers cannot overlook in days to come when giving historic references of performers past and present and their accomplishments. Long before Williams and Walker, Ernest Hogan, Cole and Johnson and other colored comedians had won name and fame Mme. Jones was traversing this country singing "Suwanee River" and other numbers to the great pleasure of hundreds of music lovers. To-day her voice still possesses that sympathetic rich timbre which made her famous years ago. Singers have

come and singers have gone, but "Black Patti" continues to heed the call of the footlights and she says she has no idea of retiring at a near date.

It was Theodore Roosevelt who made popular the term "strenuous life" but Mme. Sissieretta Jones must be regarded as a devout disciple of that doctrine. Few singers have led such a strenuous existence as she. During their theatrical season over three-fourths of her itinerary consists of one-night stands, and one-night stands are not regarded with a friendly eye by performers as they encounter so many inconveniences, they say. Mme. Jones has undergone all hardships that go with one-night stands and "is still in the ring."[39]

Sissieretta spent the summer in Providence, and Voelckel, who reported that the previous season's business had been more profitable than any other, began making plans for the 1911–12 tour. The Black Patti troupe would have company touring the sunny South in the upcoming season. The *New York Age* said more "colored" shows from the East would visit "Dixieland" than ever before. "The colored citizens below Mason and Dixon's line have evidently become enthusiastic theatergoers to the great delight of managers in recent years, for no less than half a dozen shows will be sent South from New York to provide entertainment for the Southerners. The oldest and most prominent organization will be the Black Patti Musical (Comedy) Company." Other shows included the Smart Set Company, headed by brothers Salem Tutt Whitney and Homer Tutt, and two minstrel shows—Down in Dixie Minstrels and Voelckel's Dandy Dixie Minstrels. Voelckel announced plans for the Dandy Dixie Minstrels to begin rehearsals on 21 August and to open 4 September at the Howard Theatre.[40]

Rehearsals for the new Black Patti show began on 27 July 1911 at the Music Hall in Goshen, New York. The book for the new three-act musical comedy, *In the Jungles,* was written by former longtime Black Patti Troubadours members Will Cooke and Al F. Watts and based on work by the late J. Ed. Green. Composer Will Marion Cook wrote the musical score, and Alex Rogers penned the lyrics. Julius Glenn, the "Wang Doodle Comedian," was hired as principal comedian, replacing "Jolly" John Larkins. Jerry Mills continued to serve as stage manager. The cast included twenty-five to thirty actors in addition to Sissieretta and Glenn. The company, "quartered in their private car," attended daily rehearsals in preparation for their opening night 8 August.[41]

While the Black Patti troupe was finishing up their rehearsals, they received news of the death of former Troubadour Bob Cole. Cole, forty-three, drowned on Wednesday, 2 August 1911, near his family residence in Catskill, New York. One newspaper suggested he may have committed suicide.[42] Cole, who had been treated at the Amityville Sanitarium on Long Island following a nervous breakdown a year earlier, had been released from the institution, accompanied by his mother, Dora B. Cole, at the end of July. Two days before his death, Cole had reported that he was feeling well, both mentally and physically. "According to reports from Catskill, N.Y., the comedian after dinner informed his mother that he was going to take a short walk. In less than fifteen minutes word was brought to her that her son had drowned in a creek nearby," the *New York Age* reported. "Spectators say they saw the deceased swim about with his clothes on and then suddenly disappear. He was heard to yell aloud when going down for the last time."[43] Cole, who had written and played in the inaugural show of the Black Patti Troubadours in 1896, had gone on to become one of the best-known black entertainers, composers, and playwrights of black musical comedy shows, including a couple of the Troubadours' shows in the early 1900s. With Cole's death three of the famous early black entertainers—Ernest Hogan, George Walker, and now Cole— were gone.

After the Black Patti Musical Comedy Company opened its 1911–12 season on 8 August at the Music Hall in Goshen, Voelckel sent a telegram about the opening performance to the *New York Age.* He said that hundreds had to be turned away because the turnout was so good. He praised his new comedian, Julius Glenn, saying he was "positively my best comedian in five years." Sissieretta sang Cook's new songs, "My Jewel of the Big Blue Nile" and "Love Is King," in a charming manner. Voelckel said the show was "beautifully staged" by Jerry Mills and had new and elaborate sets and costumes. He said it was a "most pretentious production befitting the most excellent route before me."[44]

The plot of *In the Jungles* had a story line similar to the past show *A Trip to Africa,* which the company performed the two previous seasons. The new show was about members of a Baptist missionary society interested in a young woman who had been lost in the jungles. Members of the organization find her later living among the jungle natives, who have made her their queen. Eventually she is brought back to her home by a confidence man, a lawyer detective, and the detective's valet, whose name is Count de Rocky Ford. The jungle scene was set in Zambesia, a village home of the fictional Gumbula tribe in Central Africa.[45]

In the Jungles played three days (21–23 August) in Indianapolis at the Park Theatre. J. D. Howard wrote a lengthy review of the show for the *Indianapolis Freeman* in which he commended the quality of the show's book and music as well as the "gorgeous" scenery, particularly the jungle sets. He said the music of *In the Jungles* had a "gingling, whistling" character that stayed with folks long after they had left the theater. The chorus numbers were "beautiful" and well executed "by a bunch of the liveliest girls and the best costumed

Sissieretta poses during a photography session to make it look as though she is sailing on a ship. Photograph courtesy of the Dr. Carl R. Gross Collection, Moorland-Spingarn Research Center, Howard University.

that have appeared with a colored show here for some time." Howard said female theatergoers would not want to miss seeing the beautiful gowns in the show designed by "Eaves, the New York costumer." The last act, he said, represented "a galaxy of wealth and beauty marvelous to behold." He noted, "Madame Sissieretta Jones (Black Patti) appeared in several big numbers. She has lost none of her pristine grace and perfect gesticulations. Her songs have been carefully selected and she renders them with a soulfulness of expression that brings forth great applause at the conclusion of each number. Her first song, 'My Jewel of the Nile,' rendered amid the environment and character-izations of a Gumbula tribe of Africans in Central Africa, was simply an eye opener of what was to follow. In the third act the biggest song of the show was rendered by the Madame, called 'Love is King.' In this act 'Baby Rose,' a pretty ditty by the Madame and entire chorus, was also repeatedly encored. The gowns worn by the Madame are the talk of all Indianapolis."

Howard said that Glenn, a former member of the "Whangdoodle Four Quartette," was "excruciatingly funny." Glenn, who had made a reputation for himself on the western burlesque circuit, sang a humorous song, "Plant a Watermelon on My Grave and Let the Juice Ooze Through," that was a "riot." Howard said this piece "recalled vividly the famous song of the late Ernest Hogan, 'O, Say Wouldn't That Be a Dream.'" Howard also singled out a new member of the cast, Tillie Seguin, describing her as "one of the most fetching little bits of femininity seen here for some time." He talked about her duet with Charles Bougia called "My Dreamland Rose," which was one of the best-received numbers in the show. "In fact this was the only love song duet rendered by colored performers I ever saw 'go' in the Park Theatre. As a rule such numbers by colored performers in this house are at best but tacitly toler-ated and are never applauded, but in this instance the performers were called back three times—a very good showing indeed," Howard said.

The critic said *In the Jungles* reminded him of certain scenes and situations in the late J. Ed. Green's musical comedy *The Queen of the Jungles,* which had been successfully produced at the Pekin Theatre in Chicago several years be-fore. Voelckel always gave partial playwright credit to Green whenever he advertised or talked about the writers of *In the Jungles.* Howard said, "'In the Jungles' presents to the American Negro pictures of our people that are within themselves studies in natural history. A great educational value is contained in every act. It is also one of the most amusing comedies I have ever had the pleasure of witnessing." Howard closed his review with words of praise for Voelckel, who had been managing successful "colored shows" for sixteen years.[46]

The highlight of the Black Patti Company's tour during the first half of the season was the two weeks the show played in Chicago—first a week at the Alhambra Theater beginning 24 September and then a week at the Bijou The-atre, 1–7 October. Sylvester Russell reviewed the opening performance at the Alhambra for the *Indianapolis Freeman.* The headline and underline for his review read, "Black Patti at the Alhambra Theater; The Famous Diva Makes Her First Chicago Appearance as a Musical Comedy Star, In Speaking Part Successfully, Julius Glenn Blossoms as a Real Comedian." Russell said that there was a "football rush" to the box office to get tickets for the show. He provided a lengthy description of Sissieretta's performance:

Black Patti, who is not named in the cast of characters, a mistake of the playwrights, enters as the star in the second act and it was at once discovered that her work as an actress has now broadened to such an extent that she can be termed an artist and her present day experience is equal if not greater and more capable than the average white actress in musical comedy. In a speaking part she was surprisingly at ease in a short but well written course of dialogue. Her first song, "My Jewel of the River Nile," once more revealed the fact that this woman as a singer is the marvel of her day, so remarkable has been the preservation of her voice. Her finished method of phrasing and perfect articulation is still superior to any female singer of her race. Her rendering of "Home, Sweet Home," very appropriate, but in an improper scene, brought her volleys of applause, as was also accorded her on her entrance. Her jungle costume was a rare object of admiration and her gown in the last act was of blue satin, with short en train covered with beaded lace and embroidered with gilded fringe.

Russell called comedian Julius Glenn "promising" and said that Voelckel, who had "brought out" Hogan, "is still an expert in the discovery of good comedians." The critic had positive remarks for Seguin, the leading soubrette; Watts, in the role of a confidence man; and Cooke, who played a tramp disguised as a detective and lawyer. Russell said the greatest musical number in the show was the song "Love Is King," sung by Sissieretta, Bougia, Jeanette Murphy, and others. The music of Cook, Russell said, "while not quite up to his past record, gave considerable proof of his capability in the quartette of the last act. The opening chorus of the second act was tuneful and the first number allotted to Black Patti was recitative and lacked the flow of melody at times which attracts the ear when a well known composer's new music seeks acquaintance." Russell summed up the show this way: "The new Patti show as a whole is exceptionally good and only suffers in lack of size but as large companies are going out of fashion people will soon get used to seeing a small show with real artists. If there is not always a scream there is a constant flow of humor, which makes you laugh at real Glenn comedy and scenes created by the authors, which all told makes the "Jungles" a winner."[47]

On Tuesday evening, 26 September, while the show was still playing at the Alhambra, the Black Patti Company had another onstage wedding. This time the bride and groom were cast members Tillie Seguin and Zel Bledseaux. "The wedding was one of the grandest affairs of its kind ever conducted on the stage," said Bledseaux, the company's correspondent to the *New York Age*. The house was filled with friends and relatives of the bride and groom. Cast member Estelle Cash Watts served as bridesmaid, and John Grant as best man.

The Reverend Dr. Roberts of Bethel A.M.E. Church officiated. After the show the groom's uncle held a reception for the couple at his home.[48]

While in Chicago, Voelckel and Sissieretta may have read an interesting article about black actors written by Lester Walton in the 5 October 1911 issue of the *Age*. The drama critic's column was devoted to the new phenomenon of using black actors to play black roles in some white theater productions. "The idea of using colored actors to play Negro roles is still young and in its infancy, but as the ice has been broken and several managers have been brave enough to employ colored performers to work in dramatic companies composed of white Thespians, as the venture has not been hurtful, there is much likelihood of the public seeing real colored people playing Negro parts in the majority of dramatic productions before many seasons have passed," Walton wrote. White producer William Brady had cast a black man to play a black steward on a steamer in a comedy called *Over Night*. Although some were opposed initially to hiring a black man to play the role rather than using a white actor in blackface, they were swayed, Walton said, by Brady's argument that people who traveled on steamers were used to seeing black stewards working on the ships. The first use of a black actor to play a black role was so successful that Brady hired other black actors to play black characters. "The presence of colored performers in a white company is particularly pleasing for many reasons," Walton wrote. "Aside from the fact that colored artists are given an opportunity to make a living, their connection with white theatrical organizations should tend to counteract much of the damage done in the past by white imitators." Walton said black stewards and waiters were known for being "all dignity itself." White actors portraying black stewards would "overdo" the part, and their "inclination to exaggerate has always been in the nature of ridicule which has never done the race any good," Walton wrote. He had high praise for theatrical producers who used black actors for black roles.[49]

Following their two-week run in Chicago, the Black Patti Company toured through Missouri and Kansas for the rest of October and Arkansas, Oklahoma, and Texas in November. They spent almost the entire month of December playing one-night stands in Texas. In late November, Voelckel and his Dandy Dixie Minstrel partner, Walter Forbish, acquired another show—the Royal Sam Company, which starred former Black Patti comedian "Jolly" John Larkins. "For several weeks, the Royal Sam Company has been leading a precarious existence, and it cannot be said that the members were always certain of three square meals a day," the *Age* reported. Four members of the company had initiated "attachment proceedings" against the show's owner, the Picker Amusement Company, for back salary when the show played in Columbus, Georgia. The suit against the company was dismissed when the show's ownership passed to Larkins on 4 October 1911. Once Voelckel and Forbish purchased the company, the show began playing to full houses again.[50]

As was customary around Christmastime, the *Age* and the *Indianapolis Freeman* published special Christmas issues that focused on the major black shows and their performers. Often the companies would buy large advertisements or submit articles to be included in these issues. The Black Patti Musical Comedy Company had a large advertisement in the 21 December 1911 issue of the *Age* that featured five photos of Sissieretta in various poses and one of "Happy" Julius Glenn. The ad began with text that read, "A Merry Christmas to the Profession. All glittering new except its fame. Now Booking, 17th season, 1912–1913. The Original Black Patti Show." In the middle of the ad between the photographs, a block of text read, "Sissieretta Jones, the Original 'Black Patti.' Whose marvelous voice and lyric triumphs are unparalelled [*sic*]. The most popular Prima-Donna in the world, with the people of all nations and races. Countless millions in every part of civilization have been charmed by her phenomenal voice. H. M. King Edward VII, the Duke of Cambridge, and other members of the Royal Family of England have honored her with their distinguished patronage. Was also present at several White House functions in Washington. A Grand New Show By Brand New People." At the bottom of the ad, the closing words read, "Shows may come, shows may go, but the 'Black Patti' show goes on forever."[51] The ad copy, likely written by Voelckel, greatly exaggerated Sissieretta's place in the world of music when it called her the "most popular Prima-Donna in the world," but it must have made her feel good, especially after such a long, successful career, to be recognized as the preeminent musical star she had become.

A similar ad ran in the *Freeman's* Christmas issue. It had much of the same text but carried only three photos of Sissieretta and two of Glenn.[52] In addition the newspaper carried short articles about Sissieretta, Glenn, and Voelckel. The one about Sissieretta was headlined, "Black Patti's Years of Success, Still Maintains a Remarkable Voice and Is Happy." It read: "There is no singer on the face of the globe who enjoys a better reputation than Mme. Sissieretta Jones, better known as 'Black Patti.' No woman ever born has been known to sing 'Suwanee River' with as much sweetness of expression as she. But the most remarkable thing about her is her talent to maintain such a powerful voice after nearly twenty years of night after night concert work. Nowhere over this broad land can one go but where the name of this noted diva is not praised and for many years to come her name will be a household word."[53]

As for Voelckel, the *Freeman* called him a "veteran in the show world" and said he had "stood the test as a successful showman." It is unknown whether someone at the newspaper penned the article about Voelckel or whether someone from the Black Patti Company wrote it: "In all the colored show world no name stands out above all as does R. Voelckel. For over twenty years his name has been linked with Negro minstrelsy and he is esteemed as the father of the Negro musical comedy. He is sole owner of the famous Black Patti show—a show that has existed longer than any other musical comedy, be they black or white. For seventeen years this company has traveled on and on without the slightest interruption, while countless numbers of colored theatrical aggregations have lived and died. Many of these were larger and created a great stir but only for a short time, but Black Patti went on under the flag of R. Voelckel."[54]

As the new year commenced, the Black Patti show began two months of mostly one-night stands throughout the South. Most reviews were favorable, and their audiences were primarily made up of black patrons. While the company was performing in North Carolina, former Troubadour Salem Tutt Whitney, star of the Smart Set show, wrote an article in the 24 February issue of the *Freeman* that provides some insight into black audiences of the South. Whitney said his show's managers, for the first time, had made it possible for black theater patrons to sit anywhere in the house to view the Smart Set show at theaters in Albany and Americus, Georgia; Orangeburg, South Carolina; and Florence, Wilmington, Raleigh, Winston-Salem, and Greensboro, North Carolina. "To break down the inherited prejudice of a Southern white man and induce him by any line of reasoning to admit a Negro upon terms of equality is no small accomplishment," Whitney said. "The financial results to the theater and the show proved the wisdom of this experiment." Black theatergoers showed their appreciation for the seating change, Whitney said, by filling "every inch of the spacious auditorium." This made good business sense, as more black patrons probably wanted to see the Smart Set show than white patrons. Whitney said he was thrilled with the quality of black patrons in southern audiences. He said they were people of "intelligence, refinement, and culture" who were well dressed and well mannered. "The ubiquitous theater nuisance who laughs longer and louder than anyone else and comments upon the show in a loud voice was missing from these all-colored audiences," Whitney wrote. "The wealthy Negroes of the South—and there are many—travel to all parts of the country, see and hear the best, consequently they are not easily hoodwinked," he added. Whitney said he did not understand why northern performers thought it was easier to please a southern audience than a northern one. Blacks are at home in the South, and the competition there is great because there are so many who are natural-born singers, dancers, and comedians, Whitney wrote. The comedian closed by commending black southern ministers for their mostly liberal views of black shows. "Many of them encourage their [church] members to attend," he wrote. "They seem to realize the remarkable influence for good that a clean, intelligent, up-to-date colored show has upon any community."[55]

When the Black Patti show finished its tour of the South in early March, the company headed northward for a number of week-long runs in cities such as Washington, D.C., Baltimore, Boston, Newark, Philadelphia, Brooklyn, and Atlantic City. One of the show's week-long engagements was at the Imperial Theatre, 25–30 March, in Sissieretta's city of residence, Providence. Audiences for the shows were reported to be large. It must have been gratifying for Sissieretta to perform in black hometown, where her mother, stepfather, and friends could attend one of her performances. A short review from Providence published in the *New York Dramatic Mirror* said, "Madame Sissieretta Jones has the feature role, and supported by a most capable company, presents one of the best musical comedies seen at this house this season."[56] Following the week in Providence, the company traveled a short distance up the road to Boston to play a week, 1–6 April. On the day the show closed in Boston, an article in the *Freeman* called for Voelckel to hire a writer to create a new play for Sissieretta and the company. The article began with a description of Sissieretta's musical and personal achievements:

> Black Patti is still the undisputed "queen of song" in the Negro race, and everybody here is proud of her. She is the pioneer that blazed the pathway from the local choir to grand opera for the colored singer, and proved that stage life could be made clean and wholesome, if there is a disposition on the part of the woman herself to travel the right road and command respect. She has opened the door of opportunity to the ambitious young Negro performer of all types. Nearly every one of the stars, living and dead, has at some time or other, been numbered as a member of the "Black Patti Troubadours," which has been in the field since the memory of man runneth to the contrary. She has worked hard and has won her way upward by sheer merit and the courage to triumph over difficulties, without unnecessary fret and worry. All this is to say that Mme. Sissieretta Jones herself is "all right;" but she must have a new play.

The writer said the show, *A Trip to Africa*, had been seen in various "guises" numerous times with "such distressing frequency" that the public would soon declare that "somebody has got to quit kicking this houn' dog around." Sissieretta did not deserve any blame for the play, the writer said. Voelckel needed to part with some money and hire someone to come up with a new, original play for the company. "We have the artists and we have the writers. 'Black Patti' deserves a strong setting for her work, and the players need situations that are not only new, but which enable them to display the talent that they really possess, and to show that they are on a par with their white contemporaries," the writer said, adding that he hoped Voelckel would take the hint in the spirit in which it was offered.[57] For sixteen seasons Voelckel had employed a winning formula that kept audiences coming back year after year to see the Black Patti show, but some, like the unnamed author of this article, were ready for a change. Voelckel, being the astute businessman he was, probably considered the writer's suggestion and weighed it against what he thought audiences were looking for when they came to see the Black Patti Company.

As the Black Patti show's 1911–12 season neared its end, the company played a week, 13–18 May, at the Grand Opera House, one of the largest theaters in New York City. Sissieretta and her troupe had not appeared in the city for several seasons. The company arrived in New York City at the same time as the Smart Set Company, which played two weeks at Hurtig and Seamon's Harlem Music Hall, a burlesque house. Lester Walton said that "colored shows" had not played New York City for sometime, adding that patrons who wanted to see a black production had to travel to Newark. The only reason the Black Patti Company and the Smart Set Company were playing in New York City was because the theaters in which they appeared had closed their regular seasons and the managers were willing to add these shows after the season finished, Walton said. Managers at the two theaters had promised that black patrons could buy tickets to any part of the theater; however when Walton attended performances of the two shows, he found black patrons segregated from white patrons. At the Harlem Music Hall black theatergoers were seated on the ground level off to the left side, while white patrons were seated in the middle and on the right. At the Grand Opera House, only white patrons were seated in the first twelve rows.[58] Walton's review of the Black Patti show said that the large houses at the Grand proved Sissieretta was still a "big drawing card." He said that although Sissieretta had been doing "one nighters" for many seasons, she could "continue to lay claim to being the leading singer of her race without fear or trembling. When one hears her and then recalls what a strenuous and hard lot it is traveling about the country for fifteen [actually sixteen] seasons, seldom staying in one town more than one night, you are compelled to marvel at this singer, whose tones are yet clear, bell-like and full of vigor."[59]

Sissieretta and her troupe finished their season at Hurtig and Seamon's Harlem Music Hall, 3–8 June 1912. The forty-four-year-old Sissieretta had completed another successful season and planned to come back for her seventeenth road tour after spending the summer in Providence. She showed no signs of tiring of life on the stage and the demanding travel schedule that it required. She likely awaited word from Voelckel to see what her role in next season's show would be.

There were no major changes for the Black Patti Musical Comedy Company's 1912–13 season other than a new play, set in the Philippine Islands, that had thematic similarities to those of the past several seasons. During the summer Will A. Cooke revised a three-act musical comedy, *Captain Jasper,* originally written by the late J. Ed. Green in 1907 but never produced on stage during his lifetime. As with the Black Patti Company's previous productions, the show had a thin plot that provided opportunities for musical numbers and dancing. The show's plot revolved around the theft of important papers and the search to find the thief and recover the documents. Sissieretta played the role of Cheteka, "queen of a Philippine tribe." Her featured vocal numbers were "Sun Blest Are You, O Golden Land," "The Nightingale," and "Belle of New York." Julius Glenn, the head comedian, played the role of Jasper Charcoal. In addition to Sissieretta and Glenn, there were about twenty-two other cast members along with ancillary staff.[60] It remained to be seen whether audiences would turn out to see Sissieretta and the Black Patti show like they had in the past, given the growing popularity of inexpensive vaudeville and moving-picture shows around the country. By 1912 approximately five million people a day in the United States went to the cinema to view a silent movie.[61]

The Black Patti show opened on 26 August 1912 in Goshen, New York, after which the company's tour got off to a typical start—a series of one-night stands in Pennsylvania, Indiana, and Ohio, with their annual three-day engagement at the Park Theatre in Indianapolis. Then the company worked its way south, arriving in Nashville on 19 September for a two-night run at the Majestic Theatre. This thousand-seat theater, owned by an African American, was run exclusively for black patrons. More and more frequently black-owned and black-managed theaters were sprouting up around the country. An unnamed Black Patti cast member, in a report to the *Indianapolis Freeman,* said the show was a hit with the audience, and "Madame Jones took them by storm upon her appearance in the second act." She had to sing several encores beyond her regular repertoire. Sissieretta had been suffering from a severe throat infection, although it was not noticeable when she sang, the cast member wrote.[62]

By late October the Black Patti Company reached Little Rock, where they played to mostly black patrons for two days. The cast member who served as correspondent to the *Freeman* said that the entire theater was available to black theatergoers, who turned up in large numbers. The unnamed cast member had high praise for Sissieretta: "Madam S. Jones, the Black Patti, seems to grow younger. To hear her sing and not see her, you would imagine you were listening to her sixteen years ago: the same voice and mannerisms, only a bit more matured; she has that rare gift that others of our race have not, personality, magnetism, poise, that is the reason she has stood the storm of time and still retains that beautiful and remarkable voice. Everybody seems to appreciate her singing more this season that [sic] they have in several seasons and that speaks well for everybody. Her popularity has been growing more, and more among the whites, as they don't attend colored shows as a rule. They have been or are becoming educated to the fact that the Negro men and women performers can really do something worth going to see and hear."[63]

Although this cast member may have exaggerated Sissieretta's youthful singing, he obviously was proud of her voice and stage presence. His comments about her popularity with white theatergoers indicates that she was continuing to perform before mixed-race audiences despite the fact that many reviews of her show during this later part of her career suggested she was playing more and more to mostly black audiences. Sissieretta's success fostered race pride among black theatergoers and may have helped dispel negative black stereotypes among her white admirers.

By early October the troupe had started a long series of one-night stands throughout Texas, which included a two-night engagement, 11–12 October, at the Majestic Theatre in Fort Worth. A review from the *Fort Worth Star-Telegram* said Black Patti's appearance in that city was always an important event, especially to black theatergoers. This visit was no exception. Large crowds of black patrons filled the balcony and gallery to "overflowing." The audience was thrilled, the review said, when Sissieretta appeared "majestically" dressed in a large white picture hat, white serge suit, white gloves, and white shoes. "As she is booked in the play as 'Cheteka,' queen of a Philippine tribe, this was rather more clothes than might have been expected, especially as the scene was laid in the summertime." The review said Sissieretta's numbers were well received, as was a song in the show named "It's a Long Lane That Has No Turning" and a dance number by the chorus called "The Shaky Rag."[64]

As December began the Black Patti Company was scheduled to play one-night stands most of the month in Georgia and Florida, with a one-week engagement, 20–26 December, in Tampa. Several of their scheduled performances were changed or canceled, as were those of other black road shows playing in the South, particularly Salem Tutt Whitney's Southern Smart Set, because of bad feelings among whites about the actions of black prizefighter Jack Johnson.[65] Johnson, the first black heavyweight champion, had been a controversial figure ever since he won the title from a white man, Tommy Burns, on 26 December 1908 in Sydney, Australia. In 1910 Johnson successfully defended his title against another white man, former heavyweight champion Jim Jeffries. Johnson, who was married to a white woman, Eta Duryea, had also been associating openly with a white prostitute, Lucille Cameron.

Government officials planned to use his relationship with Cameron to prosecute him for violating the Mann Act, which prohibited transporting women across state lines for immoral purposes. On 14 September 1912 Johnson's wife committed suicide. Three months later the fighter married Cameron, which kept her from testifying against him, as wives could not be forced to testify against their husbands. Johnson's marriage to a second white woman stirred up racial feelings about mixing the races and upset many white as well as black people. "The white public was outraged beyond words."[66] Officials later found another white prostitute, Belle Schreiber, who had been Johnson's girlfriend "on and off" for years and used her to prosecute him for violating the Mann Act. He was found guilty in 1913 and sentenced to a year and a day in prison. While on bail he skipped the country and went to Europe. He lived there until 1920, when he returned to the United States to serve his sentence.[67]

Lester Walton, writing in the *New York Age,* said the black race had looked upon Johnson as a hero when he won his title fight and as someone who would play an important part in breaking down racial prejudice. "But we have been greatly disappointed in him. Instead of lessening prejudice he has increased it. It is unfortunate in this country that the entire race is subjected to criticism when one member does something discreditable. It is not so with the white race, however."[68] The Johnson affair hurt black shows such as Sissieretta's company and the Southern Smart Set and black entertainers, particularly those who worked in the South. In addition some managers of smaller vaudeville circuits in the East said they would not be able to use "colored acts" for some time, the *New York Age* reported.[69] Russell, in his annual review of the stage published in the *Age,* said the "greatest blow" to show business during the 1912 season was the "horrible racket created by the champion Negro pugilist." He said Johnson's injury to "colored" performers had been "far reaching."[70]

With all the negative press about Johnson and how his actions had stirred up racial prejudice and hurt black entertainers and black shows, a piece in the *Indianapolis Freeman* (28 December 1912) provides an interesting look at another aspect of race in the theatrical business—the relationship between white managers and the black shows they directed. Whitney wrote an article about the Smart Set's white manager, English-born Trevor L. Corwell. Corwell had worked with Voelckel and Nolan a couple of seasons as musical director of the Black Patti Troubadours (1904–5, 1908–9) and later with the Dandy Dixie Minstrels. Whitney's comments about Corwell and his relationship with the black company he managed provide insight into the complex relationship Voelckel must have had over the years with the Black Patti Troubadours and later the Black Patti Musical Comedy Company. Whitney said it required courage, honesty, diplomacy, intelligence, an ability to judge human nature, and a "liberal view upon the race problem" for a white man to manage a black company:

> The psychological side of the question is overlooked by so many white men who would manage colored shows. A white man at the head of a colored company is regarded with suspicion by the majority of its members: sometimes these suspicions are unjustified, but they exist nevertheless. Especially is this true of a colored company playing through the South. I heard the following remark made of a certain white manager by members of a colored company. "He is all right in the North, but wait until he gets you down in 'Bam."
>
> In the South members of a colored company are continually confronted by evidences of race prejudice and restrictions. Although openly insulted and imposed upon, they know that justice and redress are denied them. The white man reigns supreme in the South, and the members of the company know that they are entirely within the manager's power. The color of his face gives him every advantage. This is why I say it takes a conscientious, liberal-minded, sympathetic man to manage a colored company. A man too big to take advantage of his color to humiliate his people. A man with a heart large enough to sympathize with them in their difficulties.

Whitney added that a white manager traveling in the South with a black troupe is often insulted by whites and subject to racial slurs such as "nigger lover." The manager has to have the "courage and forbearance" to withstand the insults, because his reactions or efforts to retaliate would likely have a negative effect on the black company.[71]

Voelckel apparently possessed all the qualities necessary to be a good manager of a black company. By the end of 1912, he had been with Sissieretta and her company for seventeen years, and most of those years were spent traveling in the South. The few times he was mentioned in newspaper articles, the comments about him, made mostly by cast members who worked for him, were complimentary. Sissieretta had remained under his management all that time, and Voelckel's Black Patti show was the longest-lasting black road show in the business. Ironically, as 1912 came to a close, the first hint of possible trouble ahead for the Black Patti Musical Comedy Company surfaced in a short, gossipy piece in the *Indianapolis Freeman* (28 December 1912). The article, written by Billy Lewis, said that Sissieretta had been appearing "to better advantage" this season and that her singing was the best in years, but Lewis raised some questions about the overall health of the company. He said the company's singing was "sprightlier" and "perhaps better" than in previous years, but the play, *Captain Jasper,* was "no more striking" than in past seasons.

"The company doesn't seem to be in so good circumstances as usual. This is according to report. The Madame, however, is all right. She has always been well paid. If things go to pieces, she will be in the cyclone cellar."[72] Another piece about trouble within the Black Patti Company appeared in the next issue of the *Freeman*. This article concerned two cast members, James P. Reid and Marie Hendricks, who claimed they had left the Black Patti show because of the company's financial difficulties. Voelckel disputed their claims and, in an effort to set the record straight, sent the *Freeman* a copy of a receipt dated 4 December 1912, signed by J. P. Reid, that said he had been paid in full. The newspaper article said, "The *Freeman* takes pleasure in correcting the bad impression made through its columns. Mr. Voelckel makes serious charges against the two, the reasons for the termination of their contract." Three weeks later, as the Black Patti Company made its way through a series of one-night stands in South Carolina, North Carolina, and Virginia, another short item regarding the health of the company appeared in the *Freeman*. This one said that Will A. Cooke would soon start writing a new play for the show's next season. It also said that according to Cooke, "the company is all right."[73] It is impossible to know whether Voelckel was having financial difficulties or whether the recent press reports were simply the result of two disgruntled actors in the show seeking their revenge in the press. Times were certainly difficult for black road shows, but from all indications the Black Patti Company appeared to have a full schedule ahead to finish out the season. They played 3–8 February in Washington, D.C., and spent the rest of the month doing one-nighters in West Virginia, Kentucky, Indiana, and Illinois. In March the company toured Illinois, Ohio, and Missouri. During the first week of the month, the company performed a series of one-night stands and finished the month with week-long engagements in Chicago, Kansas City, St. Louis, and Dayton.

On 23 March the Black Patti Company began a week's run at the Globe Theatre in Chicago, and Russell came to review the opening night performance. He said the show lacked "thunder" but had enough music and comedy to keep the audience entertained. Russell commended the cast and complimented Voelckel for the way "he has sustained the record of his company for nearly fifteen years." As always he had high praise for Sissieretta. "The chief aim in musical art-culture, which has been so long centered in Mme. Sissieretta Jones, the original Black Patti, again brought forth the same message of truth that her wonderful preservation and perfect schooling still ranks her as supreme in vocal distinction. 'Sun-Blest Are You, O Golden Land,' and 'The Nightingale,' brought her a rousing reception," he said. "In 'The Belle of New York,' in the last act, her pale silk costume embroidered with beaded lace, diamonds and a white plume were rich to behold," Russell added.[74]

In April the Black Patti Company performed in Ohio, West Virginia, and Maryland before they closed the month with a week-long engagement at the Apollo Theatre in Atlantic City. By mid-May the company returned to the Grand Opera House in New York City to close their season. *Captain Jasper* opened on Monday night, 19 May 1913, to a large audience with all the seats on the lower floor filled as well as those in the balcony and gallery. A review by "The Owl" in the *Indianapolis Freeman* commended the performances of Glenn, George Terrant, Watts, and Sarah Green. He said the chorus's singing was not as strong as it could be, but other parts of the show made up for it. "The Owl" closed his review with a paragraph of praise for Sissieretta. "When the curtain went up on the second act we knew we would soon hear of yore: that we would again listen to a voice so far famed and one that we deem a rare treat to hear. Mme. Patti has an exceptional gift as a vocalist, and added to this her appearance in carefully selected and costly costumes charmed the audience," the review said. "As she smilingly stepped forth and began to sing, the reception she received halted her for a moment, but she acknowledged it with the grace of a real duchess and began to sing. I need say no more of her singing, as we all know she stands in a class by herself."[75]

A week after this review appeared in the *Freeman,* the *Age* published a column about Sissieretta completing her seventeenth consecutive season as star of the Black Patti Company. The review, likely written by Lester Walton, was accompanied by two photographs—one of Sissieretta and the other of actors in a scene from *Captain Jasper.* "When it comes to awarding a medal or a blue ribbon for durability, reliability and sticktoitiveness on the stage," it noted, "Mme. Jones should be declared winner without hesitancy. Mme. Jones enjoys a record of which no other performer in this country can boast. For seventeen years she has appeared at the head of the Black Patti Company, and not once has she been forced to leave the troupe on account of illness. Her company always has a long season, usually opening in August and closing in May. And then, most of the Black Patti Company's booking is one-night stands. Yet year after year she has toured the South, Southwest, Middle West and sometimes West, also some cities in the North, which is going some."[76]

In the uncertain world of show business, while other black actors and entertainers had come and gone, Sissieretta had worked steadily for seventeen years. The *Age* said Voelckel had announced plans for Sissieretta to begin her eighteenth season as star of the Black Patti Company in August. Sissieretta went to Rhode Island to spend the summer, as always, with her mother. It was ironic that the 1912–13 season closed with this tribute to her longevity and her ability to stay healthy all those years, for little did Sissieretta and Voelckel know that the seventeenth season would be her last full season on the stage.

11

The Last Tour
1914–1915

While Sissieretta was relaxing in Rhode Island during the summer of 1913, Voelckel sent press releases in July to the *New York Age* and the *Indianapolis Freeman* announcing that the eighteenth season of the Black Patti Musical Comedy Company would open on 8 September in Goshen. Plans called for a forty-week tour in the South and Midwest, as well as a twelve-week tour from the Missouri River to California and back. Voelckel said the show would play the better class of the Stair and Havlin circuit's week-long stands in cities such as Chicago, Cincinnati, Louisville, Indianapolis, Dayton, Columbus, Pittsburgh, Baltimore, Philadelphia, Newark, Brooklyn, and Boston. Sissieretta would head the company, and Julius Glenn would return as the leading comedian. Glenn and Will A. Cooke were going to write a new version of the previous year's three-act musical comedy, *Captain Jasper,* which Voelckel said would have many "novel features" as well as new songs and stage settings. The new show was supposed to give Sissieretta a "better opportunity to show off her talent." The cast was to include thirty performers and a "bevy of stage beauties whose special duties will be to introduce to the Southern folk the latest turkey trot and tango dances."[1]

Voelckel's big plans for the 1913–14 season were dashed, however, when Sissieretta, for the first time in her career, had to postpone her season opening because of illness. She was supposed to start the 1913–14 season on 8 September but was instead recovering from throat surgery, according to the *New York Age* (11 September 1913). An article in the paper said her "condition" was not serious, but her doctors had ordered her not to work for several weeks. In addition Sissieretta's mother was in ill health, which contributed to her decision to postpone the opening of her eighteenth season until October or the first of November.[2] Sissieretta's recovery took longer than expected. An article in the *Indianapolis Freeman* (1 November 1913) said she was recovering "nicely from a severe attack of sore throat" but was expected to be ready to start a twenty-week tour at the end of November. By mid-December she had "entirely" recovered from her illness, but instead of starting a tour of the Black Patti Musical Comedy Company so late into the season, she planned to make her debut as a vaudevillian and perform in several vaudeville shows for the remainder of the season.[3] Sissieretta sent a letter on 14 December to the *Age* and the *Freeman* and asked the newspapers to print it. It said:

> If space permits, will you please announce through the columns of your valuable paper my sincere thanks and appreciation to my many friends for their kind letters of sympathy during my recent illness. I am happy to state that I have entirely recovered from my indisposition and shortly before the holidays I shall appear in a limited number of vaudeville engagements for the balance of the current season. For the season of 1914–15 my managers are arranging for a new three-act musical comedy of pretentious order and magnificent production, to be given at the better class of theatres in the United States and Canada.
> With kind personal regards, I am,
>
> > Yours very truly,
> > Sissieretta Jones (Black Patti)[4]

In addition to her letter, Sissieretta bought a large display advertisement in the Christmas issue of the *Freeman* that said, "Merry Xmas to all my Professional Friends and Others, Sissieretta Jones, The Original Black Patti."[5] Sylvester Russell, as he usually did every year, published his annual stage review in the *Freeman*'s Christmas issue, which included a section on the future of "colored shows" and a mention about Sissieretta. Russell said it had been a long time since big "colored" road shows "held sway." Although prejudice played a big part in their demise, he said, moving pictures had hurt the road shows "to such an extent that even big white comedy stars are forced to struggle and wane in popularity." Russell said that nothing but "pleasant memories can now reward the past achievements of Williams & Walker, Cole & Johnson and Ernest Hogan. Black Patti (Sissieretta Jones), who has long since held the greatest female record as a singer of her race, has been eliminated by illness, and if she will have to retire it will be with the distinction of having been the greatest stage woman of her race and time and it is only hoped that she has done what I had long since advocated, saved her earnings for the rainy seasons of future enforced rest."[6] About a month after Russell's review was published, news came that Sissieretta had to cancel her plans to perform in vaudeville for the remainder of the season. Her mother was "seriously ill," and she was needed at home to care for her.[7] For the first time in eighteen years, Sissieretta spent the entertainment season at home in Rhode Island rather than on the road. With the rising popularity of the movies and waning interest in black road shows, it was a critical time for her to be away from the stage. One newspaper writer called her temporary retirement from the stage a "'solar plexis' blow to the colored road shows and all but made them take the count."[8]

Sissieretta disappeared from the entertainment scene and was not heard of again until late July 1914, when her photograph and a small article appeared in the *New York Age*. It said she was going to appear in a new "musical production" for the 1914–15 season. Although Rudolph Voelckel had secured bookings for the Black Patti show, he had not yet selected members of the company.[9] By the end of August, Sissieretta was in New York rehearsing at the Crescent Theater Hall for the upcoming season, which was scheduled to open 11 September 1914 in Plainfield, New Jersey. A young comedian, Harrison Stewart, had been hired to costar with Sissieretta in a new three-act musical called *Lucky Sam from Alabam,* written by Stewart. The supporting cast, described as the "strongest" Black Patti had ever had, included Will A. Cooke, Tillie Seguin, Charles Gilpin, Viola Stewart, John Lackaye Grant, and Jeanette Murphy, along with a chorus of singers and dancers. Plans called for the show to play a week, beginning 21 September, at the Lafayette Theatre in Harlem and later in Washington and Philadelphia.[10]

The Lafayette Theatre at 7th Avenue and 131st Street was on the edge of the black residential district in Harlem. Until May 1914 the theater had been leased by Martinson and Nibur, but they had to give up their lease for nonpayment of the yearly rental of twenty-five thousand dollars. Theater critic Lester Walton and a partner took over the lease for the theater and unsegregated it. The pair achieved success with their theater venture by providing a six-act vaudeville show with three acts by African American performers and three acts by white showmen. An article from *Variety,* reprinted in the *New York Age,* said there was talk that plans were "afoot" to form a circuit of black theaters throughout the country, with the Lafayette in New York as the "keystone" of the proposed chain. Black theaters in cities such as Philadelphia, Baltimore, Washington, D.C., Richmond, Norfolk, Memphis, Nashville, Atlanta, New Orleans, Jacksonville, Pittsburgh, Columbus, Indianapolis, Cincinnati, Chicago, St. Louis, and Kansas City would be part of the black theater circuit. Although there had been talk in the past about such a circuit, it had never developed. The *Variety* article said that interest in the proposed circuit had reached a "fever point" and might finally happen. "There are plenty of theatres available for the culmination of the project and sufficient colored population in the cities mentioned to give the proper paying patronage," the article said. Such a circuit would greatly benefit black performers.[11] African American entertainer Sherman H. Dudley had organized a black-controlled circuit for black vaudevillians in 1913, but it would take another three years before he joined with others to form the Southern Consolidated

Circuit, a network of twenty-eight theaters in the South, East, and Midwest that provided better bookings for black performers.[12]

Voelckel pulled out all the stops when advertising the upcoming week-long Black Patti Musical Comedy Company's performance at the Lafayette in Harlem. Voelckel's ad, published in the *New York Age* four days before *Lucky Sam from Alabam* opened at the Lafayette on Monday, 21 September 1914, featured Sissieretta prominently. In addition to promoting the three-act musical comedy's two stars—Sissieretta and Harrison Stewart—the ad promised special scenery and "electrical effects" would be included in the show.[13] Several days after *Lucky Sam* opened, Lester Walton, who now had a financial interest in the Lafayette Theatre, wrote a glowing review that must have given everyone involved with the Black Patti Company a feeling of well-being and a sense that the season would be a financial success.

Despite a late September heat wave with temperatures reaching ninety-one degrees, "immense crowds" filled the Lafayette Theatre for every performance of *Lucky Sam from Alabam,* breaking all previous attendance records at the venue. In his review Walton said Harrison Stewart, the comedy star who had also written the show, had borrowed elements from several of his previous vaudeville sketches and bound them together "with some semblance of a plot." He included many musical numbers he had performed before at the Lafayette Theatre, which made the show seem familiar to New York audiences. Walton predicted Stewart's mixture of dialogue and musical numbers would "prove a winning combination and score strongly in other cities." Three things made this show stand out, according to him—Sissieretta's singing, Stewart's comedy work, and J. Lackaye Grant's and Estelle Williams's dancing. Walton, who called Sissieretta "one of the marvels of the stage," said Black Patti's year-long vacation from the stage seemed to have benefited her. After eighteen strenuous seasons on the road, Sissieretta was "just as spry and vivacious as a decade ago, and her voice retains much of its sweetness, roundness and brilliancy." Emphasizing her longevity on the stage, Walton said that she was a star before Williams and Walker, Cole and Johnson, and Ernest Hogan became famous, and that few white stars who began their careers eighteen years earlier still figured prominently on the stage. As usual Sissieretta's gowns had "set the women folks to talking, as they are the very latest creations and worn by one who knows the art of dressing as well as the art of singing." Walton said Sissieretta not only sings, but also "talks and walks about the stage like one who had been accustomed to acting for years." Her vocal selections included her first number, Luckstone's "Delight," followed by an encore of "Goodbye," by Tosti. Walton said Sissieretta had the only "new song of merit" in the show, a ballad called "No One," in which she was backed up by the chorus. He closed his review with words that surely delighted Voelckel, Sissieretta, Stewart, and the rest of the cast. "'Lucky Sam from Alabam' is a pleasing show, the best both scenically and from a comedy standpoint that Manager Rudolph Voelckel has taken South in twelve years. In every respect it is the strongest attraction Black Patti has been identified with for many a day. 'Lucky Sam from Alabam' should bring luck to the Black Patti Musical Comedy Company."[14]

After a successful week in Harlem, the company played a "record-breaking" week at the New American Theater in Washington, D.C., beginning 5 October 1914. The American Theater, managed by Sherman H. Dudley and A. J. Thomas, had once been a burlesque house but had been transformed into a "playhouse for the best classes." A lengthy review by "Ar W. Tee" printed in the *Indianapolis Freeman* (24 October 1914) said that Sissieretta, who sang better than ever, received an ovation when she first walked onto the stage on opening night. When she had finished her first number, she was presented with a huge basket of flowers. Tee said Sissieretta's high notes and her middle and lower register "were as much the wonder of the connoisseur as they were in the early '90's when she emerged from the choir box at Providence, R.I." The critic said Sissieretta played her role of Miss Inez Pride, "Supervising Principal of the Colored Schools," well and delivered her dramatic lines with ease. He commented on the three gowns she wore during the show, calling them "stunning creations" that made the ladies in the audience "gasp in rapt admiration as they took in every detail of the rich combinations of color, texture, design, diamonds and plumes." While Sissieretta was in Washington, many callers came to visit her and "to congratulate her upon the continuation of her success in the arena of opera and musical comedy." Tee commended many others in the cast and gave his assessment of the play, which he said lacked a consistent and well-developed plot.[15]

While the Black Patti Company was entertaining audiences nightly in Washington, they learned that dancer and performer Aida Overton Walker, age thirty-four, had died on 11 October 1914. A member of the Black Patti Troubadours during its first season, 1896–97, Aida Overton later married George Walker and became affiliated with the Williams and Walker Company. After her husband died, she joined the Cole and Johnson Company for the 1908–9 season and the Smart Company the following season. In the two years before her death, she spent more time producing acts than performing. A front-page article in the *New York Age* said that Walker had been sick from kidney disease for a long time.[16] News of her death surely saddened Sissieretta and others in the troupe.

During the rest of October, the Black Patti Company played week-long engagements at the Orpheum in Baltimore, the Wells Theatre in Norfolk, and the Academy in Richmond. Then they headed south to North Carolina, Florida, Louisiana, and Tennessee, arriving in Memphis late December 1914.[17]

During this time a report in the *New York Dramatic News,* a newspaper that focused primarily on white show business, said theater attendance had been very poor in New York as well as in many other regions around the country. The newspaper attributed the poor business to the war in Europe, which had broken out during the summer.[18] If white shows were having trouble filling theaters, black shows were surely experiencing similar difficulties, as Voelckel learned when the Black Patti Musical Comedy Company left the success and comfort of week-long engagements in major cities and headed South, where the company typically had done well in the past. Business was "disastrous" as the troupe began performing in the South and reached crisis proportions in Memphis at the Church Park Auditorium, a 2,200-seat black theater owned and managed by Robert R. Church Jr.[19] Sissieretta had performed at this venue several times since Church's father, Robert R. Church Sr., a wealthy African American businessman and political leader, had first opened the two-story theater in 1899.[20] Located on Beale Street, near Fourth Street, the auditorium had one of the largest stages in the South. The Black Patti Company arrived in Memphis sometime in late December, about a month after Robert Church Jr. had reopened the theater, which had been closed following the death of his father in 1912.

The first hint of trouble with the troupe surfaced in the *Indianapolis Freeman* (2 January 1915), in a story published shortly after the Black Patti Company completed its two-day engagement in Memphis. The newspaper said it appeared that the Black Patti show had closed, but "no one seems to know anything as to the condition of the show." The newspaper reported that Voelckel was sick in bed with rheumatism and that the company's advance agent, Mr. Collins, was thinking about taking the show out on the road again. A week after the first article appeared in the *Freeman,* a lengthy account in the 9 January issue of the newspaper detailed the final days of the Black Patti Musical Comedy Company. It began, "'Lucky Sam from Alabam' has lost his 'luck.' Also he has put a hoodoo on Black Patti and called in a hooting owl against the peace of her show. The Black Patti aggregation is in tears, Voelckel is in retreat and Black Patti is en route." The article said the company had been in Memphis for three weeks, when Voelckel, Sissieretta, and leading actors Stewart and Cooke finally left town, stranding the rest of the troupe. Voelckel got into trouble when he could not pay his bills, including money he owed Church. Church responded by attaching the Black Patti Company's private railcar. The article said that Church helped the remaining cast by giving them food and a place to stay and sending telegrams for them so they could get help. The article said Voelckel never made a serious effort to get help for his company. Although a man with the last name of Oppenheimer from St. Louis had come to town to see about aiding Voelckel and the company, he had left in disgust, the newspaper said. Several of the stranded performers, while going through some papers Voelckel left behind, claimed they found a note indicating that he had contemplated suicide. The newspaper article said, "Voelckel was expected to do something like this, but there is great surprise that Black Patti would desert the company without so much as a sigh, a tear or a 'fond goodbye.'"[21] A short article in the 21 January issue of the *New York Age* said that traveling theatrical companies were having a difficult time in the "Southland" this season and that the Black Patti Company "was no exception." The newspaper said that members of the company were making their way eastward, appearing in vaudeville. Four previous members of the Black Patti Company—Stewart and his wife, W. A. Cooke, and Jeanette Murphy—were appearing in a show at the Booker Washington Theatre in St. Louis. Billy E. Jones of the *Indianapolis Freeman* reported that Sissieretta was living in Providence and had "embraced religion at the Congdon Street Baptist Church and has, according to reports, severed her relations with the stage and its attractions."[22]

More details about the demise of the Black Patti Company in Memphis surfaced in the black press in February when Voelckel wrote a letter to the *Age* with his side of the story and Church responded to Voelckel's letter two weeks later with a letter of his own. A column in the *Age's* theater page, titled "A Disastrous Season," began with a short introduction, likely written by Lester Walton. The newspaper said that Voelckel's former business representatives and members of the Black Patti Company placed sole responsibility for the company's dissolution on him, while Voelckel blamed some members of the cast. "In all probabilities 'hard times' did more to occasion adverse conditions than anything else. Had business been good Manager Voelckel would have been able to meet his financial obligations, there would have been no attachment proceedings instituted by Robert R. Church, and some of the members of the company would not have become disagreeable and acted outrageously, as charged," the *Age* said.[23]

Voelckel, who addressed his letter to the *Age's* dramatic editor, began by summarizing the opening months of the troupe's 1914–15 season. He said that the week-long engagements in New York, Philadelphia, Washington, and Norfolk had been successful, but when the company headed South, business was "very disastrous." Voelckel said he had a contract with Church to rent the Church Park Auditorium for two evening performances and one matinee, for a fee of two hundred dollars. Voelckel said he had two advance men "properly" advertise the show and did not, as Church claimed, neglect advertising and promotion, as local managers often asserted when business was poor. Voelckel said there was talk (he did not say by whom) that some of the performers playing minor roles were intoxicated, the performance was disappointing, the comedian was a failure, and the vocal numbers were poor except songs sung by Black Patti. "This adverse report became so widely circulated that managers of theatres where the company was booked to appear wired in cancellations, stating they would not play any drunken colored show in their theatres," Voelckel said. "As soon as Mr. Church found this out he immediately attached my scenery, electrical effects, and private sleeping car. I begged him to wait a few days for his $200 rental, and I even went so far as to pay the expense of his representative and allow him a salary until he collected Mr. Church's debt," Voelckel said. "I appealed to him on three different occasions and pointed out to him that if he insisted in carrying out his intentions the oldest colored musical comedy company would close, which would work a severe hardship on some of my people, as my purse was depleted and my contract, the same as others, did not require me to defray their expenses back to New York should the show close."

Voelckel said that he made every effort to continue the season and that two men from St. Louis came to Memphis to try and help, but when they arrived at the Church Park Auditorium, they were "informed of the disgraceful performance given by the intoxicated members of the show." The men became discouraged and left the next morning. While the troupe was idle, all but ten members left Memphis and headed home, "then the actions of the balance became so unbearable that Mme. Jones (Black Patti) and her maid left for Providence, R.I., where she is receiving medical attention," Voelckel said. "In conclusion, I sincerely regret to state that I deeply deplore the circumstances which brought about such an abrupt end to the nineteenth season of the oldest colored musical comedy company on earth and caused the greatest of all colored stars to leave the company; and in closing, I must further state that I was never connected with such a degraded lot of drunkards during my experience, which fact may be verified by Mme. Jones."[24]

Two weeks after Voelckel's letter appeared in the *Age,* Lester Walton published a letter (25 February) from Robert Church, who responded to Voelckel's version of the facts surrounding the end of the Black Patti Company. In his short introduction before presenting Church's letter, Walton said that Voelckel's statement of the facts had "raised a hornet's nest and brought forth an avalanche of denials in which the question of veracity is raised." Church's letter, like Voelckel's, was addressed to the dramatic editor of the *Age.* Church accused Voelckel of false statements and of leaving his cast among strangers, in wintertime, with no food or lodging. He said that he attached Voelckel's railcar and theatrical scenery and equipment because Voelckel had made no effort to pay his debts, which included fees to rent the auditorium, bills from a local printer, hotel bills, and fees for hiring a bill-posting company in Memphis and Jackson, Mississippi. "Mr. Voelckel did not visit either performance at the Auditorium and did not make his appearance in the office of the Auditorium until more than a week after he had stranded here. He kept to his nest and had couriers to fetch and take the tidings of hope and distress," Church said. Further, the Memphis businessman said, Voelckel had not returned "a pauper's penny" of the money the auditorium had advanced him so that he could feed the company but instead used it to leave town. Church said no men from St. Louis came to the auditorium, therefore they could not have heard anything there that was detrimental about the show. The men, Church said he later learned, had talked with Voelckel's advance man, Mr. Collins, and after talking to him, the two men from St. Louis "balked not at the behavior of the company, but rather at the methods employed by the Patti management." Church said he attached Voelckel's railcar the night of the closing performance, not days later as Voelckel had stated. "The assault Mr. Voelckel makes on his company is no affair of the Auditorium's; certainly not, but we did what we could to help them," Church said. "Our personal compliments to them we shall not here dwell upon, but we will say that we gave the leading characters work at a salary equal to the salary they were supposed to get from the show, and from time to time, employed many of the chorus. While here all had meat to eat and shelter from the cold, and Mr. Voelckel provided neither."[25]

Church said he had more to tell, should it become necessary. At the close of Church's letter, Walton wrote that the *Age* took no side in the controversy but instead "served as a medium for the expression of all views on the incident" without bias or prejudice on the matter. The editor promised to publish letters in future weeks from others with something to say about the show's closing, but none appeared.[26]

Sissieretta's eighteen-year career as star of the Black Patti Musical Comedy Company and Black Patti Troubadours was finished.[27] She must have been sad and disheartened, especially after the abrupt and disquieting way the company disbanded. Perhaps she had been aware of Voelckel's growing financial difficulties during the season and had predicted something like this might happen. Her thoughts, as she traveled back to her home in Providence, probably included concern for her colleagues and manager, but the forty-seven-year-old diva likely also spent a lot of time wondering what was ahead for her.

12

Retirement and Tributes

A weary, and likely discouraged, Sissieretta arrived back in Providence in January 1915 and went to her home on Wheaton Street[1] to recover from the contentious breakup in Memphis of the Black Patti troupe as well as to care for her mother, who was in ill health. It appears, given available press reports, that Sissieretta did not perform on stage again until the week beginning 20 September 1915, when she sang during a vaudeville show for sold-out audiences at the Grand Theatre in Chicago.[2] Sylvester Russell, a longtime admirer of Sissieretta, wrote a glowing review of her opening performance that Monday night.

> When the great diva entered there was a loud, prolonged reception to greet her. The stage was set in a parlor scene, including a piano. Her first number, "Luckstone's Delight Waltz," was played by the orchestra with two pianos, and was a difficult mezo [sic] number for articulation. Her second number was a plaintive folklore, "Nobody But You." Then came "The Swanee River," which brought a better conception of her great vocal embellishments to the front, was encored, and in the song "Rose in the Bud" was a voice painting in vocal culture and vowel and consonant and dyssyllable [sic] pronouncing, which is scarcely understood or fully appreciated by many of the present day theatergoers. What is proof that her art is supreme is that she held the house spellbound in each number, and her art in vocal reading was a rich school for students, for it is true that Black Patti is still blessed with a middle and lower register, yet rare in its maturity and sweetness.[3]

At the end of Sissieretta's opening night performance, H. W. Lyons, who was sitting in a theater box with several other fans of Sissieretta, presented the singer with a large, horseshoe-shaped arrangement of roses. Russell said that Lyons, a white man who co-owned the Pompeii Café in Chicago, and those in his party had come to honor "the greatest singer the colored race has produced for a period of over thirty years." Sissieretta, touched by the gift, carried a photograph of the floral arrangement with her when she left Chicago. While she remained in the city, she kept to herself and "politely" turned down all invitations from well-wishers as she was worried about her mother back in Rhode Island. At the end of Sissieretta's week-long engagement, Russell accompanied the famous vocalist and her maid, S. E. Collier, to the train station, whereupon she told Russell that her concern for her mother's health had prompted her to cancel all the western engagements on her schedule so she could head home.[4]

Several weeks after returning from Chicago, Sissieretta gave what would be her final stage appearance at the black-run Lafayette Theatre in Harlem, where she was hired to head a "monster vaudeville bill" for the week beginning Monday, 18 October. Prior to her opening, Lafayette manager Lester Walton and his partner announced in the New York Age that they would pay Sissieretta five hundred dollars for the week, "which amount marks a new era for salaries in colored theatrical circles." The newspaper said, "Never before has this much money been given a performer to appear in what is generally termed a 'colored theatre.'" The Age said Sissieretta's appearance at the Lafayette would be the "celebrated singer's initial bow as a vaudevillian, although numerous efforts have been made by colored and white managers to induce her to enter the vaudeville field."[5]

Sissieretta was a hit with the crowds who attended the vaudeville show at the Lafayette that week. The Age, which published what likely would become the final theater review of Sissieretta's long career, praised her performance:

From a standpoint of quality the bill at the Lafayette Theatre the first half of the week equalled that of any big time house in New York. Every act was classy and entertaining and the many loyal patrons of Harlem's popular theatre found much to enthuse over. First in importance was the appearance of Mme. Sissieretta Jones (Black Patti), whose engagement at the Lafayette in vaudeville during the week is regarded as a big event in theatrical circles. Hundreds of enthusiastic admirers of the celebrated singer turned out the first half of the week to pay her honor, and the tribute must have warmed the cockles of her heart. Strange to relate, a large number of Harlemites labored under the impression that "the real Black Patti" was not singing at the Lafayette Theatre and had to be convinced that the management was presenting the "real thing." Why such an impression should have prevailed is not known.

Mme. Jones rendered four numbers. "Twas No Vision," a difficult piece, colorless and void of melody or anything inspiring, did not show the renowned soloist at her best. The song is more suitable for concert work than vaudeville. "Nobody But You," was delightfully put over by

Mme. Jones, while "Suawanne [*sic*] River" and the "Rose in the Bud" were sung as only a real artist can. Nobody [can] sing "Suawanee [*sic*] River" like Mme. Jones, and her rendition of "Rose in the Bud" was a treat to all real lovers of music. Mme. Sissieretta Jones' appearance at the Lafayette this week is an artistic triumph, and her engagement at this house has undeniably given additional tone [to] what is generally regarded as the classiest and most refined "colored theatre" in the country.[6]

The review of Sissieretta's performance demonstrated the dilemma she might have faced had she decided to continue singing on the vaudeville stage. Although she sang popular favorites that vaudeville audiences could embrace, she still wanted to include pieces more suitable to the concert stage, which did not play as well in vaudeville shows. She had been able to slip in classical and operatic selections as star of the Black Patti Troubadours and the Black Patti Musical Comedy Company, but these types of songs likely would not have been accepted in vaudeville performances. The review also showed Sissieretta's reputation was equated with class and refinement, something that was becoming more and more important to the field of black theater as black entertainers, particularly comedians, attempted to shed the derogatory stereotypes they had been forced to play in the past in order to break into show business. Her star quality would have been a big attraction to vaudeville managers. Had her mother been in better health, Sissieretta might have resumed her career and tried to adapt to life on the vaudeville stage. However, given her family responsibilities and her strong relationship with her mother, Sissieretta left show business behind and lived a quiet life in Rhode Island caring for her mother until Henrietta's death on 17 March 1924 at the age of sixty-six.[7] Sissieretta's stepfather, Daniel Crenshaw, continued to live with Sissieretta at 7 Wheaton Street, as did a couple of boarders, one of whom, Thomas Wilson, remained there until 1930. Crenshaw left Sissieretta's home sometime in 1929 or early 1930, at the start of the Great Depression.[8]

Once Sissieretta left the stage, she was out of the public eye and no longer featured in the press, thus little is known about her final years. The few reports about her life during her retirement years indicate that she lived quietly and frugally. One report said she worked as a cook for a wealthy family on the east side of Providence sometime during the 1920s. Others said she took in homeless children, watched neighborhood children when their parents had to run errands,[9] and enjoyed working in her rose garden. Most reports said she kept largely to herself, occasionally singing with the choir at the Congdon Street Baptist Church, which was a short walk from her home. An article in the *Providence Sunday Journal* written in 1980, many years after Sissieretta's death, included some remembrances by Rhode Islanders who were children when she lived in Providence. Their memories help shed more light on Sissieretta's life in Rhode Island.[10]

— Philip Addison, a member of the Providence City Council in 1980, told the newspaper he grew up on Wheaton Street and recalled as a child seeing lots of black actors and celebrities come to Sissieretta's house when they came to perform in Providence. He also remembered that Sissieretta liked children but was always stern with them. "We loved her and feared her," he said.
— Mary Hopkins, who lived across the street from Sissieretta, said the famous singer had "beautiful clothes, furs, and large hats with feathers." Hopkins liked to sing, and she recalled that when she did so, Sissieretta would peek out from behind the shutters.
— Martha Greene, who lived on Meeting Street, remembered that Sissieretta was kind, "well-liked, and respected." Greene said she did not think Sissieretta was too close to anyone. She said Sissieretta often kept her blinds drawn. "She also spent hours each day in her rose garden, tending to her flowers and humming to herself," Greene said.

Sissieretta supported herself during her retirement years by selling off her valuable jewelry—most of her silver, all but three of her medals—four pieces of rental property, and other belongings. When she became ill during the last two years of her life, she had to rely on help from William P. H. Freeman, a black realtor and past president of the local NAACP chapter, who loaned her money to help pay her property and water taxes, wood and coal bills, and other incidentals. Freeman also saw to it that Sissieretta was buried in Grace Church Cemetery rather than in a pauper's grave.[11] Following Sissieretta's death on 24 June 1933, the Probate Court of Providence made Freeman custodian of her estate.

When Sissieretta died, her death was listed in the death notices section of the *Providence Journal,* but there was no obituary to mark her extraordinary life. Her funeral was held at her home and was followed by services at Congdon Street Baptist Church. By July several articles about Sissieretta's death appeared in various publications—the *Afro-American* (New England edition), the *Baltimore Afro-American,* the *Norfolk Journal and Guide,* and the *Providence Sunday Journal.* Lydia T. Brown, the Providence correspondent to the weekly New England edition of the *Afro-American,* described Sissieretta's estate, which included four large paintings by famous artists—a painting of the Grand Canal of Venice by C. Vallets, a work by Corot, a seascape by Murot, and a painting of an old mill with a brook beside it by C. Ruetta. Brown reported that Sissieretta's furniture included gilt chairs, a gold clock, gold candlesticks, settees covered in "rich red brocade with gold fleur de lis," and a walnut piano covered with autographed photographs of famous black performers such as Cole and Johnson. Some of Sissieretta's other belongings were "two beautiful fur coats and her wonderful wardrobe of her evening gowns, loaded with sequins."[12] Although this description of her personal belongings sounded like it might be worth a lot, in truth it did not amount to much when it was professionally appraised months later when her estate was being settled.

Baltimore's *Afro-American,* published the week of 1 July 1933, focused on Sissieretta's career, describing her as "one of the pioneer singers of the race." The newspaper said Sissieretta died after a short illness and that she had been living with friends on Wheaton Street before her death, although other sources said she had been sick for two years and lived alone in her home with a parrot she had gotten in South America long ago when she performed there early in her career.[13] Black Patti, the *Afro-American* said, was one of the greatest attractions on the American stage. "Colored patrons in Baltimore and other Southern cities paid as high as two dollars a seat to climb to the peanut galleries of theatres to hear her in the days when this was considered an enormous price to pay for entertainment." She had spent "considerable time" in Baltimore, so much so, according to the newspaper, that many believed she was a native of that city. "Mme. Jones was an aristocrat of the stage and her shows were always of a high order and had none of the risque and suggestive material so common in modern shows," the newspaper said. "She was most famous for her rendition of 'Suwanee River.' She would always include a classic in her repertoire to show the remarkable range and control of her voice."[14]

The *Afro-American* ran another article about Sissieretta the following week (8 July 1933) that focused on her connections with Baltimore. The article noted how the world had forgotten about the once-famous singer. "Black Patti, the elegant Madame Sissieretta Jones, is dead and the world that once sang her praises had to stop and scratch its head when that announcement was made last Saturday from Providence, R.I. This worldly forgetfulness can not be criticized too severely, however, when we recall that most anybody who spends much of his time in Providence, R.I. is likely to be forgotten." The newspaper recalled Sissieretta's marriage to Dick Jones of Baltimore, describing him as a "race-horse and gambling man," whom Sissieretta later divorced "after he had had a swell time spending her money." Sissieretta had always been a big hit when she played at the old Holliday Street Theatre in Baltimore, the newspaper said. Admirers of both races would stand around the stage door waiting to get a glimpse of her. When Sissieretta was in Baltimore, she sometimes visited the home of the only African American city councilman, Harry Cummings. Sissieretta moved "in the very best" social circles, the newspaper said, despite the fact that stage celebrities in those days were not highly regarded by many people.[15]

The *Afro-American* closed the article about Sissieretta with a story about one of her visits to Baltimore during her concert years in the mid-1890s. Although the truth of the story is unknown, it makes an enjoyable tale about the celebrated singer:

> The story is told how upon one occasion the famous singer came to town to give a recital at a fashionable Madison St. Presbyterian Church, white, which was the gospel cafeteria of the first families who traced their ancestry back to the Calverts and the Cabots. Madame Jones arrived at the church in the afternoon and was holding a little private rehearsal, and her thrilling voice drifted to the ears of one of the city's dowagers of great wealth who was entertaining her club just across the way. She inquired whose voice it was and was surprised to learn that it was the great Black Patti. "Oh," she ohed. "I must do something for her. I'll allow her to sing for our party."
>
> The party was graced with the matrons who represented a line of generations of bankers, importers, planters, and other Maryland blue gores [bloods]. It would be quite an honor for this "Patti person" to yodel into such distinguished ears. The social columns would mention it to the undying credit of the hostess, adding another star in her crown as the city's most brilliant social entertainer. The grand lady tripped to the kitchen and dispatched her colored cook to invite Black Patti over. The black singer who had sung before crowned heads of Europe, had been honored by President Harrison and was the toast of royalty, looked at the cook with an air of aloofness and said: "Tell your mistress if she will write my managers in New York and arrange an engagement I will be happy to sing for her. It will be seven or eight months, however, as my schedule is quite full." The cook returned the message and were the faces of the blue-bloods red![16]

By mid-July 1933 the Providence newspaper finally wrote an article about Sissieretta. The article, "The Closing Chapters of the Life of 'Black Patti,'" written by F. C. Terry, included information about her early years in Rhode Island, her rise to fame, her many accomplishments, and her retirement years. Terry said that Sissieretta had left the stage to care for her ill grandmother and mother in Providence and gave them "every comfort and devotion" before their deaths. "A friend who spent years in the family says her [Sissieretta's] disposition was wonderful. She was always the same," Terry wrote. "In the face of adversity she would smilingly say, 'The sun is shining,' even during her suffering it was the same."[17]

The most touching article following Sissieretta's death appeared in the *Norfolk Journal and Guide* (15 July 1933), in which several family members, as well as Portsmouth neighbors who remembered Sissieretta as a "musically gifted little girl," were interviewed about the famous singer. The family members mentioned in the article were said to be Sissieretta's closest relatives— Melvina Colden, a first cousin; Melvina Newsome, Mrs. Colden's daughter; and William Colden, Mrs. Colden's brother and Sissieretta's first cousin. Mrs. Colden said life had not been easy for the Joyners when Sissieretta and her brother, Jerry, were small. Sissieretta's mother had been forced into "drudgery" to afford schooling for the children. Mrs. Colden recalled that Sissieretta enjoyed singing from a very young age. "Even then she showed possibilities as a singer and would fill the air with melody on the slightest provocation." Sissieretta's family told the newspaper that she loved her church in her final years. Mrs. Newsome shared a letter with the newspaper that Sissieretta had sent her in December 1932.

> Dear Sister,
>   I sincerely trust that your mother, yourself and all the folks are well and getting along during these hard times. With it all God has been mighty good to us. He has spared us to live to see another Christmas so near. We have everything to be thankful for. I am feeling fine, thanks to the Lord, and I shall continue to thank Him and pray and trust Him, until I am called. Give my love to your mother and do write and tell me how she is and Arthur also.
>
>   Love to all,
>   Cousin Sis[18]

Mrs. Newsome gave the newspaper a second letter, dated 13 March 1933, that Sissieretta wrote two months before her death. Sissieretta told her cousin she had been very sick and looked to the Lord to give her strength. "I shall continue to pray and trust in the Lord and serve Him until He is ready for me." She said she was pretty much alone except for two "troublesome" boys, fourteen and fifteen years old, the state of Rhode Island sent to stay with her.[19] Sissieretta did not include the names of these youngsters or provide any other information about them.

After Sissieretta's death the probate court of the City of Providence appointed her friend William P. Freeman to serve as custodian of her estate. Sissieretta had drawn up a will in 1914 leaving everything to her mother but had not updated the document since her mother's death in 1924. Only two people contacted the court about Sissieretta's estate—her cousin, Melvina Colden, and the young man, Lawrence Smith Jones, who apparently believed he was Sissieretta's son. By the time her debts were reconciled, there was no money left from her $1,054.36 estate for any family members. Two court-appointed appraisers had determined the value of Sissieretta's personal property—furniture, a walnut piano, four paintings, and two fur coats (which turned out to be spoiled and of no commercial value)—at $200.00. In addition to her personal property, Sissieretta had $228.92 in her bank account and a life insurance policy worth $577.03. Freeman, himself a creditor, filed a claim for $693.03 in loans he had made Sissieretta during the last two years of her life. The loans included $97.21 toward her property taxes, $236.00 in mortgage payments, and $130.62 in personal loans for small amounts of cash (such as $2.00, $5.00, and $10.00) at various times, as well as $2.83 for Christmas cards (19 December 1932) and $1.00 for a cab ride to the hospital just before she died. By the time Freeman finally settled Sissieretta's estate in 1936, he accepted $186.60 as payment for the loans.[20]

At some point after Sissieretta's estate was closed, Freeman contacted Dr. Carl R. Gross, an African American physician living in Providence who was interested in Rhode Island's black history and who had "personally" known Sissieretta. Freeman shared his remembrances about Sissieretta with Gross and gave him some of the remaining pieces of Sissieretta's property—three of her medals, her scrapbook, and some photographs. Freeman told Gross that he feared the items would get thrown out after he died and did not want them lost to posterity.[21] In 1966 Gross wrote a six-page "Brief History of the Life of Matilda Sissieretta (Joyner) Jones, 'The Black Patti,' 1869–1933," which he shared with Sissieretta's first biographer, Willia Daughtry, who used the material in her 1968 doctoral dissertation about Sissieretta. Gross also provided the brief life history of Sissieretta to William Lichtenwanger from the music division at the Library of Congress, who included some of the information in the entry he wrote about her for the 1971 biographical dictionary, *Notable American Women*. Eventually Gross donated Sissieretta's scrapbook, medals, and some photographs, along with his short biography of her life, to the Moorland-Spingarn Research Center, Manuscript Division, at Howard University in Washington, D.C., where these items remain today.

Since Daughtry's dissertation and Lichtenwanger's biographical dictionary entry, there has been renewed interest in Sissieretta. Short biographical entries about her life have been included in many biographical encyclopedias, dictionaries, and other reference books. Daughtry published a book in 2002 about Sissieretta (*Vision and Reality: The Story of "Black Patti" Matilda Sissieretta Joyner Jones*), and music professor John Graziano wrote an extensive article ("The Early Life and Career of the 'Black Patti': The Odyssey of an African American Singer in the Late Nineteenth Century") about her for the fall 2000 issue of the *Journal of the American Musicological Society*. In addition to printed materials about Sissieretta, information about her appears on many websites on the Internet, although much of it is inaccurate and incomplete. One website, BlackPatti.com, is devoted to selling recordings made on the Black Patti record label, a label that only lasted one year (1927) but produced fifty-five different discs. Sissieretta had no interest in or relationship with this record company that capitalized on her stage name.[22] The old 78 records with the purple label depicting a peacock on it are highly collectible, and some are worth thousands of dollars today. Memorabilia related to Sissieretta appears periodically on sites such as eBay and auction house websites such as Swann Galleries in New York, where these photographs and ephemera (playbills, theater programs, etc.) often sell for hundreds, and sometimes thousands, of dollars.

Sissieretta has also been the subject of several plays or musical shows in recent years. Playwright Ricardo Pitts-Wiley wrote and directed a show called *Waiting for Bessie Smith,* which features information about Sissieretta. The show played in Providence in 2004. In 2009 soprano Angela Dean Baham wrote and performed a one-woman musical drama called *The Unsung Diva: Impressions of the Life and Time of Sissieretta Jones a.k.a. the Black Patti,* which played in several cities around the country. As for awards and other recognitions, black music composer and "Father of the Blues" W. C. Handy wrote a tribute song to Sissieretta, "In Memory of Black Patti," in 1940. More recently Sissieretta was inducted in 1977 into the Rhode Island Heritage Hall of Fame, which honors people who have contributed to the state's history.[23] The year before the Rhode Island recognition, a plaque honoring Sissieretta was placed in Portsmouth, Virginia, Sissieretta's birthplace, at the Portsmouth Library.[24] In recent years the Rhode Island Black Heritage Society began giving an annual award in Sissieretta's honor called the Matilda Sissieretta Jones Award for the Humanities with a Focus on Cultural Literacy and the Arts. The Rhode Island Black Heritage Society also has two of Sissieretta's dresses, which had been on display at the society's small museum but are now in storage since the museum closed. The dresses were given to the society in the 1970s by Dorothy Britte, whose grandmother, Georgia Johnson, got them from Sissieretta in the 1920s when the two reportedly worked together for a wealthy family on Providence's East Side. Sissieretta was the cook, and Johnson the laundress. They became friends, and Sissieretta decided to give Johnson two handmade evening gowns—a black taffeta dress with a lace train and a beige moire taffeta gown. Johnson kept them in her closet for years, and eventually they were passed down to Johnson's granddaughter, who contacted the Black Heritage Society. The society restored the dresses and exhibited them at the Outlet Company department store in the early 1970s.[25] In 2003 the dresses were displayed during a special history exhibit in Providence called "Rhode Island Treasures."

Although there has been more interest about Sissieretta in recent years and more attention given to her accomplishments, she is still largely unknown by many who are knowledgeable about music and entertainment history. She might have been a familiar name in the world of opera had she not been born black. She was blessed with a magnificent and powerful voice, which, given more training and encouragement, could have led to an operatic career had the prevailing prejudice against the African American race not kept her from the chance to perform with established groups such as the Metropolitan Opera Company. Instead given the limitations white society imposed on African Americans, Sissieretta seized what opportunities were available to her and carved out a successful and prosperous life on the stage for twenty-eight years.

Even as a child Sissieretta had a dream to sing. She once said, "I love to sing; singing is to me what sunshine is to the flowers. The flowers absorb the sunshine because it is their nature. I give out melody because God filled my soul with it."[26] In a world where most African American women of her day who worked outside of their homes were destined to be laundresses, cooks, or servants for white people, Sissieretta aspired to more. She wanted to use her God-given voice and sing on the stage, and she was willing to work hard to achieve her goal. Her magnificent voice, her determination and perseverance, along with several lucky breaks along the way, helped make a musical career possible. She was able to get musical training early in her career that helped her develop and preserve her voice. Then Flora Batson and her manager-husband, John Bergen, recognized her talent as early as 1886 and provided her with an opportunity to sing in Bergen's shows. Two years later she got a chance to sing in a musical group performing in the West Indies and South America. She earned American fame in 1892 when her husband found a way to get her a featured singing spot in the Grand Jubilee at Madison Square Garden in New York City. Soon after that event, she signed with a white manager, Maj. James Pond, who helped make her famous throughout the United States with white and black audiences. Several years later she went to Europe and won accolades there, making her an international star. Even when opportunities on the concert stage diminished in the late 1890s, Sissieretta was able to keep singing as star of the Black Patti Troubadours and later with the Black Patti Musical Comedy Company.

Although Sissieretta had good fortune in her professional life, her personal life was touched by sadness and loss—the death of her only child at age two; little or no relationship with her father during her adult years; divorce from her gambling, drunken husband; the long illness and death of her beloved mother; and poverty and sickness in her own final years. Despite it all she maintained a positive attitude and persevered. She had achieved what she set out to do—sing on the stage—and, in the process, had become famous. She acquired her fame by traveling from one city and town to another, day after day, month after month, year after year. Her singing impressed various newspaper writers and critics, who wrote reviews describing her magnificent voice, her graceful manner, and the stunning gowns and jewels she wore. In the days before radio, television, records, and the Internet, Sissieretta earned her fame the hard way—one performance at a time—along with the help of the black press such as the *Age* and the *Freeman* that carried news about black entertainers. In her twenty-eight years on the stage, Sissieretta sang in forty-six of the forty-eight contiguous United States, according to newspaper articles and performance schedules, apparently missing only South Dakota and Vermont. Her home nine months of the year for nearly sixteen years was her private stateroom aboard the Black Patti railcar as it traveled across the United States, and her family during those months were her colleagues and her longtime manager, Rudolph Voelckel.

From the beginning of her career, Sissieretta became a role model for her race and helped lower the racial boundaries that prejudice imposed on her and other African Americans. She taught white Americans that black people could sing classical music and popular standards and sound as elegant and breathtaking as white vocalists, and she showed them that African Americans could achieve fame and prosperity. In her nineteen years as head of the Black Patti Troubadours and Black Patti Musical Comedy Company, she could find satisfaction that her troupe had been a training ground for and provided employment to hundreds of aspiring black singers, comedians, dancers, composers, and playwrights. At one time or another, any number of famous black entertainers of her day were in her troupe.

Sissieretta truly was a pioneer in the field of black entertainment. She paved the way for other African American female vocalists to reach for the stars, whether it be in blues, jazz, or opera. She has earned her place in music history and deserves recognition for her achievements.

APPENDIX A

Sissieretta Jones's Selected Repertoire

This list of musical selections appeared in newspaper reviews about Sissieretta Jones written between 1888 and 1915. The list is by no means a complete account of her repertoire. When known, composers have been provided. Misspellings printed in newspaper reviews have been corrected.

CONCERT YEARS (1888–1896)

"Swanee River (Old Folks at Home)," Stephen Foster
"Home, Sweet Home," Sir Henry Bishop
"Robert, Toi Que J'aime," from *Robert le Diable,* Giacomo Meyerbeer
An aria from *L'Africaine,* Giacomo Meyerbeer
A selection from *Les Huguenots,* Giacomo Meyerbeer
"Grand Aria," Pietro Centemeri
"Sempre Libera," from *La Traviata,* Giuseppe Verdi
"Maggie, the Cows Are in the Clover," Al. W. Filson
"The Cows Are in the Corn," (also known as "Morning"), Henry Tucker
"Bobolink" or "The Song of the Bobolink," Sir Henry Bishop
"Ave Maria," Charles Gounod
"Ave Maria," Harrison Millard
"Every Rose Must Have Its Thorn," Woolson Morse
"Valse-Ariette," Charles Gounod
"Magnetic Waltz Song," Luigi Arditi
"Ecstasy," Luigi Arditi
"Il Bacio," Luigi Arditi
"Nobil Donna" and "Nobil Signor," from *Les Huguenots,* Meyerbeer
"Comin' thro' the Rye," Scottish folk song
"Venzano Waltz," Luigi Venzano
"Deep in My Heart," Pietro Centemeri
"The Night Birds Cooing"
"The Ship on Fire," Henry Russell

"Marguerite's Farewell"

"When the Blue Birds Build Again," Charles A. White

"No Sir"

"La Farfalla," Ettore Gelli

"The Last Rose of Summer"

"In Old Madrid," Henry Trotère

"The Waltz Song" (also called "The Patti Waltz Song"), J. N. Pattison

"Ocean Thou Mighty Monster," from *Oberon,* Carl Maria von Weber

"Fleur des Alpes," J. B. Wekerlin

"Killarney," Michael William Balfe

"The Star-Spangled Banner"

"Inflammatus," from Rossini's *Stabat Mater*

"Message d'Amour"

"The Idol of My Heart"

Aria from *La Sonnambula,* Vincenzo Bellini

"Bolero," Arditi

Cavatina from *La Reine de Saba,* Gounod

Black Patti Troubadour and Black Patti Musical Comedy Company Years (1896–1915)

"Swanee River (Old Folks at Home)," Stephen Foster

"My Old Kentucky Home," Stephen Foster

"Miserere" and "The Anvil Chorus," from *Il Trovatore,* Giuseppe Verdi

"The Sabre Song," from *The Grand Duchess of Gerolstein,* Jacques Offenbach

Aria from *I Lombardi,* Giuseppe Verdi

Selections from *The Queen's Lace Handkerchief,* John Strauss

"Tar and Tartar," a medley of national airs, including "The Star-Spangled Banner," "Dixie," "Yankee Doodle," "The Campbells Are Coming," and "God Save the Queen"

"In Days of Yore"

Series of songs called "Songs of Dixie"

"Honey, Stay in Your Own Back Yard"

"Waltz Song" (also called "The Patti Waltz Song"), J. N. Pattison

"You Can't Pick Plums from My Plum Tree"

Selections from *Rigoletto,* Giuseppe Verdi

Opening chorus from *Orpheus in the Underworld,* Jacques Offenbach

"Ole Man Moon," Lyn Udall

"Sorry Her Lot, Who Loves Too Well," and "Farewell, My Own," from *H.M.S. Pinafore,* William S. Gilbert and Sir Arthur Sullivan

"My Dear Southern Home"

Selections from *The Chimes of Normandy,* Robert Planquette

"Good Night, Marie," Salem Tutt Whitney and Homer Tutt

"I Dreamt I Dwelt in Marble Halls" and "The Wound upon Thine Arm,"
    from *The Bohemian Girl,* Michael William Balfe
"Red, Red Rose"
"Gay Butterfly Waltz"
"Dream Song," from the comic opera *Fatinitza,* Franz von Suppé
"Dixie Land Is Good Enough for Me"
Sextet from *Lucia di Lammermoor,* Gaetano Donizetti
Quartet from *Rigoletto,* Giuseppe Verdi
"My Jewel of the Big Blue Nile," Will Marion Cook
"Love Is King," Will Marion Cook
"Baby Rose"
"Home, Sweet Home," Sir Henry Bishop
"Sun Blest Are You, O Golden Land"
"The Nightingale"
Selection from the musical comedy *The Belle of New York,* Gustave Kerker
"Delight," Isidore Luckstone
"Goodbye," Paulo Tosti
"No One"
"Nobody but You"
"Rose in the Bud," Dorothy Forster
"Twas No Vision"

APPENDIX B

1901–1902 Black Patti Troubadours' Tour
"A Filipino Mis-Fit"

Date	Location	Venue
AUGUST 1901		
14	Newburg, N.Y.	Academy of Music
15	Cohoes, N.Y.	
16	Saratoga Springs, N.Y.	Broadway Theatre
17	Schenectady, N.Y.	Van Curler Opera House
18	Troy, N.Y.	Rand's Opera House
19	Middletown, N.Y.	
20	Port Jervis, N.Y.	Grand Opera House
22–23	Asbury Park, N.J.	Auditorium
24	New Brunswick, N.J.	
25–31	Newark, N.J.	Empire Theatre
SEPTEMBER 1901		
2	Charlottesville, Va.	Auditorium
3	Staunton, Va.	Staunton Opera House
4	Roanoke, Va.	Academy of Music
5	Danville, Va.	Academy of Music
6	Newport News, Va.	Academy of Music
7	Norfolk, Va.	Academy of Music
9	Raleigh, N.C.	
10	Charlotte, N.C.	
11	Greenville, S.C.	Grand Opera House
12	Asheville, N.C.	Grand Opera House
13	Spartanburg, S.C.	Opera House
14	Elberton, Ga.	Neal's Opera House

September 1901 (continued)

Date	Location	Venue
16–18	Atlanta, Ga.	Columbia
19	Athens, Ga.	New Opera House
20	Augusta, Ga.	Grand Opera House
21	Columbia, S.C.	Theatre
23	Sumter, S.C.	Academy of Music
24	Charleston, S.C.	Academy of Music
25	Savannah, Ga.	Theatre
26	Brunswick, Ga.	Grand Opera House
28	Albany, Ga.	Sale-Davis Opera House
30	Americus, Ga.	Glovers Opera House

OCTOBER 1901

2	Macon, Ga.	Academy of Music
3	Montgomery, Ala.	McDonald's Theatre
4	Selma, Ala.	Academy of Music
5	Birmingham, Ala.	Jefferson Theatre
7	Chattanooga, Tenn.	The New Opera House
8	Nashville, Tenn.	Masonic Theatre
9	Evansville, Ind.	People's
10	Mattoon, Ill.	Theatre
11	Decatur, Ill.	Power's Grand Opera House
12	Bloomington, Ill.	Grand Opera House
13	Chicago, Ill., or Racine, Wis.	
14	Sheboygan, Wis.	Opera House
15	Green Bay, Wis.	Theatre
16	Oshkosh, Wis.	Grand Opera House
17	Ashland, Wis.	Grand Opera House
18	Duluth, Minn.	Lyceum Theatre
19	W. Superior, Wis.	Grand Opera House
21–26	St. Paul, Minn.	Grand Opera House
27–2 November	Minneapolis, Minn.	Bijou Opera House

NOVEMBER 1901

4	St. Cloud, Minn.	Davidson Opera House
5	Little Falls, Minn.	
6	Crookston, Minn.	Opera House
7	Grand Forks, N.D.	Metropolitan Theatre
8–9	Winnipeg, Man. (Canada)	Theatre

Date	Location	Venue
11	Fargo, N.D.	Opera House
12	Casselton, N.D.	
14	Billings, Mont.	Opera House
15	Bozeman, Mont.	
17	Helena, Mont.	Theatre
18	Butte, Mont.	Sutton's New Grand
19	Anaconda, Mont.	Theatre Margaret
21	Spokane, Wash.	Auditorium
23	Tacoma, Wash.	Lycem Theatre
24–30	Seattle, Wash.	Third Avenue

DECEMBER 1901

2	Victoria, B.C.	
3	Vancouver, B.C.	
4	New Westminster, B.C.	
5	New Whatcom, Wash.	
6	Everett, Wash.	
8–14	Portland, Ore.	Cordray's Opera House
16	Salem, Ore.	Temple Grand Opera House
17	Eugene, Ore.	
18	Roseburg, Ore.	
19	Ashland, Ore.	
20	Red Bluff, Calif.	
21	Chico, Calif.	
23	Marysville, Calif.	
25	Stockton, Calif.	Yosemite Theatre
25	Sacramento, Calif.	Clunie Opera House
26	Vallego, Calif.	
26–27	Oakland, Calif.	MacDonough Theatre
27	Woodland, Calif.	Opera House
29–4 January	San Francisco, Calif.	California Theatre

JANUARY 1902

6–7	San Diego, Calif.	Fisher Opera House
8	Santa Anna, Calif.	
9	Riverside, Calif.	
10	San Bernardino, Calif.	Opera House
11	Pomona, Calif.	
12–15	Los Angeles, Calif.	Theatre
16	Pomona or Pasadena, Calif.	

Date	Location	Venue
17	Santa Barbara, Calif.	
18	Ventura, Calif.	
20	Bakersfield, Calif.	
21	Tulare, Calif.	
22	Visalia, Calif.	
23	Fresno, Calif.	Barton Opera House
24	San Jose, Calif.	
25	Stockton, Calif.	
27	Nevada City, Calif.	
28	Grass Valley, Calif.	
29	Virginia City, Nev.	Piper's Opera House
30	Reno, Nev.	McKissick's Opera House

FEBRUARY 1902

Date	Location	Venue
1	Ogden, Utah	Grand Opera House
3–5	Salt Lake City, Utah	Grand Theatre
6	Park City, Utah	Dewey Theatre
7	Provo, Utah	
9	Leadville, Colo.	Elk's Opera House
10	Salida, Colo.	
12	Canon City, Colo.	
13	Pueblo, Colo.	Grand Opera House
14	Cripple Creek, Colo.	Grand Opera House
15	Colorado Springs, Colo.	Grand Opera House
16–22	Denver, Colo.	Denver Theatre
24	Cheyenne, Wyo.	
25	Kearney, Neb.	
26–27	Lincoln, Neb.	
28–1 March	St. Joseph, Mo.	Lyceum Theatre

MARCH 1902

Date	Location	Venue
2–8	Kansas City, Mo.	Gillis
9	Leavenworth, Kans.	Crawford Opera House
10	Topeka, Kans.	Crawford's Opera House
11	Emporia, Kans.	Whitley Opera House
12	Wichita, Kans.	Crawford Theatre
13	Wellington, Kans.	Woods' Opera House
14	Perry, Okla. Territories	
15	Gutherie, Okla. Territories	

Date	Location	Venue
16	Oklahoma City, Okla. Territories	Overholser Opera House
17	Ardmore, Indian Territories	
18	Ft. Worth, Tex.	Greenwall's Opera House
19	Dallas, Tex.	Theatre
20	Corsicana, Tex.	
21	Waco, Tex.	Auditorium
22	Temple, Tex.	
23–24	San Antonio, Tex.	Grand Opera House
25	Austin, Tex.	Hancock Opera House
26	Galveston, Tex.	Grand Opera House
27	Houston, Tex.	Sweeney & Comb's
28	Beaumont, Tex.	Kyle Opera House
29	Lake Charles, La.	Opera House
30–5 April	New Orleans, La.	Crescent Theatre

APRIL 1902

Date	Location	Venue
6	Donaldsville, La.	
7	Baton Rouge, La.	Elks' Theatre
8	Natchez, Miss.	Temple Opera House
9	Vicksburg, Miss.	Walnut Street Theatre
10	Monroe, La., or Greenville, Miss.	
11	Pine Bluff, Ark.	Opera House
12	Hot Springs, Ark.	Grand Opera House
14	Little Rock, Ark.	Capital Theatre
14–16	Memphis, Tenn.	
17	Jackson, Tenn.	
18	Cairo, Ill.	Opera House
19	Vincennes, Ind.	McJimsey's Theatre
21–23	Indianapolis, Ind.	Park Theatre
24–26	Columbus, Ohio	High Street Theatre
28	Newark, Ohio	Auditorium
29	Zanesville, Ohio	
30	Cambridge, Ohio	Colonial Theatre

MAY 1902

Date	Location	Venue
1–3	Wheeling, W.V.	
5	Steubenville, Ohio	Olympic Theatre
6	East Liverpool, Ohio	Grand Opera House

May 1902 (continued)

Date	Location	Venue
7	McKeesport, Pa.	White's Opera House
8	Uniontown, Pa.	Grand Opera House
9	Connelsville, Pa.	Theatre
10	Mt. Pleasant, Pa.	Grand Opera House
12	Greensburg, Pa.	
13	Latrobe, Pa.	
14	Johnstown, Pa.	Cambria Theatre
15	Altoona, Pa.	Eleventh Ave. Opera House
16	Tyrone, Pa.	
17	Reading, Pa.	Academy of Music
19–24	Baltimore, Md.	Holliday Street Theatre
26	Havre de Grace, Md.	
27	Wilmington, Del.	Grand Opera House
28	West Chester, Pa.	Assembly Building
29	Chester, Pa.	
30–31	Atlantic City, N.J.	

JUNE 1902

2–7	New York City, N.Y.	New Star Theatre

End of Season

NOTES

PROLOGUE

1. The loan for the cab ride is documented in the papers of the *Estate of Matilda S. Joyner,* packet 2, document 24, filed 27 March 1934.

2. Certificate of Death, Matilda Sissieretta Joyner, R.I. Public Health Commission, filed 27 June 1933.

3. Lichtenwanger, "Matilda Sissieretta Joyner Jones," 289–90.

4. The author queried the music library at the University of Washington about any recordings Sissieretta might have made. The library said no recordings were made and cited its source as K. J. Kutsch and Leo Riemens's *Grosses Sängerlexikon,* 3rd ed., 7 vols. (Munich: Saur, 1997–2002), a biographical dictionary of singers, from the famous to the near-forgotten ones. A newspaper item, "The Stage," *IF,* 25 December 1897, 2, stated that the Black Patti Troubadour Sextette was doing a "land office business" with Edison Phonograph agents, yet there is no evidence that this group, Sissieretta, or the Black Patti Troubadours ever issued a commercial Edison cylinder, according to Brooks, *Lost Sounds,* 499–500.

5. Sissieretta's scrapbook (hereafter referred to as SJScrapbook) contains press clippings, mostly from 1892–96. It is located in the Dr. Carl R. Gross Collection at the

Moorland-Spingarn Research Center, Manuscript Division, Howard University, Washington D.C.

6. Lester Walton, "Music and the Stage, Theatrical Comment," *NY Age,* 4 May 1911, 6.

1. RHODE ISLAND

1. No birth certificate has yet been found to verify Matilda Sissieretta Joyner's birth date. Various sources give different dates for her birth. The most common date has been 12 January 1869, which was listed in several articles and on her death certificate in Rhode Island. Strangely the 12 January date on her death certificate was crossed out by someone and the date 25 December 1869 substituted. The 1870 federal census lists Sissieretta as being two years old and her younger sister as nine months old, which indicates Sissieretta was born in 1868. The 1880 federal census also estimated her birth year to be 1868, although Sissieretta reported in the 1905 Rhode Island census that she was thirty-four years old and born on 5 January 1871. Willia Daughtry, whose 1968 doctoral dissertation about Sissieretta said her birth date was 5 January 1869, later revised the date to 5 January 1868 in her book *Vision and Reality.* Sissieretta, in an interview in the *New York Dramatic Mirror* (11 January 1896) says she was born in 1869. Professor John Graziano, in his article, "The Early Life and Career of the 'Black Patti,'" also believes she was born 5 January 1868. Like Graziano and Daughtry, this author believes Sissieretta's birth date was 5 January 1868.

2. Portsmouth Bureau, "Passing of Famed 'Black Patti' Deep Loss to Those Who Knew Her as a Child in Portsmouth," *Norfolk (Va.) Journal and Guide,* 15 July 1933, 1.

3. SJScrapbook, newspaper clipping, n.n., n.d.

4. 1870 Norfolk County (Portsmouth) Va. Census, Jefferson Ward, 12 August 1870, 479B.

5. *Jeremiah Joyner v. Henrietta Joyner.*

6. Portsmouth Bureau, "Passing of Famed 'Black Patti' Deep Loss to Those Who Knew Her as a Child in Portsmouth," *Norfolk (Va.) Journal and Guide,* 15 July 1933, 1.

7. Register of Deaths, City of Portsmouth (Va.), 1870 [for Isabella Joiner (*sic*)], and 1876 [for Jerry M. Joyner].

8. "Ridgeway Theater," *Colfax (Wash.) Gazette,* 25 November 1904, 5.

9. Newby-Alexander, Breckenridge-Haywood, and the African American Historical Society of Portsmouth, *Black America Series,* 8.

10. Shifflett, *Victorian America,* 22.

11. McLoughlin, *Rhode Island,* 146.

12. Daughtry, *Vision and Reality,* 3.

13. *1878 Providence City Directory,* listing for Jeremiah M. Joyner.

14. Armstrong, *Community of Spirit,* 38.

15. 1880 United States Federal Census, Providence, Rhode Island: Roll: T9_1212; Family History Film 1255212; page 312.3000; Enumeration District 19, http://www .Ancestry.com (accessed 4 June 2007). Jeremiah Joyner's name did not appear in Providence city directories again until 1882, when he was listed as a carpet cleaner living at 82 Mathewson Street.

16. *Jeremiah Joyner v. Henrietta Joyner.*

17. *Providence City Directories,* 1882–93.

18. "Music Knows No Color," *Evening Herald,* n.d., n.p., in SJScrapbook.

19. F. C. Terry, "The Closing Chapters of the Life of 'Black Patti,'" *Providence Sunday Journal,* 16 July 1933, E2.

20. "Music Knows No Color."

21. W. Allison Sweeney, "The Black Patti," *IF,* 29 August 1891, Columbian Exposition edition, 2, and "A Successful Singer," *NY Age,* 8 February 1890, 2. A search of Providence City directories did not show any listings for an Academy of Music, Baroness Lacombe, or a Mr. Monros.

22. David Richard Jones and Matilda Sissie Joyner, Marriages Registered in the City of Providence, R.I., for the year ending 31 December 1883, 536.

23. Mabel Adelina Jones, 8 April 1884, Births Registered in the City of Providence, recorded July 1884, 211.

24. "Providence Driftings," *NY Freeman,* 10 January 1885, 1.

25. "Providence People," *NY Age,* 28 April 1888, 1.

26. "Providence Driftings," *NY Freeman,* 31 January 1885, 1.

27. "Providence People," *NY Age,* 28 April 1888, 1; and "Providence Driftings," *NY Freeman,* 31 January 1885, 1.

28. "State Election Providence May 26," *NY Freeman,* 30 May 1885, 4.

29. Doris E. McGinty, "Flora Batson Bergen," in Logan and Winston, *Dictionary of American Negro Biography,* 32–34.

30. "The Star Company," *NY Freeman,* 24 October 1885, 4.

31. Story, *And So I Sing,* 33.

32. Gable-Wilson, "Let Freedom Sing!," 62–77.

33. Story, *And So I Sing,* 25–28.

34. Ibid., 28.

35. Brooks McNamara, "Popular Entertainment," in Wilmeth and Bigsby, *Cambridge History of American Theatre,* 391 and 388.

36. James V. Hatch, "American Minstrelsy in Black and White," in Hill and Hatch, *History of African American Theatre,* 93 and 107.

37. Ibid., 107.

38. *Providence Evening Telegram,* quoted in "'Richard Himself Again,'" *NY Freeman,* 7 November 1885, 4.

39. "Grand Selika Concert" (advertisement), *NY Freeman,* 19 December 1885, 3.

40. Mabel Adeline [*sic*] Jones, City of Providence Death Records, Providence, R.I., 1886, 714.

41. "Providence Driftings," *NY Freeman,* 27 February 1886, 1.

42. "Providence Letter," *NY Freeman,* 2 May 1886, 1.

43. "Providence Paragraphs," *NY Freeman,* 21 August 1886, 1.

44. Sissieretta probably studied at one of these schools, the New England Conservatory or the Boston Conservatory, or she may have studied privately with a faculty member, as Professor Graziano has suggested. Based on various newspaper reports, it appears she studied in Boston from August 1886 until late 1887.

45. Providence City Directory 1887, listings for David R. Jones and Henrietta Joyner.

46. "Rhode Island Citizens," *NY Age,* 31 December 1887, 4.

47. Southall, *Blind Tom,* 1.

48. Abbott and Seroff, *Out of Sight,* 47.

49. Logan and Winston, *Dictionary of American Negro Biography,* 43, and "Rhode Island Citizens," *NY Age,* 31 December 1887, 4.

50. "The Odd Fellows' Concert," *NY Age,* 14 April 1888, 1.

51. "Quaker City Gossip," *NY Age,* 12 May 1888, 1.

52. W. Allison Sweeney, "The Black Patti," *IF,* 29 August 1891, 2.

53. Graziano, "Early Life," 550.

54. Southern, *Music of Black Americans,* 242.

55. "Grand Concert to Buy Loaves," in SJScrapbook, n.n., n.d. Although the article has no name or date of the newspaper, it was obviously, from the context, published in New York, and someone wrote the date 15 June 1892 on the clipping.

56. "Providence News," *NY Clipper,* 4 August 1888, 327.

57. "Local Gossip," *NY Age,* 4 August 1888, 3, and "Grand Concert to Buy Loaves," in SJScrapbook.

58. Graziano, "Early Life," 550, and "Theatrical Gossip," *NYT,* 2 August 1888, 2.

59. Sweeney, "Black Patti."

60. "Local Gossip," *NY Age,* 4 August 1888, 3.

61. Graziano, "Early Life," 566, and "'Brown' and 'Black Pattis,'" *Cleveland Gazette,* 22 October 1892, 2.

62. "She's a Great Artist," *Detroit Evening News,* n.d., in SJScrapbook.

63. Southern, *Music of Black Americans,* 225–27.

2. West Indies and South American Tours

1. *Daily Gleaner,* 13 August 1888 and 16 August 1888, quoted in Graziano, "Early Life," 552–53.

2. "Theatrical Gossip," *NYT,* 27 August 1888, 8.

3. "The Stage, Mr. Will H. Pierce Interviewed," *IF,* 13 July 1889, 8.

4. Graziano, "Early Life," 555.

5. "History of Colón."

6. Harding, *History of Panama,* 23–24.

7. "The Stage," *IF,* 22 June 1889, 5.

8. Graziano, "Early Life," 555–56.

9. *Globe* (Barbados), 15 November 1888, quoted in Graziano, "Early Life," 556.

10. Graziano, "Early Life," 557.

11. Ibid.

12. "The Stage, Mr. Will H. Pierce Interviewed," *IF,* 29 June 1889, 5.

13. Graziano, "Early Life," 557.

14. "The Stage, Mr. Will H. Pierce Interviewed," *IF,* 13 July 1889, 8; and "The Stage, Mr. Will H. Pierce Interviewed," *IF,* 29 June 1889, 5.

15. *Daily Chronicle* (Georgetown, British Guyana), 16 December 1888, quoted in Graziano, "Early Life," 558.

16. Graziano, "Early Life," 559.

17. "American Artists Abroad," *NY Age,* 30 March 1889, 1.

18. Graziano, "Early Life," 558.

19. "The Stage, Mr. Will H. Pierce Interviewed," *IF,* 29 June 1889, 5.

20. Graziano, "Early Life," 559, and "The Stage, Mr. Will H. Pierce Interviewed," *IF,* 29 June 1889, 5.

21. "New York City News," *NY Age,* 16 February 1889, 3.

22. Florence Williams, "A Singer's Triumph," *NY Age,* 16 February 1889, 1.

23. "The Stage," *IF,* 22 June 1889, 5; and "The Stage, Mr. Will H. Pierce Interviewed," *IF,* 29 June 1889, 5.

24. "American Artists Abroad," *NY Age,* 30 March 1889, 1.

25. "The Tennessee Concert Company," *NY Age,* 6 April 1889, 1.

26. Florence Williams, *NY Age,* 13 April 1889, 2.

27. "Irish Home Rule," *Providence Journal,* 4 April 1889.

28. "Black Patti at Home," *Chicago Evening Post,* n.d., and "Queen of Song," newspaper clipping, n.n., n.d., both in SJScrapbook. Another newspaper clipping, "Madame S. Jones," n.n., n.d., in SJScrapbook, mistakenly said she had appeared at Boston Music Hall in 1887 to benefit the "Parnell Defence [*sic*] Fund."

29. The "Providence Friends" medal is one of three medals kept in the Dr. Carl R. Gross Collection, Collection 41–1 to 42–1, Moorland-Spingarn Research Center, Manuscript Division, Howard University, Washington, D.C.

30. Abbott and Seroff, *Out of Sight,* 33.

31. "Mme. Matilda S. Jones" (advertisement), *NY Age,* 4 May 1889, 3

32. "The Stage," *IF,* 18 May 1889, 5.

33. "Providence People," *New York Age,* 3 August 1889, 4; and "The Stage," *IF,* 13 July 1889, 8.

34. "Musical and Dramatic," *NY Age,* 27 July 1889, 2.

35. "Musical and Dramatic," *NY Age,* 6 July 1889, 4.

36. "The Stage," *IF,* 9 November 1889, 5; and "Off to the West Indies," *NY Age,* 26 October 1889, 1.

37. "A Successful Singer," *NY Age,* 8 February 1890, 2.

38. "The Stage," *IF,* 14 December 1889, 7.

39. A. E. Lunan, "Miss Williams' Troupe" (letter), *NY Age,* 1 February 1890, 3.

40. "Off to the West Indies," *NY Age,* 22 March 1890, 3.

41. Florence Williams, "The Tennessee Jubilee Singers in the West Indies," *NY Age,* 5 April 1890, 1.

42. "On Their West Indian Tour," *NY Age,* 3 May 1890, 4.

43. Florence Williams, "Weird West Indian Legend," *NY Age,* 24 May 1890, 4.

44. "New York City News," *NY Age,* 14 June 1890, 3.

45. "Journalistic and Personal," *NY Age,* 13 September 1890, 2.

46. Florence Williams, "Guests of Gen. Hyppolite," *NY Age,* 27 December 1890, 1; and "The Stage," *IF,* 17 January 1891, 3.

47. Florence Williams, "Guests of Gen. Hyppolite," *NY Age,* 27 December 1890, 1.

48. Ibid.

49. Letter from D. R. Jones, *IF,* 1 November 1890, 6; and Florence Williams, "Guests of Gen. Hyppolite," *NY Age,* 27 December 1890, 1.

50. The medal is part of the Dr. Carl R. Gross Collection, Moorland-Spingarn Research Center, Howard University.

51. Florence Williams, "At Beautiful St. Thomas," *NY Age,* 24 January 1891, 1.

52. Graziano, "Early Life," 562.

53. *Bulletin* (St. Thomas), 18 April 1891, quoted in Graziano, "Early Life," 562.

54. "Another Colored Patti," *Detroit Plaindealer,* 17 July 1891, 1.

55. Graziano, "Early Life," 565.

56. Ibid.

57. Abbott and Seroff, *Out of Sight,* 30.

58. Graziano, "Early Life," 565.

59. "The Black Patti," *IF,* 29 August 1891, Columbian Exposition edition, 2.

60. Ibid.

3. "I Woke Up Famous," 1892

1. "Bergen Star Concerts," *NY Age,* 17 October 1891, 1; and "Personal," *NY Age,* 23 October 1891, 3.

2. "The Stage," *IF,* 4 December 1891, 6.

3. "Mme. Wilson's Testimonial," *NY Age,* 27 February 1892, 1.

4. "The Race's Patti," *Cleveland Gazette,* 5 March 1892, 1, and *IF,* 5 March 1892, 1.

5. Kirk, *Musical Highlights,* 73; "Madame Sissieretta at the White House," *Washington Post,* 25 February 1892, 8; Kirk, *Music at the White House,* 151; and "The Race's Patti," *Cleveland Gazette,* 5 March 1892, 1.

6. Kirk, *Music at the White House,* 151, and Kirk, *Musical Highlights,* 77.

7. "Patti's Colored Rival," *Washington Post,* 28 February 1892, 5.

8. "The Great Prima Dona [*sic*]," *Washington Bee,* 27 February 1892, 3.

9. Sylvester Russell, "Death of Flora Batson," *IF,* 15 December 1906, 1+.

10. "A Negro Jubilee," *NYDM,* 2 April 1892, 5.

11. "Notes of the Stage," *NYT,* 24 April 1892, 13; and "Theatrical Gossip," *NYT,* 26 April 1892, 8.

12. Riis, *Just Before Jazz,* 44.

13. Morgan and Barlow, *From Cakewalks,* 26.

14. "Notes of the Stage," *NYT,* 24 April 1892, 13; and "Theatrical Gossip," *NYT,* 26 April 1892, 8.

15. "The 'Black Patti' and a Cakewalk," *NY Herald,* 27 April 1892, 6.

16. "Theatrical Gossip," *NYT,* 26 April 1892, 8.

17. Durso, *Madison Square Garden,* 78.

18. Ibid., 73–77.

19. "The 'Black Patti' and a Cakewalk," *NY Herald,* 27 April 1892, 6.

20. Ibid.

21. Gross, "Brief History," 2.

22. "The Colored Jubilee," *NYDM,* 7 May 1892, 5.

23. Ibid.

24. "Patti's Dusky Rival," newspaper from New York, n.n., 27 April 1892, in SJScrapbook.

25. "A Patti with a Soul," *Detroit Plaindealer,* 20 May 1892, 5.

26. Johnson, *Black Manhattan,* 100; and Story, *And So I Sing,* 14.

27. Sylvester Russell, "Death of Flora Batson," *IF,* 15 December 1906, 1+.

28. Hughes and Meltzer, *Black Magic,* 336, 338.

29. "Madame S. Jones," *Message,* 14 May 1892, in SJScrapbook.

30. *James B. Pond v. Sissieretta Jones and David R. Jones.* Information about the terms of the contract are contained in a "Memorandum of Agreement" between Sissieretta and David Jones of Providence, R.I., and James B. Pond, of New York City, an affidavit to this lawsuit.

31. Officer and Williamson, "Purchasing Power."

32. Ibid.

33. United States, and Social Science Research Council, *Historical Statistics,* 92.

34. Rob Hudson (associate archivist, Carnegie Hall), e-mail messages to author, 10 February 2009 and 16 January 2010. Hudson confirmed the Society of the Sons of New York's concert was the second time African Americans had performed in any part of Carnegie Hall. Henry (Harry) T. Burleigh was among the first African Americans to perform there. He and two African American vocalists (Tillie Jones Thomas and Deseria Plato) appeared during a recital given by pianist W. T. Talbert on 16 May 1892 in the Chamber Music Hall (known today as Weill Recital Hall), the smallest auditorium in the facility, located adjacent to the main auditorium.

35. "Sons of New York at Carnegie's Recital Hall," *New York Echo,* n.d., page unknown, e-mailed to author 10 February 2009 by Rob Hudson, associate archivist, Carnegie Hall. Hudson also provided information from a concert program performed 15 June 1892 at Carnegie Hall's Recital Hall.

36. "Notes of the Stage," *New York Times,* 26 June 1892, 13.

37. Graziano, "Early Life," 570–71.

38. "A Wonderful Performance," *Saratoga (N.Y.) Union,* 6 August 1892, in SJScrapbook, and also reprinted in "Black Patti in Saratoga," *Washington Bee,* 1 October 1892, 2.

39. "The 'Black Patti' Concert Troupe," *Springfield (Ill.) Republican,* n.d., in SJScrapbook. A short biography of Princess Lily Dolgorouky in this newspaper article says that she was born in Seville, Spain, "morganatically related" to the reigning family in Russia, studied in Russia, and conducted the orchestra that played for the country's empress. *Morganatically* describes a marriage in which a man of high rank marries a woman of lower rank with the stipulation that neither she nor her children will have any claim to the man's rank or property. The newspaper opined that, in addition to being a fine conductor, Princess Dolgorouky was "without question" a superior violinist and a high-ranking artist.

40. "Return to Asbury Park," *Asbury Park (N.J.) Daily Journal,* 12 August 1892, in SJScrapbook; and "A Real Russian Princess," *Asbury Park (N.J.) Daily Press,* 12 August 1892, in SJScrapbook.

41. "In Summer's Whirl," *Daily Saratogian* (Saratoga Springs, N.Y.), 16 August 1892, in SJScrapbook.

42. Ibid.

43. "The Black Patti," *Buffalo Inquirer,* 18 August 1892, in SJScrapbook.

44. "Black Patti," *Daily Saratogian* (Saratoga Springs, N.Y.), 29 August 1892, in SJScrapbook.

45. Graziano, "Early Life," 572.

46. Kelley and Lewis, *To Make Our World Anew,* 3, 10–11, 27.

47. Ibid., 24.

48. Ibid., 28, 32.

49. "Her Color No Bar," *Empire* (Toronto), n.d., in SJScrapbook.

50. Ibid.

51. "Pittsburg's Pride," *Pittsburg* [*sic*] *Press,* 7 September 1892, 1; and "Pittsburg's Big Show," *Pittsburg* [*sic*] *Press,* 8 September 1892, 4.

52. "Black Patti," Pittsburgh newspaper clipping, n.n., 25 September 1892, in SJScrapbook.

53. "Quick Words," *Pittsburgh Chronicle Telegraph,* 26 September 1892, 2.

54. "The Black Pearl," *Pittsburgh Chronicle Telegraph,* 27 September 1892, 2.

55. "Proving Attractive Features," *Pittsburg* [*sic*] *Press,* 27 September 1892, 4.

56. "Our Pattis, Madame Selika at Cleveland and Madame Jones in Pittsburgh," *Cleveland Gazette,* 1 October 1892, 1.

57. "Queen of Song," *Pittsburgh Dispatch,* n.d., in SJScrapbook.

58. Daughtry, *Vision and Reality,* 4.

59. F. C. Terry, "The Closing Chapters of the Life of 'Black Patti,'" *Providence Sunday Journal,* 16 July 1933, E2.

60. "Black Patti Success," *Pittsburgh Post,* 27 September 1892, 2.

61. *Pittsburgh Chronicle Telegraph,* 29 September 1892, 2.

62. "Adieu Sweet Singer," a Pittsburgh newspaper clipping, n.n., n.d., likely published in early October 1892, in SJScrapbook.

63. "A Grand Farewell," a Pittsburgh newspaper clipping, n.n., n.d., likely published in early October 1892, in SJScrapbook; and *Pittsburgh Chronicle Telegraph,* 3 October 1892, 2.

64. *Pittsburgh Chronicle Telegraph,* 30 September 1892, 2.

65. *Pittsburg* [*sic*] *Press,* 2 October 1892, 15.

66. "Black Patti," *Pittsburgh Chronicle Telegraph,* 15 October 1892, 2; and "Great Attractions Secured," *Pittsburgh Chronicle Telegraph,* 17 October 1892, 2.

67. "Black Patti Captured Her Audience Once More," *Pittsburgh Chronicle Telegraph,* 18 October 1892, 2.

68. "A Prime Favorite," *Pittsburgh Chronicle Telegraph,* 19 October 1892, 2.

69. "The Black Patti," *Cleveland Gazette,* 19 November 1892, 3.

70. Ibid.

71. "The Rounder's Chat," *Cleveland Gazette,* 26 November 1892, 1.

72. Ibid.

73. "The Rounder's Chat," *Cleveland Gazette,* 3 December 1892, 1.

74. "Star Course Opening," *Boston Journal,* 10 October 1892, in SJScrapbook.

75. Graziano, "Early Life," 573; "She's a Great Artist," *Detroit Evening News,* n.d.,

in SJScrapbook; and "Not Pleased, the Black Patti Thinks Her People Not Well Treated," *Louisville Commercial*, n.d., in SJScrapbook.

76. "'Brown' and 'Black Pattis,'" *Cleveland Gazette*, 22 October 1892, 2.

77. Abbott and Seroff, *Out of Sight*, 214.

4. TROUBLE ON THE HORIZON, 1893

1. *IF*, 21 January 1893, 3.

2. "Musical Notes," *Chicago Journal*, n.d., in SJScrapbook.

3. "Black Patti" (advertisement), *Chicago Tribune*, 7 January 1893, 3; and "She Has a Wonderfully Rich Voice," *Chicago Tribune*, 6 January 1893, 3.

4. "Amusements, Central Music Hall," *Chicago Inter-Ocean*, n.d., in SJScrapbook.

5. Ibid.

6. *Chicago Times*, n.d., in SJScrapbook.

7. *Chicago Tribune*, n.d., in SJScrapbook.

8. "Music and Drama," newspaper clipping from Chicago, n.n., n.d., in SJScrapbook.

9. *Chicago Times*, n.d., in SJScrapbook.

10. "Amusements, Central Music Hall."

11. "Black Patti," *Brantford (Ontario) Courier*, 3 February 1893, in SJScrapbook.

12. "She Is a Gem," *Daily Expositor*, n.p., 3 February 1893, in SJScrapbook; and "Black Patti," *Brantford (Ontario) Courier*, 3 February 1893, in SJScrapbook.

13. "The Black Patti," *Daily Expositor*, n.p., 4 February 1893, in SJScrapbook.

14. "Patrons of Music," *Detroit Plaindealer*, 25 July 1890, 1.

15. "The 'Black Patti' Sings," *Cleveland Gazette*, 18 February 1893, 4.

16. "Of Local Interest," *Detroit Plaindealer*, 17 February 1893, 5.

17. Hill and Hatch, *History of African American Theatre*, 154–56.

18. Abbott and Seroff, *Out of Sight*, 278, 281.

19. "At the World's Fair," *IF*, 11 February 1893, 5.

20. "Notes of Music," *NYT*, 29 January 1893, 13; and "In Aid of Cook's Opera Scheme," *NYT*, 10 February 1893, 9.

21. Jaycox, *Progressive Era*, 37–38.

22. "In Aid of Cook's Opera Scheme," *NYT*, 10 February 1893, 9.

23. "The Sissieretta Jones Concert," *New York Review*, n.d., in SJScrapbook; and Rob Hudson (associate archivist, Carnegie Hall), e-mails to author, 11 February 2009 and 16 January 2010.

24. Program, Carnegie Hall Concert, 13 February 1893, provided by Rob Hudson (associate archivist, Carnegie Hall); "The Sissieretta Jones Concert," *New York Review*, n.d., in SJScrapbook; "The Black Patti," *Commercial Gazette*, n.d., in SJScrapbook; and Abbott and Seroff, *Out of Sight*, 280.

25. "Woman's World," *IF*, 11 March 1893, 3.

26. "Mr. Jones's Absence," newspaper clipping, n.n., n.d., in SJScrapbook.

27. "She Sings Well," newspaper clipping from Cincinnati, n.n., n.d., in SJScrapbook.

28. "Mr. Jones's Absence," newspaper clipping, n.n., n.d., in SJScrapbook.

29. "This Is Too Bad," *Detroit Plaindealer,* 31 March 1893, 4.

30. "Mr. Jones's Absence," newspaper clipping, n.n., n.d., in SJScrapbook, which includes a letter to the editor by Sissieretta Jones that carried a dateline, "Columbus, O., 21 March."

31. " Black Patti," *Dayton (Ohio) Herald,* n.d., in SJScrapbook.

32. "The Black Patti," *Dayton (Ohio) Evening Press,* n.d., in SJScrapbook; and "'Black Patti' Sings," *Cleveland Gazette,* 1 April 1893, 3.

33. "Not Pleased, the Black Patti Thinks Her People Not Well Treated," *Louisville Commercial,* n.d., in SJScrapbook.

34. Ibid.

35. "Woman's Work and Ways," *Detroit Plaindealer,* 14 April 1893, 8.

36. "The Theaters," Louisville newspaper clipping, n.n., n.d., in SJScrapbook.

37. *Louisville Post,* n.d., in SJScrapbook; and *Louisville Times,* n.d., in SJScrapbook.

38. "The Theaters," Louisville newspaper clipping, n.n., n.d., in SJScrapbook.

39. Ibid.

40. "A Great Editor and 'Black Patti,'" *St. Louis Globe Democrat,* 1 April 1893, in SJScrapbook.

41. *IF,* 15 April 1893, 3.

42. *James B. Pond v. Sissieretta Jones and David R. Jones.*

43. Ibid.

44. Jaycox, *Progressive Era,* 39.

45. Shifflett, *Victorian America,* 56.

46. Sworn affidavit by David R. Jones, 13 May 1893, *James B. Pond v. Sissieretta Jones and David R. Jones.*

47. *Cleveland Gazette,* 24 December 1892, 3.

48. Sworn affidavit by David R. Jones, 13 May 1893, *James B. Pond v. Sissieretta Jones and David R. Jones.*

49. Ibid.

50. Sworn affidavit by M. Sissieretta Jones, 15 May 1893, *James B. Pond v. Sissieretta Jones and David R. Jones.*

51. Sworn affidavit by James H. Durham, 9 May 1893, *James B. Pond v. Sissieretta Jones and David R. Jones.*

52. Abbott and Seroff, *Out of Sight,* 279.

53. Sworn affidavit by Charles B. Morris, 12 May 1893, *James B. Pond v. Sissieretta Jones and David R. Jones.*

54. Sworn affidavit by D. W. Robertson, 16 May 1893, and sworn affidavit by Georgiana Wilson, 15 May 1893, *James B. Pond v. Sissieretta Jones and David R. Jones.*

55. Order of Chief Judge John Sedgwick, 17 May 1893, *James B. Pond v. Sissieretta Jones and David R. Jones.*

56. "In Other Cities, Providence," *NYDM,* 3 June 1893, 5.

57. Order of Judge David McAdam, Special Term of the Superior Court of New York, 10 June 1893, *James B. Pond v. Sissieretta Jones and David R. Jones.*

58. Judge McAdam's final order was incomplete in the existing New York court records. The judge's ruling was published in "Pond Enjoins the Black Patti," *NYDM*, 8 July 1893, 4.

59. Bruce Abrams (Division of Old Records, County Clerk and Clerk of the Supreme Court's Office), letter to the author, 9 February 2009. Abrams wrote that "the remarks recorded in the newspaper would have been recorded if there had been a transcript of the court hearing, but transcripts are never prepared unless the case is appealed," and this case does not appear to have been appealed.

60. "Pond Enjoins the Black Patti," *NYDM*, 8 July 1893, 4.

61. "Major Pond and Mme. Jones," *Cleveland Gazette*, 15 July 1893, 3.

62. "Sissieretta Jones," *IF*, 9 September 1893, 8.

63. "Black Patti's Success," *Asbury Park (N.J.) Press*, 3 August 1893, in SJScrapbook.

64. Abbott and Seroff, *Out of Sight*, 281.

65. "Ida B. Wells-Barnett" (biography), Black History Month, Gale Cengage Learning website, http://www.gale.com/free_resources/bhm/bio/wells_1.htm (accessed 11 September 2011).

66. Abbott and Seroff, *Out of Sight*, 279.

67. "Colored World's Fair Opera Company," *Detroit Plaindealer*, 3 March 1893, 4.

68. Abbott and Seroff, *Out of Sight*, 280.

69. "Colored World's Fair Opera Company," *Detroit Plaindealer*, 3 March 1893, 4.

70. Abbott and Seroff, *Out of Sight*, 280.

71. "To Tole with Watermelons," *Cleveland Gazette*, 22 July 1893, 1.

72. John H. Cook, "Secretary John H. Cook, Chicago, Writes the Freeman to Deny Certain Rumors," *IF*, 12 August 1893, 2.

73. Abbott and Seroff, *Out of Sight*, 283.

74. "The Watermelons Absent," *Cleveland Gazette*, 26 August 1893, 2.

75. Abbott and Seroff, *Out of Sight*, 283; and "Honor to Their Race," *Chicago Inter-Ocean*, 26 August 1893, quoted in Abbott and Seroff, *Out of Sight*, 283.

76. "Chicago the World's Mecca," *IF*, 12 August 1893, 1.

77. "Honor to Their Race," quoted in Abbott and Seroff, *Out of Sight*, 284.

78. "Douglass Is Bitter," *Chicago Herald*, 26 August 1893, quoted in Abbott and Seroff, *Out of Sight*, 284.

79. Rambler, "Rambler Writes," *Chicago Conservator*, 9 September 1893, in SJScrapbook.

80. Ibid.

81. Ibid.

82. Abbott and Seroff, *Out of Sight*, 283–84. These two scholars found no trace of a manuscript of Cook's opera of *Uncle Tom's Cabin* and doubt he ever actually completed it.

83. White and Igleheart, *World's Columbian Exposition*, 445–49.

84. Walter B. Hayson, "World's Fair Music," *Cleveland Gazette*, 21 October 1893, 3.

85. "Pittsburg's Show," *Pittsburg [sic] Press*, 6 September 1893, 7; and Graziano, "Early Life," 579.

86. "The Gates Opened," *Pittsburg [sic] Press*, 7 September 1893, 5.

87. "Six Days More," *Pittsburg* [*sic*] *Press,* 15 October 1893, 7.

88. "Grand Stand Playing," *Pittsburg* [*sic*] *Press,* 16 October 1893, 6.

89. "Nearing the End," *Pittsburgh Chronicle Telegraph,* 16 October 1893, 2.

90. "Black Patti's Triumph," *Commerce Gazette,* n.d., in SJScrapbook.

91. Graziano, "Early Life," 579.

92. Officer and Williamson, "Purchasing Power."

93. Graziano, "Early Life," 579.

94. Johnson, *Black Manhattan,* 99.

95. Newspaper clipping, n.n., n.d., in SJScrapbook. Based on a sentence in this small, incomplete newspaper clipping that mentioned a concert manager named Neumann, it is likely that Sissieretta's comments were made after her January 1893 concerts in Chicago, which were managed by F. Wight Neumann.

5. THE ROAD TO EUROPE, 1894–1895

1. "Dvorak Leads for the Fund," *NY Herald,* 24 January 1894, in SJScrapbook.

2. "A Conservatory Concert," newspaper clipping, n.n., n.d., in SJScrapbook.

3. "Dvorak Leads for the Fund," *NY Herald,* 24 January 1894, in SJScrapbook.

4. "Negro Melodies," *Cleveland Gazette,* 3 June 1893, 1.

5. "Dvorak Leads for the Fund," *NY Herald,* 24 January 1894, in SJScrapbook.

6. Ibid.

7. Ibid.

8. "Hear 'The Old Folks at Home,'" unidentified newspaper clipping, n.n., n.d., in SJScrapbook.

9. "Dvorak Leads for the Fund," *NY Herald,* 24 January 1894, in SJScrapbook.

10. Howard, *Stephen Foster,* 188–97.

11. Foster, *Swanee River.*

12. Misinformation in Sissieretta's scrapbook has led to much confusion about the actual date of this concert. An article in her scrapbook about the Free Bread Fund, sponsored by the *New York World,* is dated 9 February 1894; however, this article could not be found in the *World* when this author carefully reviewed newspapers from January 1894 through April 1894. Information gathered from other sources confirmed that by February 1894 the *World* was trying to raise money to buy poor people bread, but no information could be found to indicate Sissieretta sang in a concert in early February to benefit the Free Bread Fund. The concert must have taken place sometime later in the year. Adding to the confusion is another unidentified, undated newspaper clipping from Sissieretta's scrapbook that describes the concert the day after it took place. It appears Dr. Carl R. Gross, who preserved Sissieretta's scrapbook after her death, wrote in the wrong date on this clipping as he attempted to identify when the article was published. He wrote "6–15–92," which could not have been the case because the article mentions a special guest, New York state treasurer Addison B. Colvin. Colvin did not start serving until 1 January 1894, which would indicate that the article in Sissieretta's scrapbook identified as being from the *World* had to be published sometime after that date. Another article in Sissieretta's scrapbook about a Sons of New York concert at the Standard Theatre to benefit the Free Bread Fund contains another handwritten note with the date "6–15–92." The note further says "? *New York*

World, June 10, 1892, date on medal," and it bears the initials C. R. G. (Carl R. Gross). Sissieretta did perform in a concert on 15 June 1892 sponsored by the Society of the Sons of New York and was given a medal for her participation, but that concert was held at the Recital Hall at Carnegie Hall and not at the Standard Theatre as stated in the article on which Gross wrote these notes.

13. "It Was a Great Benefit," newspaper clipping, n.n., n.d., in SJScrapbook.

14. Ibid.

15. "Local Department," *Cleveland Gazette,* 31 March 1894, 3.

16. "Correspondence, Pennsylvania, York," *NYDM,* 28 April 1894, 10.

17. "Correspondence, Pennsylvania, Greensburg," *NYDM,* 12 May 1892, 11. She canceled her concert in Greensburg on 26 April, the day of the concert, and then canceled all dates west of Tyrone, Pennsylvania. No reason was given, although the newspaper said the advanced ticket sales for her 26 April concert in Greensburg were large.

18. "The Entertainers," *NYDM,* 31 March 1894, 18.

19. "Correspondence, New York, Saratoga Springs," *NYDM,* 25 August 1894, 6.

20. *Cleveland Gazette,* 11 August 1894, 2.

21. "At New York's Famous Spa," *NYT,* 26 August 1894, 12.

22. "A Chat with the Black Patti," *NYDM,* 11 January 1896, 17.

23. "Mme. Sissieretta Jones," *NY Age,* 24 December 1908, Dramatic sect., 1

24. Rudolph Voelckel, U.S. Passport Application, No. 20117, filed in New York, 4 February 1895. U.S. Passport Applications, 1792–1925 (online database), http://www .Ancestry.com (accessed 2 February 2009).

25. "Grand Transcontinental Tour," *NYDM,* 10 November 1894, 20.

26. "The Black Patti's Tour," *NYDM,* 10 November 1894, 3.

27. Rob Hudson (associate archivist, Carnegie Hall), program information e-mailed to author on 10 February 2009.

28. "'Black Patti' Gives a Concert," *NY Herald,* 19 November 1894, 8.

29. "The Black Patti's Tour," *NYDM,* 24 November 1894, 7.

30. "Plays This Week," *Brooklyn Eagle,* 25 November 1894, 9.

31. "Notes of Music," *NYT,* 9 December 1894, 13.

32. "The 'Black Patti' Here, Also," *Cleveland Gazette,* 22 December 1894, 2; and "The Black Patti Sang," *Cleveland Gazette,* 29 December 1894, 2–3.

33. "In Other Cities, Atlanta," *NYDM,* 9 February 1895, 4.

34. "Personals," *NYDM,* 16 February 1895, 12.

35. Rudolph Voelckel, U.S. Passport Application, No. 20117, filed in New York, 4 February 1895. U.S. Passport Applications, 1792–1925 (online database), http://www .Ancestry.com (accessed 2 February 2009).

36. Graziano, "Early Life," 582–83. Graziano said Sissieretta implied in an 11 January 1896 interview with the *New York Dramatic Mirror* that she traveled to Europe on her own. This author does not interpret Sissieretta's statement that way.

37. "Mme. Sisserretta [*sic*] Jones," *IF,* 4 May 1895, 1.

38. *Borsen-Courier,* quoted in "Mme. Sisserretta [*sic*] Jones," *IF,* 4 May 1895, 1.

39. "Mme. Sisserretta [*sic*] Jones," *IF,* 4 May 1895, 1.

40. Ibid.

41. "A Diamond Cross," *Cleveland Gazette,* 11 May 1895, 1.

42. "Easter at the Music Halls," *Era* (London), 13 April 1895, 16.

43. "Palace Theatre," *Daily Telegraph* (London), 16 April 1895, 7.

44. "Palace Theatre," *Times* (London), 16 April 1895, 4.

45. "The London Music Halls," *Era* (London), 20 April 1895, 16.

46. *Entr'acte* (London), 20 April 1895, 5.

47. "The London Music Halls," *Era* (London), 20 April 1895, 16.

48. "Music Hall Gossip," *Era* (London), 27 April 1895, 17; and "London Day by Day," *Daily Telegraph* (London), 23 April 1895, 7. Various newspapers over the years have said she gave a command performance for the Prince of Wales, although the reports have never given a specific date or details of the event.

49. "Music Hall Gossip," *Era* (London), 25 May 1895, 17.

50. Frederic Edward McCay, "From London and Paris," *NYDM,* 20 July 1895, 2.

51. "Afro-American Notes," *New York Morning Advertiser,* 26 August 1895, 5.

52. "About the Theaters," *Los Angeles Times,* 12 July 1896, 21.

53. "Theatrical Gossip," *NYT,* 3 October 1895, 8.

54. "Some Race Doings," *Cleveland Gazette,* 26 October 1895, 4.

55. "A Chat with the Black Patti," *NYDM,* 11 January 1896, 17.

56. "Black Patti's Success," *NYDM,* 28 March 1896, 20.

57. "Is a Singer by Nature," *San Francisco Call,* 4 July 1896, 5.

58. "Proctor's Pleasure Palace," *NYDM,* 3 August 1895, 17; and "Manager Proctor's New Theatre," *NYT,* 28 July 1895, 11.

59. "Theatrical Gossip," *NYT,* 19 November, 1895, 8.

60. "Black Patti's Contracts," *NYDM,* 30 November 1895, 20.

61. Haley, *Afro-American Encyclopedia,* 225.

62. "Walter Damrosch, 1862–1950, Biography."

63. "The Damrosch Opera Tour," *NYDM,* 21 September 1895, 3.

64. "Proctor's Pleasure Palace," *NYDM,* 7 December 1895, 19.

65. "Last Week's Bills, Proctor's Pleasure Palace," *NYDM,* 21 December 1895, 19.

66. "A Chat with the Black Patti," *NYDM,* 11 January 1896, 17.

6. A New Career

1. "The Black Patti" (advertisement), *NYDM,* 11 January 1896, 18.

2. Stein, *American Vaudeville,* xi, xiii; and Easton, "Vaudeville!"

3. "Dates Ahead, Vaudeville," *NYDM,* 29 February 1896, 20; and "Vaudeville Jottings," *NYDM,* 9 May 1896, 18.

4. "Amusements," *Washington Bee,* 28 March 1896, 8.

5. Graziano, "Early Life," 585. Graziano based his weekly pay estimate on information from an article in the 7 March 1896 edition of the *New York Dramatic Mirror.* The article described a court judgment Sissieretta had won against a Mrs. M. G. Dahl, proprietress of Dahl Conservatory of Music, New York, for failing to pay her seventy-five dollars for a concert Sissieretta gave at the conservatory on 31 December 1895. Graziano estimated that if Sissieretta charged seventy-five dollars per performance and sang a minimum of four nights a week, she would earn three hundred dollars in a week.

6. Southern, *Music of Black Americans,* 244.

7. "A Big Organization," *NYDM,* 27 June 1896, 17.

8. Ibid.; and "Variety and Minstrelsy," *NY Clipper,* 27 June 1896, 262.

9. Charters, *Nobody,* 52.

10. Graziano, "Early Life," 586.

11. Southern, *Music of Black Americans,* 296.

12. Graziano, "Early Life," 587; and the *Colored American* (Washington, D.C.), 9 July 1898, as reprinted in Wright and Southern, "Sissieretta Jones," 201.

13. Hill and Hatch, *History of African American Theatre,* 94, 107–13.

14. Woll, *Black Musical Theatre,* 2.

15. Abbott and Seroff, *Ragged but Right,* 3, 7.

16. Ibid., 11, 14.

17. Hill and Hatch, *History of African American Theatre,* 130.

18. Woll, *Black Musical Theatre,* 4.

19. Ibid.

20. Hill and Hatch, *History of African American Theatre,* 142; and Abbott and Seroff, *Ragged but Right,* 4, 35.

21. "Amusements," *San Francisco Examiner,* 5 July 1896, 5, and 11 July 1896, 5; and "Amusements," *San Francisco Chronicle,* 4 July 1896, 5.

22. "Is a Singer by Nature," *San Francisco Call,* 4 July 1896, 5.

23. "About the Theaters," *Los Angeles Times,* 12 July 1896, 21.

24. "At the Playhouses," *Los Angeles Times,* 22 July 1896, 6.

25. "Variety and Minstrelsy," *NY Clipper,* 25 July 1896, 326, and 8 August 1896, 357.

26. "Vaudeville, Burlesque, and Extravaganza," *NYDM,* 12 September 1896, 4.

27. "Correspondence, Massachusetts, Pittsfield," *NYDM,* 19 September 1896, 7.

28. Abbott and Seroff, *Ragged but Right,* 41.

29. "Black Patti's Troubadours," *IF,* 19 December 1896, Holiday supplement, 4.

30. "Correspondence, Massachusetts, Pittsfield," *NYDM,* 19 September 1896, 7.

31. "Black Patti's Troubadours" (advertisement), *NYDM,* 26 September 1896, 18.

32. "The Stage," *IF,* 10 October 1896, 6.

33. "Offense Wasn't Intended," *NYT,* 13 October 1896, 2.

34. Ibid.

35. Rob Hudson (associate archivist, Carnegie Hall) e-mailed author (10 February 2009) the 12 October 1896 program for the Zion Grand Centennial Jubilee Concert and Banquet given in the main hall at Carnegie Hall.

36. "Offense Wasn't Intended," *NYT,* 13 October 1896, 2.

37. "Black Patti's Troubadours," *NY Clipper,* 17 October 1896, 522.

38. "They Are Loyal," *NYDM,* 10 October 1896, 17; and "Variety and Minstrelsy," *NY Clipper,* 10 October 1896, 504.

39. "Won't Board Black Troubadours," *NYT,* 24 October 1896, 2.

40. "Keep Your Eye on the Dark Horse" (advertisement), *NY Clipper,* 24 October 1896, 544.

41. "Didn't Pay Job Hedges," *NYT,* 8 November 1896, 9.

42. "Black Patti on the Rack," *Brooklyn Eagle,* 8 November 1896, 5.

43. "Didn't Pay Job Hedges," *NYT,* 8 November 1896, 9.

44. "'Black Patti's' Case Ended," *NYT,* 18 November 1896, 16.

45. "Variety and Minstrelsy," *NY Clipper,* 12 December 1896, 649.

46. "In Other Cities, Indianapolis," *NYDM,* 2 January 1897, 4.

47. John Nolan, "Variety and Minstrelsy," *NY Clipper,* 30 January 1897, 762.

48. "Variety and Minstrelsy," *NY Clipper,* 16 January 1897, 730.

49. "Black Patti's Fifty Troubadours" (advertisement), *NYDM,* 16 January 1897, 20; and "Black Patti's Fifty Troubadours" (advertisement), *NY Clipper,* 16 January 1897, 739.

50. Ibid.

51. "The Stage," *IF,* 6 February 1897, 5.

52. "Variety and Minstrelsy," *NY Clipper,* 15 May 1897, 170; and "Black Patti's Success," *NYDM,* 22 May 1897, 17.

53. "Variety and Minstrelsy," *NY Clipper,* 15 May 1897, 170; and "Proctor's Pleasure Palace," *NY Clipper,* 22 May 1897, 190.

54. "The Stage," *IF,* 29 May 1897, 7.

55. "Charged with Theft," *NYDM,* 29 May 1897, 15; and "Vaudeville and Minstrel," *NY Clipper,* 29 May 1897, 203.

56. "The Troubadours' Troubles," *NYDM,* 5 June 1897, 19.

57. Logan and Winston, *Dictionary of American Negro Biography,* 121.

58. "Vaudeville and Minstrel," *NY Clipper,* 12 June 1897, 236.

59. "Bob Cole Explains," *NYDM,* 12 June 1897, 17.

60. Ralph Matthews, "Looking at the Stars," *Baltimore Afro-American,* 8 July 1933, 8.

61. "Professional Doings," *NYDM,* 18 September 1897, 2.

62. Matthews, "Looking at the Stars," *Baltimore Afro-American,* 8 July 1933, 8; and Logan and Winston, *Dictionary of American Negro Biography,* 121.

63. "Proctor's Pleasure Palace," *NY Clipper,* 5 June 1897, 222; and "Pleasure Palace," *NYDM,* 12 June 1897, 16.

64. "The Vaudeville Stage," *NYDM,* 5 June 1897, 16; and "Pleasure Palace," *NYDM,* 12 June 1897, 16.

65. "Pleasure Palace," *NYDM,* 19 June 1897, 16.

66. "Bob Cole Explains," *NYDM,* 12 June 1897, 17; and "Black Patti's Troubadours" (advertisement), *NYDM,* 26 June 1897, 17.

7. THE BLACK PATTI TROUBADOURS, EARLY YEARS, 1897–1900

1. Riis, *Just Before Jazz,* 24.

2. "The Stage," *IF,* 11 September 1897, 5.

3. Logan and Winston, *Dictionary of American Negro Biography,* 317.

4. "The Stage," *IF,* 11 September 1897, 5.

5. Fletcher, *Tom Fletcher Story,* 141.

6. "Providence Opera House" (advertisement), *Providence Evening Bulletin,* 30 August 1897, 6.

7. Howard Ripley, "In Other Cities, Providence," *NYDM,* 11 September 1897; and "Vaudeville and Minstrel," *NY Clipper,* 11 September 1897, 453.

8. *Melodic Gems.*

9. Ibid.

10. "California Theatre" (advertisement), *San Francisco Call,* 3 February 1898, 7.

11. "In Other Cities, San Francisco," *NYDM,* 26 February 1898, 3.

12. "Black Patti in San Francisco," *NYDM,* 5 March 1898, 19.

13. Ashton Stevens, "The Good Coon Song, the Bad Coon Singer, and an Emotional Comedian," *San Francisco Call,* 13 February 1898, 27.

14. "Vaudeville, the Black Patti at Los Angeles," *NYDM,* 26 March 1898, 21.

15. Sampson, *Ghost Walks,* 146–47.

16. Bill of play, Broadway Theatre and Tabor Grand Opera House, Denver, 13 March 1898, from author's collection.

17. "The Stage," *IF,* 30 April 1898, 5.

18. "Ernest Hogan Re-engaged," *NYDM,* 28 May 1898, 18; and "Ernest Hogan" (advertisement), *NYDM,* 28 May 1898, 17.

19. *Matilda Sissie Jones v. David Richard Jones.*

20. Deposition of Lawrence Smith Jones, 18 August 1933, in New York, filed in the *Estate of Matilda S. Joyner.* Jones, a minister, came forward during proceedings to settle Sissieretta's estate after her death in June 1933. He claimed to be her son. The probate court documents, located in the City of Providence Archives at Providence City Hall, include a sworn statement from John C. Simons, a minister in the Church of the Good Shepherd, New York City, who was Jones's godfather. Both Jones and Simons said singer Flora Batson, deceased, had been Jones's godmother. Jones and Simons both claimed that Sissieretta and David were Jones's parents. The Maryland State Archives does not have a birth certificate for Lawrence Smith Jones, who said he was born 25 January 1898 in Bucktown, Maryland. Sissieretta could not have been the mother as she was performing in Seattle on that day.

21. "Washington–Seattle," *NYDM,* 12 February 1898, 8.

22. "The Stage," *IF,* 8 July 1899, 5.

23. "Stage Silhouettes," *Colored American* (Washington, D.C.), 9 July 1898, 6. Based on a salary of five hundred dollars per week, Sissieretta would have made twenty-two thousand dollars for a forty-four-week tour.

24. "Vaudeville and Minstrelsy, The Black Patti Troubadours," *NY Clipper,* 27 August 1898, 423; "Vaudeville and Minstrelsy, New Jersey, Plainfield," *NY Clipper,* 3 September 1898, 441; and "Black Patti Troubadours" (advertisement), *NYDM,* 3 September 1898, 5.

25. "Vaudeville and Minstrelsy," *NY Clipper,* 27 August 1898, 423.

26. "The Black Patti Troubadours," *NYDM,* 3 September 1898, 17.

27. "The Stage," *IF,* 31 December 1898, 58; 17 September 1898, 5; and 12 November 1898, 5.

28. "The Stage," *IF,* 19 November 1898, 5.

29. "Correspondence, Canada, Winnipeg," *NYDM,* 21 January 1899, 24; "Correspondence, Montana, Butte," *NYDM,* 4 February 1899, 6; and "The Stage," *IF,* 3 December 1898, 5.

30. "Theatrical, Latest by Telegram," *NY Clipper,* 25 February 1898, 872; and "Correspondence, California, Los Angeles," *NYDM,* 18 March 1899, 4.

31. "Hogan under Contract," *NYDM,* 18 March 1899, 18.

32. "Ernest Hogan's Plans," *NYDM,* 22 April 1899, 19.

33. Fletcher, *100 Years,* 141.

34. Logan and Winston, *Dictionary of American Negro Biography*, 317.

35. "The Stage," *IF,* 15 April 1899, 5.

36. "Black Patti Troubadours" (advertisement), *NYDM,* 29 April 1899, 11.

37. "Black Patti's Troubadours" (article), *NYDM,* 29 April 1899, 21.

38. "The Stage," *Detroit Free Press,* 21 September 1899, 4.

39. "Black Patti's Season," *NYDM,* 1 July 1899, 18.

40. "The Stage," *Detroit Free Press,* 25 September 1899, 4.

41. "The Stage," *IF,* 16 September 1899, 5; "The Stage," *Detroit Free Press,* 25 September 1899, 4; and "Black Patti Troubadours" (advertisement), *Detroit Free Press,* 24 September 1899, sec. 5, 7.

42. "The Stage," *Detroit Free Press,* 25 September 1899, 4.

43. "Black Patti Troubadours" (advertisement), *Detroit Free Press,* 24 September 1899, part 5, p. 7.

44. "The Stage," *IF,* 14 October 1899, 5, and 4 November 1899, 5.

45. "Holiday Issue, Black Patti's Troubadours," *IF,* 30 December 1899, 9.

46. "Black Patti Troubadours," *San Francisco Call,* 16 December 1899, 7.

47. Ashton Stevens, "Rag-time Rages in Two Theatres," *San Francisco Examiner,* 18 December 1899, 6.

48. "In Other Cities, New Orleans," *NYDM,* 21 April 1900, 3.

49. "Negroes in Grand Opera," *NYDM,* 5 May 1900, 15.

50. "The Stage," *IF,* 2 June 1900, 5; "Black Patti's Season Ends," *NYDM,* 16 June 1900, 16; and "Black Patti Troubadour Notes," *NY Clipper,* 26 May 1900, 286.

51. "Reflections," *NYDM,* 9 June 1900, 11.

52. "Vaudeville, Ernest Hogan in a Country Coon," *NYDM,* 7 July 1900, 16.

8. The Black Patti Troubadours, 1900–1906

1. Grun, *Timetables of History,* 454–55.

2. "The Stage," *IF,* 15 September 1900, 5.

3. "The Stage," *IF,* 12 January 1901, 5.

4. Sylvester Russell, "Colored Actors," *IF,* 29 December 1900, Holiday Issue, 8.

5. "The Stage," *IF,* 24 August 1901, 5; "Los Angeles Theatre" (advertisement), *Los Angeles Times,* 12 January 1902, B1; and "The Stage," *IF,* 1 March 1902, 5.

6. "The Stage," *IF,* 26 October 1901, 5.

7. "In Other Cities, Portland, Ore.," *NYDM,* 4 January 1902, 3.

8. "The Stage," *IF,* 21 December 1901, 5.

9. "Black Patti at the California," *San Francisco Bulletin,* 30 December 1901, in SJScrapbook; and Sylvester Russell, "A Review of the Stage," *IF,* 28 December 1901, 14.

10. *Denver Times,* 17 February 1902, quoted in "The Stage," *IF,* 1 March 1902, 5.

11. *Songs as Sung.*

12. "Changes in the Bill," *NYT,* 1 June 1902, 30.

13. "Black Patti's Tour Begins," *NYDM,* 16 August 1902, 16.

14. Sampson, *Blacks in Blackface,* 186–88.

15. The author, using information from a variety of newspapers, reconstructed touring schedules for each of the Black Patti Troubadours seasons up to 1915. Using

these schedules, the author counted how many days per season the Troubadours spent in southern and southwestern states. The count is only an estimate, because some dates during several seasons were unavailable, making the schedules incomplete.

16. "Black Patti's Troubadors [*sic*]," *Colored American* (Washington, D.C.), 13 September 1902, 9.

17. "Correspondence, South Carolina, Charleston," *NYDM,* 18 October 1902, 23.

18. I. McCorker, "The 'Black Patti,' One of the World's Most Tuneful Cantatrices," *IF,* 27 December 1902, 1+.

19. Ibid.

20. "Black Patti Troubadours," *IF,* 28 March 1903, 5.

21. Sylvester Russell, "Why the Great Singers Are Declining," *IF,* 27 June 1903, 5.

22. Ibid.

23. "The Stage," *IF,* 8 August 1903, 5.

24. "The Stage," *IF,* 3 October 1903, 5; and Hill and Hatch, *History of African American Theatre,* 196.

25. Sylvester Russell, "Black Patti in Albany," *IF,* 19 September 1903, 6.

26. Stearns and Stearns, *Jazz Dancing,* 251. The Stearnses said Ida Forsyne toured with the Troubadours from 1898 until 1902, but newspaper articles and a Troubadour show program indicate Forsyne joined the Troubadours in 1899 and was with them throughout the 1904–5 season.

27. Ibid., 78.

28. Logan and Winston, *Dictionary of American Negro Biography,* 121.

29. Hill and Hatch, *History of African American Theatre,* 166.

30. *IF,* 3 October 1903, 6.

31. "Notes from the Black Patti Troubadours," *IF,* 21 November 1903, 5–6.

32. Hill and Hatch, *History of African American Theatre,* 196–97.

33. Sylvester Russell, "Annual Stage Review," *IF,* 26 December 1903, 6.

34. "Theatrical Conditions," *NYDM,* 26 December 1903, 10.

35. "Notes of the Black Patti Troubadours," *IF,* 16 January 1904, 5.

36. "Notes of the Black Patti Troubadours," *IF,* 30 January 1904, 5.

37. "Route," *IF,* 12 March 1904, 5; and "Today's News," *Fort Collins (Colo.) Weekly Courier,* 23 November 1904, 11.

38. "Amusements in Cuba," *NYDM,* 27 May 1905, 13.

39. *Fort Collins (Colo.) Weekly Courier,* 23 November 1904, 7.

40. "Brooklyn Amusements," *NYT,* 15 May 1904, 13.

41. Grun, *Timetables of History,* 456–57.

42. Hill and Hatch, *History of African American Theatre,* 129.

43. Sylvester Russell, "Coming Events, Home and Abroad," *IF,* 16 July 1904, 5.

44. "Nolan on Contract Jumpers," *NYDM,* 30 July 1904, 16.

45. "Black Patti Troubadours Open," *NYDM,* 6 August 1904, 14.

46. "The Matinee Girl," *NYDM,* 27 August 1904, 2.

47. Ibid.

48. Sylvester Russell, "The Black Patti Show," *IF,* 17 September 1904, 5.

49. J. D. Howard, "'A Swell Bunch,' Says Howard," *IF,* 1 October 1904, 5.

50. W. Milton Lewis, "Pencilings," *IF,* 8 October 1904, 2.

51. Sylvester Russell, "Annual Stage Review," *IF,* 24 December 1904, 6+.

52. "At the Academy of Music," *Charleston (S.C.) News and Courier,* 10 April 1905, 8.

53. Sylvester Russell, "A Review of the Stage," *IF,* 8 July 1905, 5.

54. Sylvester Russell, "Cole Gives Private Lecture," *IF,* 7 October 1905, 5.

55. *Songs as Sung.*

56. "Correspondence, New Jersey, Asbury Park," *NYDM,* 12 August 1905, 6; and "Madame Sissieretta Jones," *IF,* 10 February 1906, 5.

57. Sampson, *Ghost Walks,* 348.

58. "Theatre Troubles Down in Dixie," *NY Age,* 12 October 1905, 7.

59. "Madame Sissieretta Jones," *IF,* 10 February 1906, 5.

60. W. Milton Lewis, "Black Patti Troubadours," *IF,* 24 February 1906, 6.

61. "The Empire Theater," *Pittsburgh Post,* 6 March 1906, 6.

62. "Black Patti's Voice," *Pittsburgh Post,* 8 March 1906, 6.

63. "Has Sung around the World," *Pittsburgh Post,* 11 March 1906, 3.

64. Sylvester Russell, "Black Patti in New York," *IF,* 30 June 1906, 6.

65. *Songs as Sung.*

66. Russell, "Black Patti in New York," *IF,* 30 June 1906, 6.

67. Sylvester Russell, "Black Patti Interviewed," *IF,* 4 August 1906, 5.

9. THE FINAL TROUBADOUR YEARS, 1906–1909

1. "Rehearsal Call" (advertisement), *NYDM,* 21 July 1906, 17; "Initial Opening of the Dandy Dixie Minstrels," *IF,* 25 August 1906, 7; and "The Stage," *IF,* 20 October 1906, 6.

2. Sylvester Russell, "The Sixth Annual Review," *IF,* 5 January 1907, 5.

3. Sylvester Russell, "Death of Flora Batson," *IF,* 15 December 1906, 1+.

4. Logan and Winston, *Dictionary of American Negro Biography,* 33.

5. Sylvester Russell, "Death of Flora Batson," *IF,* 15 December 1906, 1+.

6. "Black Patti Not Dead; Is Due Here Next Week," *Los Angeles Herald,* 7 February 1907, 3.

7. J. D. Howard, "Jolly John Larkins," *IF,* 11 May 1907, 5.

8. Ibid.

9. Dorothy, "The Black Patti Troubadour Girls," *IF,* 18 May 1907, 6.

10. Ibid.

11. Ibid.

12. Lester A. Walton, "Theatrical People and Their Well Earned Success," *NY Age,* 27 June 1907, 6.

13. Sylvester Russell, "The Faults of Song Publishers," *IF,* 22 June 1907, 6.

14. "The Shoo-fly Regiment," *IF,* 18 May 1907, 1.

15. "The Stage," *IF,* 20 July 1907, 5; and "The Stage," *IF,* 27 July 1907, 5.

16. "The Stage," *IF,* 3 August 1907, 5.

17. Ibid.

18. "The Black Patti Troubadours," *IF,* 7 September 1907, 2; and "The Stage," *IF,* 10 August 1907, 5.

19. "Black Patti's Troubadours," *IF,* 26 October 1907, 5; and "Elysium," *New Orleans Times Picayune,* 17 February 1908, 2.

20. "Black Patti Troubadours," *IF,* 2 November 1907, 5.

21. "Black Patti Troubadours," IF, 16 November 1907, 5.

22. Charters, *Nobody,* 45.

23. Ibid. Charters claimed Voelckel and Sissieretta's relationship was more than a friendship. She said that after Sissieretta divorced her husband she "married" Voelckel but does not provide any sources for information about the relationship between the two.

24. "The Stage," *IF,* 13 July 1907, 5; and "The Elysium Theatre to Reopen," *IF,* 8 August 1907, 2.

25. "Black Patti Troubadours at the Elysium Theatre," *IF,* 30 November 1907, 5.

26. "The Stage," *IF,* 21 December 1907, 5.

27. "Elysium," *New Orleans Times Picayune,* 17 February 1908, 2.

28. "The Tramp Social Club at New Orleans," *IF,* 8 February 1908, 5; and "The Stage," *IF,* 7 March 1908, 5.

29. "About the Big Colored Shows," *NY Age,* 2 April 1908, 6.

30. "Black Patti's Dusky Crowd," *Chattanooga Daily Times,* 2 April 1908, published in *IF,* 11 April 1908, 5.

31. "Black Patti Troubadours," *IF,* 18 April 1908, 5.

32. "The Stage," *IF,* 28 March 1908, 5; and "Black Patti Troubadours," *IF,* 2 May 1908, 5.

33. "Black Patti Troubadours," *IF,* 22 August 1908, 5; "The Stage," *IF,* 19 September 1908, 5; "Jeanette Murphy the Tennessean Nightingale," *NY Age,* 24 December 1908, 6; and "In Virginia and North Carolina," *NY Age,* 1 October 1908, 6.

34. "The Stage," IF, 19 September 1908, 5.

35. Hoosier, "Black Patti Troubadours at Boonton, N.J.," *IF,* 19 September 1908, 5.

36. "In Virginia and North Carolina," *NY Age,* 1 October 1908, 6; "In North and South Carolina," *NY Age,* 8 October 1908, 6; and "Traveling in Three States," *NY Age,* 15 October 1908, 6.

37. *NY Age,* 22 October 1908, 6; and "The Stage," *IF,* 24 October 1908, 5.

38. "Notes from the Black Patti Show," *NY Age,* 29 October 1908, 6; and "Black Patti Notes," *NY Age,* 5 November 1908, 6.

39. *IF,* 7 November 1908, 5; and "Black Patti Notes," *NY Age,* 5 November 1908, 6. Margaret Voelckel and her husband were born in Germany. They moved to the United States and had four sons—Frederick, Emil, Rudolph, and Auguste. The U.S. census records for 1880 show Margaret was widowed and reared the boys on her own in Manhattan. She worked as a laundress.

40. "Correspondence, Georgia, Macon," *NYDM,* 14 November 1908, 21.

41. "Black Patti Notes," *NY Age,* 26 November 1908, 6.

42. Ibid.; and "S. Tutt Whitney," *IF,* 25 December 1908, 5.

43. "Black Patti Notes," *NY Age,* 26 November 1908, 6.

44. "Black Patti Company Notes," *NY Age,* 10 December 1908, 6.

45. "The Stage," *IF,* 12 December 1908, 5; and "Among the Comedians," *NY Age,* 24 December 1908, 6.

46. Lester A. Walton, "Seats at the Theatre," *NY Age,* 17 December 1908, 6.

47. "Mme. Sissieretta Jones," *NY Age,* 24 December 1908, Dramatic sect., 1; and Sissieretta Jones, "Negro Folk Songs," *NY Age,* 24 December 1908, Dramatic sect., 1.

48. Sissieretta Jones, "Negro Folk Songs," *NY Age,* 24 December 1908, Dramatic sect., 1.

49. Sylvester Russell, "The New Dramatic Editor," *NY Age,* 24 December 1908, Dramatic sect., 3.

50. Sylvester Russell, "Eighth Annual Review," *IF,* 9 January 1909, 5.

51. Ibid.

52. "Black Patti Notes," *NY Age,* 14 January 1909, 6.

53. "Black Patti Notes," *NY Age,* 14 January 1909, 6; 4 February 1909, 6; 18 February 1909, 6; 25 February 1909, 6; and 4 March 1909, 6.

54. "Black Patti Notes," *NY Age,* 1 April 1909, 6; and 25 March 1909, 6.

55. "Music and the Stage," *Los Angeles Times,* 15 March 1909, 17; and "Black Patti Notes," *NY Age,* 25 March 1909, 6.

56. Walter Anthony, "Sissieretta Jones Appeals to Heart," *San Francisco Call,* 5 April 1909, 5.

57. "Black Patti and Her Company at Baker," *Morning Oregonian* (Portland), 19 April 1909, 7.

58. "Ernest Hogan's Condition Serious," *NY Age,* 22 April 1909, 6; and "What Hogan Thinks of 'Black Patti,'" *IF,* 1 May 1909, 5.

59. Lester Walton, "Theatrical Comment," *NY Age,* 29 April 1909, 6.

60. Lester Walton, "Death of Ernest Hogan," *NY Age,* 27 May 1909, 6.

61. "'Black Patti' on Death of Ernest Hogan," *NY Age,* 27 May 1909, 6.

62. "Music and the Stage," *NY Age,* 15 July 1909, 6.

63. "Music and the Stage," *NY Age,* 8 July 1909, 6; "Music and the Stage," *NY Age,* 22 July 1909, 6; and "Jolly John Larkins to Star with Black Patti Trobadours [*sic*]," *IF,* 29 May 1909, 5.

64. "Black Patti's Record," *NY Age,* 19 August 1909, 6.

10. The Black Patti Musical Comedy Company, 1909–1914

1. "Black Patti's Record," *NY Age,* 19 August 1909, 6.

2. Ibid.

3. Lester Walton, "Black Patti Has a Speaking Part," *NY Age,* 23 September 1909, 6.

4. "Black Patti at the Park Theater," *IF,* 12 February 1910, 5; and "Black Patti Musical Comedy Company at Indianapolis," *IF,* 26 February 1910, 5.

5. "'A Trip to Africa' Going Big,'" *NY Age,* 7 October 1909, 6; and J. Frank Head, "New Patti Show a Hit," *NY Age,* 30 September 1909, 6.

6. "Notes from the Black Patti Company," *NY Age,* 21 October 1909, 6; and "Black Patti Musical Comedy Company," *IF,* 4 December 1909, 5.

7. *Macon (Ga.) Daily Telegraph,* as published in "Did Macon, Ga. Put Negro on Stage?" *NY Age,* 30 December 1909, 6.

8. *Tampa Morning Tribune,* 7 January 1910, as published in "The Stage," *IF,* 29 January 1910, 6.

9. "Prominent Whites Act as Ushers for Negroes," *NY Age,* 20 January 1910, 6.

10. "The Outlook for Colored Road Shows; The Moving Picture House Is Taking the Day," *IF,* 15 January 1910, 6.

11. Anthony Byrd, "Black Patti Company," *NY Age,* 24 February 1910, 6.

12. Ibid.

13. "J. Ed. Green Passes Away," *IF,* 26 February 1910, 5.

14. Lester Walton, "A Trip to Africa," *NY Age,* 28 April 1910, 6.

15. "About the Colored Shows," *NY Age,* 21 July 1910, 6. See also Poggi, *Theater in America,* 3–96, for a discussion of theatrical syndicates, economic factors affecting the theater business, and competition from the movies.

16. "Black Patty [*sic*] Musical Comedy Company," *IF,* 3 September 1910, 6; and "Black Patti Company," *NY Age,* 18 August 1910, 6.

17. "Black Patty [*sic*] Musical Comedy Company," *IF,* 3 September 1910, 6.

18. "New Show for Patti Co.," *NY Age,* 22 September 1910, 6; and "Picked Up in Passing," *IF,* 1 October 1910, 6.

19. *Arkansas Gazette,* as published in "Black Patti in Texas," *NY Age,* 6 October 1910, 6.

20. Lester A. Walton, "The Return of Cole & Johoson [*sic*]," *NY Age,* 6 October 1910, 6.

21. "Theatrical Comment," *NY Age,* 13 October 1910, 6; and "Condition of Bob Cole," *NY Age,* 20 October 1910, 6.

22. "Black Patti Company," *NY Age,* 3 November 1910, 6.

23. "Black Patti Musical Comedy Company," *IF,* 29 October 1910, 5; "Black Patti Co.," *NY Age,* 27 October 1910, 6; and "Black Patti's Musical Comedy Company," *IF,* 5 November 1910, 5.

24. "Larkins to Leave Patti Co.," *NY Age,* 1 December 1910, 6; and "Larkins and Voelckel Make Up," *NY Age,* 15 December 1910, 6.

25. "Black Patti Co.," *NY Age,* 1 December 1910, 6; and "Black Patti Co." *NY Age,* 15 December 1910, 6.

26. S. Tutt Whitney, "The Negro on the Stage," *NY Age,* 22 December 1910, 6.

27. "Black Patti Co.," *NY Age,* 5 January 1911, 6.

28. Sissieretta Jones, letter to Charles H. Page, attorney-at-law, 6 January 1911, provided to author by the Rhode Island Black Heritage Society, Providence.

29. Gross, "Brief History"; and Property Records, City of Providence, Deed Book 610, 333, Providence City Hall, Providence.

30. "Black Patti Co.," *NY Age,* 26 January 1911.

31. Tim Owsley, "Black Patti (Sissieretta Jones)," *IF,* 11 February 1911, 6.

32. "Black Patti Company," *NY Age,* 2 February 1911, 6; and "Advertisement," *NY Age,* 16 February 1911, 6.

33. Lester A. Walton, "Theatrical Comment," *NY Age,* 23 February 1911, 6.

34. Hill and Hatch, *History of African American Theatre,* 243.

35. "Black Patti Co.," *NY Age,* 16 March 1911, 6; "Black Patti Co.," *NY Age,* 23 March 1911, 6; and "'Black Patti Troubadours' Score a Hit," *IF,* 25 March 1911, 1.

36. W. P. Bayless, "Passing Show at Washington, D.C.," *IF,* 1 April 1911, 6.

37. "Black Patti Co.," *NY Age,* 23 March 1911, 6; and "'Black Patti Troubadours' Score a Hit," *IF,* 5 March 1911, 1.

38. "The Black Patti" (advertisement), *NY Age,* 27 April 1911, 6; "Dandy Dixie Minstrels" (advertisement), *NY Age,* 27 April 1911, 6; and "Voelckel a Veteran in the Show World," *IF,* 23 December 1911, 19.

39. Lester A. Walton, "Music and the Stage, Theatrical Comment," *NY Age,* 4 May 1911, 6.

40. Lester A. Walton, "Music and the Stage, Preparing for Next Season," *NY Age,* 22 June 1911, 6; and "About the Voelckel Shows," *NY Age,* 27 July 1911, 6.

41. "Patti Company Rehearsing," *NY Age,* 3 August 1911, 6; and "Correspondence, New York, Middletown," *NYDM,* 9 August 1911, 17.

42. "Well Known Colored Comedian Drowns," *IF,* 5 August 1911, 5.

43. "The Death of 'Bob' Cole," *NY Age,* 10 August 1911, 6.

44. Rudolph Voelckel, "Patti Company Opens Big," *NY Age,* 10 August 1911, 6.

45. Sylvester Russell, "Chicago Weekly Review, Black Patti at the Alhambra Theater," *IF,* 30 September 1911, 5.

46. J. D. Howard, "Black Patti," *IF,* 26 August 1911, 5.

47. Sylvester Russell, "Chicago Weekly Review, Black Patti at the Alhambra Theater," *IF,* 30 September 1911, 5.

48. "Black Patti Co.," *NY Age,* 19 October 1911, 6.

49. Lester A. Walton, "Music and the Stage, Using the Real Thing," *NY Age,* 5 October 1911, 6.

50. "Voelckel Gets Larkins' Show," *NY Age,* 23 November 1911, 6; and "Notes from the 'Royal Sam' Company," *IF,* 2 December 1911, 5.

51. "The Original Black Patti Show" (advertisement), *NY Age,* 21 December 1911, 6.

52. "Black Patti Show" (advertisement), *IF,* 23 December 1911, 6.

53. "Black Patti's Years of Success, Still Maintains a Remarkable Voice and Is Happy," *IF,* 23 December 1911, 6.

54. "Voelckel a Veteran in the Show World," *IF,* 23 December 1911, 6.

55. S. Tutt Whitney, "Seen and Heard While Passing," *IF,* 24 February 1912, 6.

56. "Correspondence, Rhode Island, Providence," *NYDM,* 3 April 1912, 19.

57. "Black Patti Needs a New Play," *IF,* 6 April 1912, 6.

58. "Black Patti at the Grand," *NY Age,* 9 May 1912, 6; and Lester A. Walton, "Two Colored Shows in Town," *NY Age,* 16 May 1912, 6.

59. Lester A. Walton, "Two Colored Shows in Town," *NY Age,* 16 May 1912, 6.

60. Billy E. Jones, "Eastern Theatrical Notes," *IF,* 17 August 1912, 6; and "The Black Patti Company in Indianapolis," *IF,* 14 September 1912, 5.

61. Grun, *Timetables of History,* 465.

62. "Black Patti Company in Nashville, Tenn.," *IF,* 5 October 1912, 6.

63. "The Black Patti Co.," *IF,* 19 October 1912, 6.

64. "At the Theatres, Black Patti at the Byers," *Fort Worth Star-Telegram,* 12 October 1912, in SJScrapbook.

65. Lester A. Walton, "Theatrical Comment," *NY Age,* 5 December 1912, 6.

66. Early, "Rebel."

67. Ibid. In July 2009 the U.S. Congress approved a resolution urging a post-humous, presidential pardon for Jack Johnson. As of 1 November 2011, President Barack Obama had not granted the requested pardon.

68. Lester A. Walton, "Jack Johnnon [*sic*]," *NY Age,* 24 October 1912, 6.

69. Walton, "Theatrical Comment," *NY Age,* 5 December 1912, 6.

70. Sylvester Russell, "Annual Stage Review," *NY Age,* 26 December 1912.

71. S. Tutt Whitney, "A White Manager with a Colored Show through the South," *IF,* 28 December 1912, 3.

72. Billy Lewis, "The Stage–Some Actor–So Forth and So On," *IF,* 28 December 1912.

73. "Gossip of the Stage," *IF,* 4 January 1913; and "Gossip of the Stage," *IF,* 25 January 1913, 6.

74. Sylvester Russell, "Black Patti at the Globe Theater," *IF,* 12 April 1913, 6.

75. "New York News," *IF,* 31 May 1913, 5.

76. "Theatrical Comments," *NY Age,* 29 May 1913, 6.

11. THE LAST TOUR, 1914–1915

1. "Patti in New Comedy," *NY Age,* 31 July 1913, 6; and "Black Patti's Eighteenth Season," *IF,* 2 August 1913, 6.

2. "Black Patti Ill," *NY Age,* 11 September 1913, 6.

3. "Negro Players of America to Go on Tour," *IF,* 1 November 1913, 6; and Lester A. Walton, "Theatrical Comments," *NY Age,* 18 December 1913, 6.

4. Lester A. Walton, "Theatrical Comments," *NY Age,* 18 December 1913, 6; and "Merry Xmas" (advertisement), *IF,* 20 December 1913 6.

5. Sissieretta Jones, "A Card of Thanks," *IF,* 20 December 1913, 5.

6. Sylvester Russell, "Annual Stage Review," *IF,* 20 December 1913, 12.

7. "Theatrical Jottings," *NY Age,* 29 January 1914, 6.

8. "Gossip of the Stage," *IF,* 8 August 1914, 6.

9. "Black Patti to Tour," *NY Age,* 30 July 1914, 6.

10. "Black Patti Rehearsing," *NY Age,* 27 August 1914, 6; and Lester A. Walton, "Theatrical Comments," *NY Age,* 27 August 1914, 6.

11. "Colored Vaudeville Circuit," *NY Age,* 20 August 1914, 6, reprinted part of an article that first appeared in *Variety,* no date given.

12. Hill and Hatch, *History of African American Theatre,* 206. In 1921 the Southern Consolidated Circuit joined the Theater Owners Booking Association.

13. "Lafayette Theatre" (advertisement) and photograph caption, *NY Age,* 17 September 1914, 6.

14. Lester A. Walton, "Lucky Sam from Alabam," *NY Age,* 24 September 1914, 6.

15. Ar W. Tee, "The Passing Show in Washington," *IF,* 24 October 1914, 4.

16. "Aida Overton Walker Is Dead," *NY Age,* 15 October 1914, 1.

17. "Movements of the Player Folk," *IF,* 24 October 1914, 6; and Rudolph Voelckel letter published in "A Disastrous Season," *NY Age,* 11 February 1915, 6.

18. "War Hurts Theatrical Business," *NYDM,* 11 November 1914, 8.

19. Voelckel, "Disastrous Season"; and Bobby L. Lovett, "Beale Street," in Van West, *Tennessee Encyclopedia.*

20. The Church Park Auditorium is no longer standing, but a granite plaque at the site of the entertainment center includes a statement that says, "Overflow crowds came to see such leading entertainers and politicians as W. C. Handy and the Black Patti Troubadours, and the Whitney Musical Company as well as Dr. Booker T. Washington, President Theodore Roosevelt, and early leaders of the Lincoln Republican League and the NAACP."

21. "Stage Notes," *IF,* 2 January 1915, 6; and "Lucky Sam from Alabam Lost Out at Memphis, Tenn.–Mr. Church's Generosity," *IF,* 9 January 1915, 5.

22. "Patti Show Closed," *NY Age,* 21 January 1915, 6; Salem Tutt Whitney, "Seen and Heard while Passing," *IF,* 23 January 1915, 6; and Billy E. Jones, "New York News," *IF,* 20 February 1915, 6.

23. Voelckel, "Disastrous Season."

24. Ibid.

25. "R. R. Church, Jr. Writes," *NY Age,* 25 February 1915, 6.

26. Ibid.

27. Several online sources say that Sissieretta's last show with the Black Patti Musical Comedy Company was in 1916 at the Gibson Theater on State Street. This information apparently stems from a 1966 interview Willia Daughtry conducted with Harry Bolden for Daughtry's 1968 dissertation (Daughtry, "Sissieretta Jones," 226–27). Bolden, who said he had been a chorus member with the "Troubadours" (which became the Black Patti Musical Comedy Company in 1909), told Daughtry about his recollections of the company's final show, which he said was in 1916. This appears to be a faulty memory, as no evidence has yet been found to indicate that the Black Patti troupe played beyond the beginning of January 1915.

12. Retirement and Tributes

1. Sissieretta's home no longer exists. In fact Wheaton Street has been renamed Pratt Street.

2. "A $500 Engagement," *NY Age,* 14 October 1915, 6; Sylvester Russell, "Chicago Weekly Review," *IF,* 25 September 1915, 5; and Gross, "Brief History."

3. Sylvester Russell, "Chicago Weekly Review," *IF,* 25 September 1915, 5.

4. Sylvester Russell, "Chicago Weekly Review," *IF,* 2 October 1915, 5.

5. "A $500 Engagement," *NY Age,* 14 October 1915, 6.

6. "Black Patti Heads Bill at Lafayette," *NY Age,* 21 October 1915, 6.

7. Death Record of Henrietta Crenshaw, City of Providence, No. 931, 199, filed 18 March 1924.

8. Providence City Directories, 1925–26, 1927–28, 1929–30, 1931–36; and Rhode Island State Census, 1925, Providence, Ward 1, 19.

9. Maureen McGetrick, "'Black Patti' Was a Success, Her Audience Was a Failure," *Providence Sunday Journal,* 28 September 1980, 14; Gross, "Brief History"; and F. C. Terry, "The Closing Chapters of the Life of 'Black Patti,'" *Providence Sunday Journal,* 16 July 1933, E2.

10. Maureen McGetrick, "'Black Patti' Was a Success, Her Audience Was a Failure," *Providence Sunday Journal,* 28 September 1980, 14.

11. Gross, "Brief History," 5, 6; and Lydia T. Brown, "Black Patti Left Only a Small Estate," *Baltimore Afro-American,* New England ed., 8 July 1933.

12. Lydia T. Brown, "Black Patti Left Only a Small Estate," *Baltimore Afro-American,* New England ed., week of 8 July 1933.

13. "Black Patti Noted Singer Buried in R.I.," *Baltimore Afro-American,* week of 1 July 1933, 1; Gross, "Brief History"; and F. C. Terry, "The Closing Chapters of the Life of 'Black Patti,'" *Providence Sunday Journal,* 16 July 1933, E2.

14. "Black Patti Noted Singer Buried in R.I.," *Baltimore Afro-American,* week of 1 July 1933, 1.

15. "Black Patti," *Baltimore Afro-American,* week of 8 July 1915, 8.

16. Ibid.

17. F. C. Terry, "The Closing Chapters of the Life of 'Black Patti,'" *Providence Sunday Journal,* 16 July 1933, E2

18. Portsmouth Bureau, "Passing of Famed 'Black Patti' Deep Loss to Those Who Knew Her as a Child in Portsmouth," *Norfolk (Va.) Journal and Guide,* 15 July 1933.

19. Ibid.

20. *Estate of Matilda S. Joyner, Administrative number 34296, Records of Probate Court, City of Providence, R.I.,* packets 1 and 2.

21. Gross, "Brief History," 6 and preface.

22. Two advertisements from the 27 May and 28 May 1927 issues of the *Chicago Defender,* republished in "Black Patti," *78 Quarterly,* no. 11 (1999): 18–19, make it appear that Sissieretta endorsed the record label, although there is no evidence that she did.

23. For more on Baham's show *The Unsung Diva,* see her website (Angela Dean Baham, http://angeladeanbaham.com). Handy, *Unsung Americans,* 106–10; and "Hall Tabs 11; Stars Absent," *Providence Journal,* 17 May 1977, A10.

24. Daughtry, *Vision and Reality,* xi.

25. Maureen McGetrick, "'Black Patti' Was a Success, Her Audience Was a Failure," *Providence Sunday Journal,* 28 September 1980, 14.

26. "Music Knows No Color," *Evening Herald,* n.d., in SJScrapbook.

BIBLIOGRAPHY

LEGAL DOCUMENTS

Estate of Matilda S. Joyner. Administrative number 34296. Probate Court of the City of Providence, R.I. Records located in the Division of Archives and History, Providence City Hall, June 1933.

James B. Pond v. Sissieretta Jones and David R. Jones. Superior Court of the City and County of New York. Filed 17 May 1893.

Jeremiah Joyner v. Henrietta Joyner. Petition for Divorce. Case number 8117. Supreme Court of State of Rhode Island and Providence Plantations, Providence, R.I. Filed 8 March 1889.

Matilda Sissie Jones v. David Richard Jones. Petition for Divorce. Case number 11643. Appellate Division of the Supreme Court in Providence, R.I. Filed 4 June 1898.

BOOKS AND ARTICLES

Abbott, Lynn, and Doug Seroff. *Out of Sight: The Rise of African American Popular Music, 1889–1895.* Jackson: University Press of Mississippi, 2002.

————. *Ragged but Right: Black Traveling Shows, "Coon Songs," and the Dark Pathway to Blues and Jazz.* Jackson: University Press of Mississippi, 2007.

Appelbaum, Stanley. *The Chicago World's Fair of 1893: A Photographic Record.* New York: Dover, 1980.

Armstrong, Jan. *Community of Spirit: African-Americans in Providence, Rhode Island, 1870–1950.* Providence: Rhode Island Black Heritage Society, 1998.

Berry, Lemuel, Jr. *Biographical Dictionary of Black Musicians and Music Educators, Volume 1.* Guthrie, Okla.: Educational Book Publishers, 1978.

Bond, Beverly G., and Janann Sherman. *Memphis in Black and White.* Charleston, S.C.: Arcadia, 2003.

Brooks, Tim. *Lost Sounds: Blacks and the Birth of the Recording Industry, 1890–1919.* Urbana: University of Illinois Press, 2005.

Cashman, Sean Dennis. *America in the Gilded Age: From the Death of Lincoln to the Rise of Theodore Roosevelt.* 3rd ed. New York: New York University Press, 1994.

Casson, Herbert N. *The History of the Telephone.* Chicago: McClurg, 1910.

Charters, Ann. *Nobody: The Story of Bert Williams.* New York: Macmillan, 1970.

Church, Annette E., and Roberta Church. *The Robert R. Churches of Memphis: A Father and Son Who Achieved in Spite of Race.* Ann Arbor, Mich.: Edward Brothers, 1974.

Cone, John Frederick. *Adelina Patti, Queen of Hearts.* Portland, Ore.: Amadeus, 1993.

Conley, Patrick T., and Paul Campbell. *Providence: A Pictorial History.* Norfolk, Va.: Donning, 1982.

Cuney-Hare, Maud. *Negro Musicians and Their Music.* New York: Da Capo, 1974.

Dannett, Sylvia G. L. *Profiles of Negro Womanhood.* Vol. 1, *1619–1900.* Yonkers, N.Y.: Educational Heritage, 1964.

Daughtry, Willia Estelle. "Sissieretta Jones: A Study of the Negro's Contribution to Nineteenth Century American Concert and Theatrical Life." Ph.D. diss., Syracuse University, 1968.

———. *Vision and Reality: The Story of "Black Patti" Matilda Sissieretta Joyner Jones.* Pittsburgh: Dorrance, 2002.

Durso, Joseph. *Madison Square Garden, 100 Years of History.* New York: Simon & Schuster, 1979.

Early, Gerald. "Rebel of the Progressive Era." *Unforgivable Blackness.* 2005. http://www.pbs.org/unforgivableblackness/rebel/ (accessed 11 September 2011).

Easton, Rick. "Vaudeville! A Dazzling Display of Hetereogeneous [*sic*] Splendor." http://xroads.virginia.edu/~ma02/easton/vaudeville/vaudevillemain.html (accessed 11 September 2011).

Effinger, Marta Jenell. "Staging Migrations toward an American West: From Ida B. Wells to Rhodessa Jones." Ph.D. diss., Northwestern University, 2000.

Elam, Harry J., Jr., and David Krasner. *African American Performance and Theater History.* New York: Oxford University Press, 2001.

Fletcher, Tom. *100 Years of the Negro in Show Business.* New York: Burdge, 1954.

Foster, Stephen Collins. *The Swanee River.* New York: Caldwell, 1887.

Foster, William. "Pioneers of the Stage; Memoirs of William Foster." In *The Official Theatrical World of Colored Artists,* 40–49. New York: Theatrical World, 1928.

Franklin, John Hope, and Alfred A. Moss Jr. *From Slavery to Freedom: A History of Negro Americans.* 6th ed. New York: Knopf, 1988.

Gable-Wilson, Sonya R. "Let Freedom Sing! Four African-American Concert Singers in Nineteenth-Century America." Ph.D. diss., University of Florida, 2005.

Glynn, Helen L. "The Life and Times of Sissieretta Jones." In *Rhode Island's Musical Heritage: An Exploration,* edited by Carolyn Livingston and Dawn Elizabeth Smith, 141–49. Sterling Heights, Mich.: Harmonic Park, 2008.

Graziano, John. "The Early Life and Career of the 'Black Patti': The Odyssey of an African American Singer in the Late Nineteenth Century." *Journal of the American Musicological Society* 53 (2000): 543–96.

———. "Sentimental Songs, Rags, and Transformations: The Emergence of the Black Musical, 1895–1910." In *Musical Theatre in America, Papers and Proceedings of the Conference on the Musical Theatre in America,* edited by Glenn Loney, 211–31. Westport, Conn.: Greenwood, 1984.

Gross, Carl R. "A Brief History of the Life of Matilda Sissieretta Joyner Jones, the 'Black Patti'" (short unpublished biography). Providence, R.I., 1966. Dr. Carl R.

Gross Collection, Collection 41–1 to 42–1, Moorland-Spingarn Research Center, Manuscript Division, Howard University, Washington, D.C.

Grun, Bernard. *The Timetables of History.* New and rev. ed. New York: Simon & Schuster, 1991.

Haley, James T. *Afro-American Encyclopedia: Or, the Thoughts, Doings, and Sayings of the Race, Embracing Lectures, Biographical Sketches, Sermons, Poems, Names of Universities, Colleges, Seminaries, Newspapers, Books, and a History of the Denominations, Giving the Numerical Strength of Each. In Fact, It Teaches Every Subject of Interest to the Colored People, as Discussed by More Than One Hundred of Their Wisest and Best Men and Women.* Nashville: Haley & Florida, 1895. Electronic edition, Chapel Hill: University of North Carolina, 2000. http://docsouth.und.edu/church/haley.html.

Handy, W. C., ed. *Unsung Americans Sung.* 2nd ed. New York: Handy Brothers, 1946.

Harding, Robert C. *The History of Panama.* Westport, Conn.: Greenwood, 2006.

Henriksen, Henry. "Black Patti." *Record Research,* no. 165–66 (1979): 4–8; 167–68 (1979): 4–8; 171–72 (1980): 4–5; 177–78 (1980): 8; and 187–88 (1981): 8.

Hill, Errol G., and James V. Hatch. *A History of African American Theatre.* New York: Cambridge University Press, 2005.

Hine, Darlene Clark, ed. *Black Women in America: An Historical Encyclopedia.* Vol. 1, *A–L.* Brooklyn: Clarkson, 1993.

"History of Colón, Panama, A." Colón.com. http://www.coloncity.com/history1 .html (accessed 11 September 2011).

Hornsby, Alton, Jr. *Chronology of African American History.* 2nd ed. Detroit: Gale Research, 1997.

Howard, John Tasker. *Stephen Foster, America's Troubadour.* New York: Crowell, 1935.

Huggins, Nathan Irvin. *Harlem Renaissance.* New York: Oxford University Press, 1973.

Hughes, Langston, and Milton Meltzer. *Black Magic: A Pictorial History of Black Entertainers in America.* New York: Bonanza, 1967.

"Ida B. Wells-Barnett." Black History Month. Gale Cengage Learning website. http://www.gale.com/free_resources/bhm/bio/wells_1.htm (accessed 11 September 2011).

Jaycox, Faith. *The Progressive Era.* New York: Facts on File, 2005.

Johnson, James Weldon. *Black Manhattan.* New York: Da Capo, 1991.

Jones, Matilda Sissieretta. Scrapbook. Dr. Carl R. Gross Collection, Collection 41–1 to 42–1, Moorland-Spingarn Research Center, Manuscript Division, Howard University, Washington, D.C.

Keiler, Allan. *Marian Anderson: A Singer's Journey.* Urbana: University of Illinois Press, 2002.

Kelley, Robin D. G., and Lewis, Earl, eds. *To Make Our World Anew.* Vol. 2, *A History of African Americans since 1880.* New York: Oxford University Press, 2005.

Kirk, Elise K. *Music at the White House: A History of the American Spirit.* Urbana: University of Illinois Press, 1986.

———. *Musical Highlights from the White House.* Malabar, Fla.: Krieger, 1992.

Knight, Franklin W., and Colin A. Palmer. *The Modern Caribbean.* Chapel Hill: University of North Carolina Press, 1989.

Lichtenwanger, William. "Matilda Sissieretta Joyner Jones." In *Notable American Women, 1607–1950: A Biographical Dictionary,* edited by Edward James, Janet Wilson James, and Paul Boyer, 2:289–91. Cambridge, Mass.: Harvard University Press, 1971.

Logan, Rayford, and Michael Winston, eds. *Dictionary of American Negro Biography.* New York: Norton, 1982.

McGowan, Louis, and Daniel Brown. *Providence.* Charleston, S.C.: Arcadia, 2006.

McLoughlin, William. *Rhode Island: A History.* New York: Norton, 1978.

Melodic Gems from Voelckel and Nolan's Black Patti's Troubadours. New York: Witmark, ca. 1897.

Morgan, Thomas L., and William Barlow. *From Cakewalks to Concert Halls.* Washington, D.C.: Elliott & Clark, 1992.

Nelson, Edward T., ed. *Fifty Years of History of the Ohio Wesleyan University, Delaware, Ohio, 1844–1894.* Cleveland: Cleveland Printing Company, 1895.

Newby-Alexander, Cassandra, Mae Breckenridge-Haywood, and the African American Historical Society of Portsmouth. *Portsmouth, Virginia.* Black America series. Charleston, S.C.: Arcadia, 2003.

Odell, George C. D. *Annals of the New York Stage.* New York: AMS, 1949.

Officer, Lawrence H., and Samuel H. Williamson. "Purchasing Power of Money in the United States from 1774 to Present." MeasuringWorth.com, 2011. http://www.measuringworth.com/ppowerus/.

Peterson, Bernard L., Jr. *The African American Theatre Directory, 1816–1960.* Westport, Conn.: Greenwood, 1997.

Platt, Raye R., John K. Wright, John C. Weaver, and Johnson E. Fairchild. *The European Possessions in the Carribean Area: A Compilation of Facts Concerning Their Population, Physical Geography, Resources, Industries, Trade, Government, and Strategic Importance.* New York: American Geographical Society, 1941.

Poggi, Jack. *Theater in America: The Impact of Economic Forces, 1870–1967.* Ithaca, N.Y.: Cornell University Press, 1968.

Pond, Major James Burton. *Eccentricities of Genius: Memories of Famous Men and Women of the Platform and Stage.* New York: Dillingham, 1900.

Providence City Directory. Providence, R.I., 1882–1936.

Riis, Thomas J. *Just Before Jazz: Black Musical Theater in New York, 1890–1915.* Washington, D.C.: Smithsonian Institution Press, 1992.

Sadie, Stanley, ed. *The New Grove Dictionary of Music and Musicians, Volume 13.* 2nd ed. Oxford: Macmillan, 2001.

Sampson, Henry. *Blacks in Blackface: A Source Book on Early Black Musical Shows.* Metuchen, N.J.: Scarecrow, 1980.

———. *The Ghost Walks: A Chronological History of Blacks in Show Business, 1865–1910.* Metuchen, N.J.: Scarecrow, 1988.

Shifflett, Crandall. *Victorian America, 1876–1913.* New York: Facts on File, 1996.

Smith, Jessie Carney, ed. *Notable Black American Women.* Detroit: Gale Research, 1992.

Songs as Sung by the Black Patti Troubadours. New York: Witmark, 1904.

Songs as Sung by the Black Patti Troubadours. New York: Witmark, 1906.

Southall, Geneva Handy. *Blind Tom, the Black Pianist-Composer, Continually Enslaved.* Lanham, Md.: Scarecrow, 2002.

Southern, Eileen. *Biographical Dictionary of Afro-American and African Musicians.* Westport, Conn.: Greenwood, 1982.

——. *The Music of Black Americans: A History.* New York: Norton, 1971; 2nd ed., 1983.

Stearns, Marshall, and Jean Stearns. *Jazz Dancing: The Story of American Vernacular Dance.* New York: Macmillan, 1968.

Stein, Charles W., ed. *American Vaudeville as Seen by Its Contemporaries.* New York: Knopf, 1984.

Stepto, Gabriel Burns. *The African American Years: Chronologies of American History and Experience.* New York: Scribner, 2003.

Stewart, Rowena. *A Heritage Discovered: Blacks in Rhode Island.* Providence: Rhode Island Black Heritage Society, 1975.

Story, Rosalyn M. *And So I Sing: African American Divas of Opera and Concert.* New York: Warner, 1990.

Tanner, Jo A. *Dusky Maidens: The Odyssey of the Early Black Dramatic Actress.* Westport, Conn.: Greenwood, 1992.

Tibbets, John C., ed. *Dvořák in America, 1892–1895.* Portland, Ore.: Amadeus, 1993.

Tsotsi, Tom, and Pete Whelan. "Black Patti." *78 Quarterly,* no. 11 (1999): 11–91.

United States, and Social Science Research Council. *Historical Statistics of the United States, Colonial Times to 1957.* Washington, D.C.: U.S. Department of Commerce, Bureau of the Census, 1960.

Van West, Carroll, ed. *The Tennessee Encyclopedia of History and Culture.* Electronic edition, Knoxville: University of Tennessee Press, 2002. http://tennesseeencyclopedia.net.

"Walter Damrosch, 1862–1950, Biography." *Performing Arts Encyclopedia.* Washington, D.C.: Library of Congress. http://lcweb2.loc.gov/diglib/ihas/loc.natlib.ihas.200035728/default.html (accessed 16 August 2006).

White, Trumbull, and William Igleheart. *The World's Columbian Exposition, Chicago, 1893.* Philadelphia: Smith, 1893.

Wilmeth, Don B., and Christopher Bigsby, eds. *The Cambridge History of American Theatre.* Vol. 2, *1870–1945.* New York: Cambridge University Press, 1999.

Woll, Allen. *Black Musical Theatre: From Coontown to Dreamgirls.* Baton Rouge: Louisiana State University Press, 1989.

"World of 1898, The: The Spanish-American War." Library of Congress, Hispanic Division, Washington, D.C. http://www.loc.gov//rr//hispanic/1898/intro.html (accessed 11 September 2011).

Wright, Josephine, and Eileen Southern, eds. "Sissieretta Jones." *Black Perspective in Music* 4 (1976): 191–201.

INDEX

British Guiana. *See* Guyana
Brooks, Ellis, 49, 77
Brown, Hattie, 15, 24
Brown, Louis L., 12, 19, 20, 22, 23
Brown, Mattie, 12, 22
Brown, Tom, 97
Brown University, 1
buck dances, 35, 103, 109, 118, 120, 131, 171
Buffalo Exposition, 42, 43
Burleigh, Harry T., 40, 58, 59, 73, 81, 82, 133
Byrd, Anthony D., 102, 118, 123, 148, 156, 193
Byrd, Sarah Green, 190, 198

cakewalk competitions, 33–34, 35, 103, 109, 113–14, 116, 123
Cappiani, Louisa, 52, 63
Carnegie Hall, 40, 59, 86
Carson, William K., 202–3
Carter, Mamie, 166
Cash, Estelle, 206
Cawtee Star Concert Company, 20
Centennial Exposition (Philadelphia), 5
Central Music Hall (Chicago), 53, 55, 56–57
Charters, Ann, 97
Chatteron, Charles F., 35
Cleveland, Grover, 31, 64
Clifford, Maud, 102
Clinton, George, 104
Cochran, J. W., 40
Colden, Melvina, 240
Colden, William, 240
Cole, Bob, 97, 102–3, 105–7, 112–13, 117, 138, 142, 147–48, 150, 154, 157, 161, 172–73, 176, 198–201
Cole, Dora B., 210
Coleman, Will, 118
Collier, S. E., 235
Collins, H. D., 148
Colored Folks Day (World's Columbian Exposition), 71–72, 73–76
Colvin, Addison, 83
Combries, Adeil Byround de, 21
Companini, Italo, 77
Congdon Street Baptist Church (Providence, R.I.), 1, 5–6, 231, 236
Cook, John H., 73

Cook, Will Marion, 58, 59, 73–76, 117
Cooke, Will A., 127, 148, 179, 183, 209, 219, 223, 225, 227, 231
coon songs, 99, 100, 103, 109, 116
Cordilia, Madame (performer), 118
Corwell, Trevor L., 157, 180
Craig, Walter F., 31, 40
Crenshaw, Daniel, 151, 236
Crosby, James, 146
Crowders, Reuben. *See* Hogan, Ernest
Cuba, 24, 153
Cummings, Harry, 238

Daisy, Lillian, 102
Damrosch, Walter, 93
Damrosch Opera Company, 93, 94
Dandy Dixie Minstrels, 167–68, 176, 188–89, 191, 209, 214
Dandy Jim (cakewalker), 34
Darkest Africa, 114
Daughtry, Willia Estelle, 2, 241
Davidson, J. W., 102
Davis and Goggins, 103
Day, George, 183
De Wolfe Sisters, 102, 103
Detroit Opera House, 57, 58
DeVere, Clementine, 49
Dill, Mollie, 102
Dittenhoefer, A. J., 68
Dixie Troubadours. *See* Dandy Dixie Minstrels
Dobbs, Georgia, 148, 150
Dolgorouky, Lily (princess), 42, 49, 261n39
Douglas, Mrs. Montrose, 171
Douglass, Frederick, 35, 58, 59, 67, 72–75
Douglass, J. H., 83
Douglass, Joseph, 73
Down in Dixie Minstrels, 198
Doyle, Jeannette, 40
Drury, Thomas, 151
Drury Opera Company, 140
Dudley, S. H., 175
Dudley, Sherman H., 198
Dunbar, Paul Lawrence, 62, 73
Dunger, Charles, 31
Durham, James H., 67
Durham, W. S., 40
Dusenberry, George M., 19

Victoria (queen of England), 8
Vilona, Emma, 78, 86
Vilona, Lilly, 78, 86
Vilona, Nina, 78, 86
Viranska, Bertha, 79, 81
Voelckel, Margaret, 181
Voelckel, Rudolph, 85, 87, 124, 126–30,
  132, 134, 138, 142; Black Patti Trouba-
  dours, 97–98, 100, 102–7, 109–16, 121,
  123–30, 132, 134, 138, 147, 154, 159, 175,
  173–75, 177–78, 180, 186, 191–92, 202;
  coon songs, 135, 161, 173; Dandy Dixie
  Minstrels, 167, 168, 174, 208; split with
  Nolan, 142, 167, 188, 189, 191
Volkmann, Paul, 81
Von Scarfa, Rudolph, 42

Walker, Ada Overton, 117, 204
Walker, George, 117, 150, 198, 201, 204,
  210
Wallace, Elizabeth, 171
Wallack's Theatre (New York), 12, 13
Walter, Mathilde, 85, 86
Walters, Alexander, 104
Walton Lester A., 2, 172, 183–85, 188–89,
  192, 197, 200, 208, 214, 235
Ward, Billy, 148
Washington, Booker T., 104
Watts, Al F., 138, 165, 171, 198–99, 206
Watts, Cecil, 138
Watts, Estelle Cash, 213
Wells, Ida B., 44, 72, 74
Western, Lille, 102

White, Stanford, 34
white audiences, 152, 155, 183. *See also*
  Jones, Matilda Sissieretta: white audi-
  ences
white newspapers, 28, 59, 70, 149, 178, 217
white-owned theaters, 162
Whitney, Emma Baynard, 171, 173, 179,
  181, 182
Whitney, Salem Tutt, 117, 171–74, 176,
  178–79, 183, 191, 198, 203, 209
Wiley, Stella, 97, 102, 103
Wilkes, Mattie, 147
Williams, Bert, 38, 97, 117, 138, 175, 185,
  198
Williams, Florence, 19–23, 25, 26, 28
Williams, Harry, 58
Wilson, Florrie, 131
Wilson, Georgiana, 31, 40, 61–63, 65, 68
Wilson, James, 131
Wilson, Thomas, 236
Wise, Hen, 102
Wise, Lena, 102
Witmark and Sons, 118, 119, 140, 141, 161
Wolford, John, 12, 15
Woodward, Sidney, 73, 83
World's Columbian Exposition, 58, 66,
  71, 73, 76, 77
Worles, James E., 142, 148, 150, 151

Zion African Methodist Episcopal
  Church, 104
Zion Grand Centennial Jubilee Concert
  and Banquet, 104, 105